STAR⇄CROSSED!!

01

JUNKO

CONTENTS

STAR⇄CROSSED!!

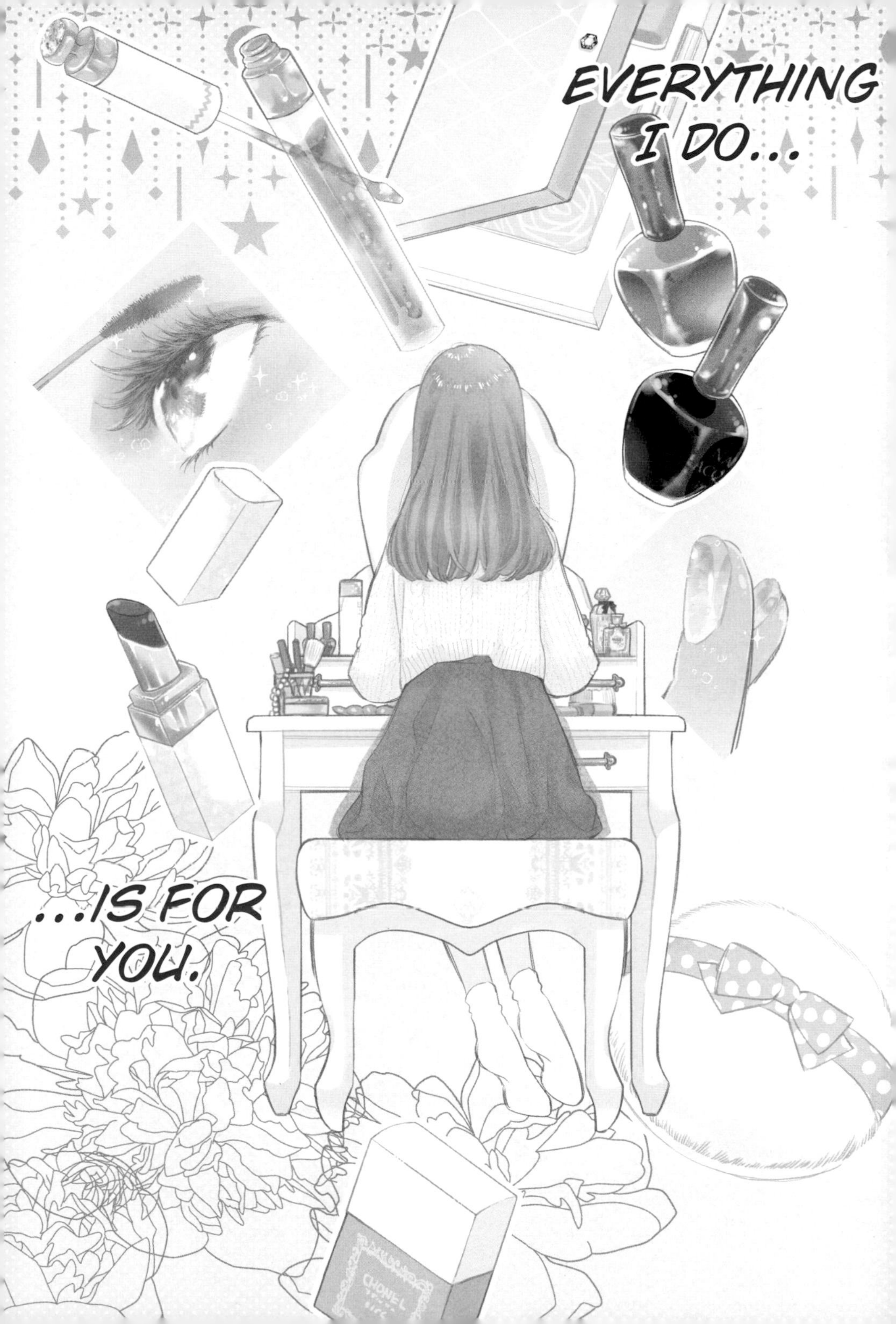
EVERYTHING I DO...
...IS FOR YOU.

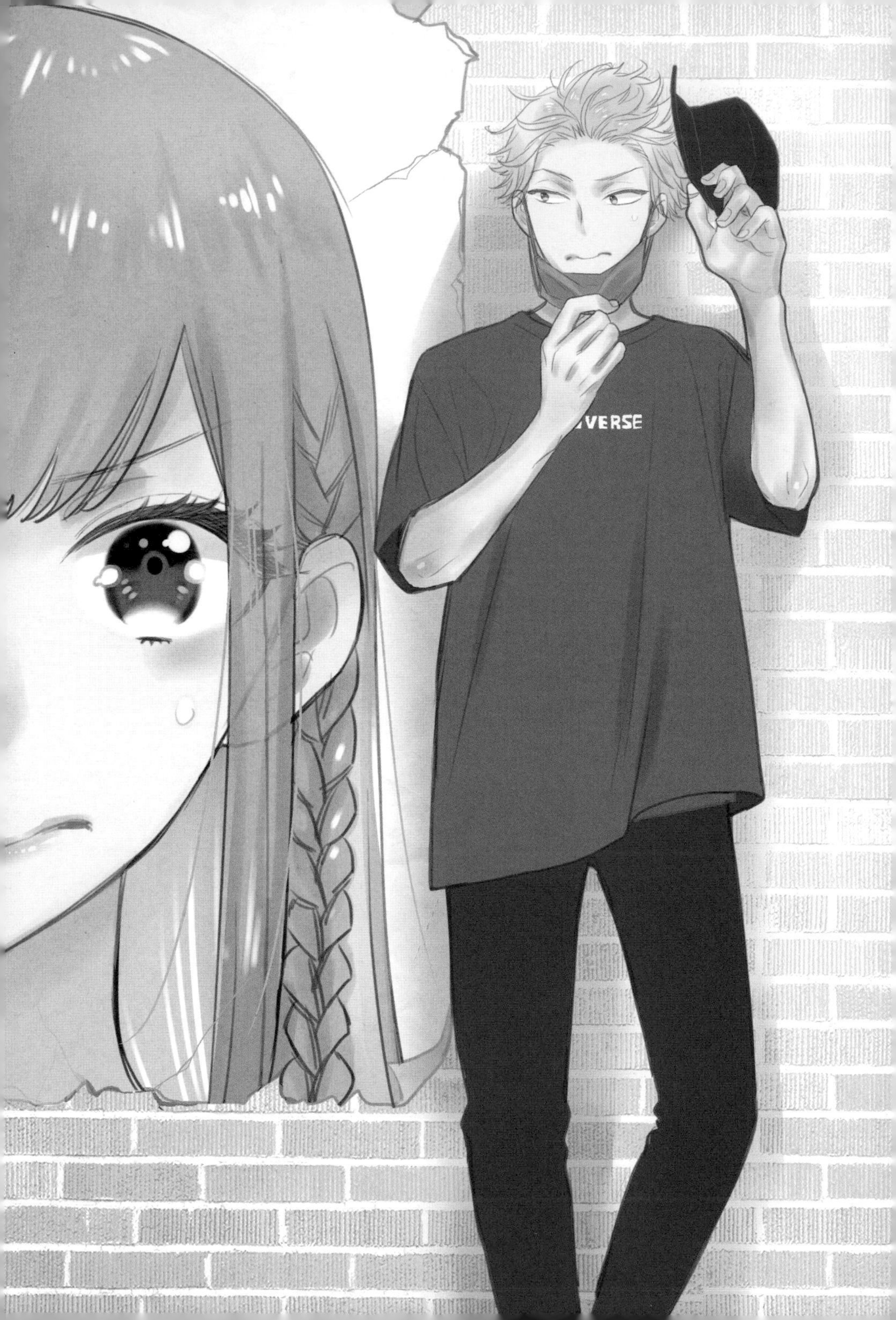

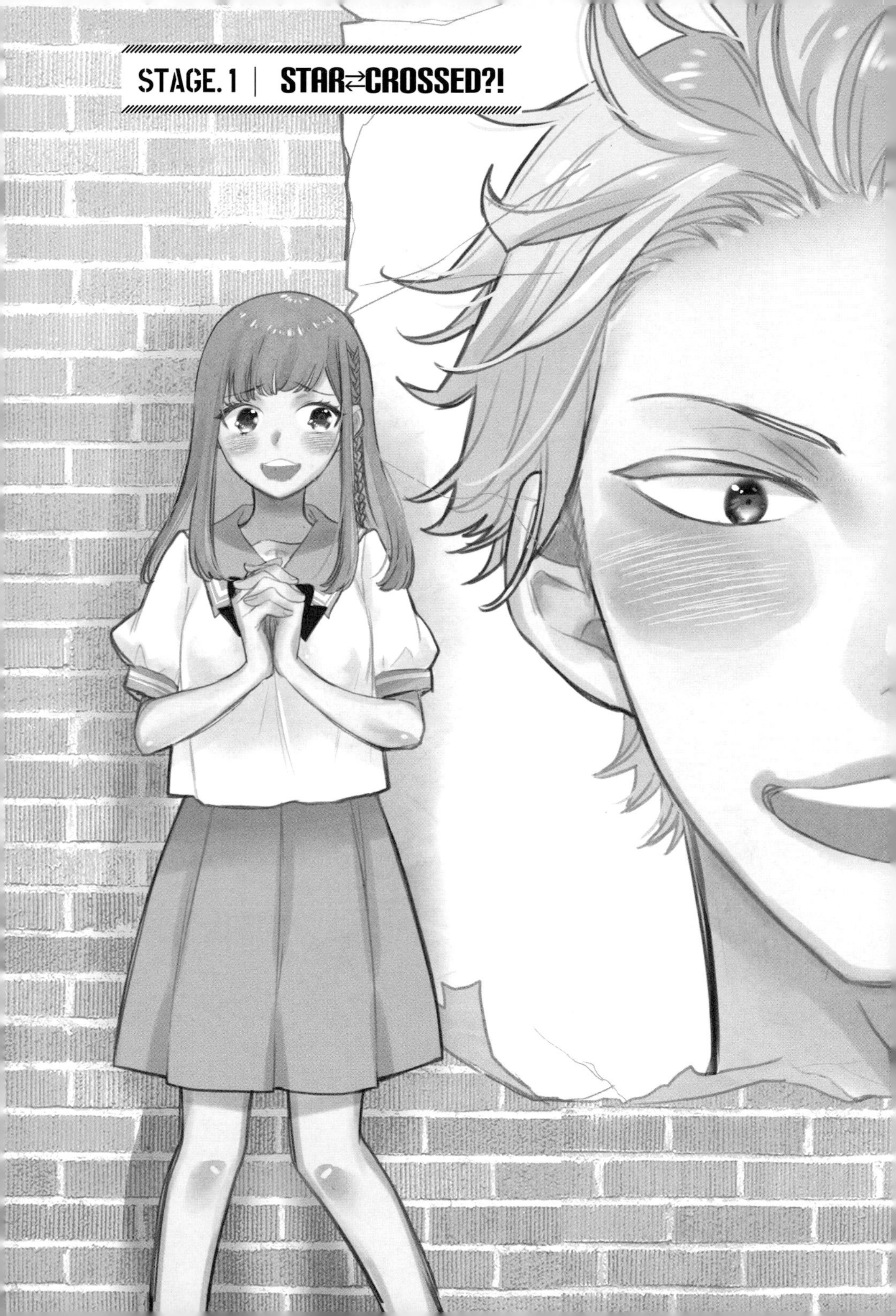
STAGE. 1 | STAR⇄CROSSED?!

R⇄CROSS

D!! STAR

AR⇄CROS

CROSSED

⇄CROSSE

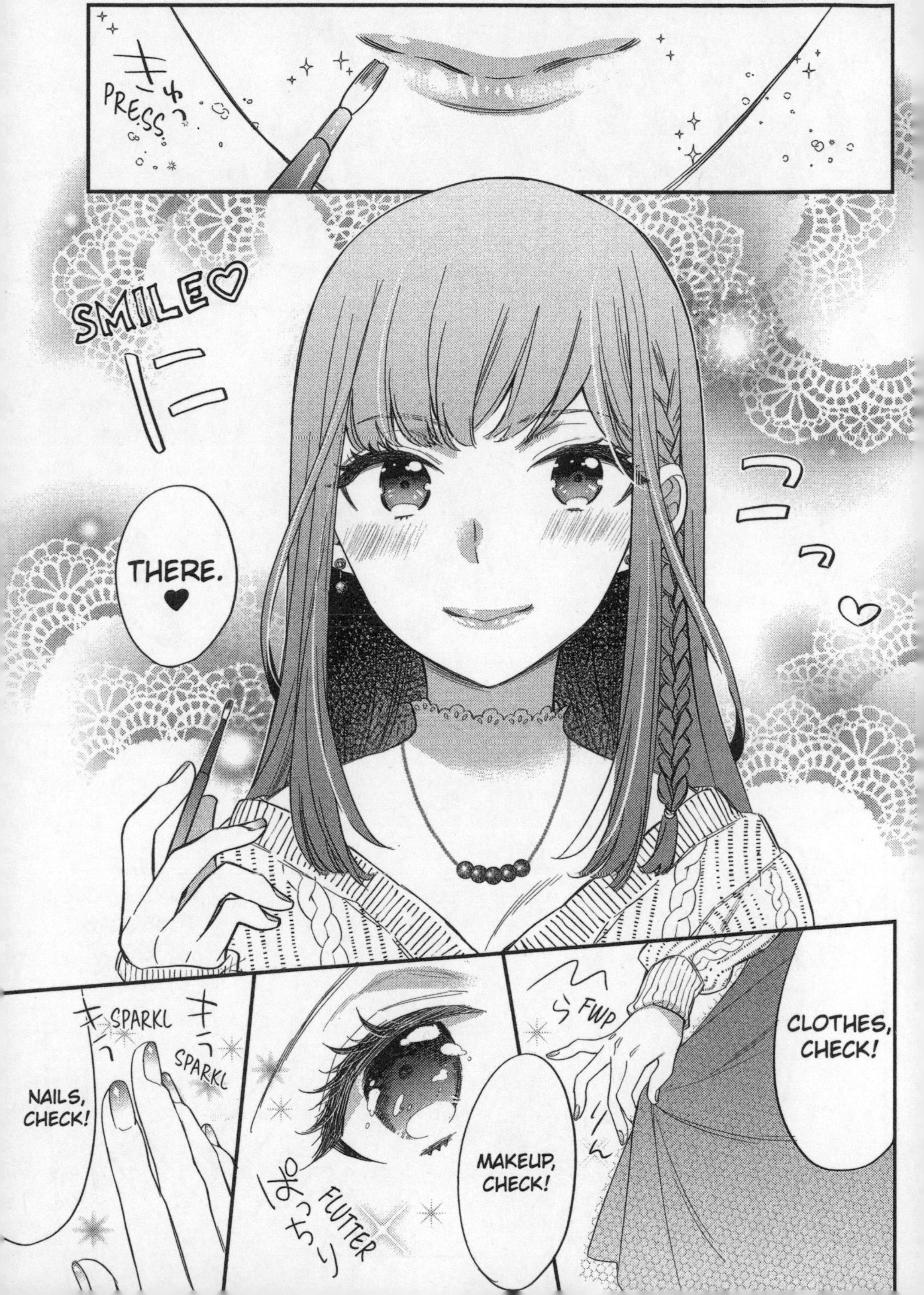
きゅっ
PRESS
SMILE♡
ニコッ
THERE. ♥
CLOTHES, CHECK!
FWP
MAKEUP, CHECK!
ぱっちり
FLUTTER
キラ
SPARKL
キラ
SPARKL
NAILS, CHECK!

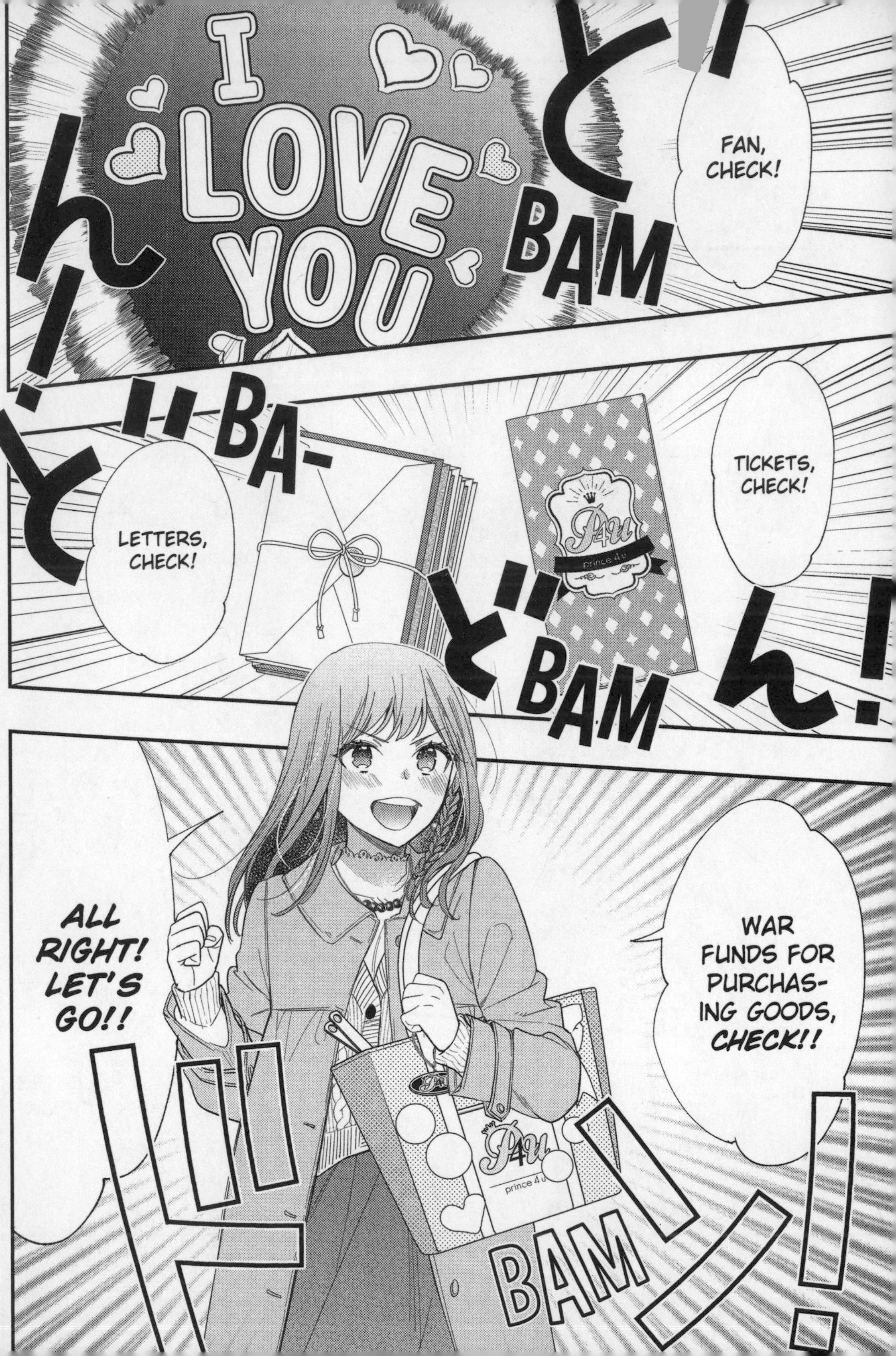
I LOVE YOU
FAN, CHECK!
BAM
TICKETS, CHECK!
BAM
LETTERS, CHECK!
BA-
WAR FUNDS FOR PURCHAS-ING GOODS, CHECK!!
ALL RIGHT! LET'S GO!!
prince 4 u
BAM

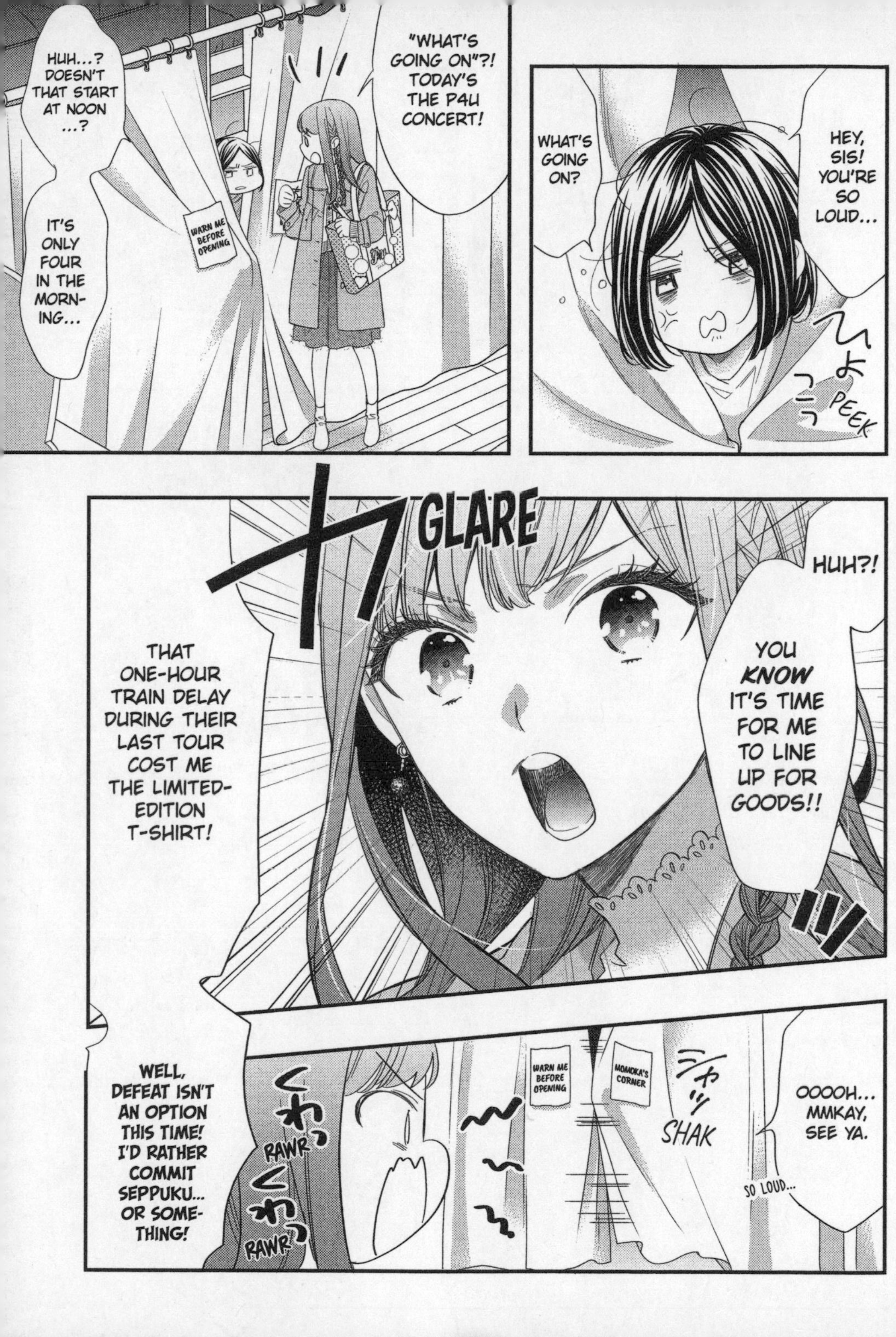
HEY, SIS! YOU'RE SO LOUD...
WHAT'S GOING ON?
PEEK
"WHAT'S GOING ON"?! TODAY'S THE P4U CONCERT!
HUH...? DOESN'T THAT START AT NOON ...?
WARN ME BEFORE OPENING
IT'S ONLY FOUR IN THE MORNING...
GLARE
HUH?!
YOU KNOW IT'S TIME FOR ME TO LINE UP FOR GOODS!!
THAT ONE-HOUR TRAIN DELAY DURING THEIR LAST TOUR COST ME THE LIMITED-EDITION T-SHIRT!
OOOOH... MMKAY, SEE YA.
SHAK
SO LOUD...
MOMOKA'S CORNER
WARN ME BEFORE OPENING
WELL, DEFEAT ISN'T AN OPTION THIS TIME! I'D RATHER COMMIT SEPPUKU... OR SOMETHING!
RAWR
RAWR

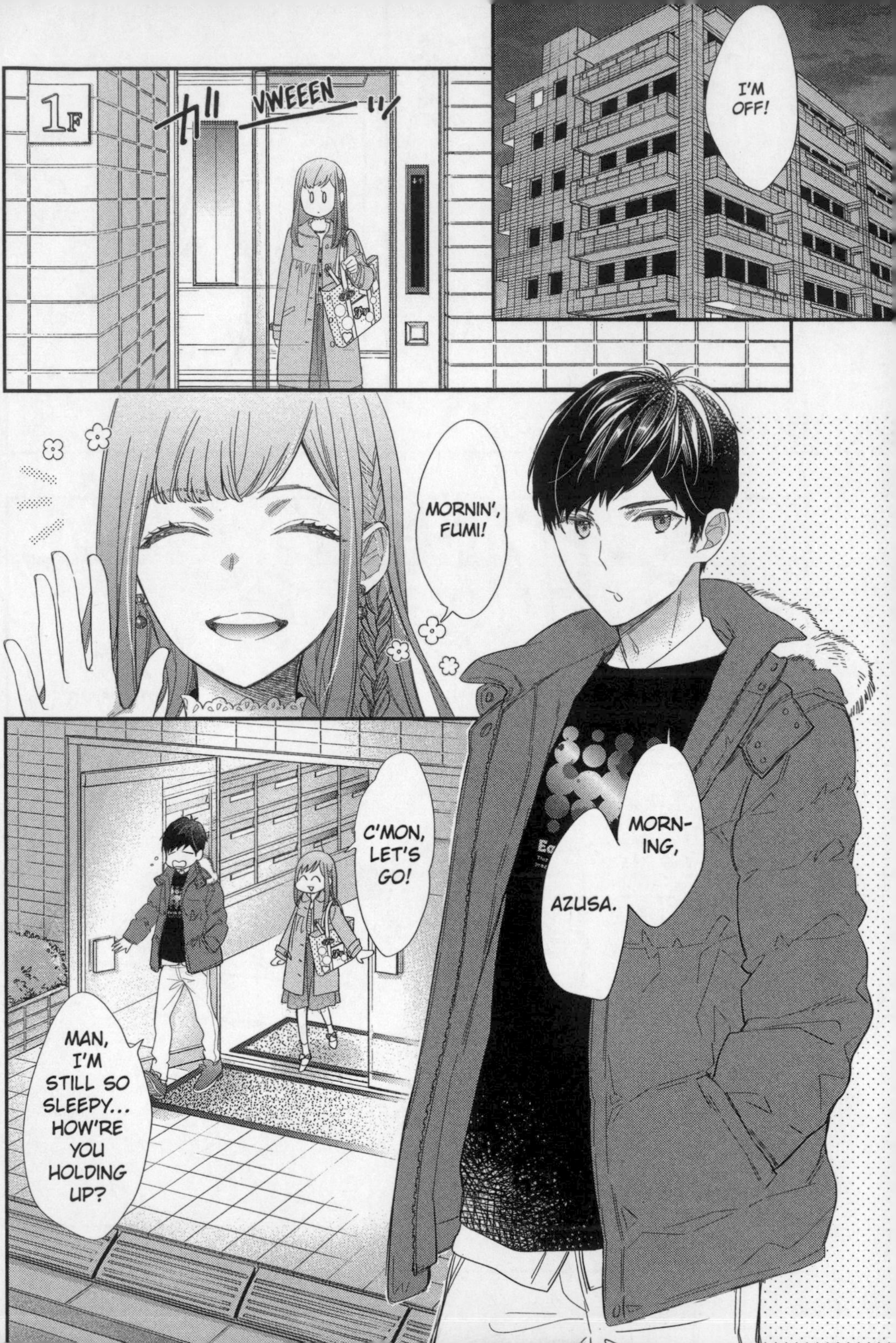
I'M OFF!
VWEEEN
MORN-ING,
AZUSA.
MORNIN', FUMI!
C'MON, LET'S GO!
MAN, I'M STILL SO SLEEPY... HOW'RE YOU HOLDING UP?

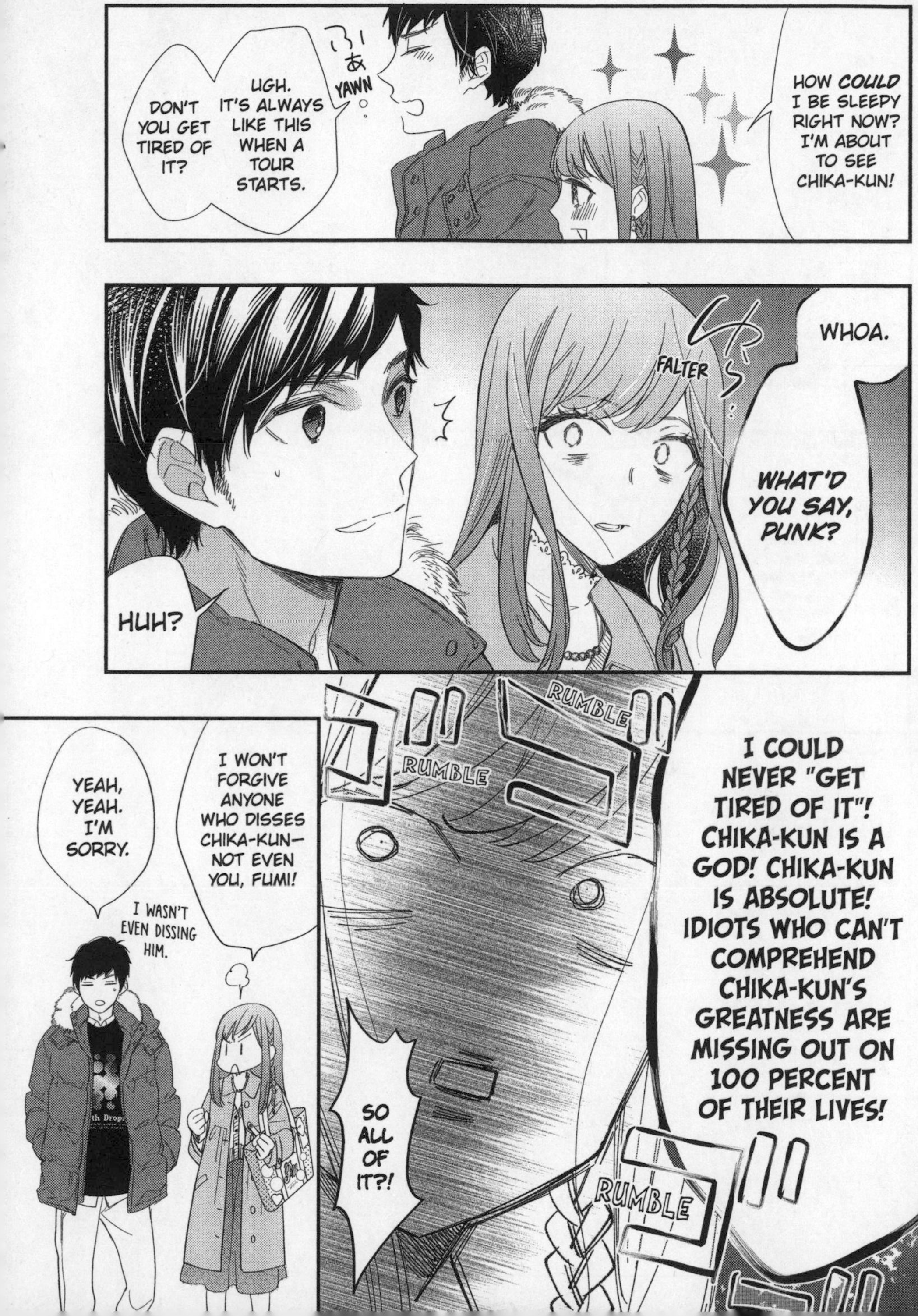
HOW COULD I BE SLEEPY RIGHT NOW? I'M ABOUT TO SEE CHIKA-KUN!
ふぁ
YAWN
UGH. IT'S ALWAYS LIKE THIS WHEN A TOUR STARTS.
DON'T YOU GET TIRED OF IT?
WHOA.
FALTER
WHAT'D YOU SAY, PUNK?
HUH?
RUMBLE
RUMBLE
I COULD NEVER "GET TIRED OF IT"! CHIKA-KUN IS A GOD! CHIKA-KUN IS ABSOLUTE! IDIOTS WHO CAN'T COMPREHEND CHIKA-KUN'S GREATNESS ARE MISSING OUT ON 100 PERCENT OF THEIR LIVES!
SO ALL OF IT?!
RUMBLE
I WON'T FORGIVE ANYONE WHO DISSES CHIKA-KUN—NOT EVEN YOU, FUMI!
YEAH, YEAH. I'M SORRY.
I WASN'T EVEN DISSING HIM.

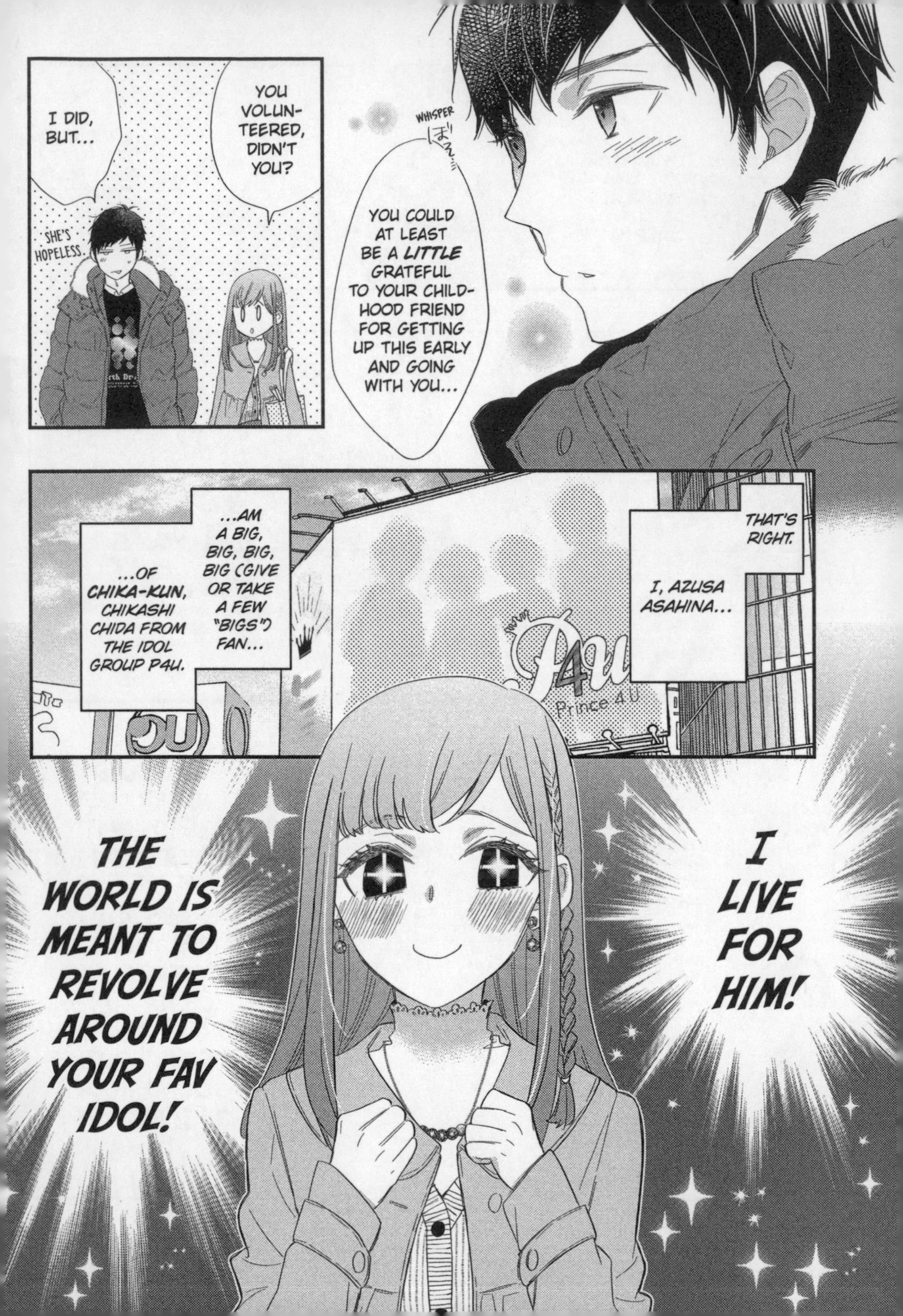
WHISPER
YOU COULD AT LEAST BE A *LITTLE* GRATEFUL TO YOUR CHILDHOOD FRIEND FOR GETTING UP THIS EARLY AND GOING WITH YOU...
YOU VOLUNTEERED, DIDN'T YOU?
I DID, BUT...
SHE'S HOPELESS.
THAT'S RIGHT.
I, AZUSA ASAHINA...
...AM A BIG, BIG, BIG, BIG (GIVE OR TAKE A FEW "BIGS") FAN...
...OF CHIKA-KUN, CHIKASHI CHIDA FROM THE IDOL GROUP P4U.
P4U
Prince 4 U
I LIVE FOR HIM!
THE WORLD IS MEANT TO REVOLVE AROUND YOUR FAV IDOL!

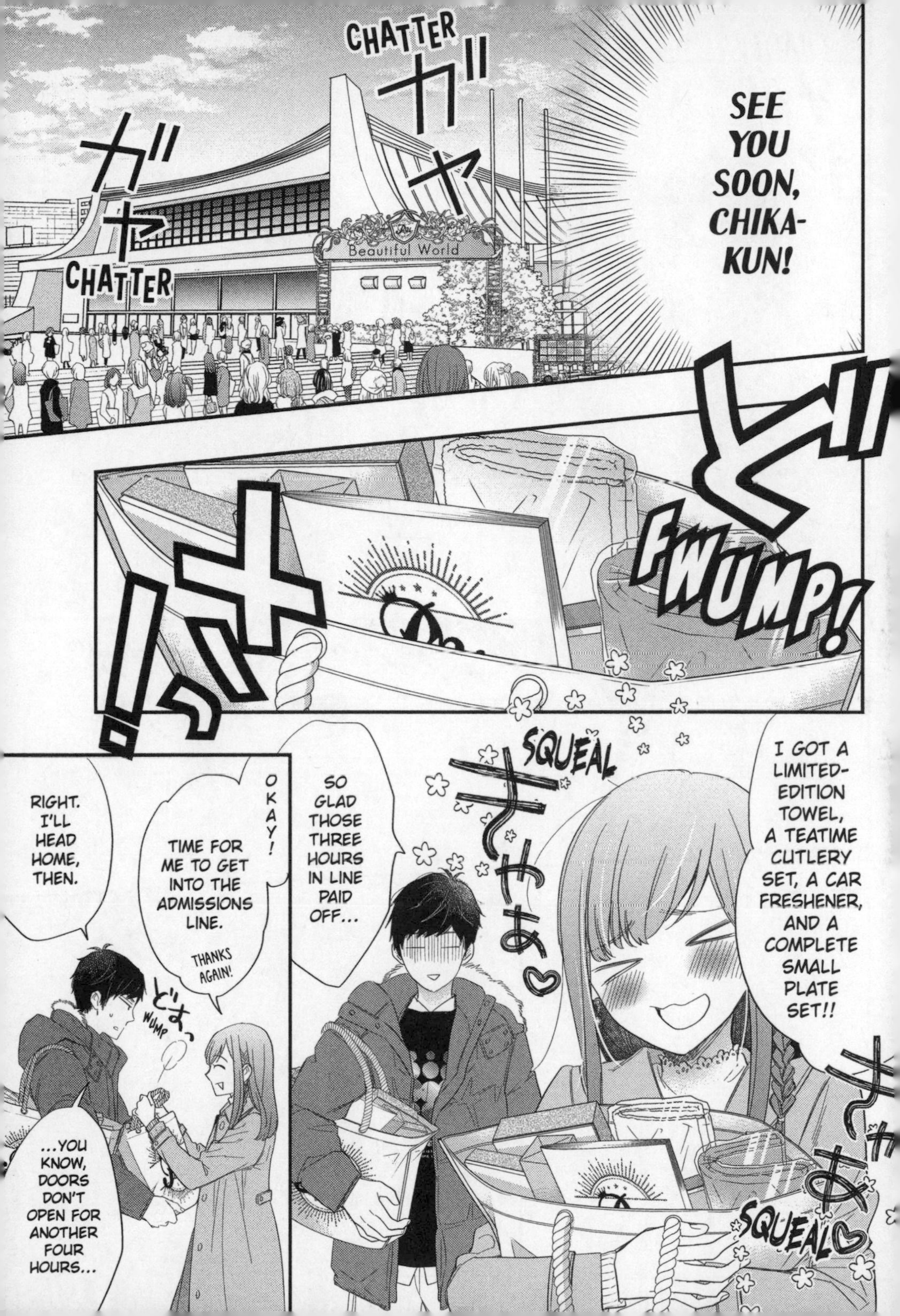
SEE YOU SOON, CHIKA-KUN!
CHATTER
Beautiful World
CHATTER
FWUMP!
SQUEAL
I GOT A LIMITED-EDITION TOWEL, A TEATIME CUTLERY SET, A CAR FRESHENER, AND A COMPLETE SMALL PLATE SET!!
SQUEAL
SO GLAD THOSE THREE HOURS IN LINE PAID OFF...
OKAY!
TIME FOR ME TO GET INTO THE ADMISSIONS LINE.
THANKS AGAIN!
RIGHT. I'LL HEAD HOME, THEN.
WUMP
...YOU KNOW, DOORS DON'T OPEN FOR ANOTHER FOUR HOURS...

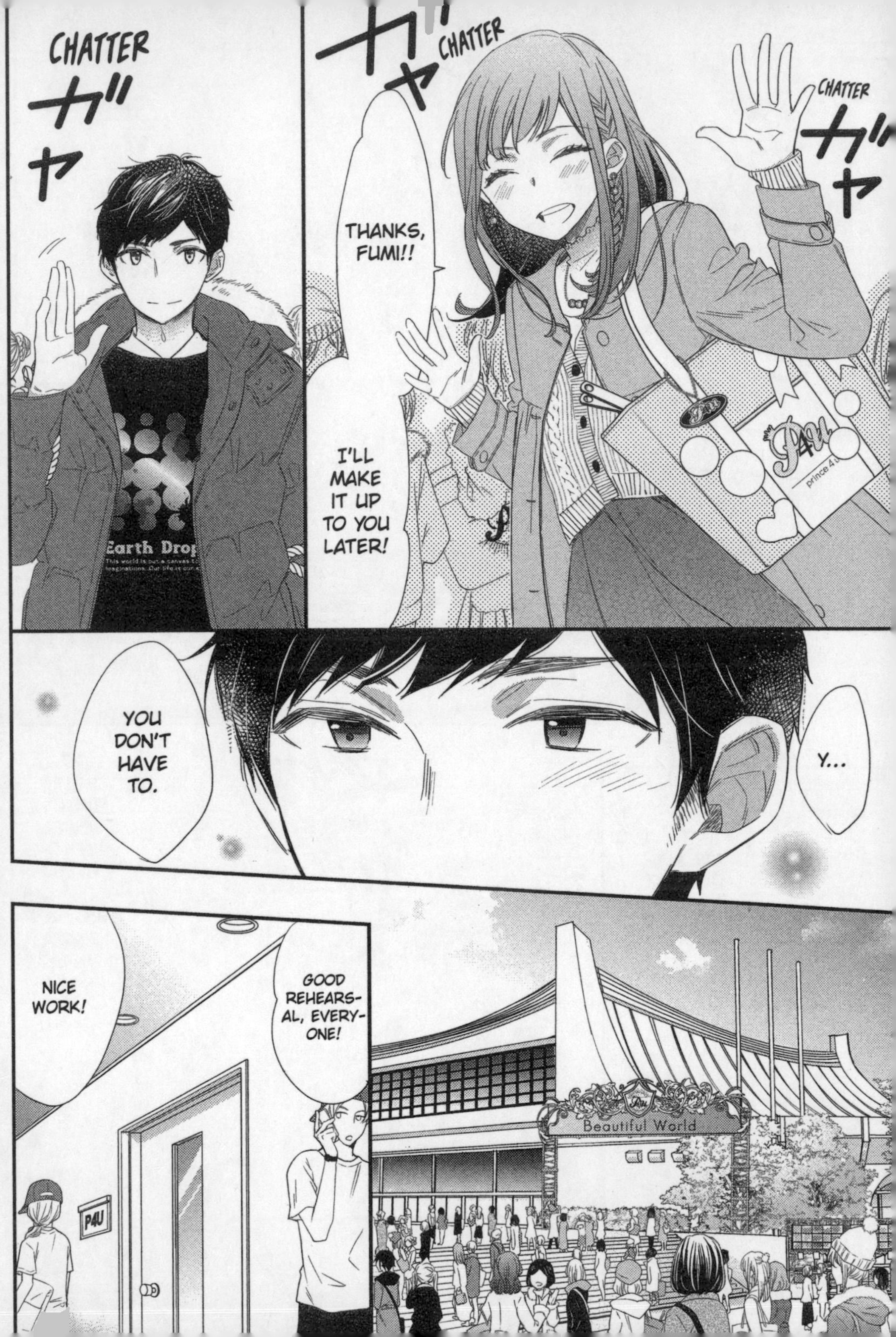
CHATTER
ガヤ
CHATTER
ガヤ
THANKS, FUMI!!
I'LL MAKE IT UP TO YOU LATER!
CHATTER
ガヤ
Y...
YOU DON'T HAVE TO.
GOOD REHEARSAL, EVERYONE!
NICE WORK!
Beautiful World
P4U

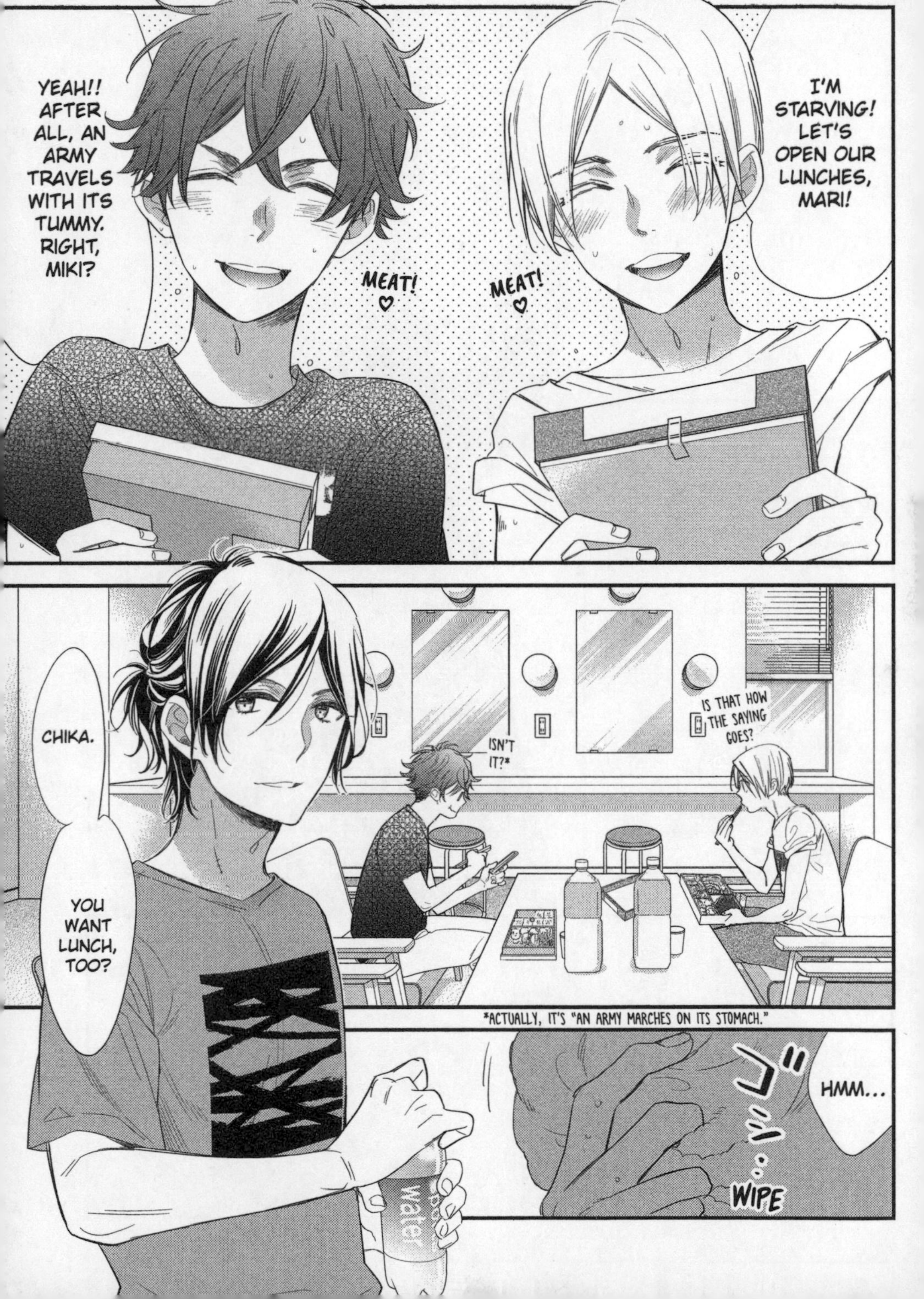
I'M STARVING! LET'S OPEN OUR LUNCHES, MARI!
MEAT! ♡
MEAT! ♡
YEAH!! AFTER ALL, AN ARMY TRAVELS WITH ITS TUMMY. RIGHT, MIKI?
IS THAT HOW THE SAYING GOES?
ISN'T IT?*
*ACTUALLY, IT'S "AN ARMY MARCHES ON ITS STOMACH."
HMM...
WIPE
CHIKA.
YOU WANT LUNCH, TOO?

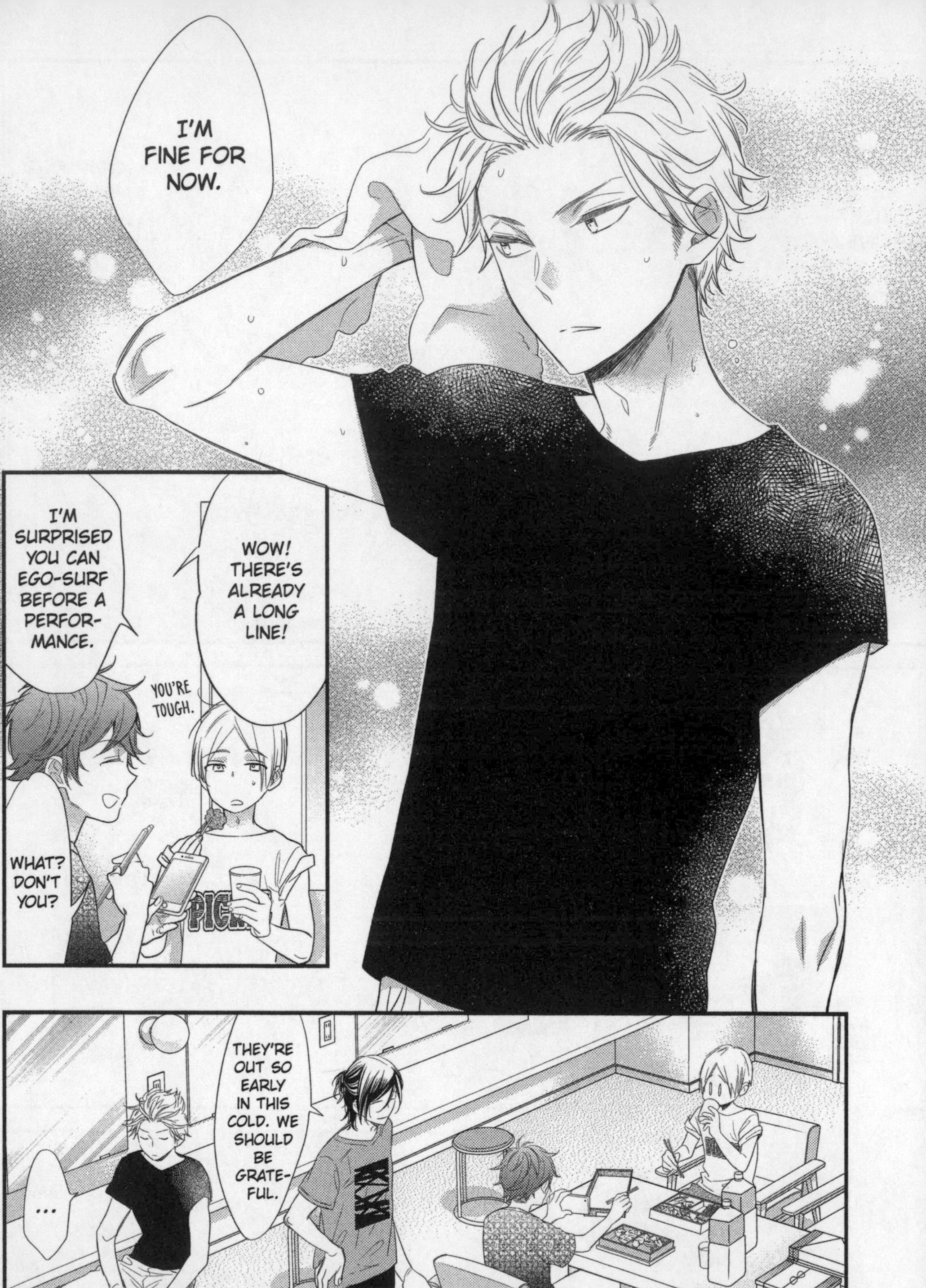
I'M FINE FOR NOW.
WOW! THERE'S ALREADY A LONG LINE!
I'M SURPRISED YOU CAN EGO-SURF BEFORE A PERFORMANCE.
YOU'RE TOUGH.
WHAT? DON'T YOU?
THEY'RE OUT SO EARLY IN THIS COLD. WE SHOULD BE GRATEFUL.
...

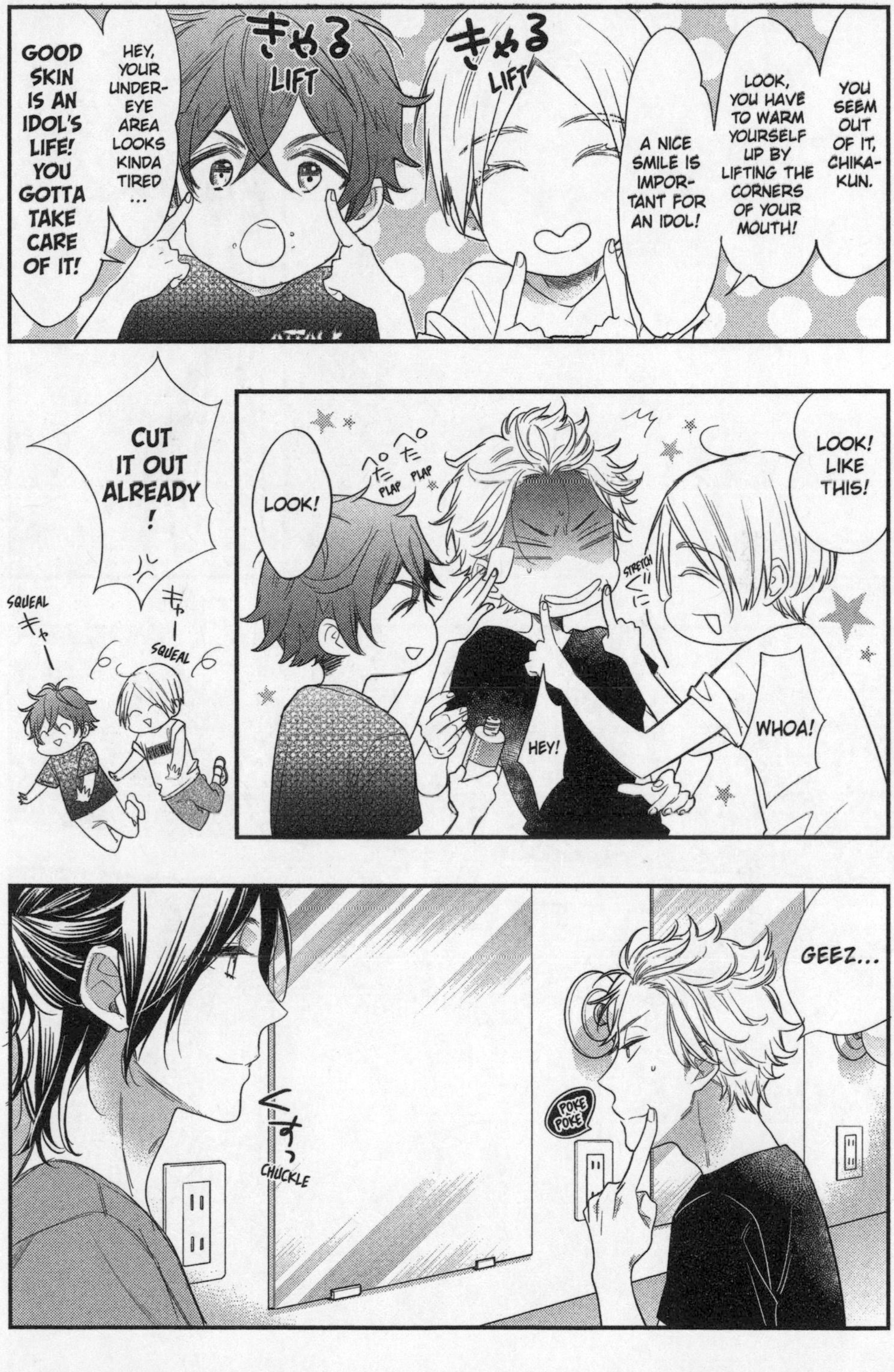
YOU SEEM OUT OF IT, CHIKA-KUN.
LOOK, YOU HAVE TO WARM YOURSELF UP BY LIFTING THE CORNERS OF YOUR MOUTH!
A NICE SMILE IS IMPORTANT FOR AN IDOL!
きゅる LIFT
きゅる LIFT
HEY, YOUR UNDER-EYE AREA LOOKS KINDA TIRED...
GOOD SKIN IS AN IDOL'S LIFE! YOU GOTTA TAKE CARE OF IT!
LOOK! LIKE THIS!
ぐに STRETCH
WHOA!
ぺた ぺた PLAP PLAP
LOOK!
HEY!
CUT IT OUT ALREADY!
きゃー SQUEAL
きゃー SQUEAL
GEEZ...
POKE POKE
くすっ CHUCKLE

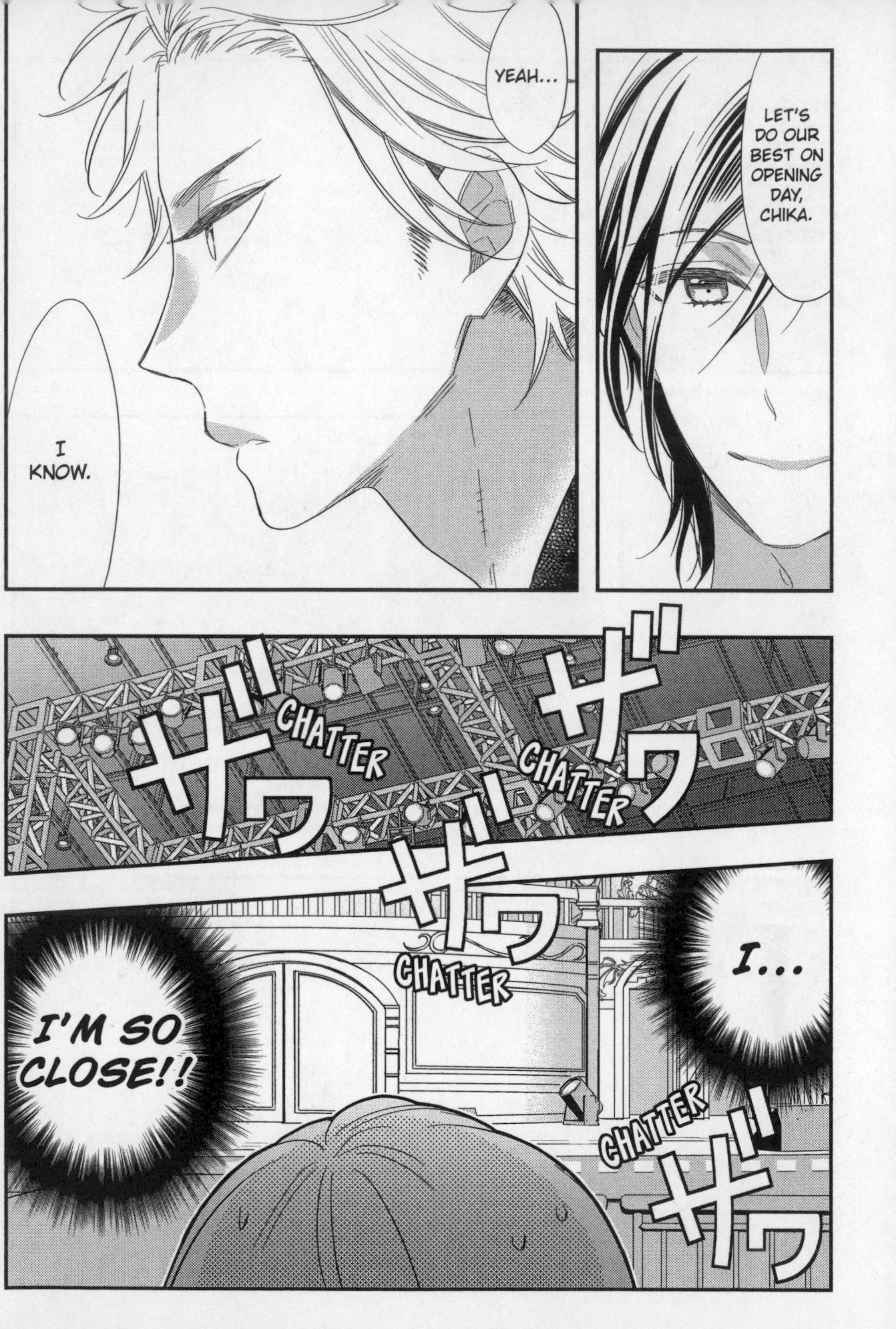
LET'S DO OUR BEST ON OPENING DAY, CHIKA.
YEAH...
I KNOW.
ザワ
CHATTER
ザワ
CHATTER
ザワ
CHATTER
I...
I'M SO CLOSE!!
ザワ
CHATTER

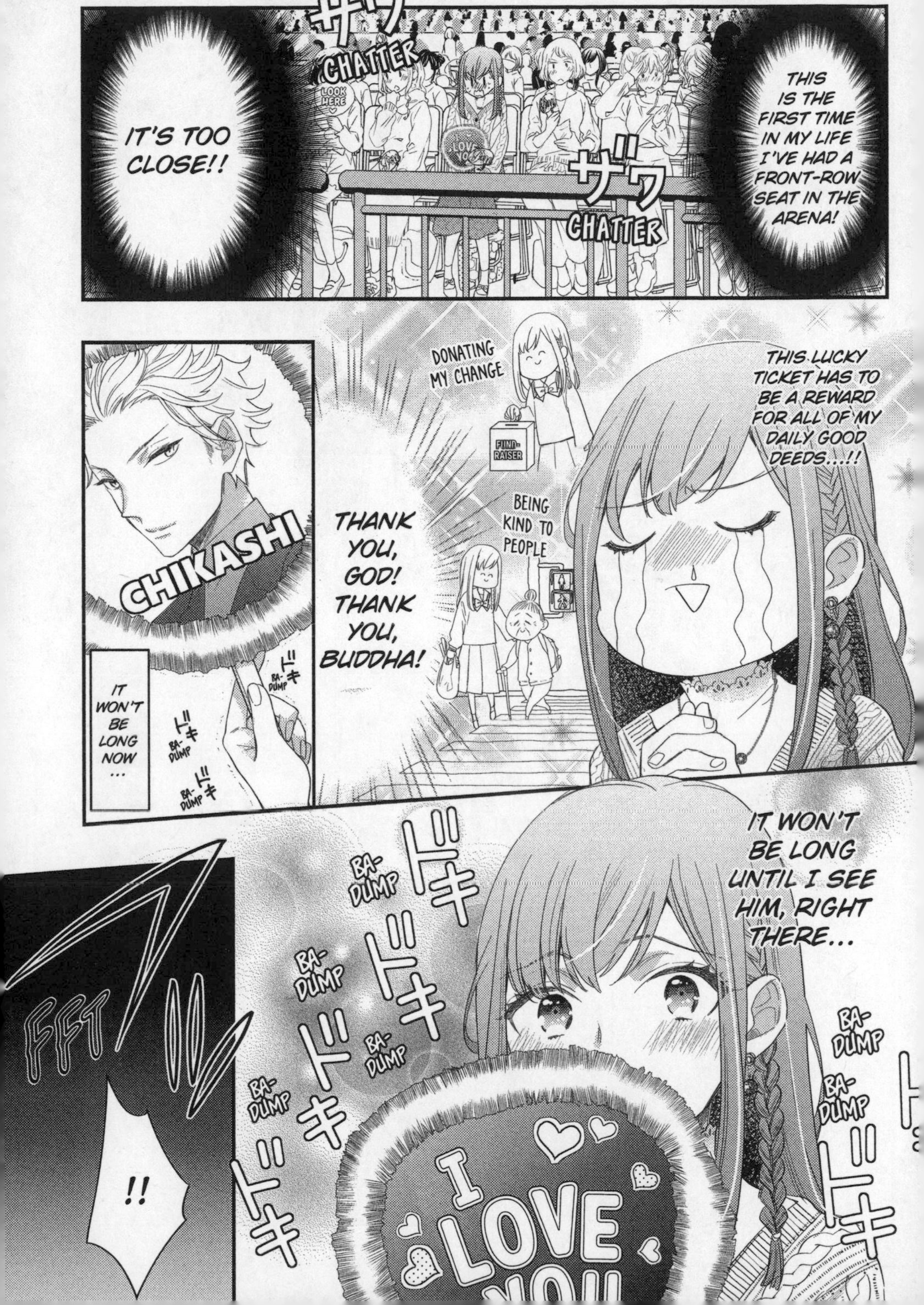
THIS IS THE FIRST TIME IN MY LIFE I'VE HAD A FRONT-ROW SEAT IN THE ARENA!
ザワ CHATTER
ザワ CHATTER
LOOK HERE
I LOVE YOU
IT'S TOO CLOSE!!
THIS LUCKY TICKET HAS TO BE A REWARD FOR ALL OF MY DAILY GOOD DEEDS...!!
DONATING MY CHANGE
FUND-RAISER
BEING KIND TO PEOPLE
THANK YOU, GOD! THANK YOU, BUDDHA!
CHIKASHI
ドキ BA-DUMP
ドキ BA-DUMP
ドキ BA-DUMP
IT WON'T BE LONG NOW...
IT WON'T BE LONG UNTIL I SEE HIM, RIGHT THERE...
ドキ BA-DUMP
ドキ BA-DUMP
ドキ BA-DUMP
ドキ BA-DUMP
ドキ BA-DUMP
I LOVE YOU
FFT
!!

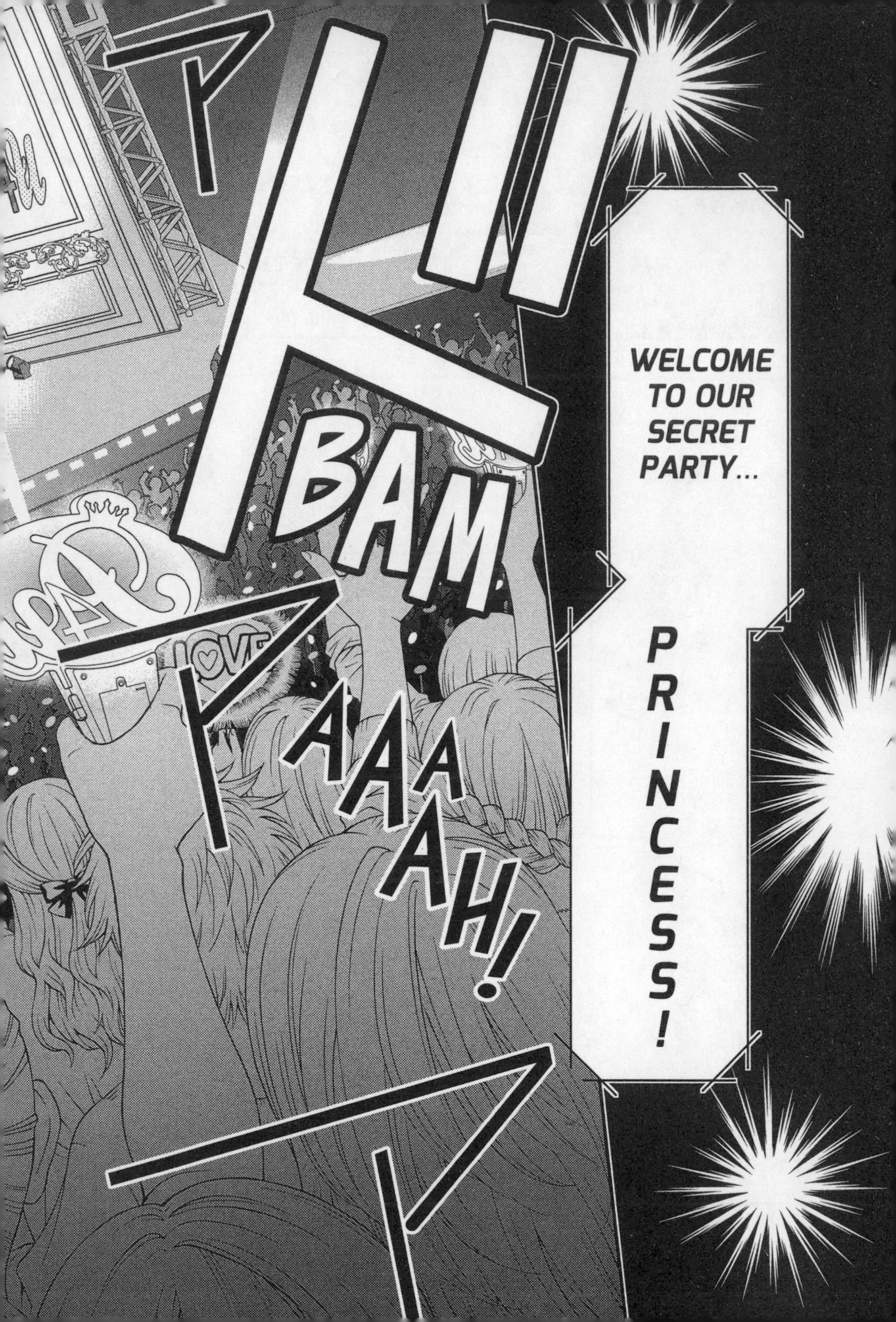
WELCOME TO OUR SECRET PARTY...
PRINCESS!
BAM
AAAAH!

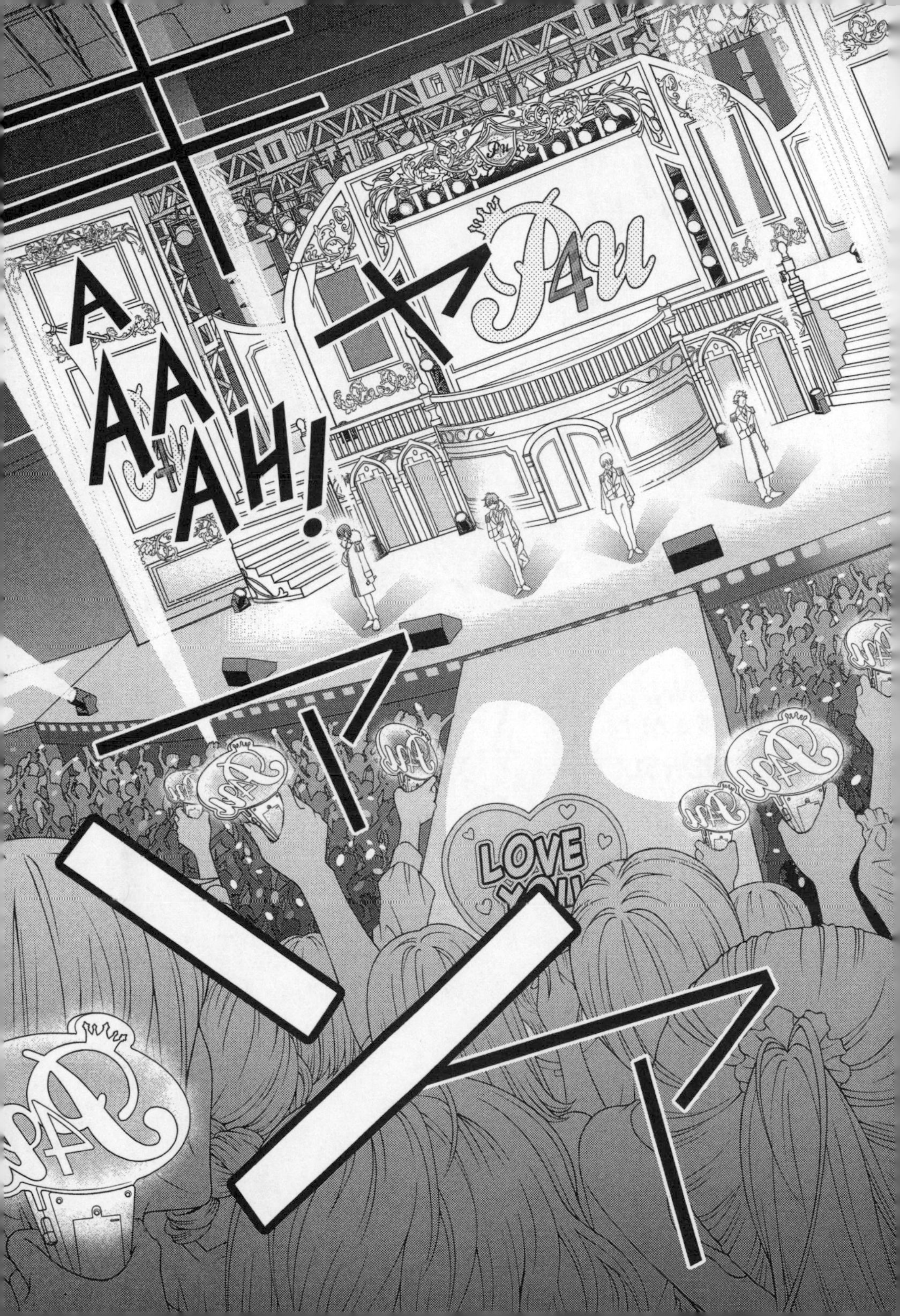
AAAAH!
LOVE

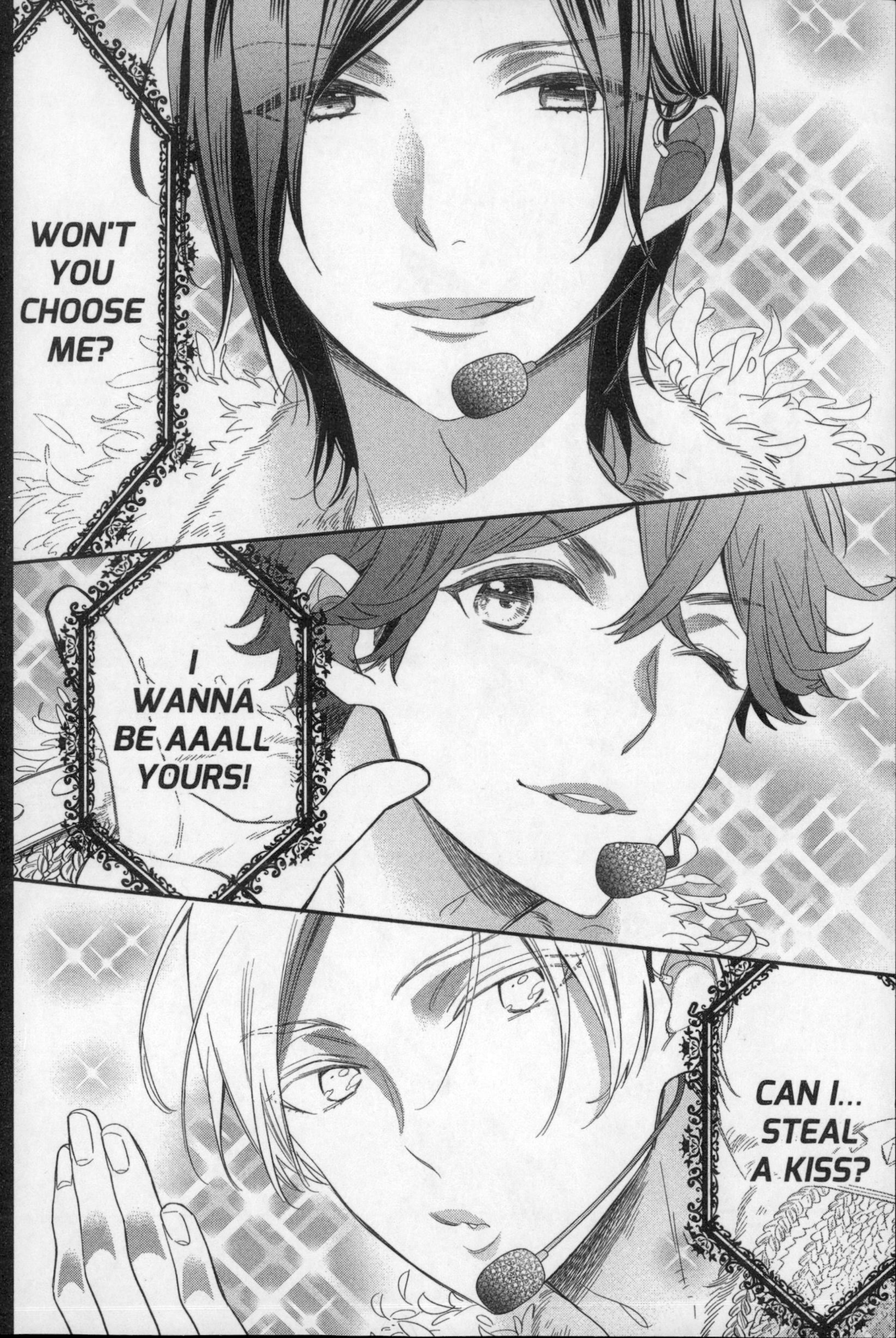
WON'T YOU CHOOSE ME?
I WANNA BE AAALL YOURS!
CAN I... STEAL A KISS?

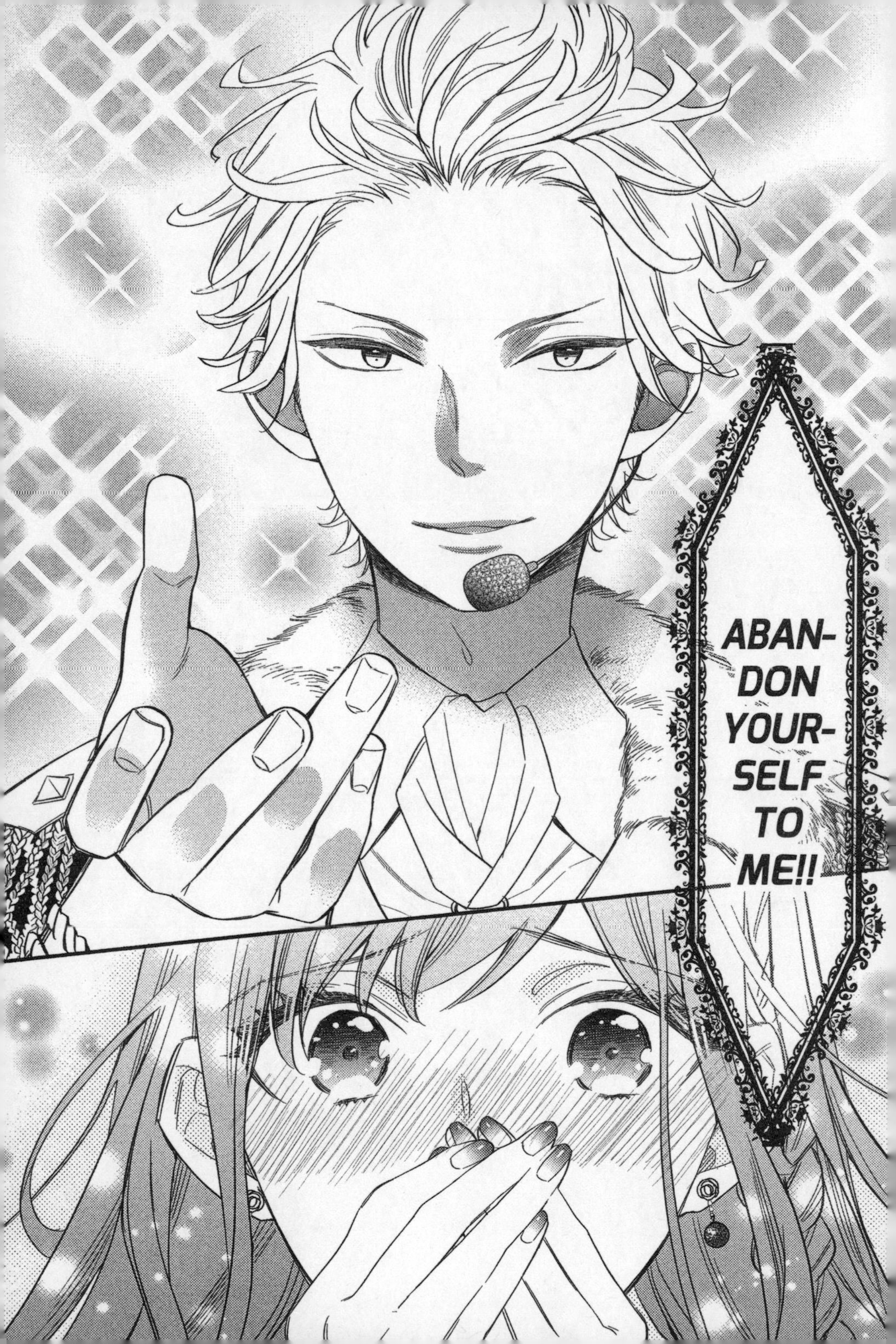
ABAN-
DON
YOUR-
SELF
TO
ME!!

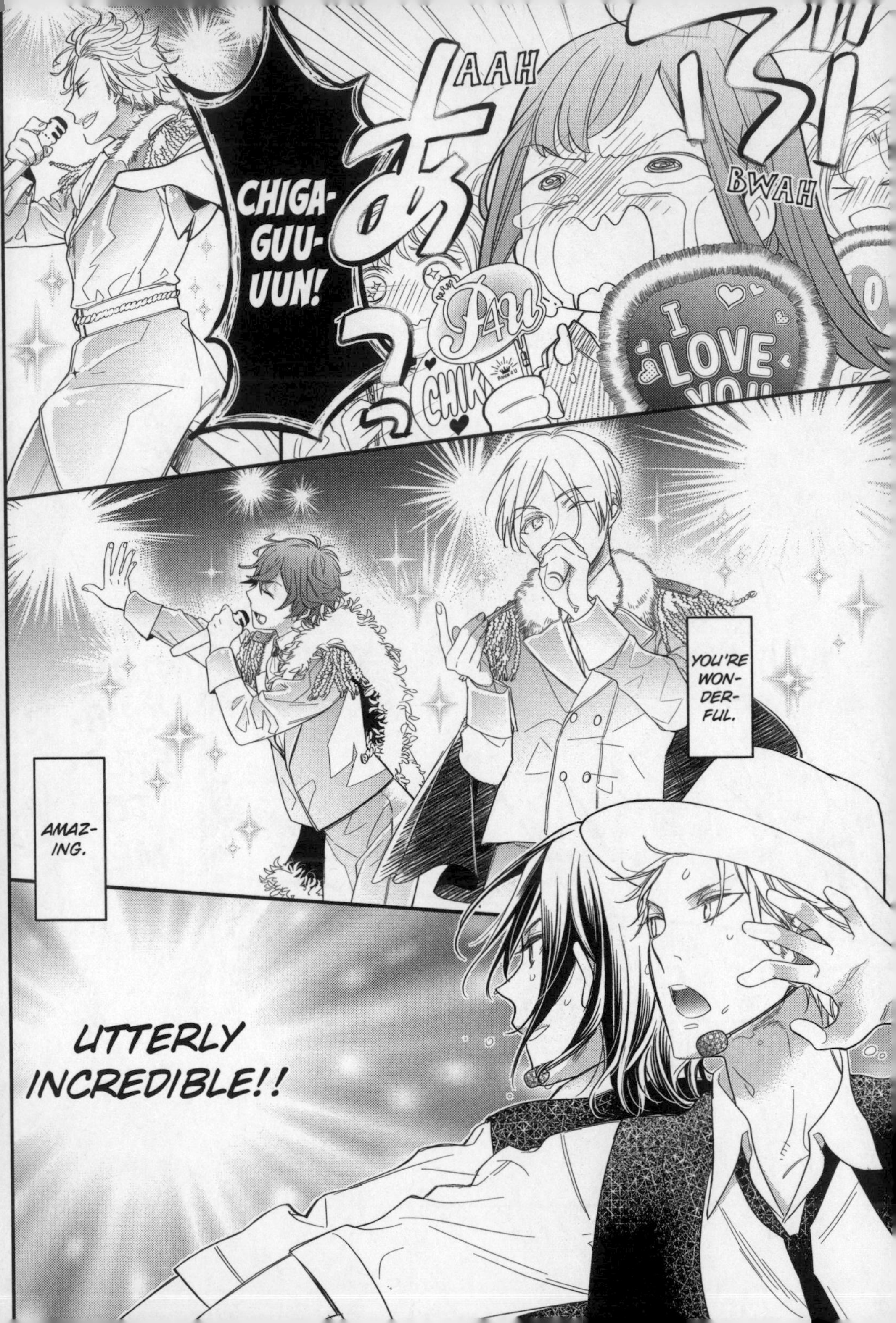

BWAH
AAH
I LOVE
P4U
CHIGA-GUUU-UUN!
YOU'RE WON-DER-FUL.
AMAZ-ING.
UTTERLY INCREDIBLE!!

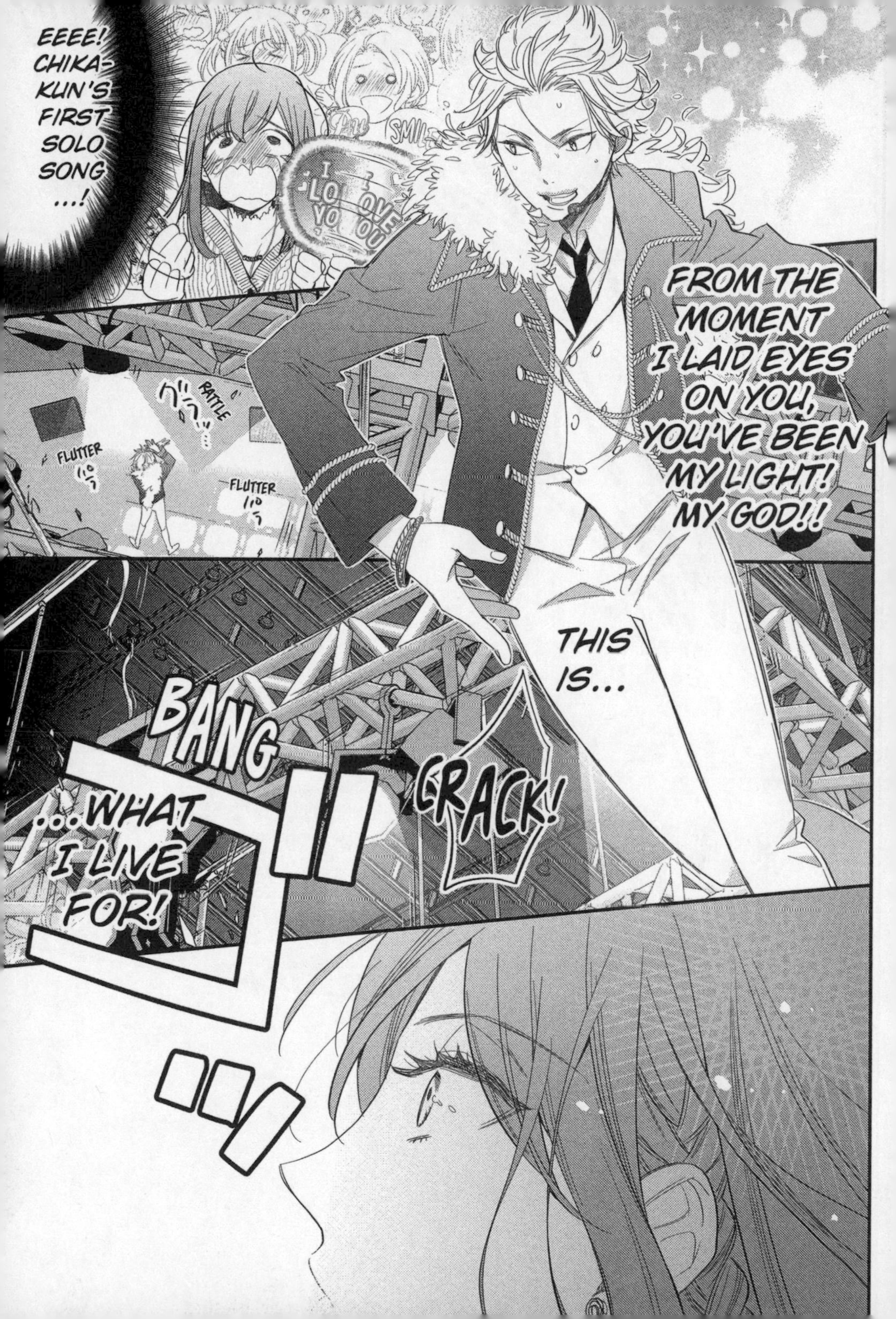
FROM THE MOMENT I LAID EYES ON YOU, YOU'VE BEEN MY LIGHT! MY GOD!!
EEEE! CHIKA-KUN'S FIRST SOLO SONG ...!
I LOVE YOU
RATTLE
FLUTTER
FLUTTER
THIS IS...
BANG
CRACK!
...WHAT I LIVE FOR!
...!!

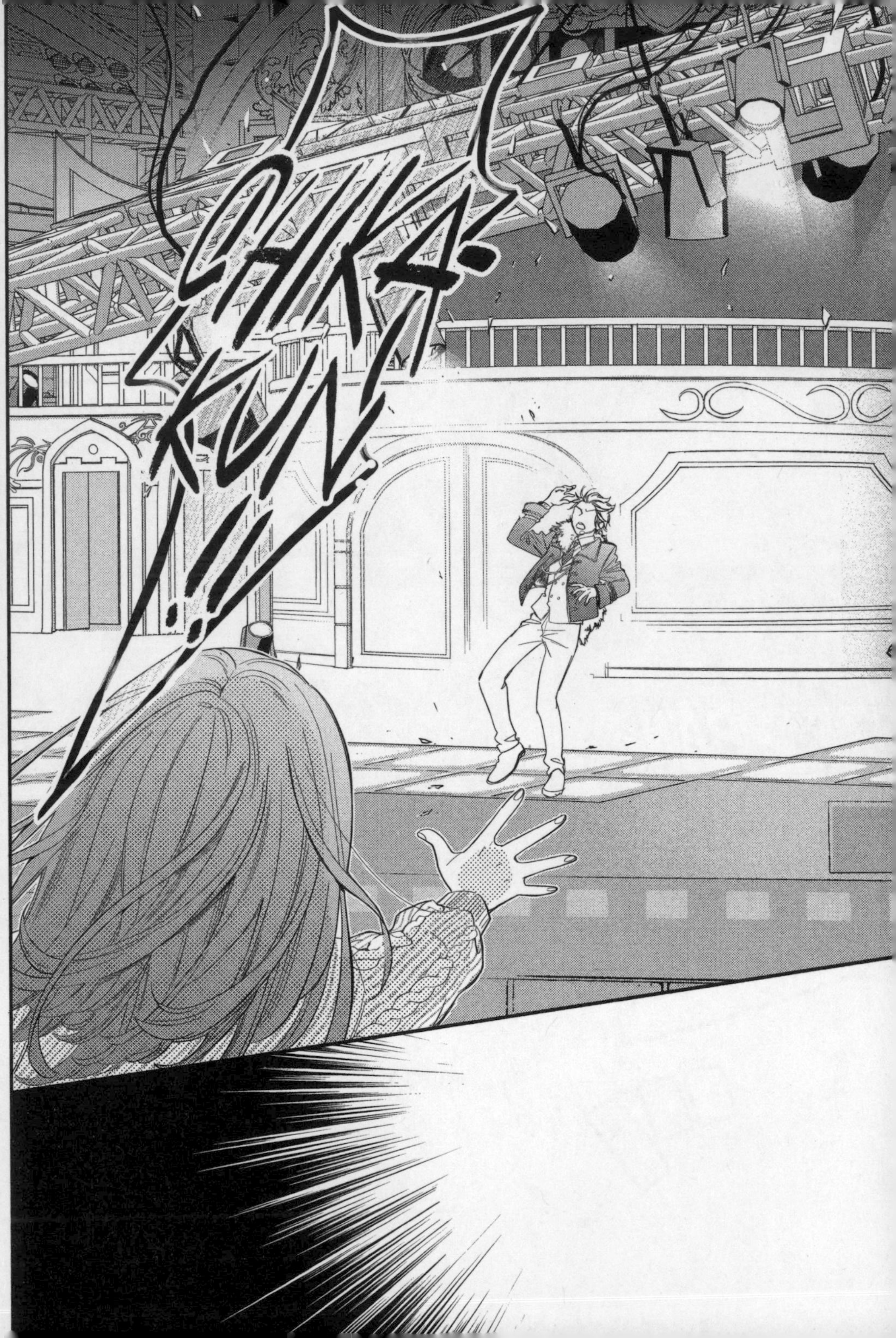
CHIKA-KUN!!

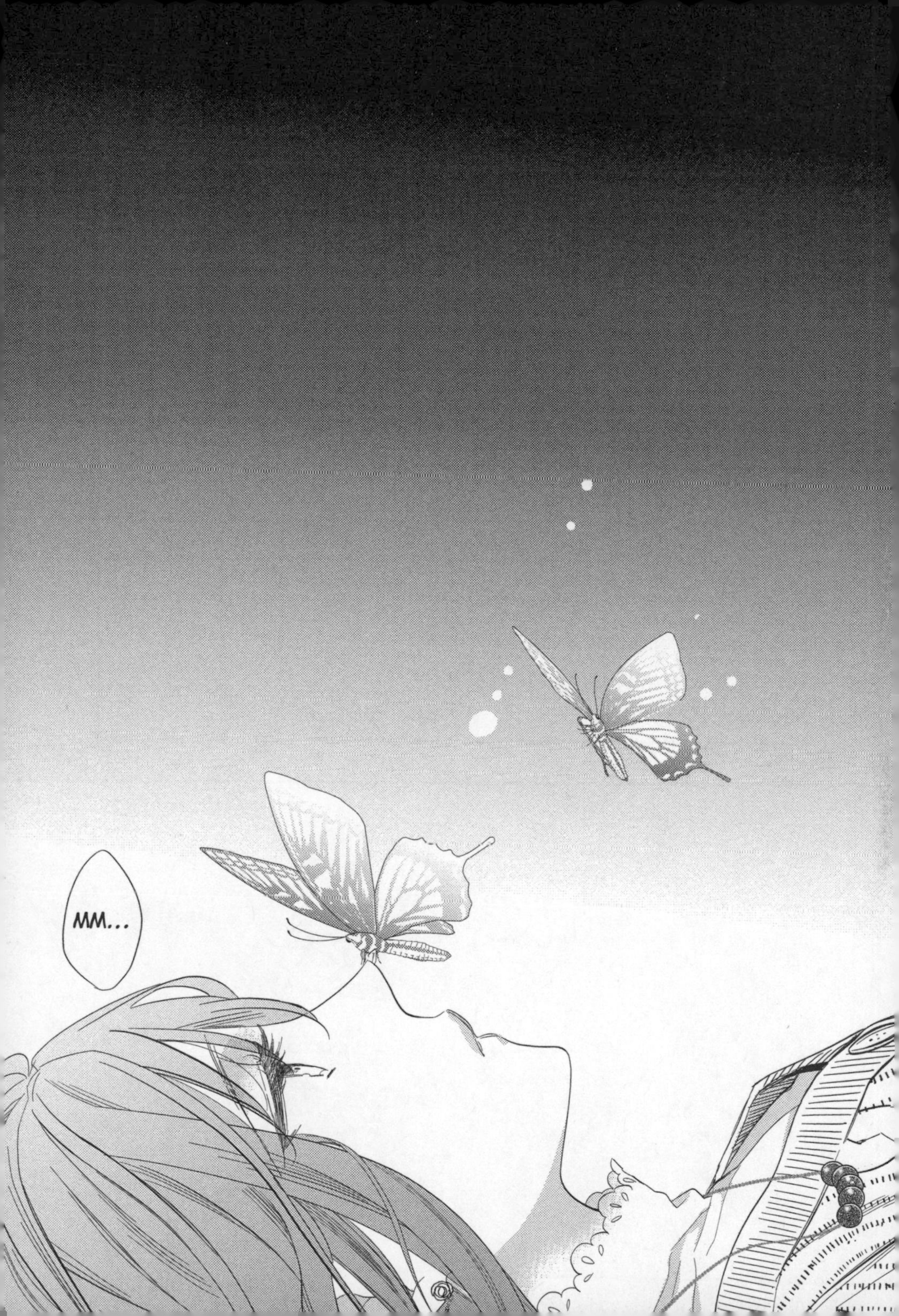
MM...

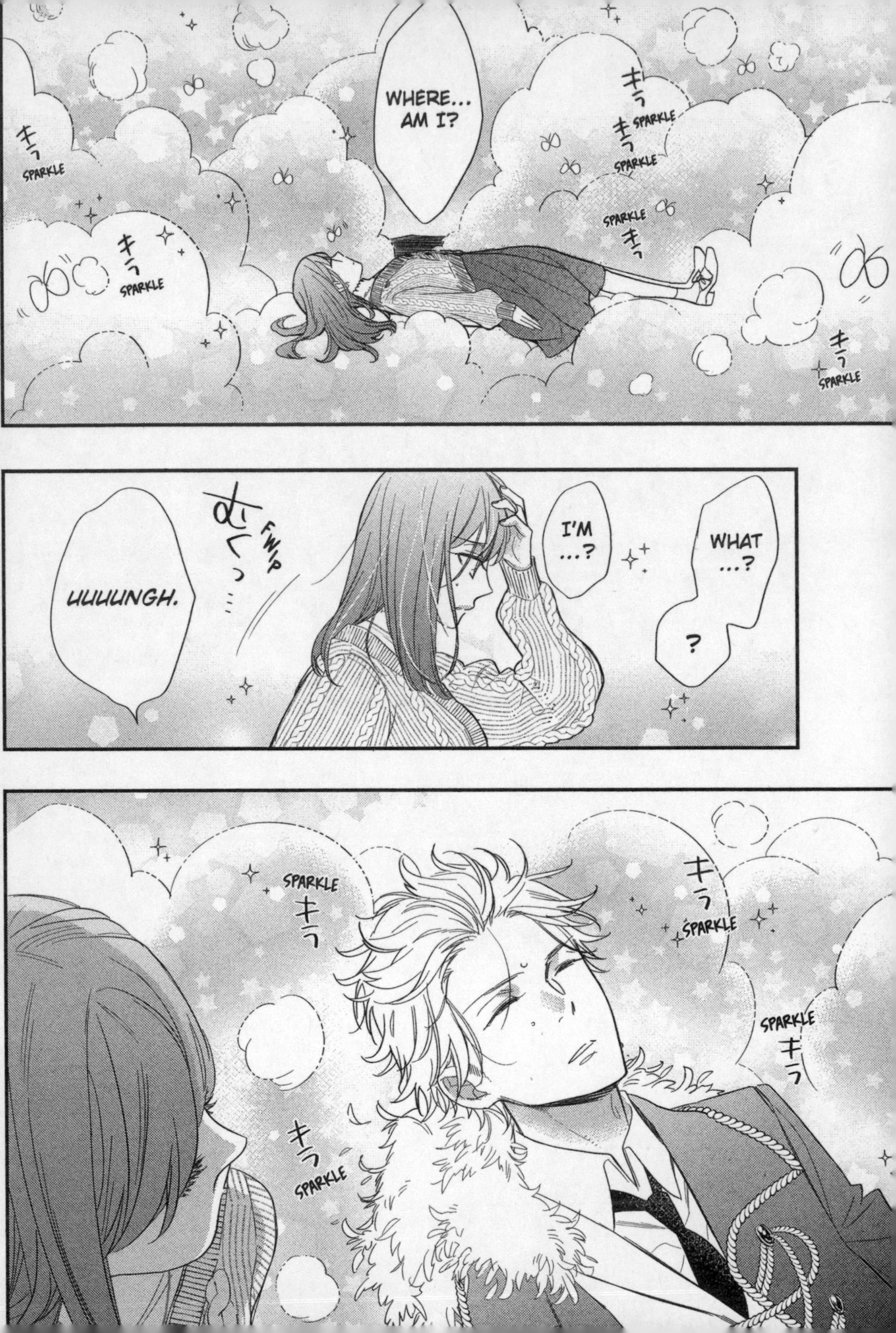

キラ SPARKLE
キラ SPARKLE
SPARKLE キラ
キラ SPARKLE
WHERE... AM I?
キラ SPARKLE
キラ SPARKLE
WHAT ...? ?
I'M ...?
ぬくっ FWIP
UUUUNGH.
キラ SPARKLE
SPARKLE キラ
SPARKLE キラ
キラ SPARKLE

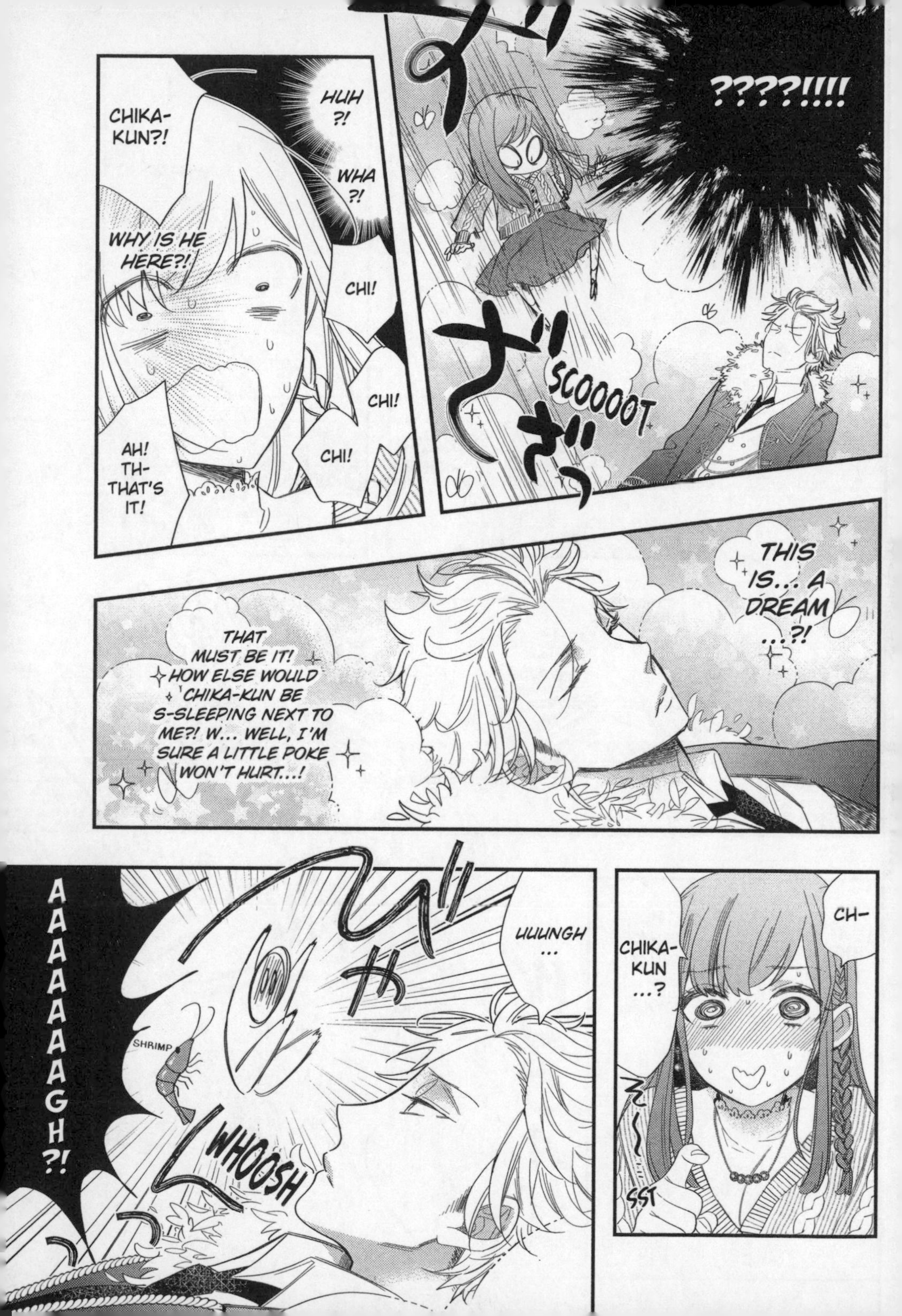

????!!!!
SCOOOOT
HUH ?!
CHIKA-KUN?!
WHA ?!
WHY IS HE HERE?!
CHI!
CHI!
CHI!
AH! TH-THAT'S IT!
THIS IS... A DREAM ...?!
THAT MUST BE IT! HOW ELSE WOULD CHIKA-KUN BE S-SLEEPING NEXT TO ME?! W... WELL, I'M SURE A LITTLE POKE WON'T HURT...!
CH-
CHIKA-KUN ...?
SST
UUUNGH ...
WHOOSH
SHRIMP
AAAAAAAAAGH?!

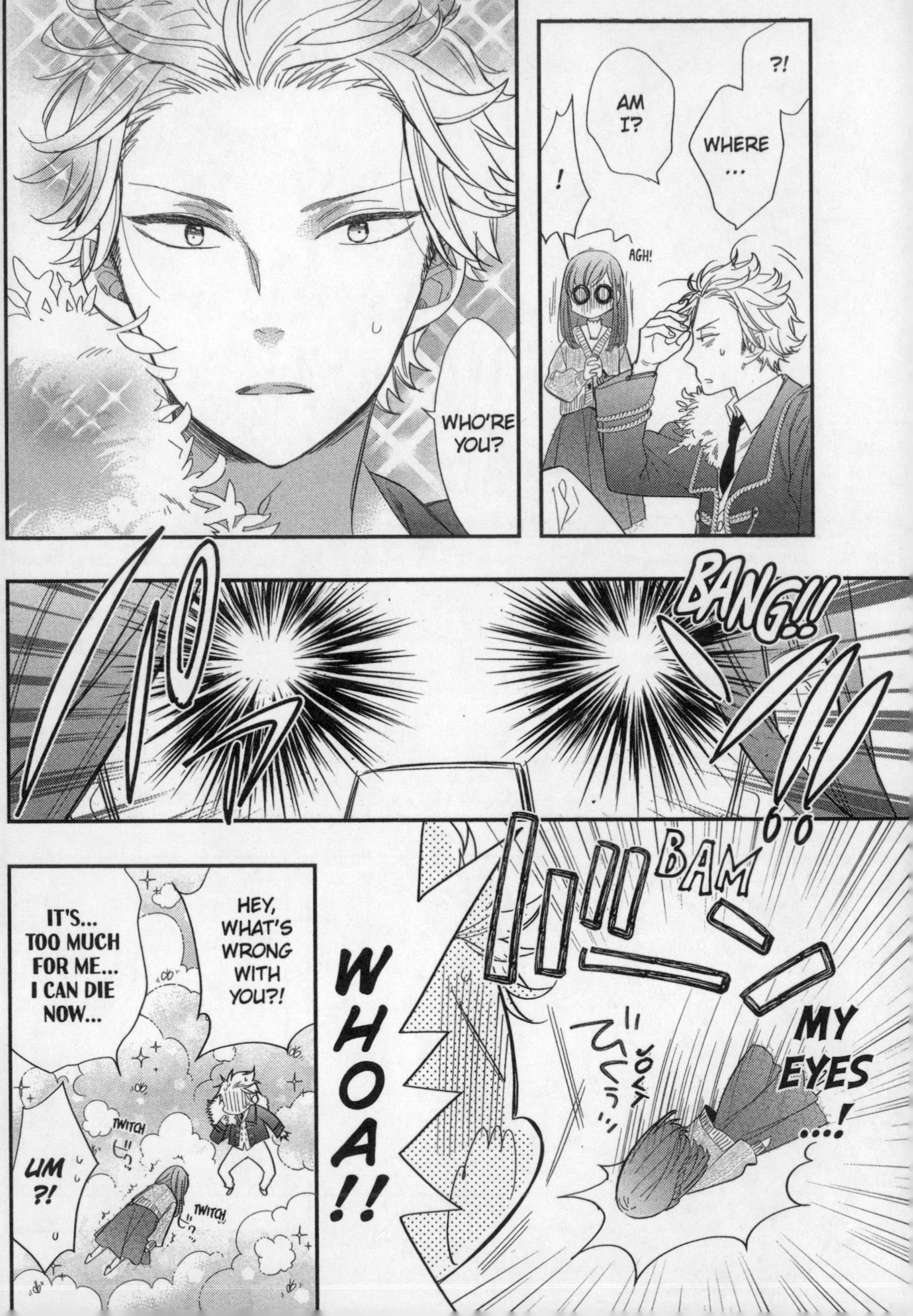
?!
WHERE...
AM I?
!
AGH!
WHO'RE YOU?
BANG!!
BAM
MY EYES...!
JOLT
WHOA!!
HEY, WHAT'S WRONG WITH YOU?!
IT'S... TOO MUCH FOR ME... I CAN DIE NOW...
TWITCH
UM ?!
TWITCH

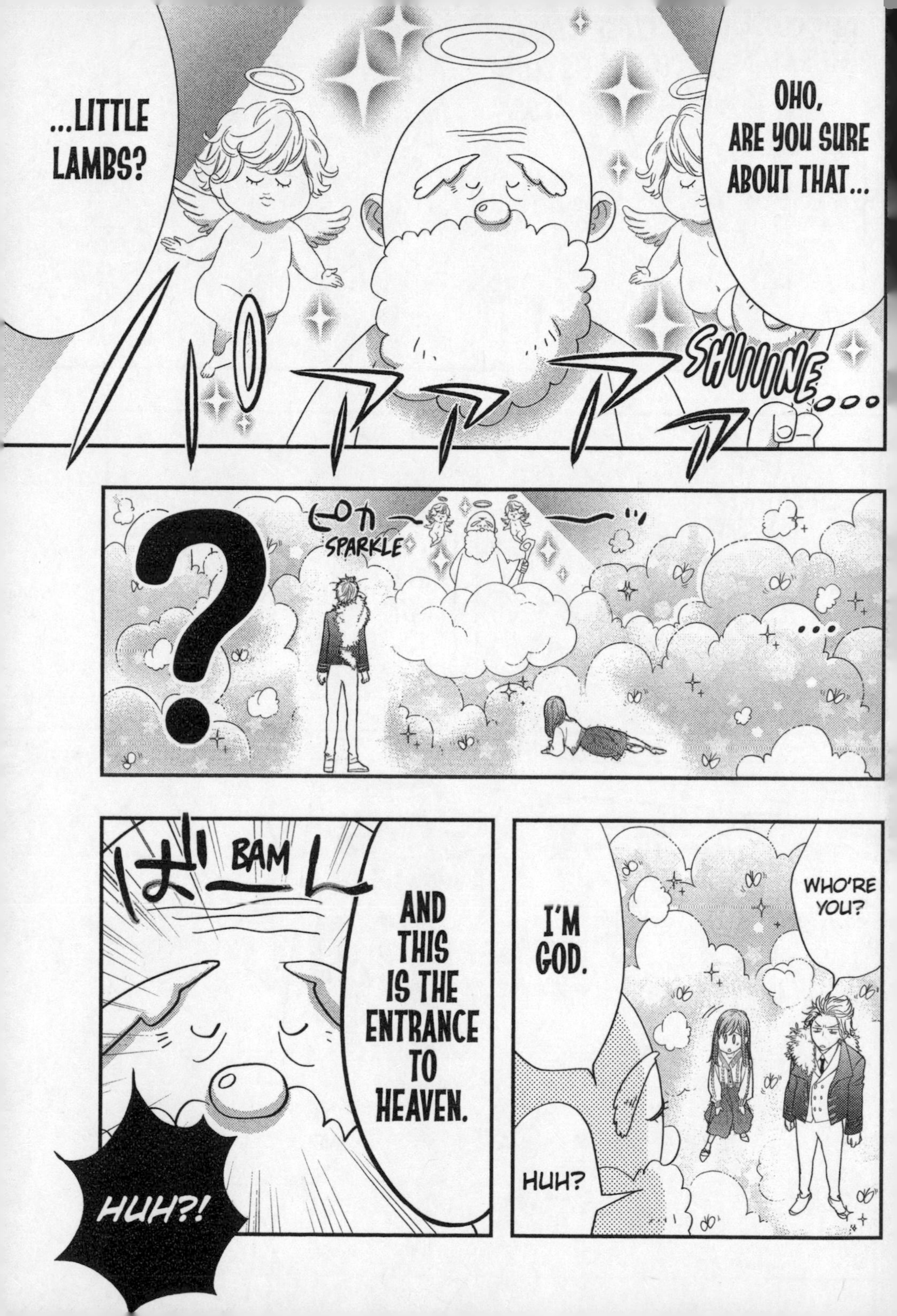
OHO, ARE YOU SURE ABOUT THAT...
...LITTLE LAMBS?
SHUIINE...
SPARKLE
...
WHO'RE YOU?
I'M GOD.
HUH?
BAM
AND THIS IS THE ENTRANCE TO HEAVEN.
HUH?!

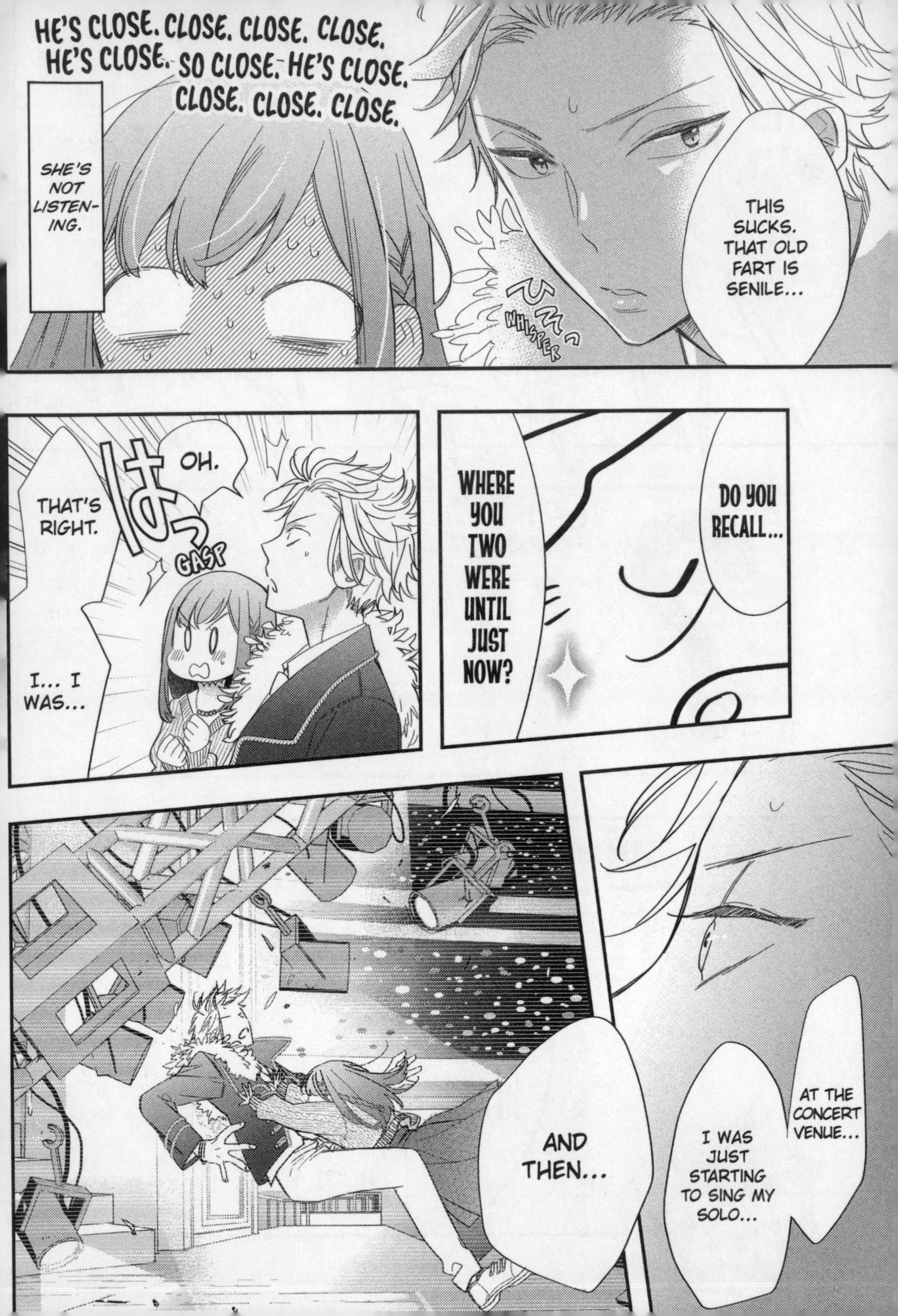
THIS SUCKS. THAT OLD FART IS SENILE...
WHISPER
HE'S CLOSE. CLOSE. CLOSE. CLOSE. HE'S CLOSE. SO CLOSE. HE'S CLOSE. CLOSE. CLOSE. CLOSE.
SHE'S NOT LISTENING.
DO YOU RECALL...
WHERE YOU TWO WERE UNTIL JUST NOW?
OH.
THAT'S RIGHT.
GASP
I... I WAS...
AT THE CONCERT VENUE...
I WAS JUST STARTING TO SING MY SOLO...
AND THEN...

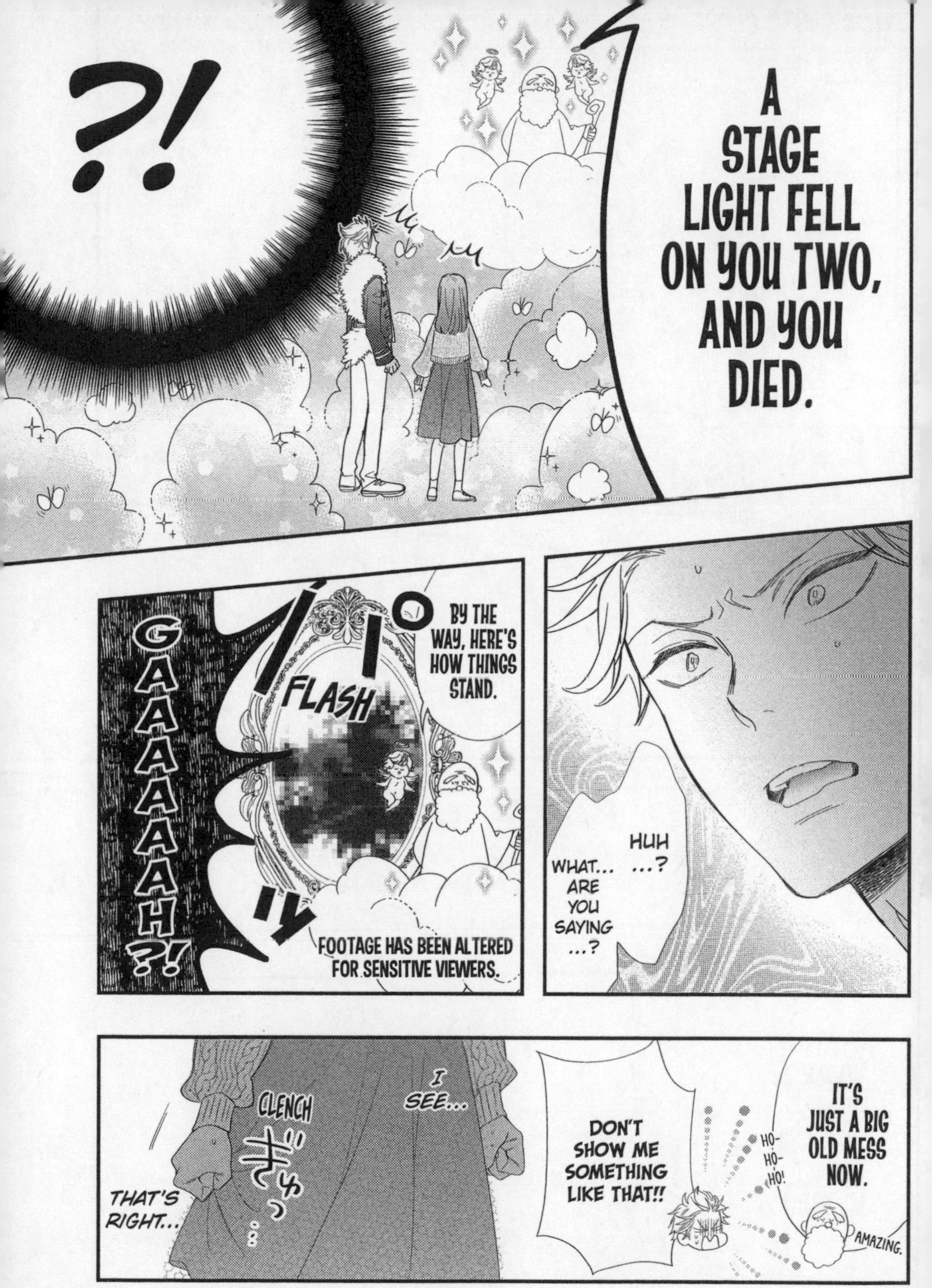
A STAGE LIGHT FELL ON YOU TWO, AND YOU DIED.
?!
HUH ...?
WHAT... ARE YOU SAYING ...?
BY THE WAY, HERE'S HOW THINGS STAND.
FLASH
GAAAAAAAAH?!
FOOTAGE HAS BEEN ALTERED FOR SENSITIVE VIEWERS.
IT'S JUST A BIG OLD MESS NOW.
HO-HO-HO!
AMAZING.
DON'T SHOW ME SOMETHING LIKE THAT!!
I SEE...
CLENCH
ぎゅっ…
THAT'S RIGHT...

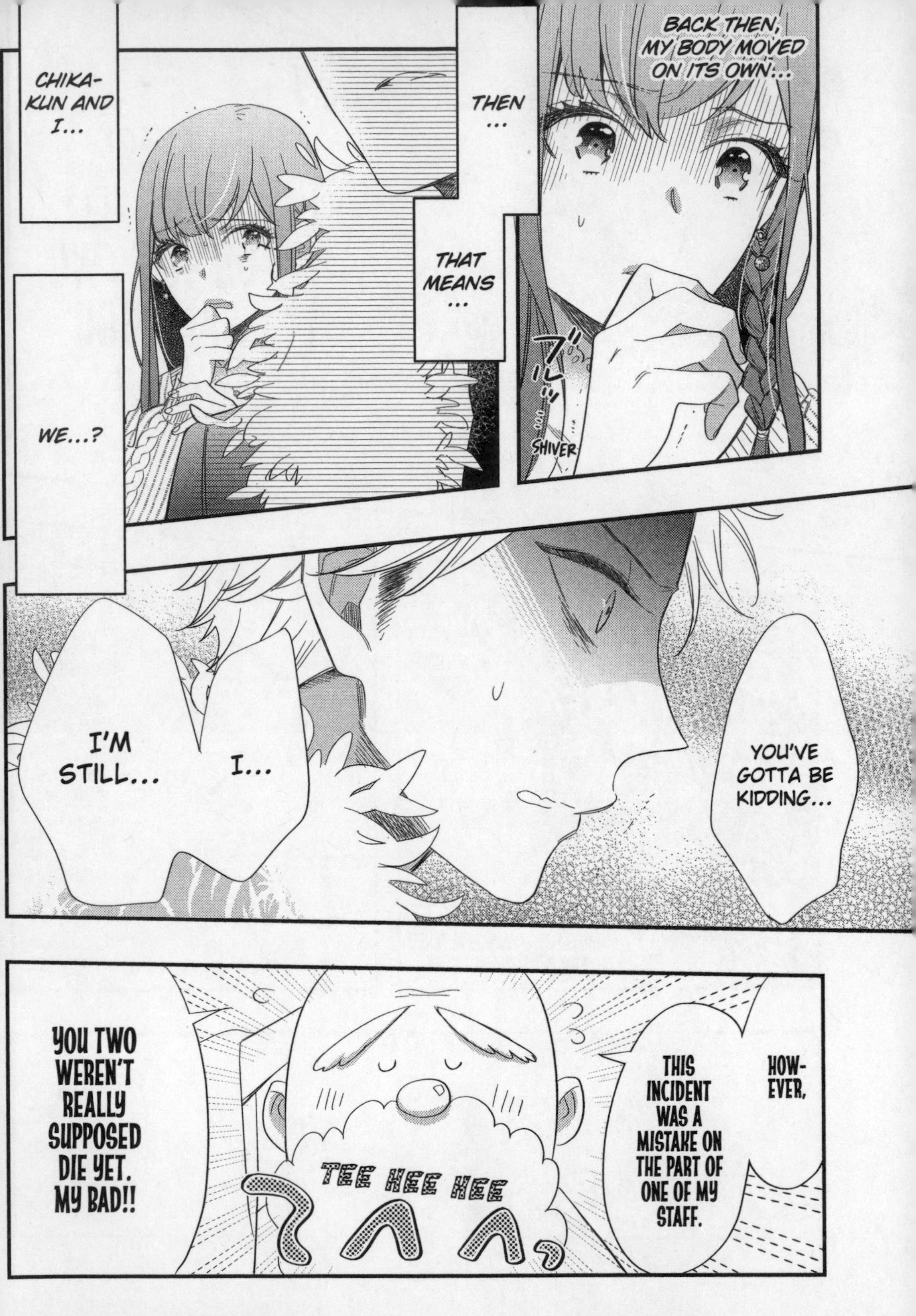
BACK THEN, MY BODY MOVED ON ITS OWN…
ブルッ
SHIVER
THEN …
THAT MEANS …
CHIKA-KUN AND I…
WE…?
YOU'VE GOTTA BE KIDDING…
I…
I'M STILL…
HOW-EVER,
THIS INCIDENT WAS A MISTAKE ON THE PART OF ONE OF MY STAFF.
TEE HEE HEE
YOU TWO WEREN'T REALLY SUPPOSED DIE YET. MY BAD!!

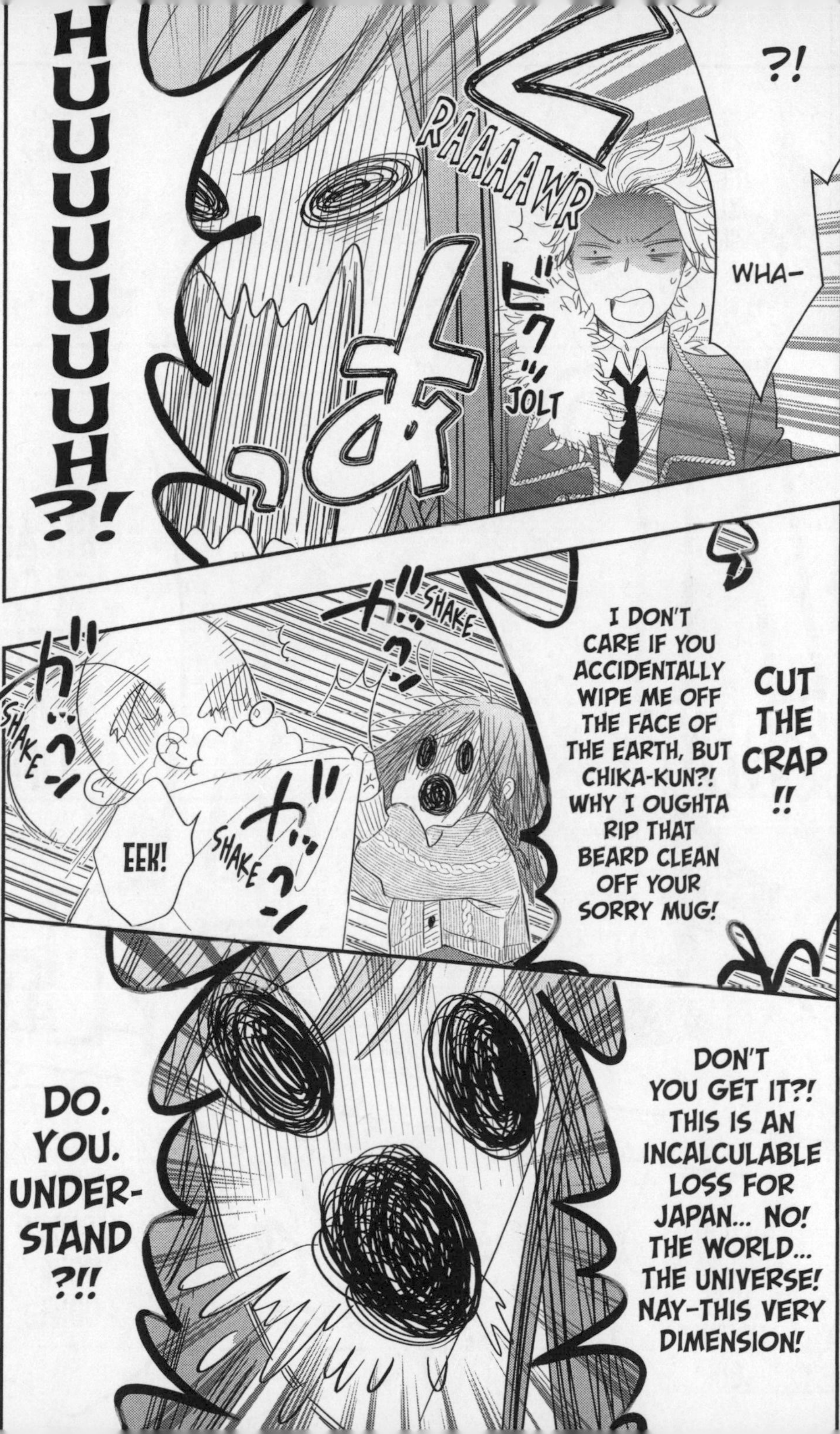
?!
RAAAAWR
WHA-
JOLT
HUUUUUUUH?!
CUT THE CRAP!!
I DON'T CARE IF YOU ACCIDENTALLY WIPE ME OFF THE FACE OF THE EARTH, BUT CHIKA-KUN?! WHY I OUGHTA RIP THAT BEARD CLEAN OFF YOUR SORRY MUG!
SHAKE
SHAKE
SHAKE
EEK!
DON'T YOU GET IT?! THIS IS AN INCALCULABLE LOSS FOR JAPAN... NO! THE WORLD... THE UNIVERSE! NAY–THIS VERY DIMENSION!
DO. YOU. UNDER-STAND?!!

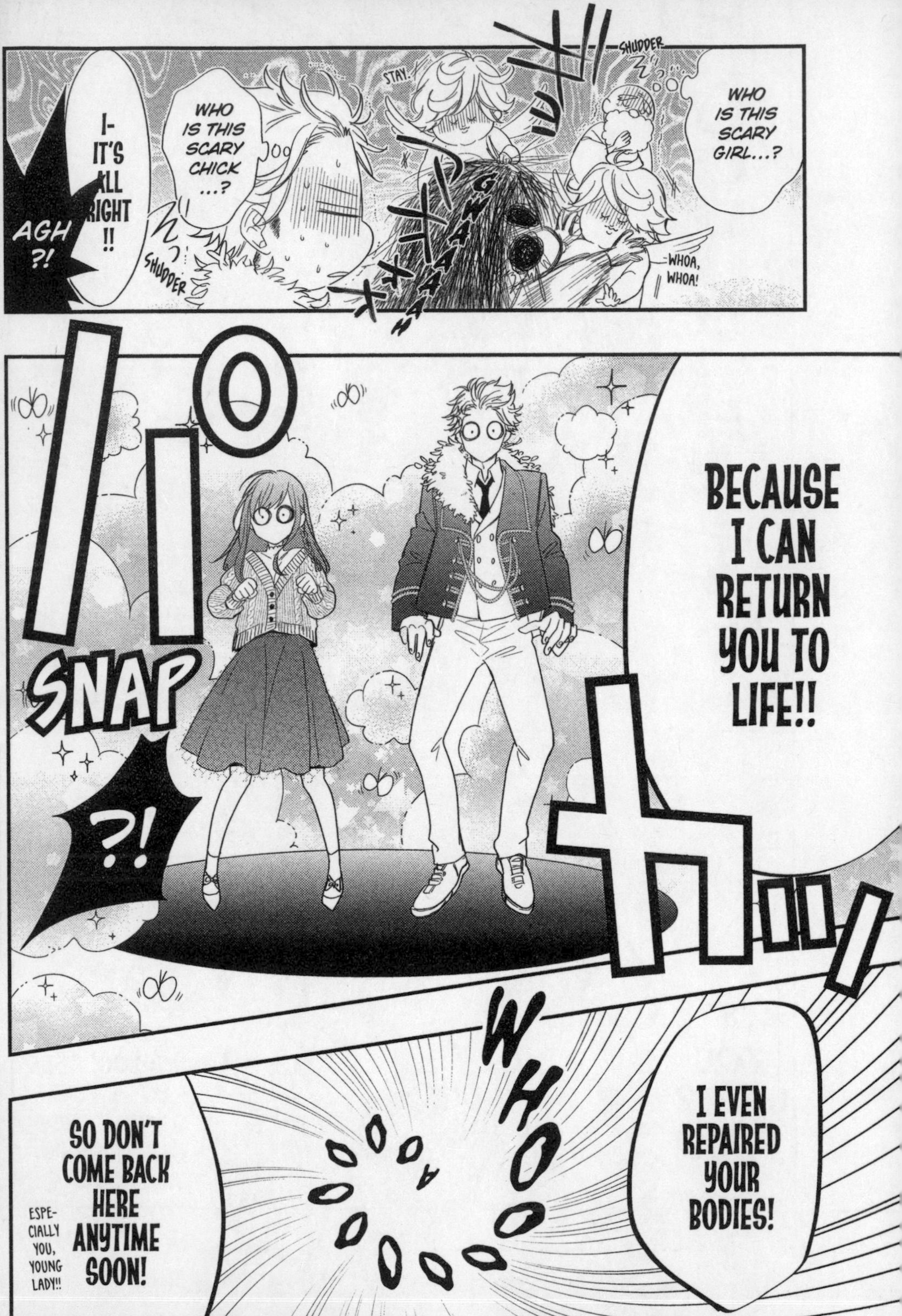
SHUDDER
WHO IS THIS SCARY GIRL...?
WHOA, WHOA!
STAY.
GWAAAAAAAH
WHO IS THIS SCARY CHICK...?
SHUDDER
I- IT'S ALL RIGHT!!
AGH?!
BECAUSE I CAN RETURN YOU TO LIFE!!
SNAP
?!
WHOOA
I EVEN REPAIRED YOUR BODIES!
SO DON'T COME BACK HERE ANYTIME SOON!
ESPE-CIALLY YOU, YOUNG LADY!!

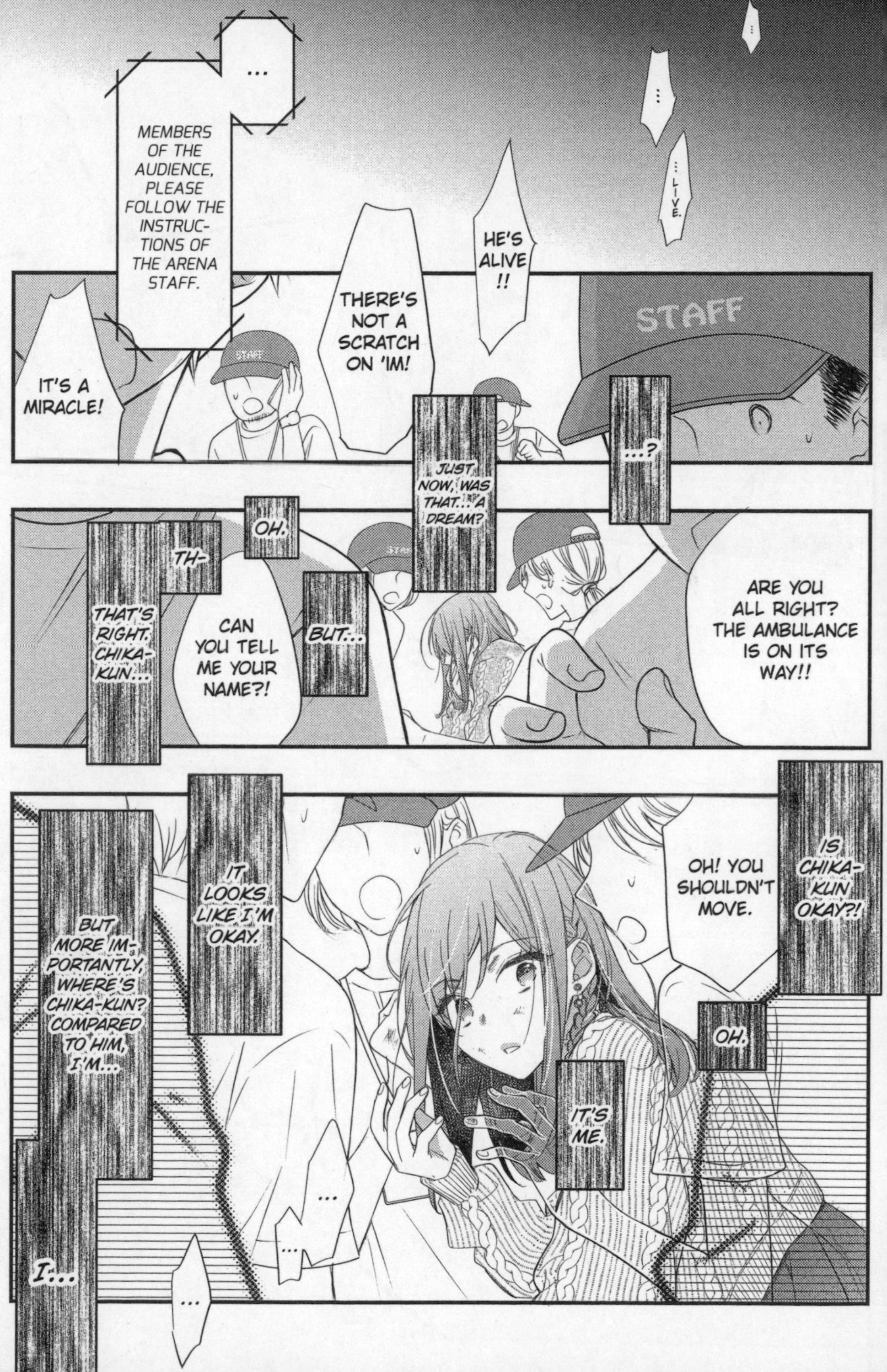
...
...
...LIVE.
HE'S ALIVE!!
...
MEMBERS OF THE AUDIENCE, PLEASE FOLLOW THE INSTRUC-TIONS OF THE ARENA STAFF.
...?
JUST NOW, WAS THAT... A DREAM?
THERE'S NOT A SCRATCH ON 'IM!
IT'S A MIRACLE!
STAFF
ARE YOU ALL RIGHT? THE AMBULANCE IS ON ITS WAY!!
OH.
BUT...
CAN YOU TELL ME YOUR NAME?!
TH-
THAT'S RIGHT, CHIKA-KUN...
IS CHIKA-KUN OKAY?!
OH! YOU SHOULDN'T MOVE.
OH.
IT'S ME.
IT LOOKS LIKE I'M OKAY.
BUT MORE IM-PORTANTLY, WHERE'S CHIKA-KUN? COMPARED TO HIM, I'M...
...
...
...
I...

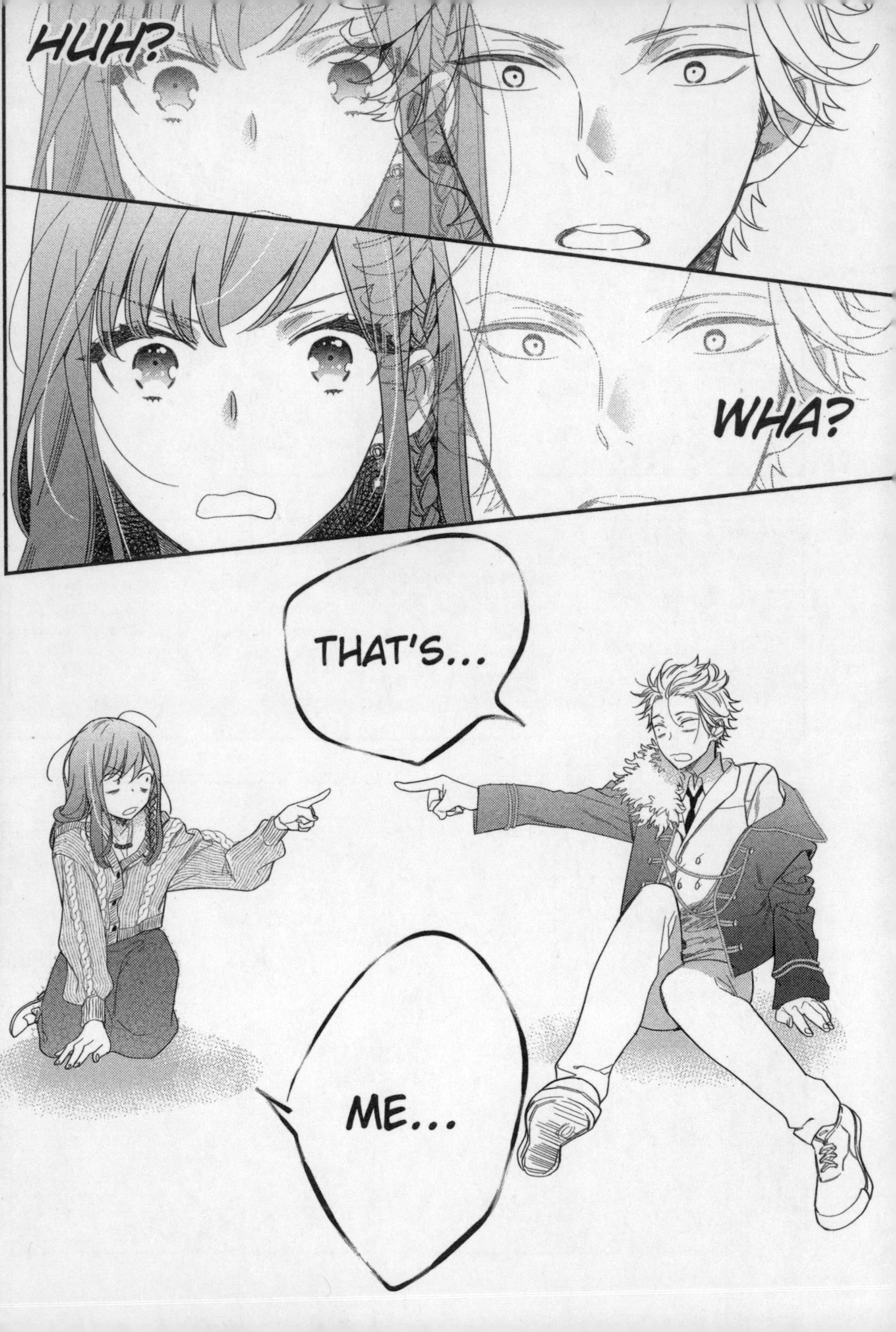
HUH?
WHA?
THAT'S...
ME...

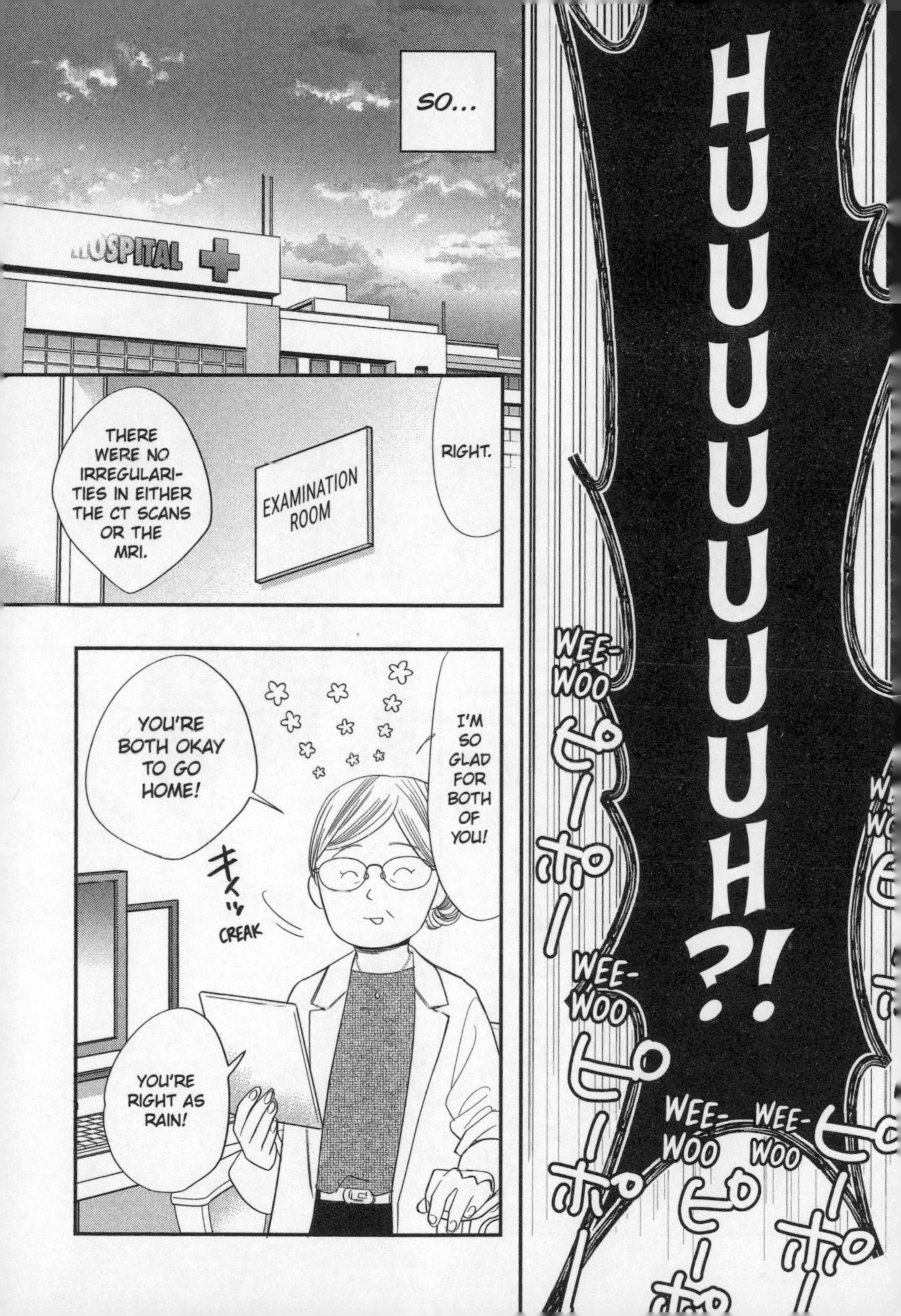
HUUUUUUUH?!
WEE-WOO
ピーポー
WEE-WOO
ピーポー
WEE-WOO
ピーポー
WEE-WOO
ピーポー
SO...
HOSPITAL
RIGHT.
THERE WERE NO IRREGULARITIES IN EITHER THE CT SCANS OR THE MRI.
EXAMINATION ROOM
I'M SO GLAD FOR BOTH OF YOU!
YOU'RE BOTH OKAY TO GO HOME!
キィッ
CREAK
YOU'RE RIGHT AS RAIN!

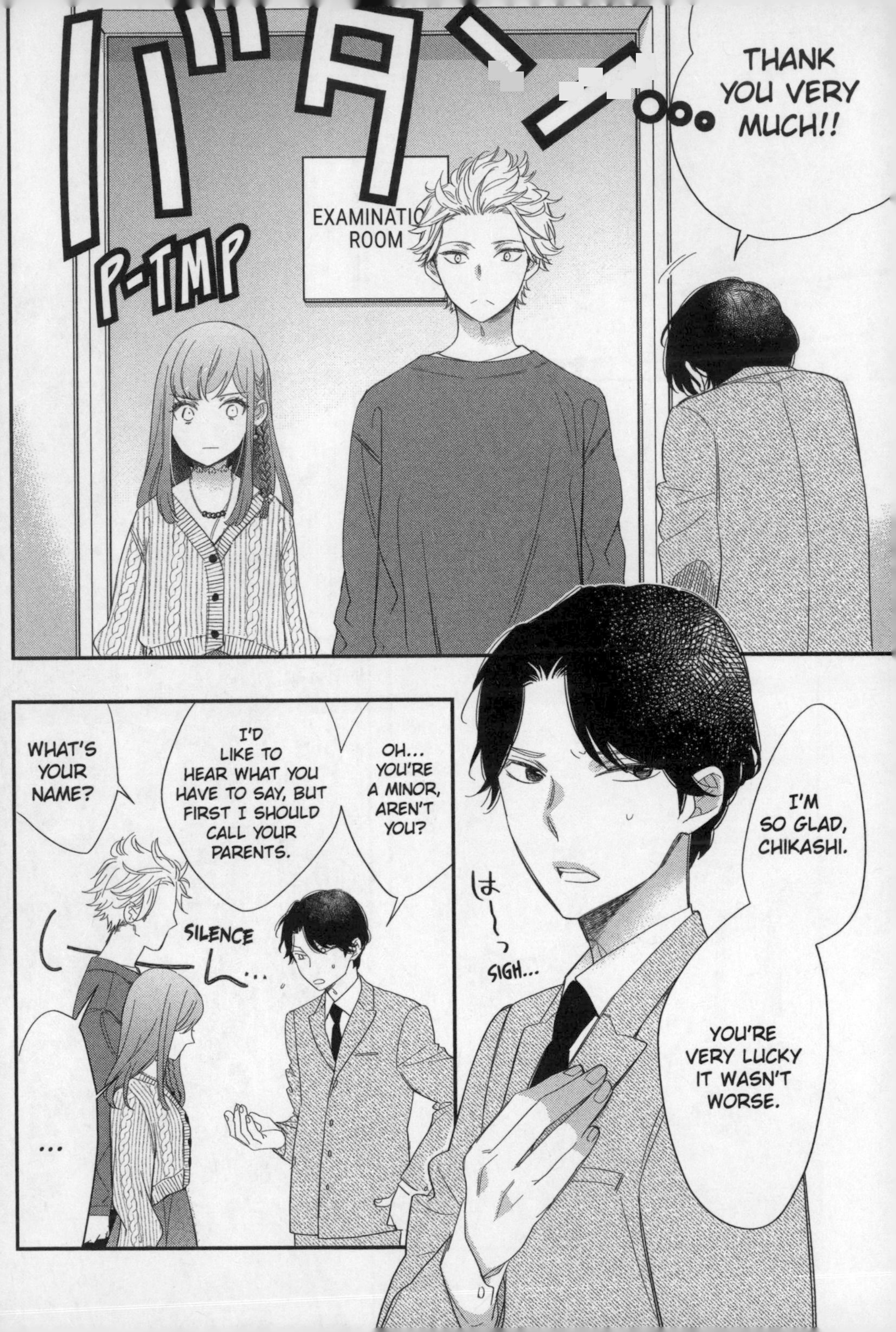
THANK YOU VERY MUCH!!
P-TMP
EXAMINATIO ROOM
I'M SO GLAD, CHIKASHI.
はーっ
SIGH...
YOU'RE VERY LUCKY IT WASN'T WORSE.
OH... YOU'RE A MINOR, AREN'T YOU?
I'D LIKE TO HEAR WHAT YOU HAVE TO SAY, BUT FIRST I SHOULD CALL YOUR PARENTS.
WHAT'S YOUR NAME?
SILENCE
...

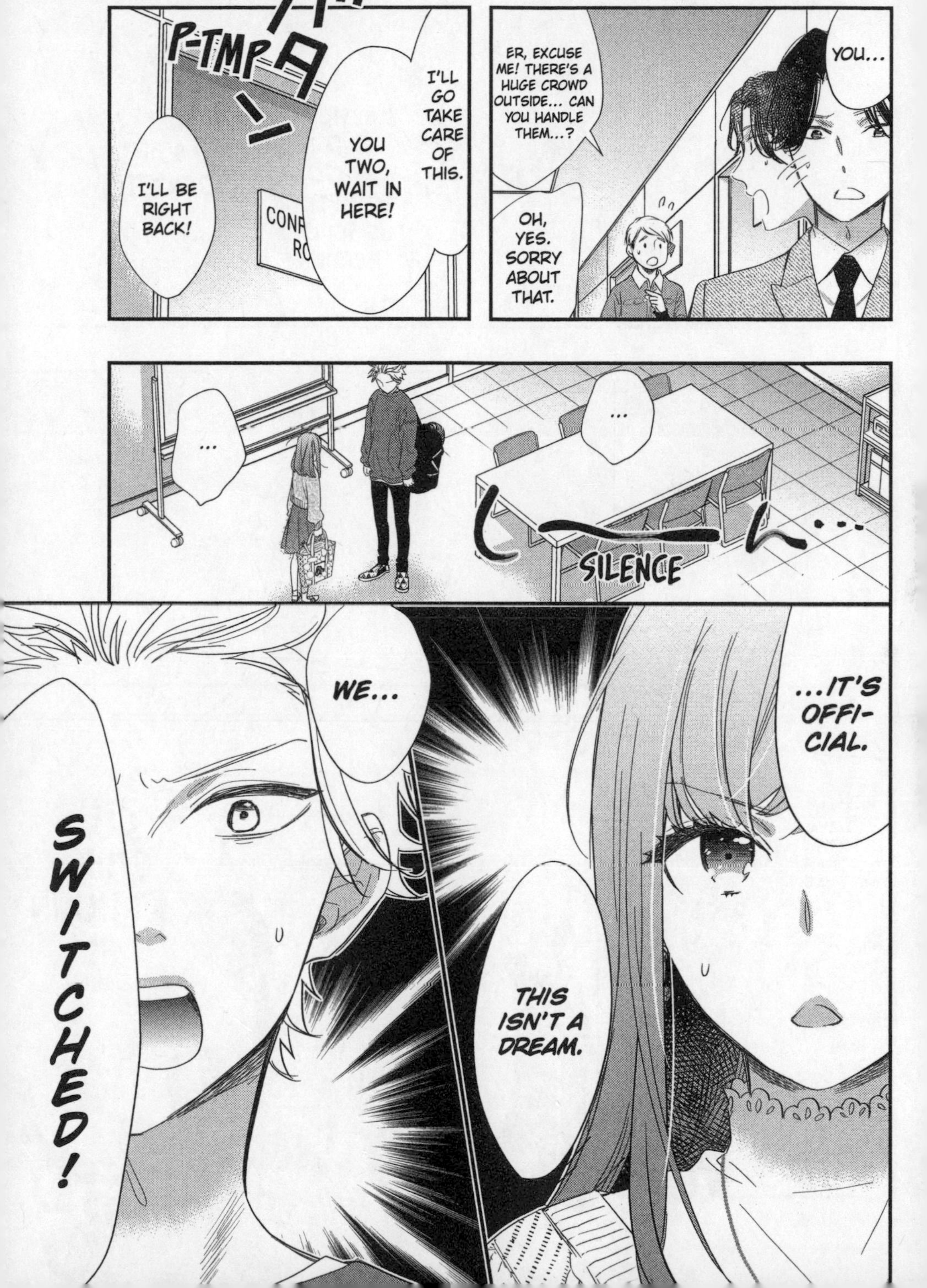
YOU...
ER, EXCUSE ME! THERE'S A HUGE CROWD OUTSIDE... CAN YOU HANDLE THEM...?
OH, YES. SORRY ABOUT THAT.
I'LL GO TAKE CARE OF THIS.
YOU TWO, WAIT IN HERE!
I'LL BE RIGHT BACK!
P-TMP
...
...
SILENCE
...IT'S OFFICIAL.
WE...
THIS ISN'T A DREAM.
SWITCHED!

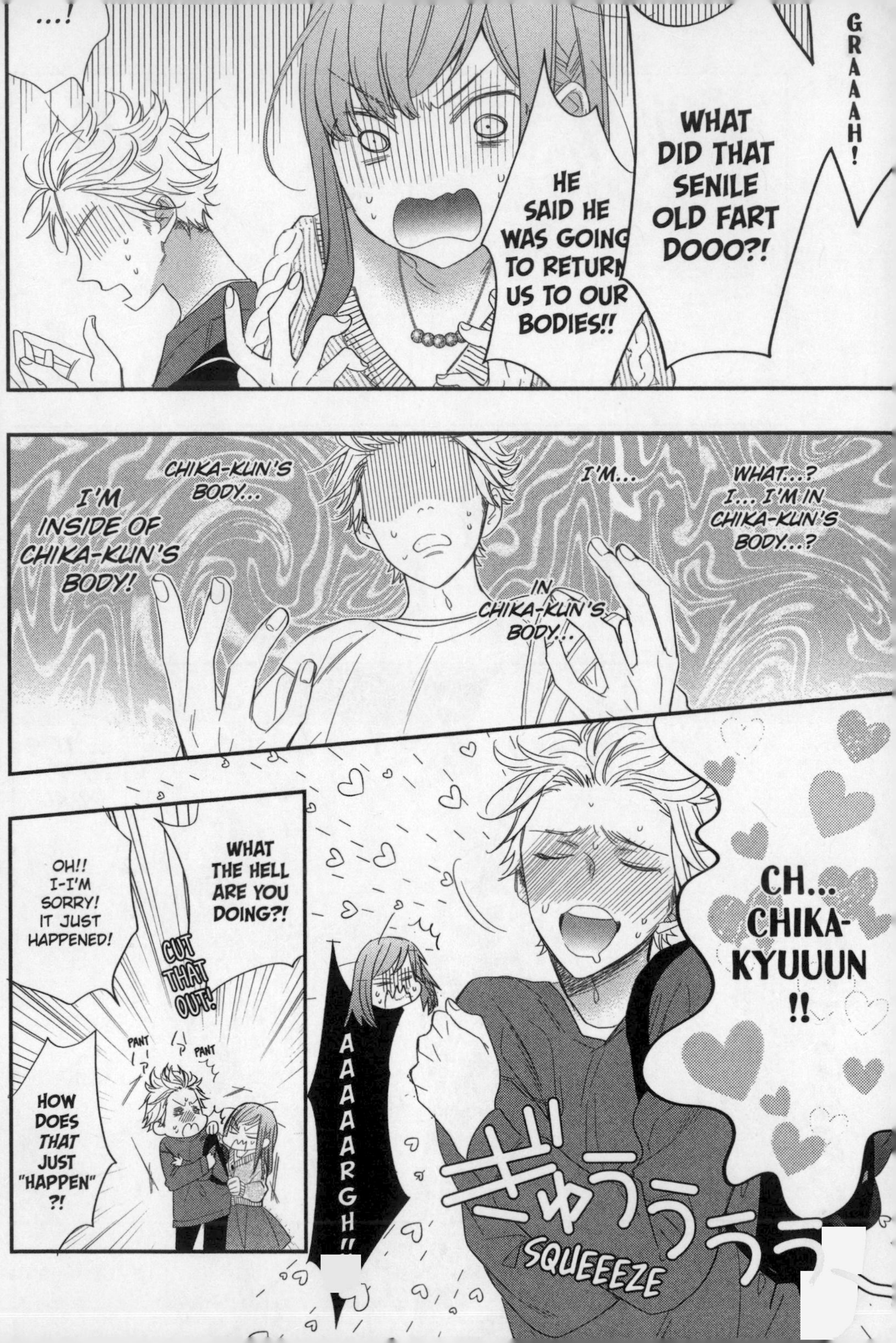
GRAAAAH!
WHAT DID THAT SENILE OLD FART DOOO?!
HE SAID HE WAS GOING TO RETURN US TO OUR BODIES!!
...!
WHAT...? I... I'M IN CHIKA-KUN'S BODY...?
I'M...
IN CHIKA-KUN'S BODY...
CHIKA-KUN'S BODY...
I'M INSIDE OF CHIKA-KUN'S BODY!
CH... CHIKA-KYUUUN!!
AAAAAARGH!!
ぎゅううう
SQUEEEEZE
WHAT THE HELL ARE YOU DOING?!
OH!! I-I'M SORRY! IT JUST HAPPENED!
CUT THAT OUT!
PANT
PANT
HOW DOES THAT JUST "HAPPEN"?!

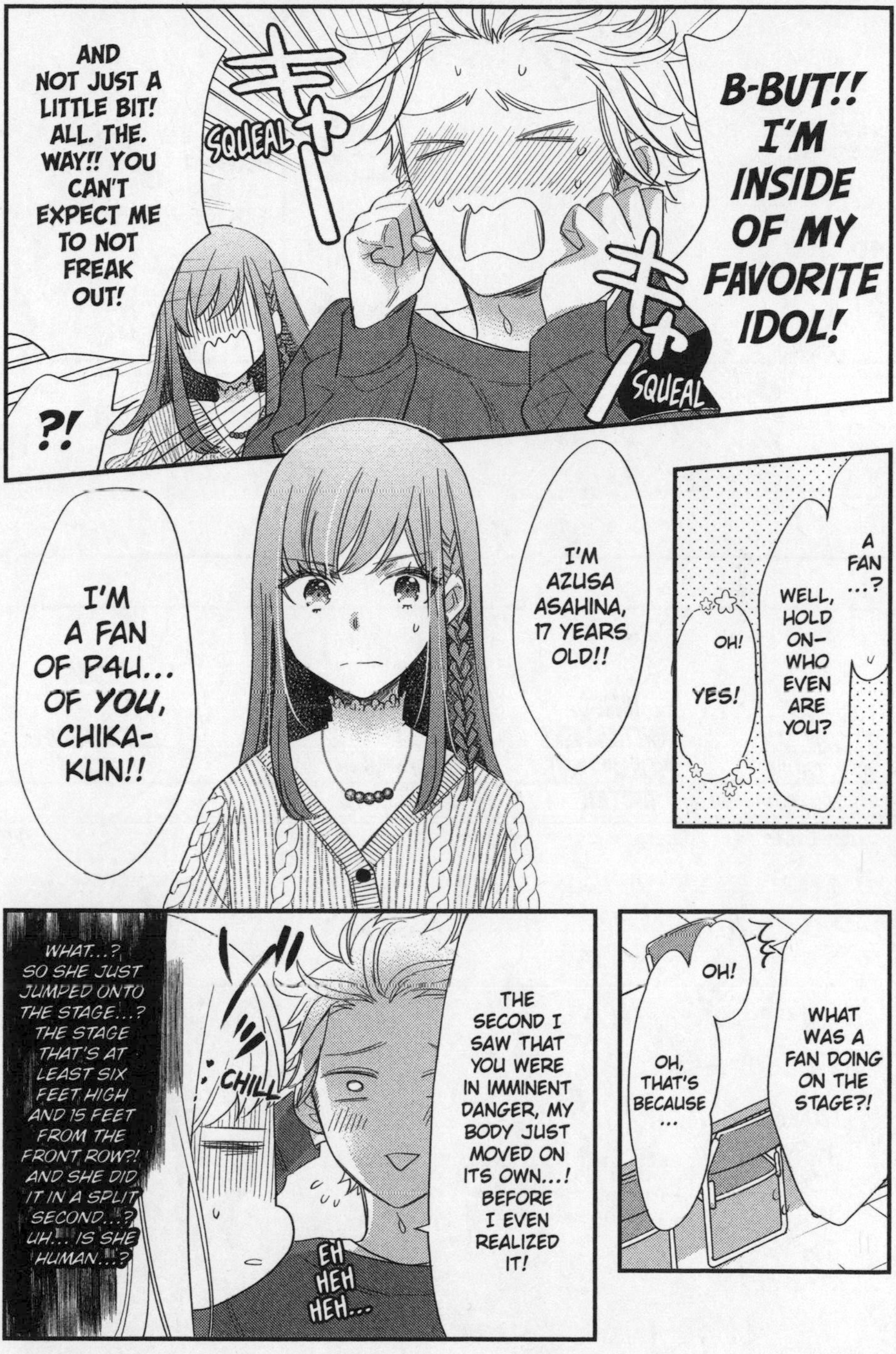
B-BUT!! I'M INSIDE OF MY FAVORITE IDOL!
SQUEAL
SQUEAL
AND NOT JUST A LITTLE BIT! ALL. THE. WAY!! YOU CAN'T EXPECT ME TO NOT FREAK OUT!
?!
A FAN ...?
WELL, HOLD ON— WHO EVEN ARE YOU?
OH!
YES!
I'M AZUSA ASAHINA, 17 YEARS OLD!!
I'M A FAN OF P4U... OF YOU, CHIKA-KUN!!
WHAT WAS A FAN DOING ON THE STAGE?!
OH!
OH, THAT'S BECAUSE ...
THE SECOND I SAW THAT YOU WERE IN IMMINENT DANGER, MY BODY JUST MOVED ON ITS OWN...! BEFORE I EVEN REALIZED IT!
EH HEH HEH...
CHILL
WHAT...? SO SHE JUST JUMPED ONTO THE STAGE...? THE STAGE THAT'S AT LEAST SIX FEET HIGH AND 15 FEET FROM THE FRONT ROW?! AND SHE DID IT IN A SPLIT SECOND...? UH... IS SHE HUMAN...?

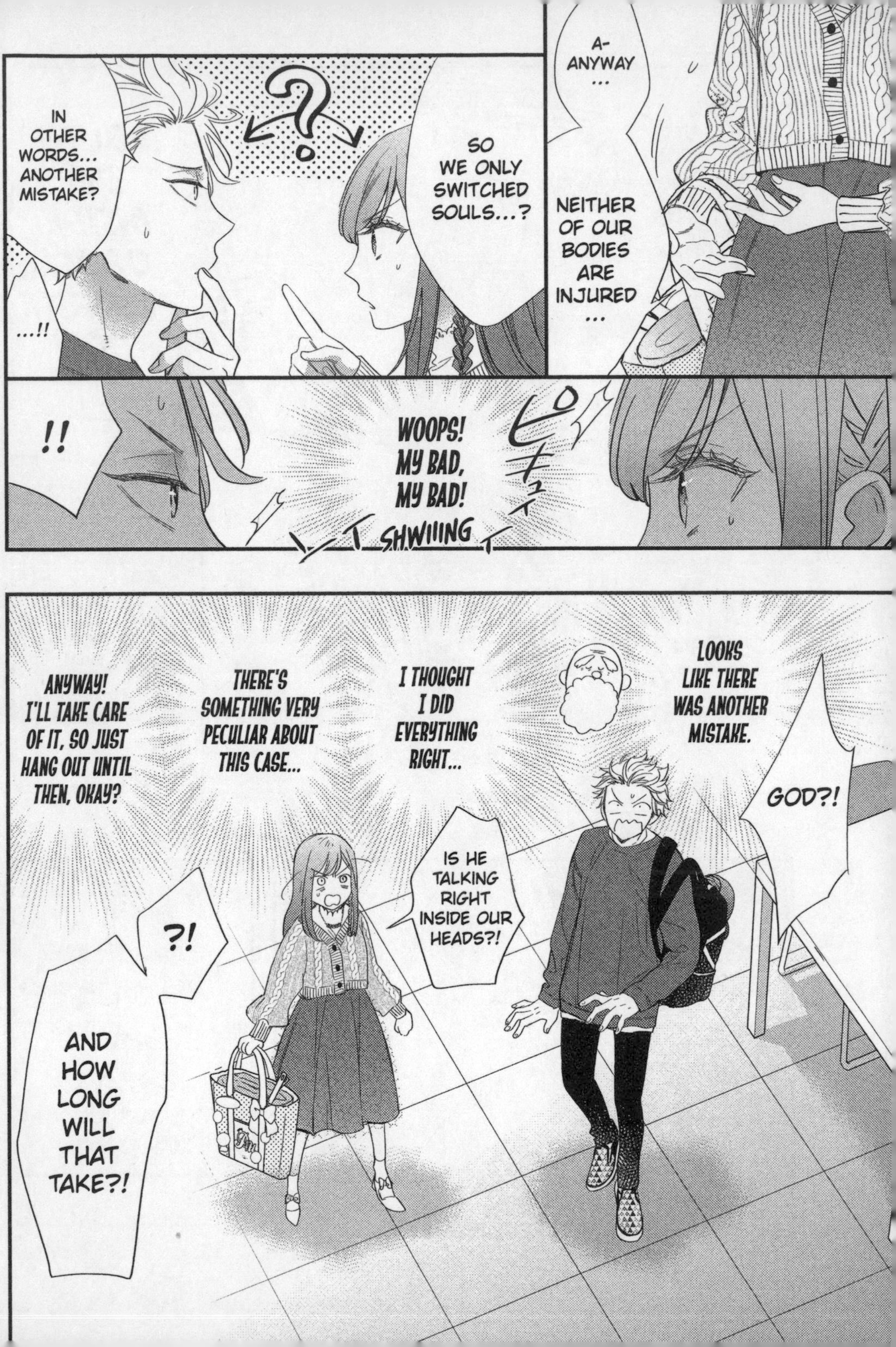
A- ANYWAY...
NEITHER OF OUR BODIES ARE INJURED...
SO WE ONLY SWITCHED SOULS...?
IN OTHER WORDS... ANOTHER MISTAKE?
...!!
WOOPS! MY BAD, MY BAD!
!!
SHWIIING
LOOKS LIKE THERE WAS ANOTHER MISTAKE.
GOD?!
I THOUGHT I DID EVERYTHING RIGHT...
THERE'S SOMETHING VERY PECULIAR ABOUT THIS CASE...
ANYWAY! I'LL TAKE CARE OF IT, SO JUST HANG OUT UNTIL THEN, OKAY?
IS HE TALKING RIGHT INSIDE OUR HEADS?!
?!
AND HOW LONG WILL THAT TAKE?!

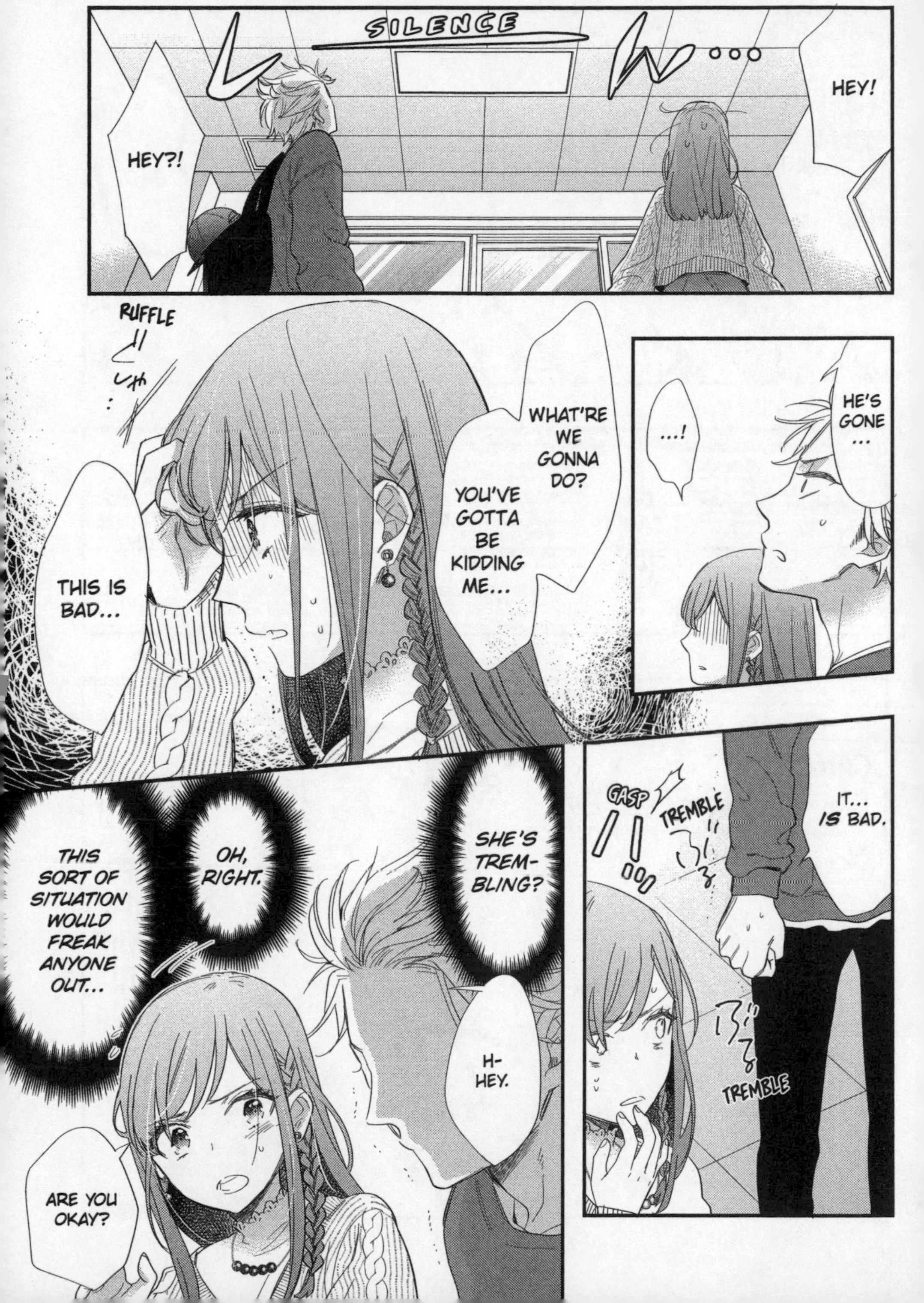
SILENCE
HEY!
HEY?!
HE'S GONE...
...!
RUFFLE
WHAT'RE WE GONNA DO?
YOU'VE GOTTA BE KIDDING ME...
THIS IS BAD...
IT... IS BAD.
GASP
TREMBLE
TREMBLE
SHE'S TREMBLING?
OH, RIGHT.
THIS SORT OF SITUATION WOULD FREAK ANYONE OUT...
H-HEY.
ARE YOU OKAY?

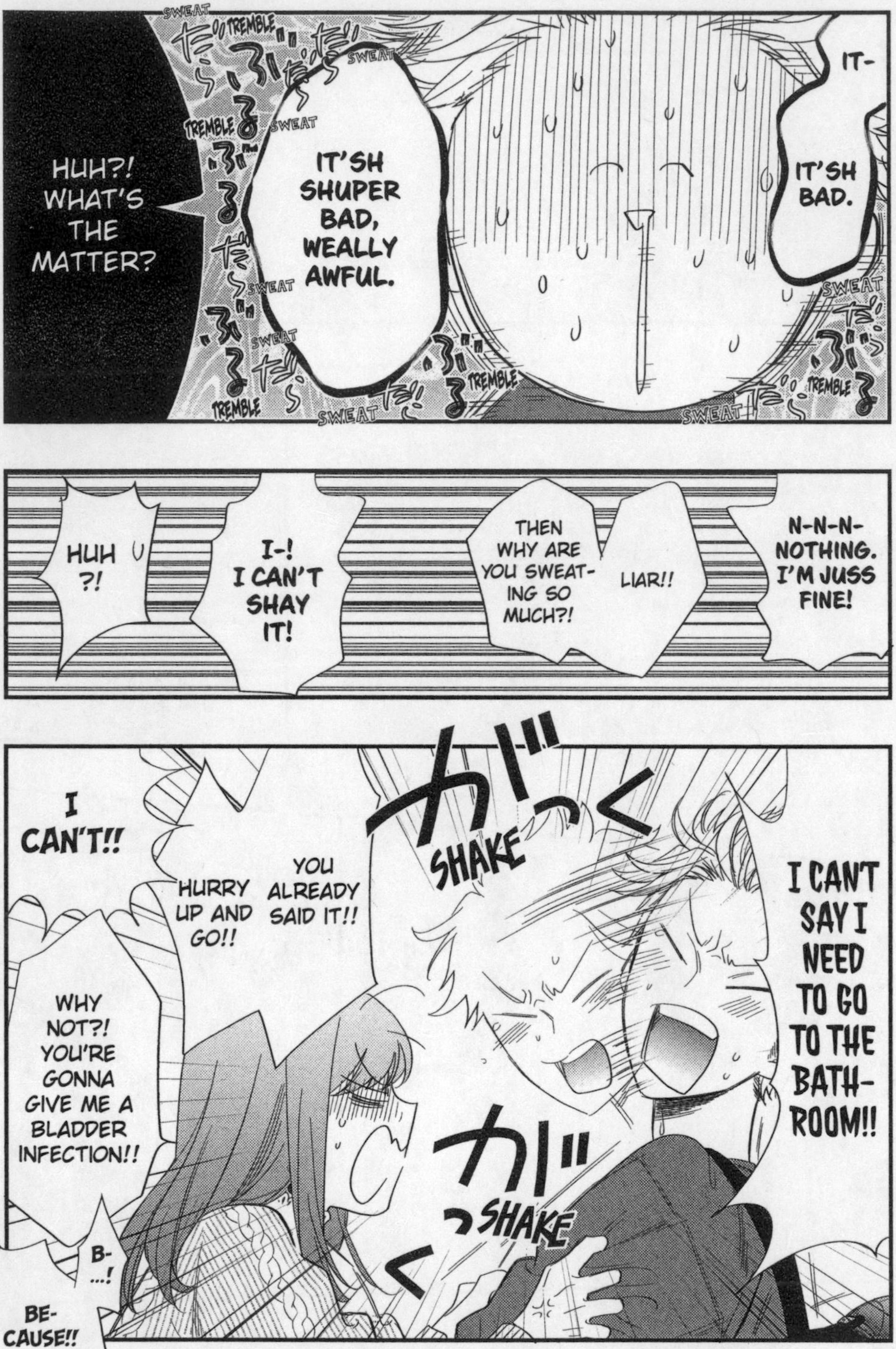
IT-
IT'SH BAD.
SWEAT
TREMBLE
IT'SH SHUPER BAD, WEALLY AWFUL.
HUH?! WHAT'S THE MATTER?
N-N-N-NOTHING. I'M JUSS FINE!
LIAR!!
THEN WHY ARE YOU SWEAT-ING SO MUCH?!
I-! I CAN'T SHAY IT!
HUH ?!
I CAN'T SAY I NEED TO GO TO THE BATH-ROOM!!
SHAKE
YOU ALREADY SAID IT!!
HURRY UP AND GO!!
I CAN'T!!
WHY NOT?! YOU'RE GONNA GIVE ME A BLADDER INFECTION!!
SHAKE
B- ...!
BE-CAUSE!!

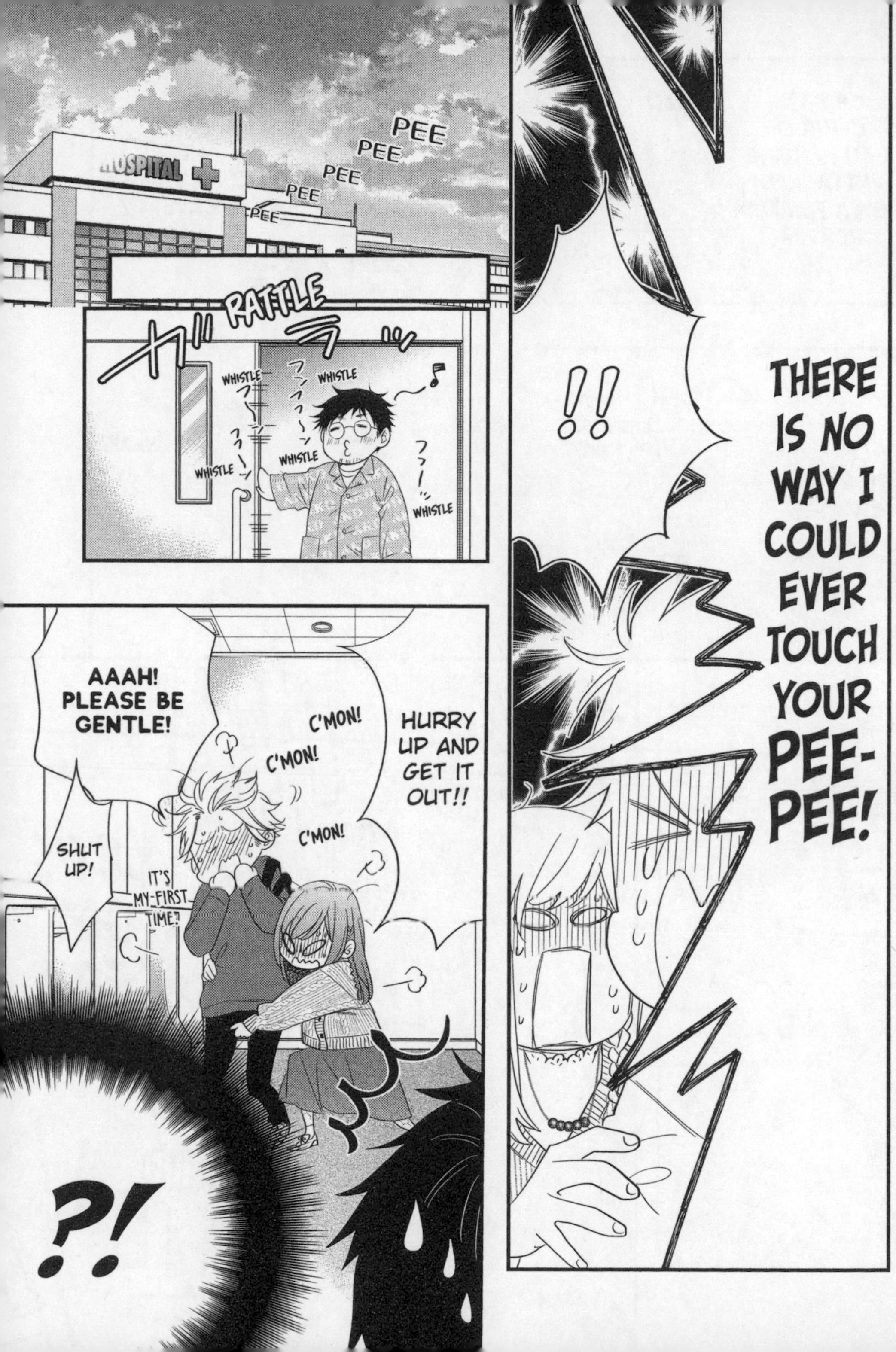
!!
THERE IS NO WAY I COULD EVER TOUCH YOUR PEE-PEE!
HOSPITAL
PEE
PEE
PEE
PEE
PEE
RATTLE
WHISTLE
WHISTLE
WHISTLE
WHISTLE
WHISTLE
HURRY UP AND GET IT OUT!!
C'MON!
C'MON!
C'MON!
AAAH! PLEASE BE GENTLE!
SHUT UP!
IT'S MY FIRST TIME!
?!

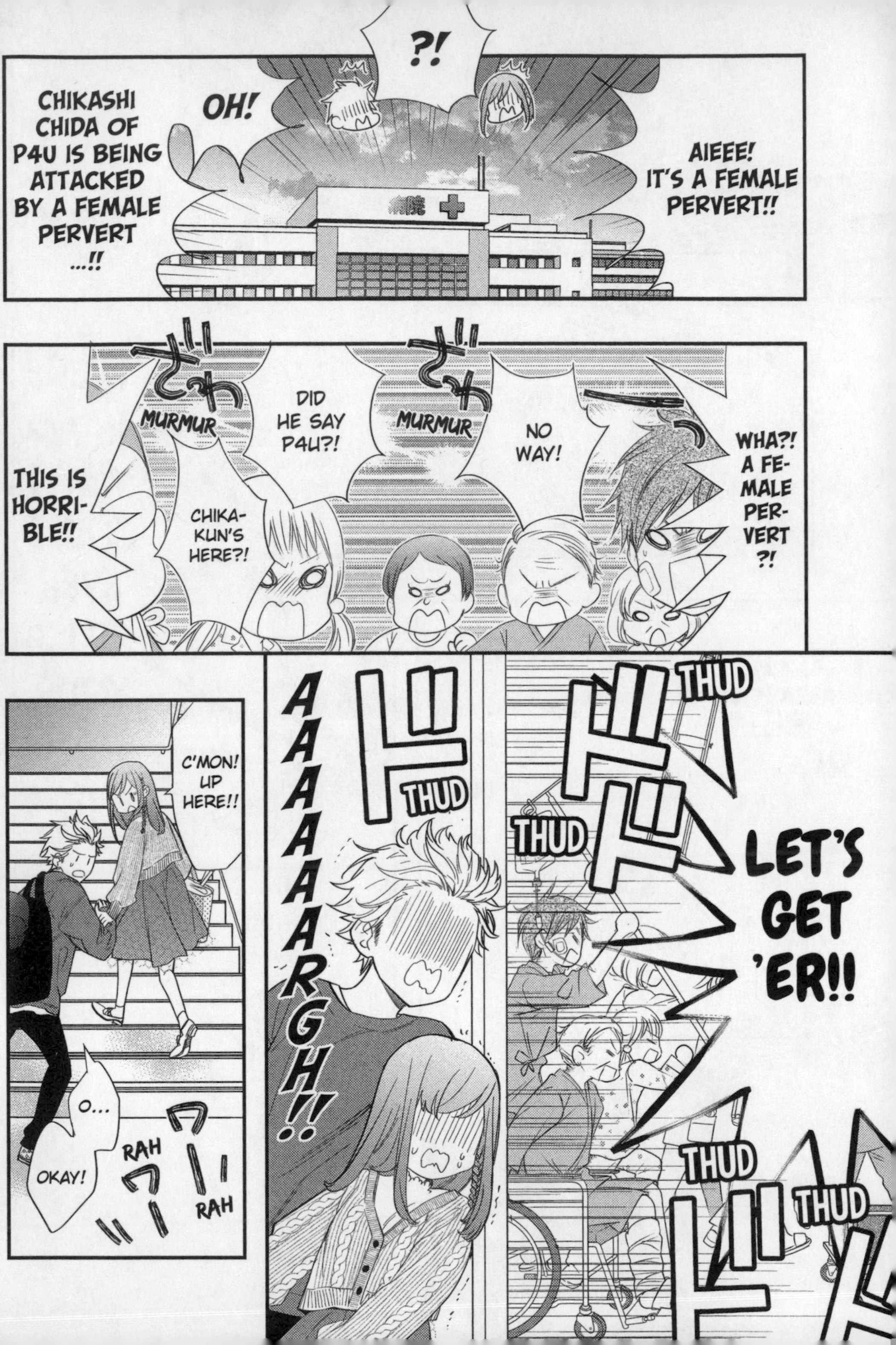
?!
AIEEE! IT'S A FEMALE PERVERT!!
OH!
CHIKASHI CHIDA OF P4U IS BEING ATTACKED BY A FEMALE PERVERT ...!!
WHA?! A FE-MALE PER-VERT ?!
NO WAY!
ざわ
MURMUR
DID HE SAY P4U?!
CHIKA-KUN'S HERE?!
ざわ
MURMUR
THIS IS HORRI-BLE!!
THUD
THUD
LET'S GET 'ER!!
THUD
THUD
THUD
AAAAAAAARGH!!
C'MON! UP HERE!!
O...
OKAY!
RAH
RAH

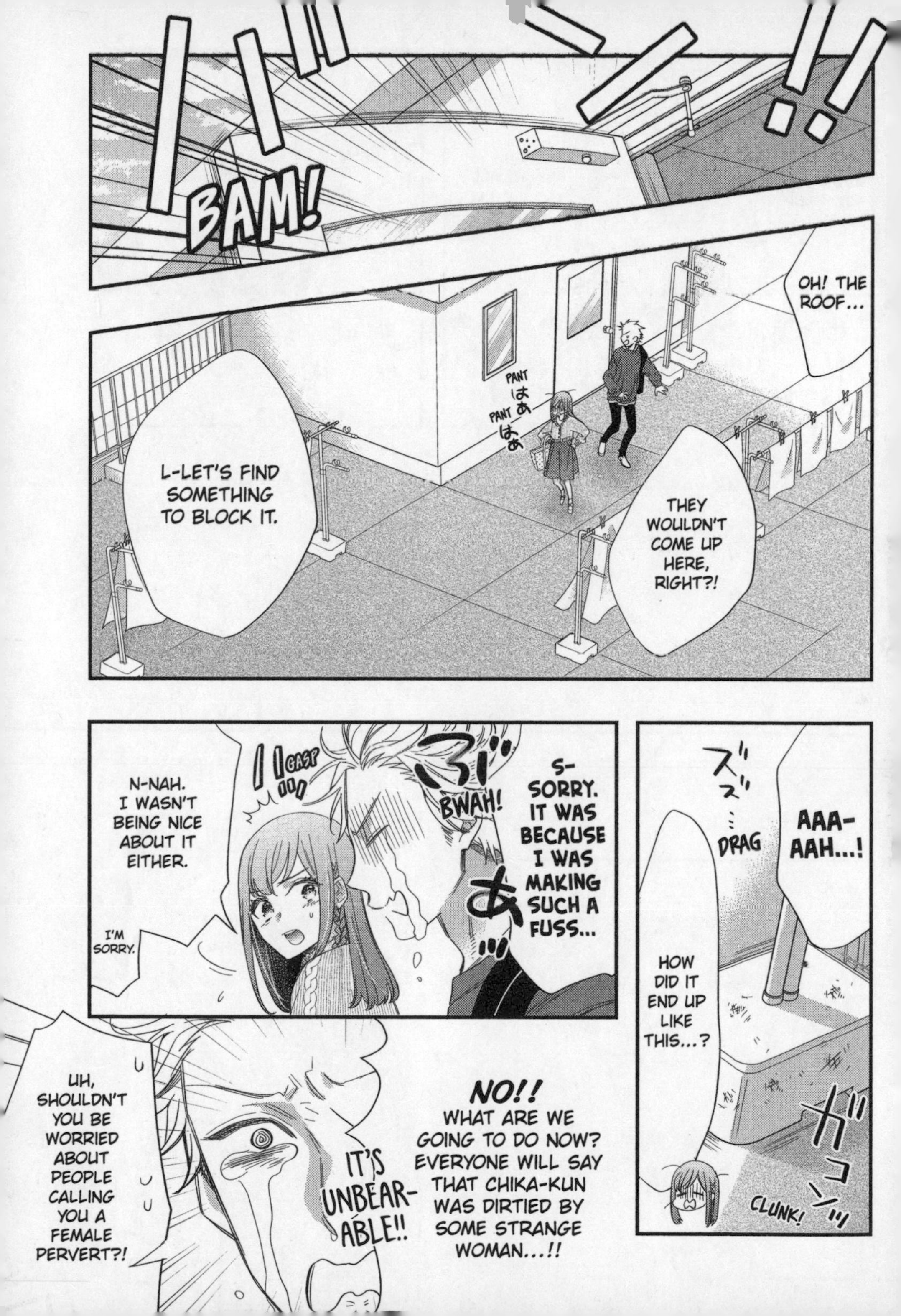
BAM!
OH! THE ROOF...
THEY WOULDN'T COME UP HERE, RIGHT?!
PANT PANT
L-LET'S FIND SOMETHING TO BLOCK IT.
AAAAH...!
DRAG
HOW DID IT END UP LIKE THIS...?
CLUNK!
S-SORRY. IT WAS BECAUSE I WAS MAKING SUCH A FUSS...
BWAH!
GASP
N-NAH. I WASN'T BEING NICE ABOUT IT EITHER.
I'M SORRY.
NO!! WHAT ARE WE GOING TO DO NOW? EVERYONE WILL SAY THAT CHIKA-KUN WAS DIRTIED BY SOME STRANGE WOMAN...!!
IT'S UNBEARABLE!!
UH, SHOULDN'T YOU BE WORRIED ABOUT PEOPLE CALLING YOU A FEMALE PERVERT?!

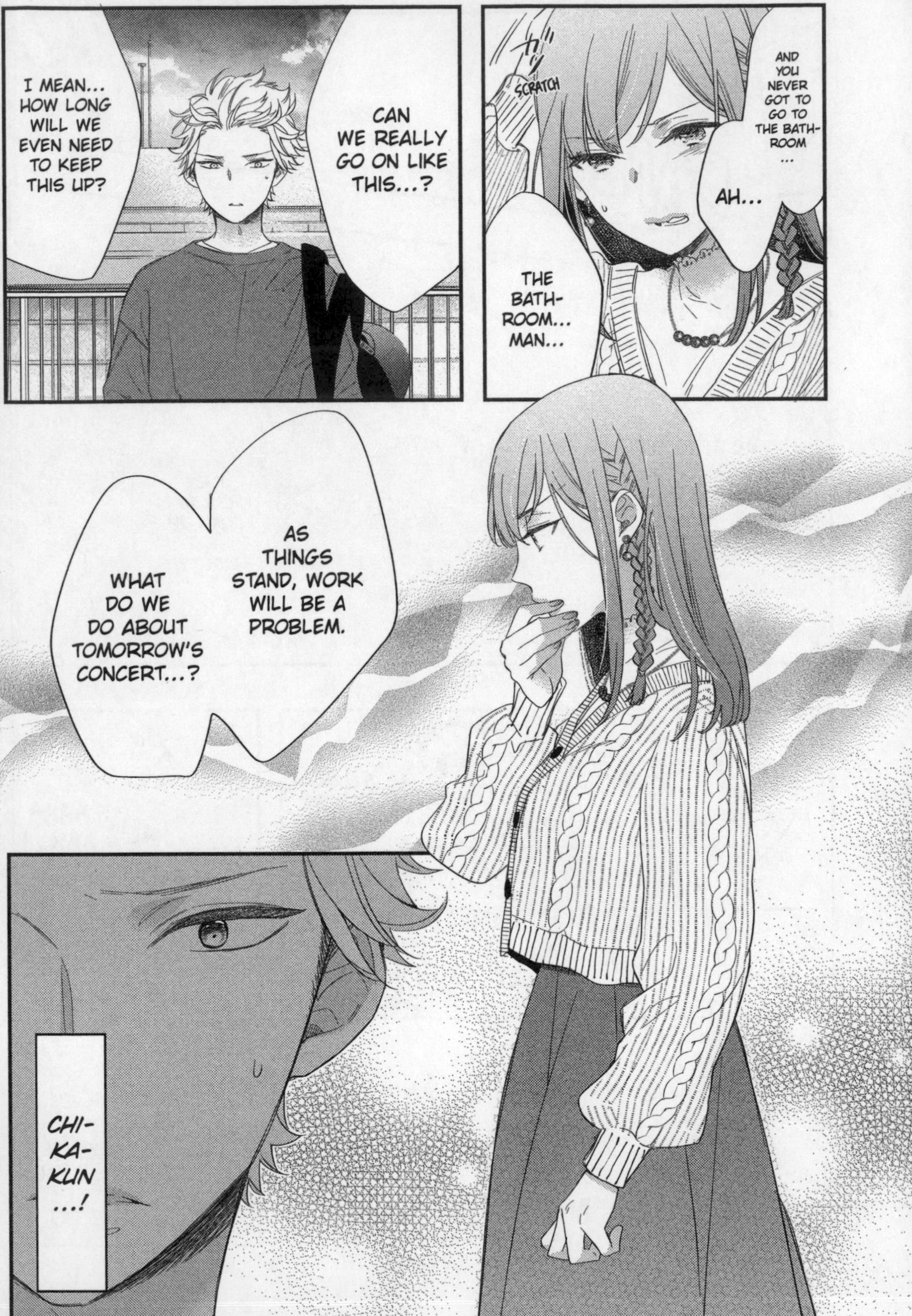
AND YOU NEVER GOT TO GO TO THE BATH-ROOM...
AH...
SCRATCH
THE BATH-ROOM... MAN...
CAN WE REALLY GO ON LIKE THIS...?
I MEAN... HOW LONG WILL WE EVEN NEED TO KEEP THIS UP?
AS THINGS STAND, WORK WILL BE A PROBLEM.
WHAT DO WE DO ABOUT TOMORROW'S CONCERT...?
CHI-KA-KUN...!

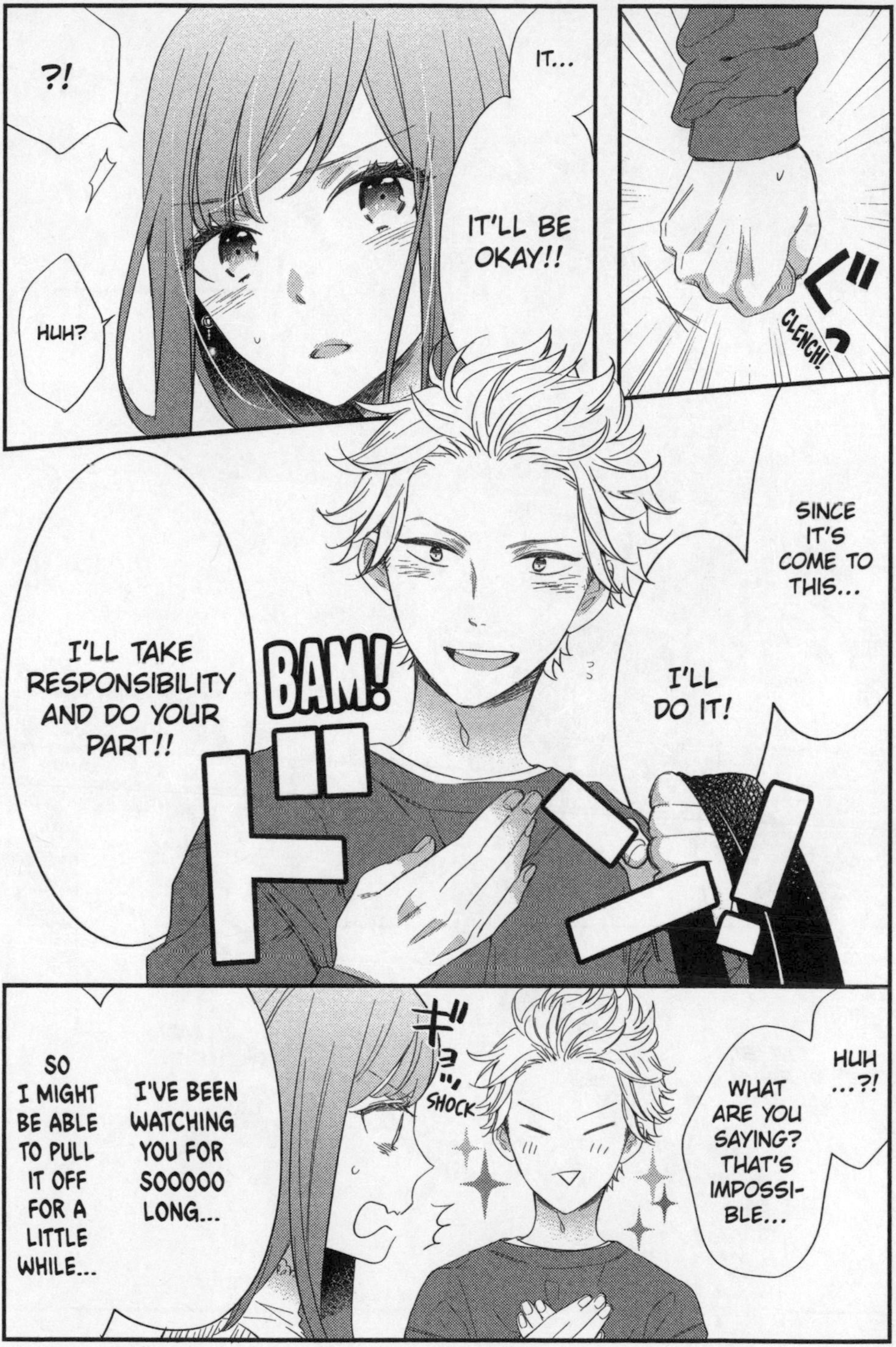
ぐっ
CLENCH!
IT...
?!
IT'LL BE OKAY!!
HUH?
SINCE IT'S COME TO THIS...
I'LL DO IT!
BAM!
ドーン!
I'LL TAKE RESPONSIBILITY AND DO YOUR PART!!
HUH ...?!
WHAT ARE YOU SAYING? THAT'S IMPOSSI-BLE...
ギョッ
SHOCK
I'VE BEEN WATCHING YOU FOR SOOOOO LONG...
SO I MIGHT BE ABLE TO PULL IT OFF FOR A LITTLE WHILE...

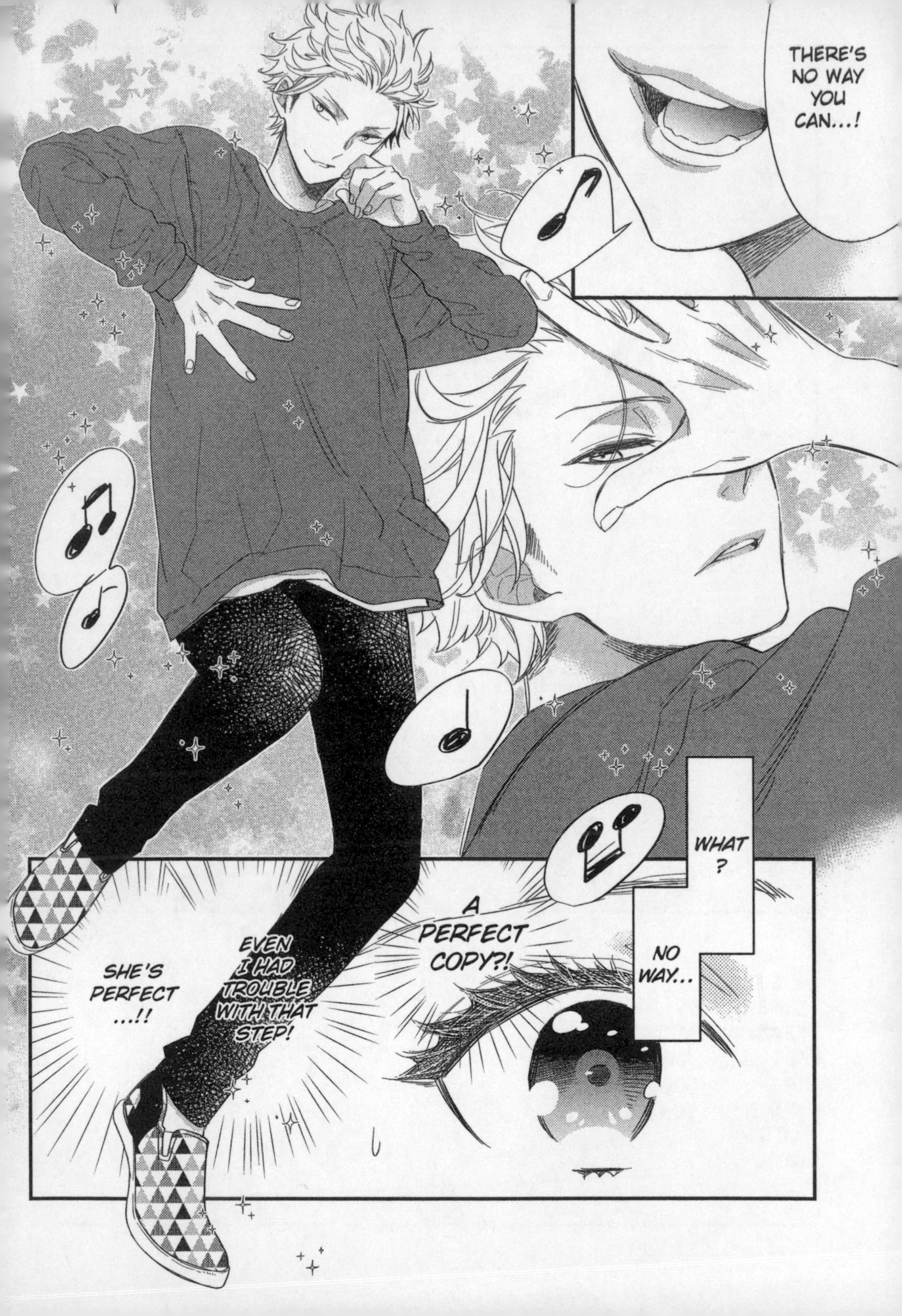
THERE'S NO WAY YOU CAN...!
WHAT?
NO WAY...
A PERFECT COPY?!
EVEN I HAD TROUBLE WITH THAT STEP!
SHE'S PERFECT ...!!

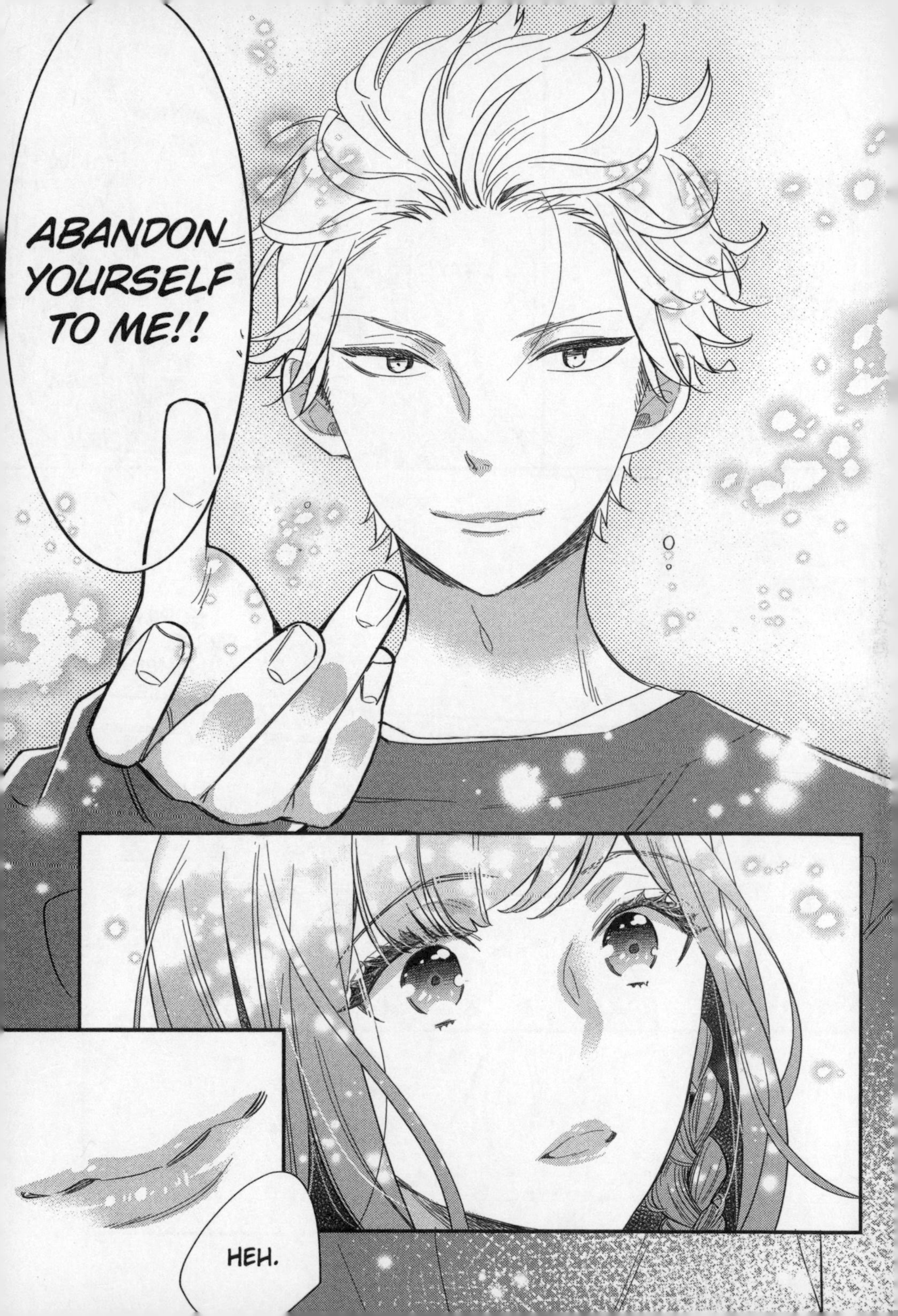
ABANDON YOURSELF TO ME!!
HEH.

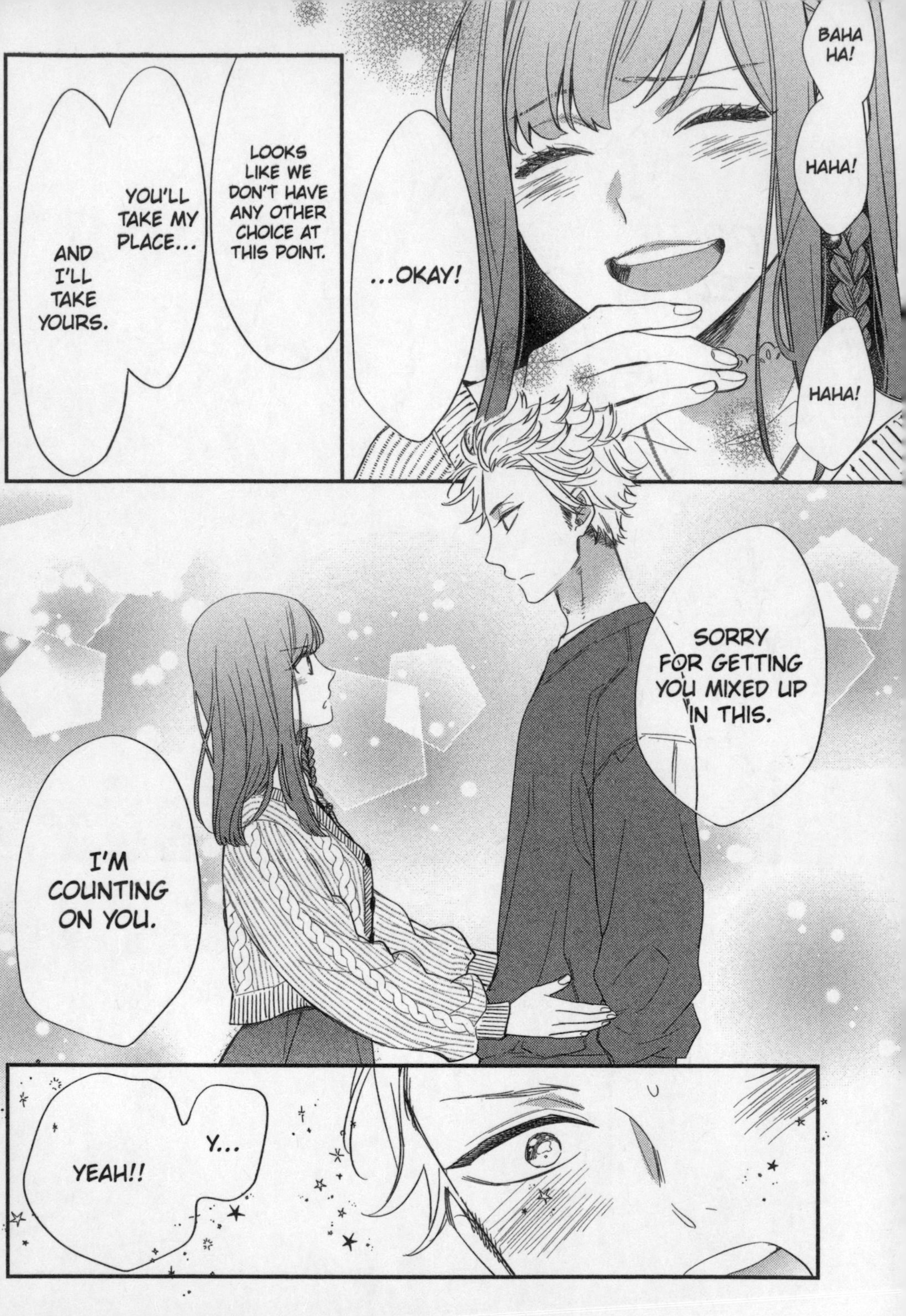
BAHA HA!
HAHA!
...OKAY!
HAHA!
LOOKS LIKE WE DON'T HAVE ANY OTHER CHOICE AT THIS POINT.
YOU'LL TAKE MY PLACE...
AND I'LL TAKE YOURS.
SORRY FOR GETTING YOU MIXED UP IN THIS.
I'M COUNTING ON YOU.
Y... YEAH!!

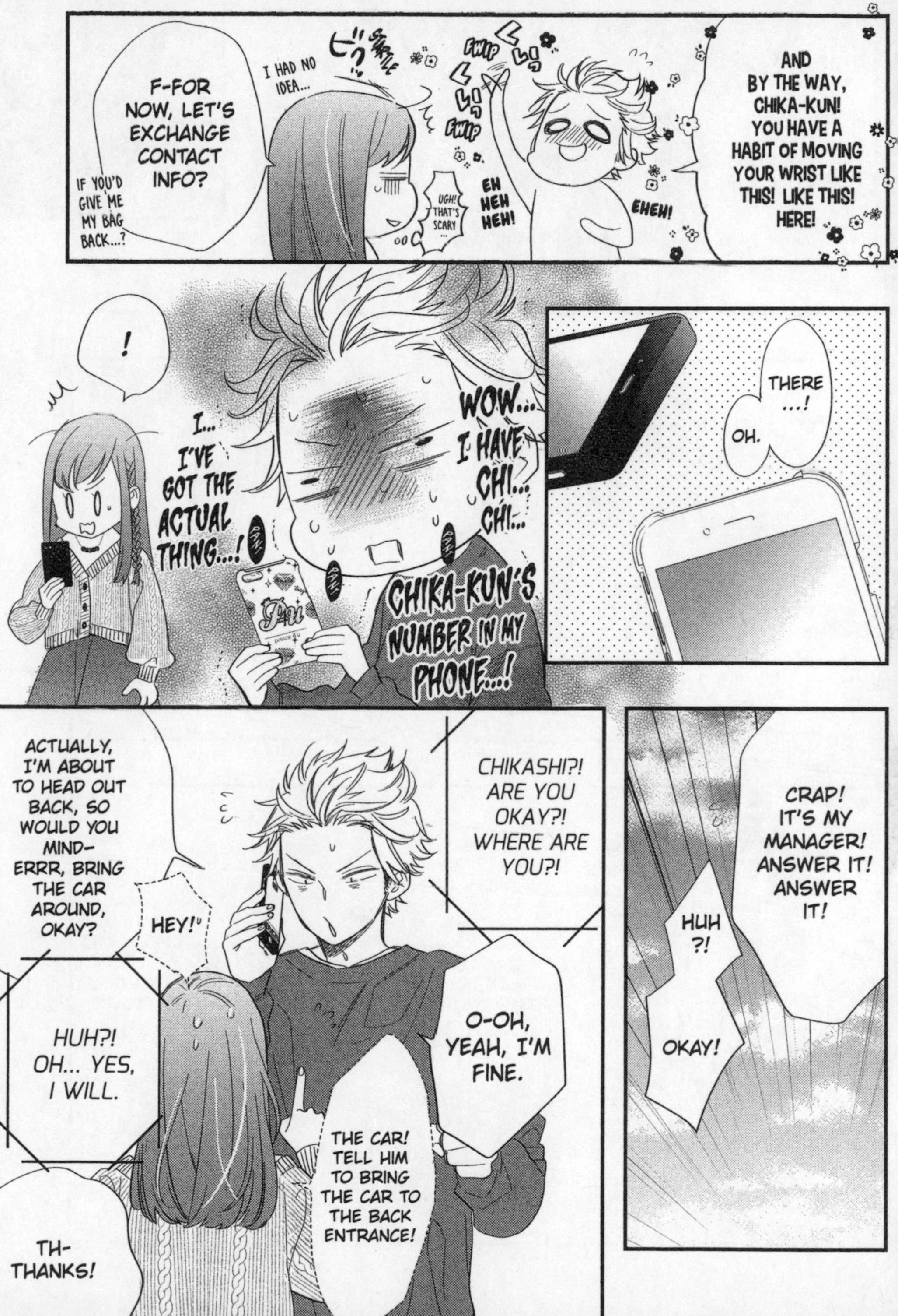
AND BY THE WAY, CHIKA-KUN! YOU HAVE A HABIT OF MOVING YOUR WRIST LIKE THIS! LIKE THIS! HERE!
EHEH!
FWIP
FWIP
EH HEH HEH!
UGH! THAT'S SCARY...
STARTLE
I HAD NO IDEA...
F-FOR NOW, LET'S EXCHANGE CONTACT INFO?
IF YOU'D GIVE ME MY BAG BACK...?
THERE...!
OH.
WOW... I HAVE CHI... CHI... CHIKA-KUN'S NUMBER IN MY PHONE...!
I... I'VE GOT THE ACTUAL THING...!
!
CRAP! IT'S MY MANAGER! ANSWER IT! ANSWER IT!
HUH?!
OKAY!
CHIKASHI?! ARE YOU OKAY?! WHERE ARE YOU?!
O-OH, YEAH, I'M FINE.
ACTUALLY, I'M ABOUT TO HEAD OUT BACK, SO WOULD YOU MIND— ERRR, BRING THE CAR AROUND, OKAY?
HEY!
THE CAR! TELL HIM TO BRING THE CAR TO THE BACK ENTRANCE!
HUH?! OH... YES, I WILL.
TH-THANKS!

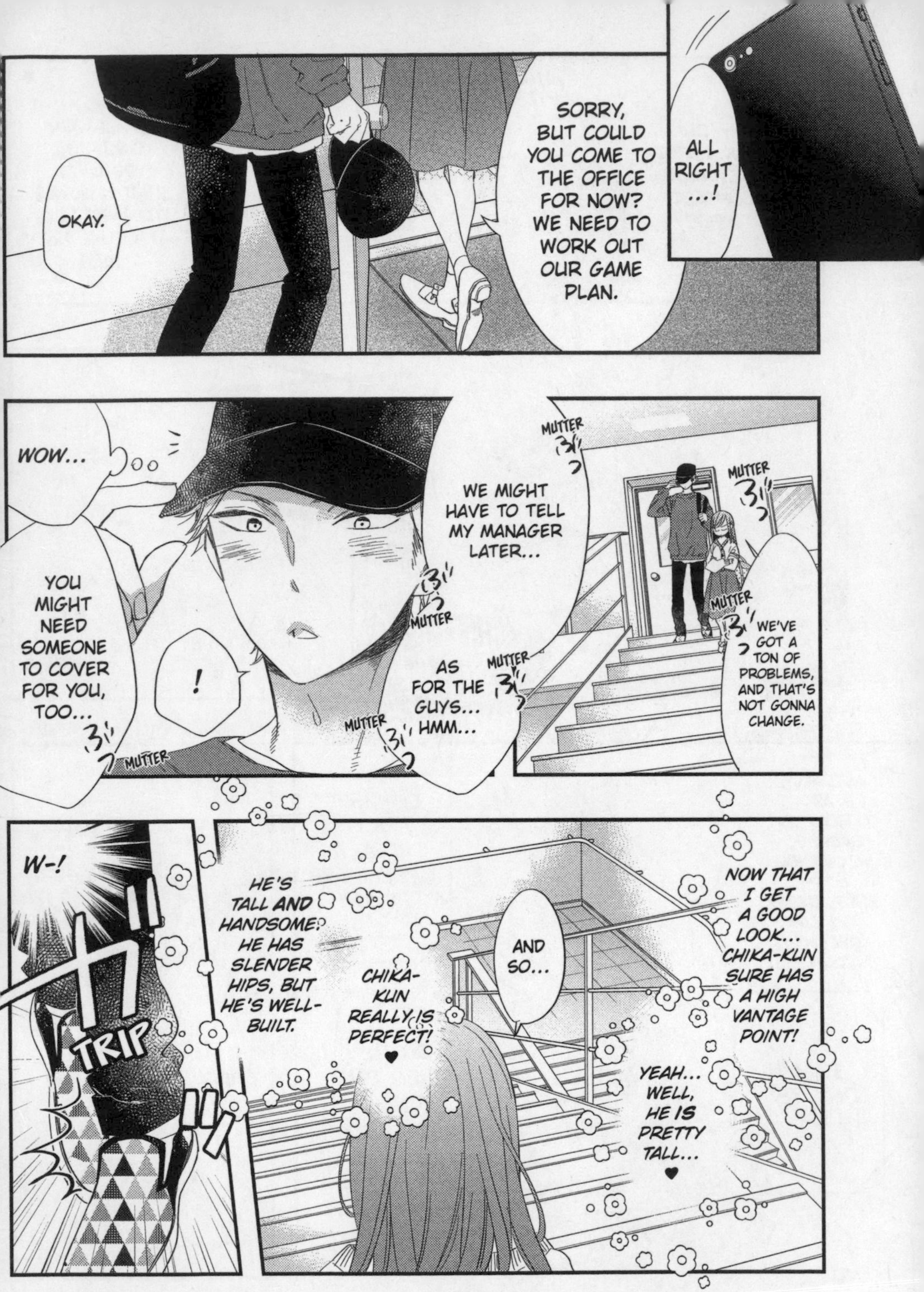
ALL RIGHT...!
SORRY, BUT COULD YOU COME TO THE OFFICE FOR NOW? WE NEED TO WORK OUT OUR GAME PLAN.
OKAY.
MUTTER
MUTTER
MUTTER
WE'VE GOT A TON OF PROBLEMS, AND THAT'S NOT GONNA CHANGE.
MUTTER
WE MIGHT HAVE TO TELL MY MANAGER LATER...
MUTTER
MUTTER
AS FOR THE GUYS... HMM...
MUTTER
WOW...
!
YOU MIGHT NEED SOMEONE TO COVER FOR YOU, TOO...
MUTTER
NOW THAT I GET A GOOD LOOK... CHIKA-KUN SURE HAS A HIGH VANTAGE POINT!
YEAH... WELL, HE IS PRETTY TALL... ♥
AND SO...
CHIKA-KUN REALLY IS PERFECT! ♥
HE'S TALL AND HANDSOME! HE HAS SLENDER HIPS, BUT HE'S WELL-BUILT.
W-!
TRIP

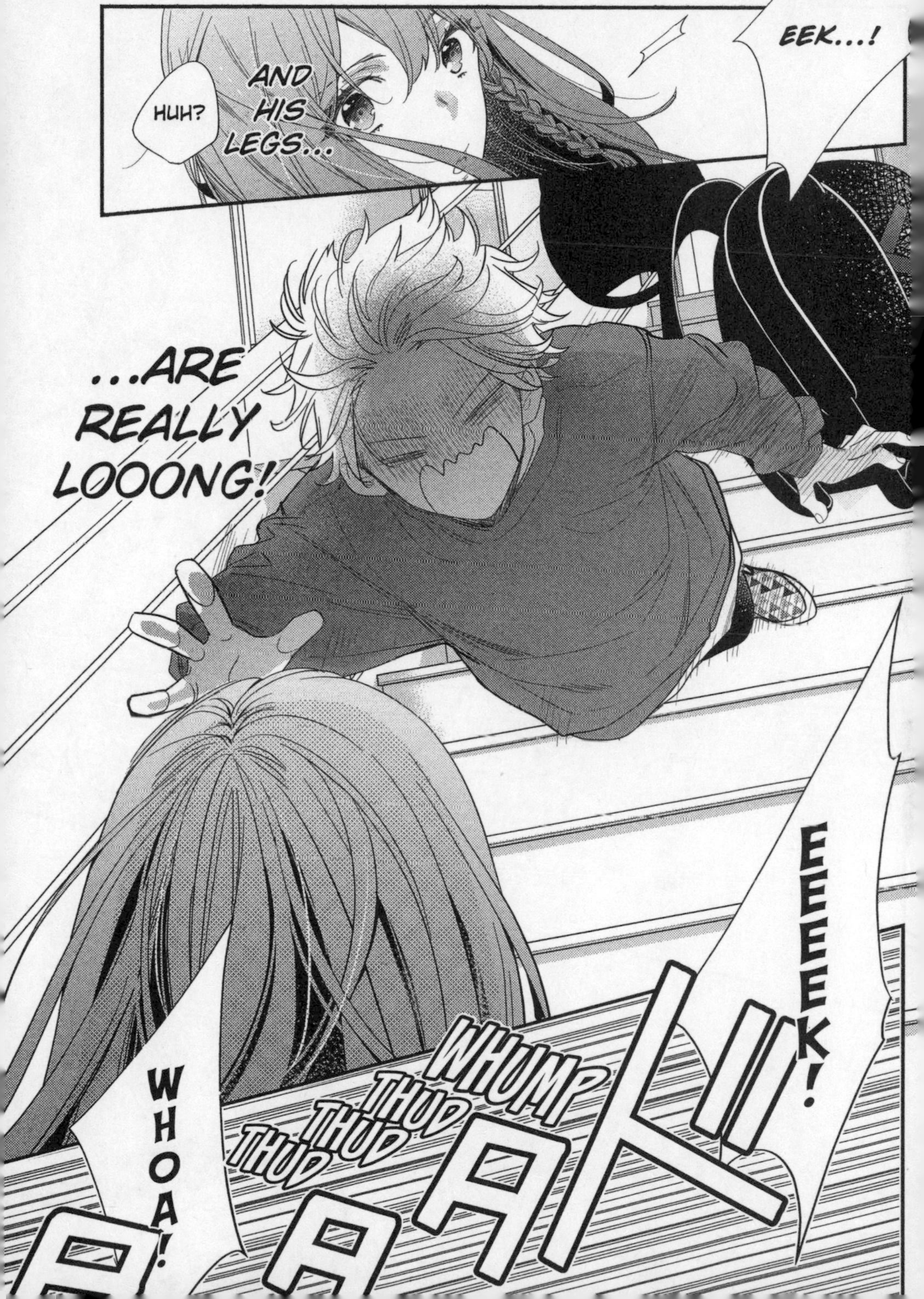
EEK...!
AND HIS LEGS...
HUH?
...ARE REALLY LOOONG!
EEEEEK!
WHUMP
THUD THUD THUD
WHOA!

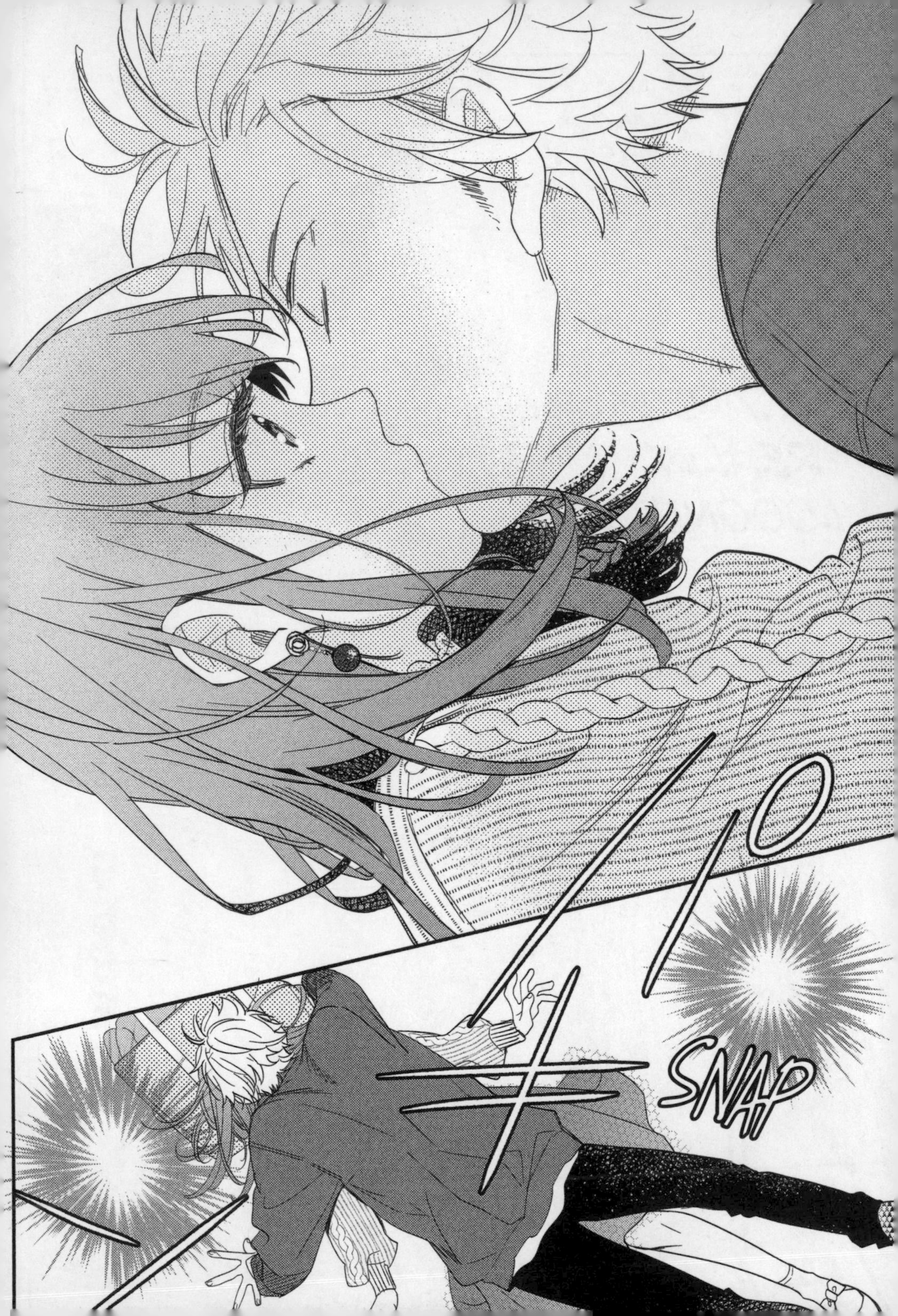
SNAP

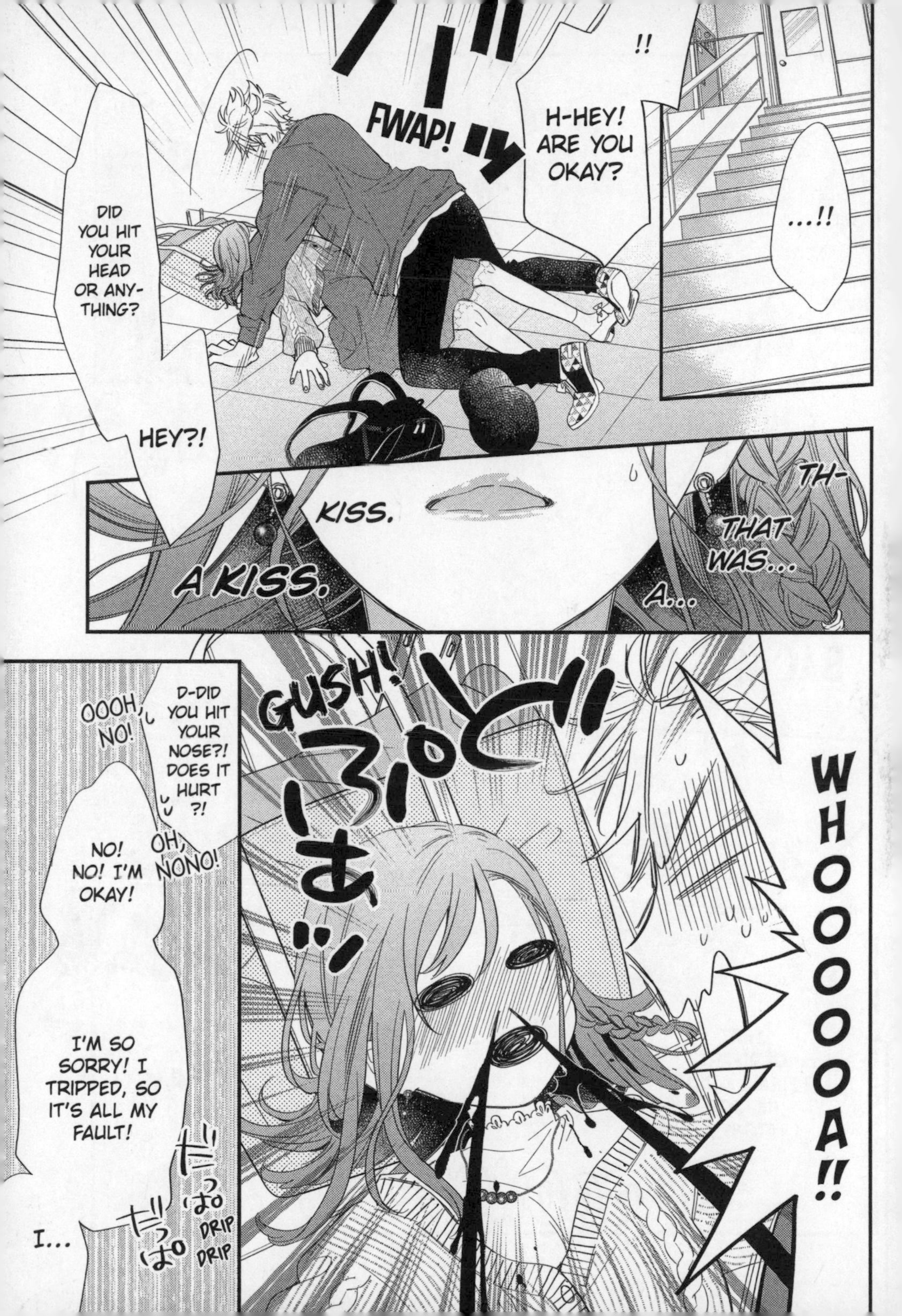
!!
H-HEY! ARE YOU OKAY?
...!!
FWAP!
DID YOU HIT YOUR HEAD OR ANYTHING?
HEY?!
TH-THAT WAS...
A...
A KISS.
KISS.
WHOOOOOOA!!
GUSH!
D-DID YOU HIT YOUR NOSE?! DOES IT HURT?!
OOOH, NO!
OH, NONO!
NO! NO! I'M OKAY!
I'M SO SORRY! I TRIPPED, SO IT'S ALL MY FAULT!
DRIP DRIP
I...

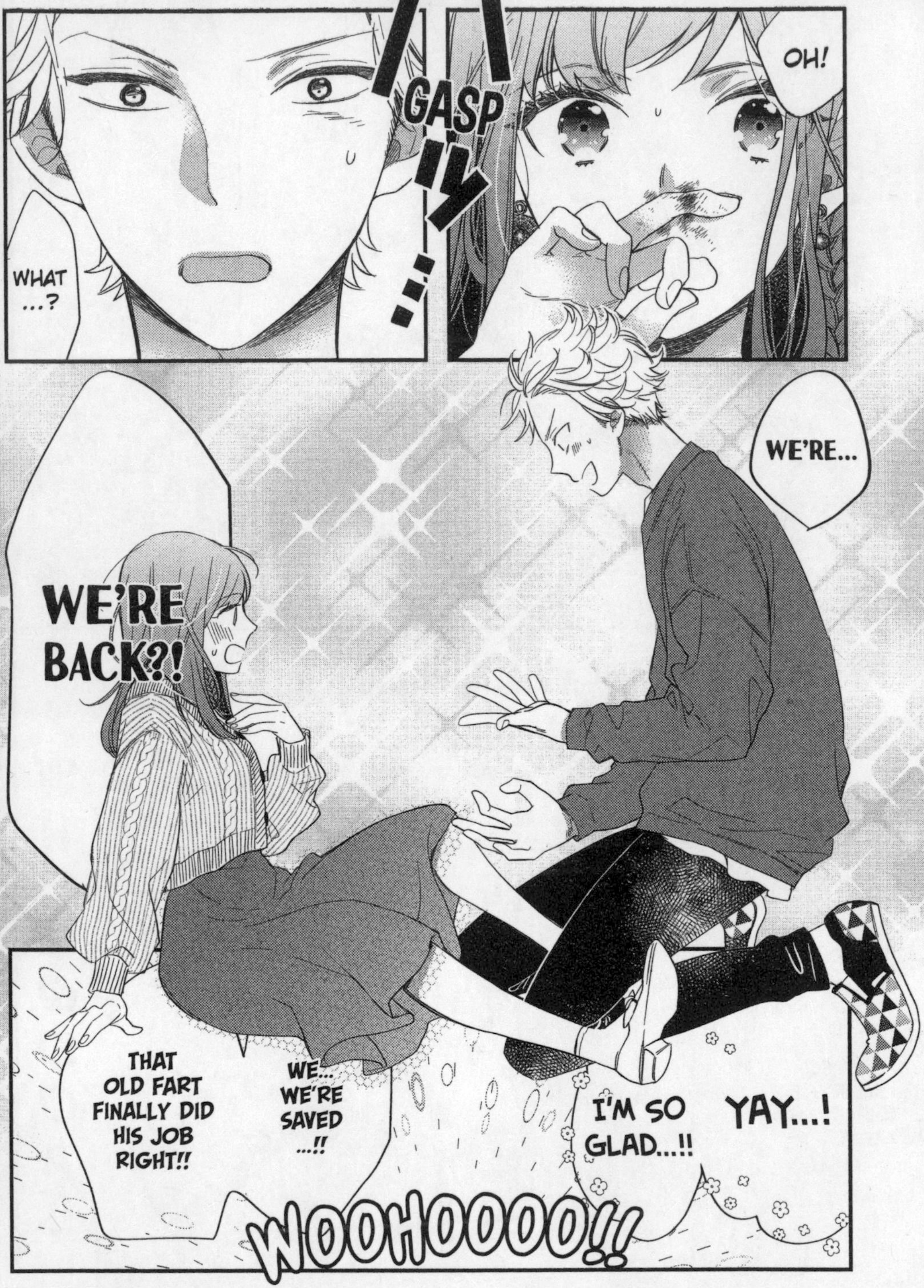
OH!
GASP
WHAT ...?
WE'RE...
WE'RE BACK?!
YAY...!
I'M SO GLAD...!!
WE... WE'RE SAVED ...!!
THAT OLD FART FINALLY DID HIS JOB RIGHT!!
WOOHOOOOO!!

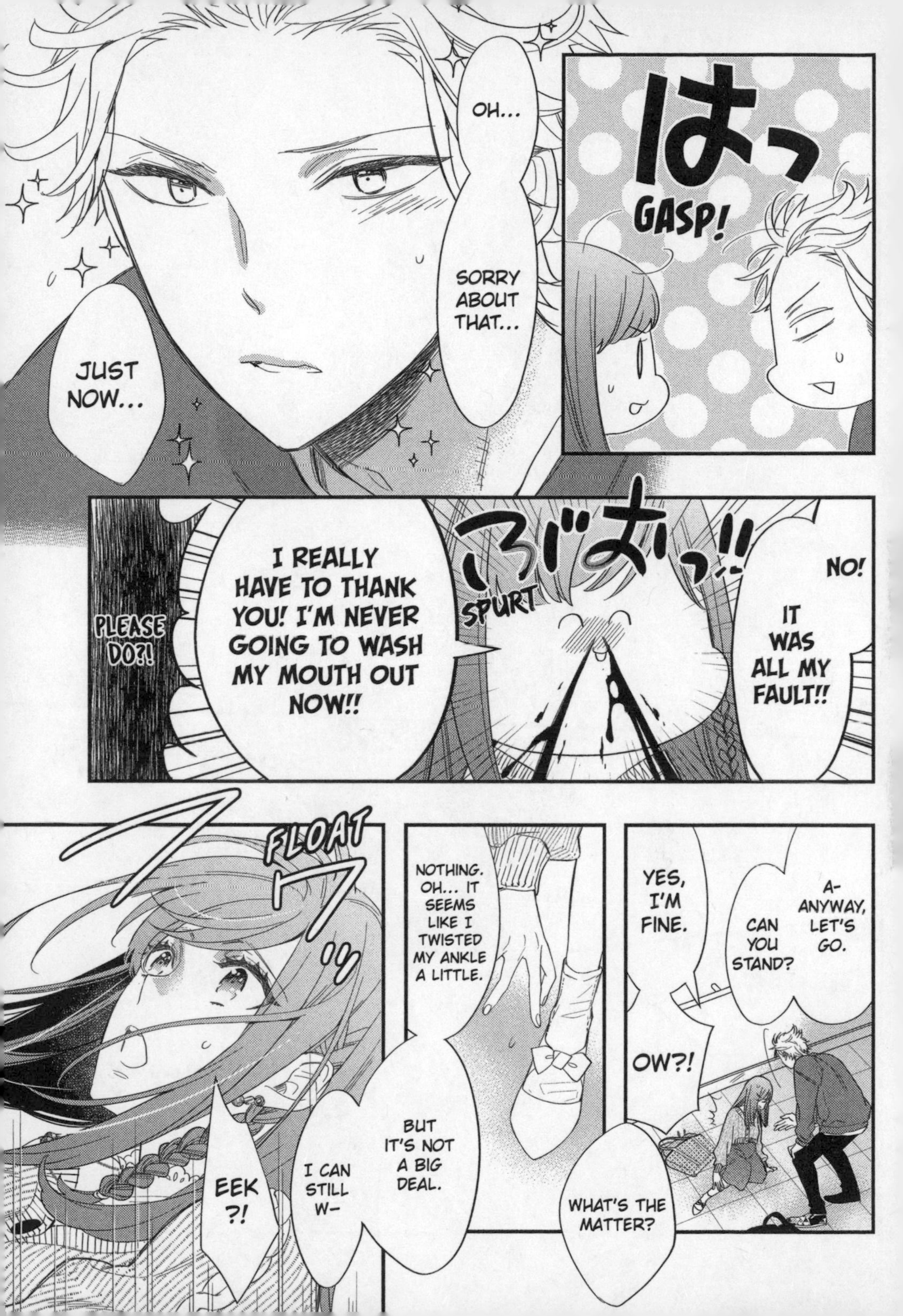
はっ
GASP!
OH...
SORRY ABOUT THAT...
JUST NOW...
NO!
IT WAS ALL MY FAULT!!
SPURT
I REALLY HAVE TO THANK YOU! I'M NEVER GOING TO WASH MY MOUTH OUT NOW!!
PLEASE DO?!
A- ANYWAY, LET'S GO.
CAN YOU STAND?
YES, I'M FINE.
OW?!
WHAT'S THE MATTER?
NOTHING. OH... IT SEEMS LIKE I TWISTED MY ANKLE A LITTLE.
BUT IT'S NOT A BIG DEAL.
I CAN STILL W-
FLOAT
EEK ?!

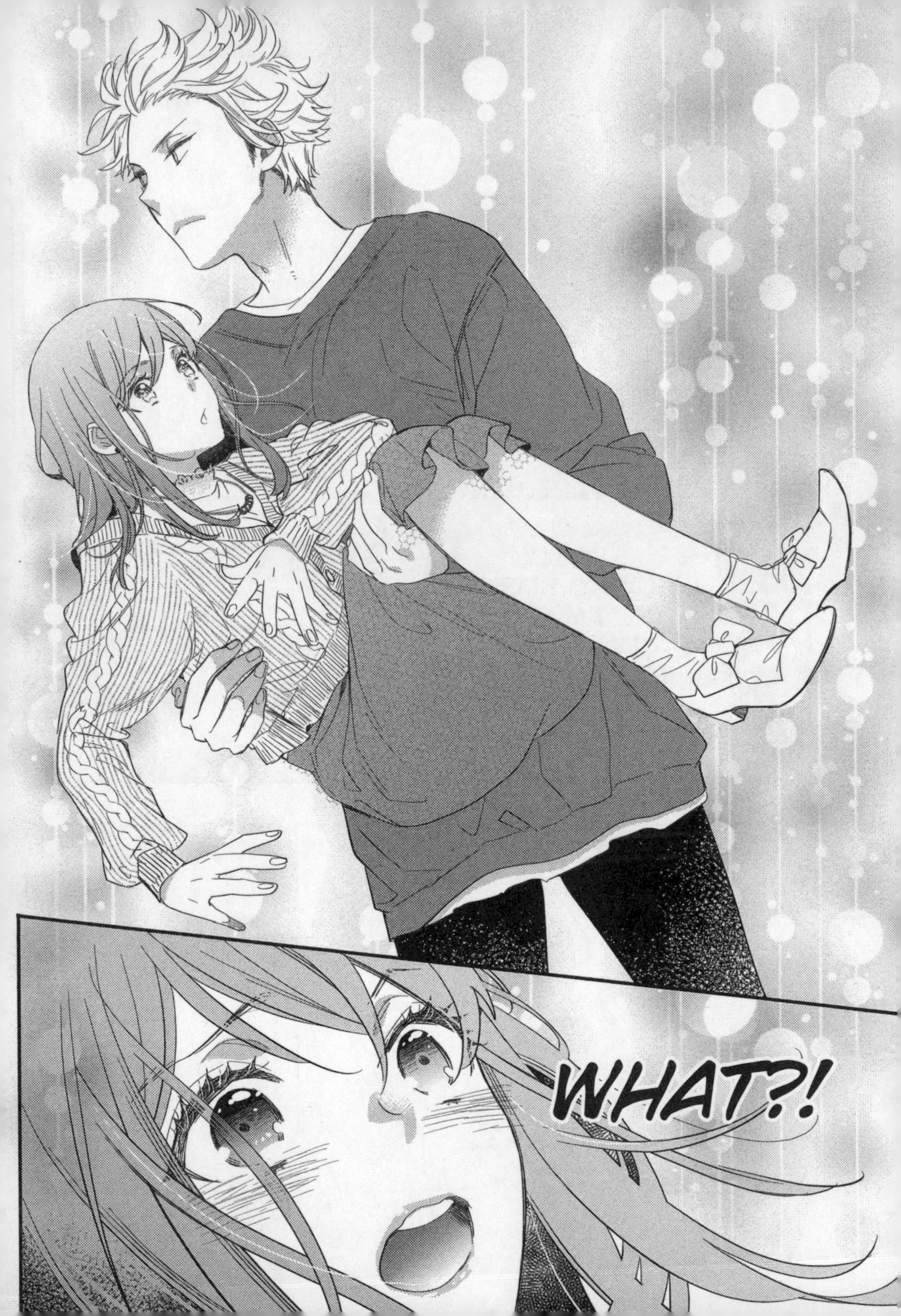
WHAT?!

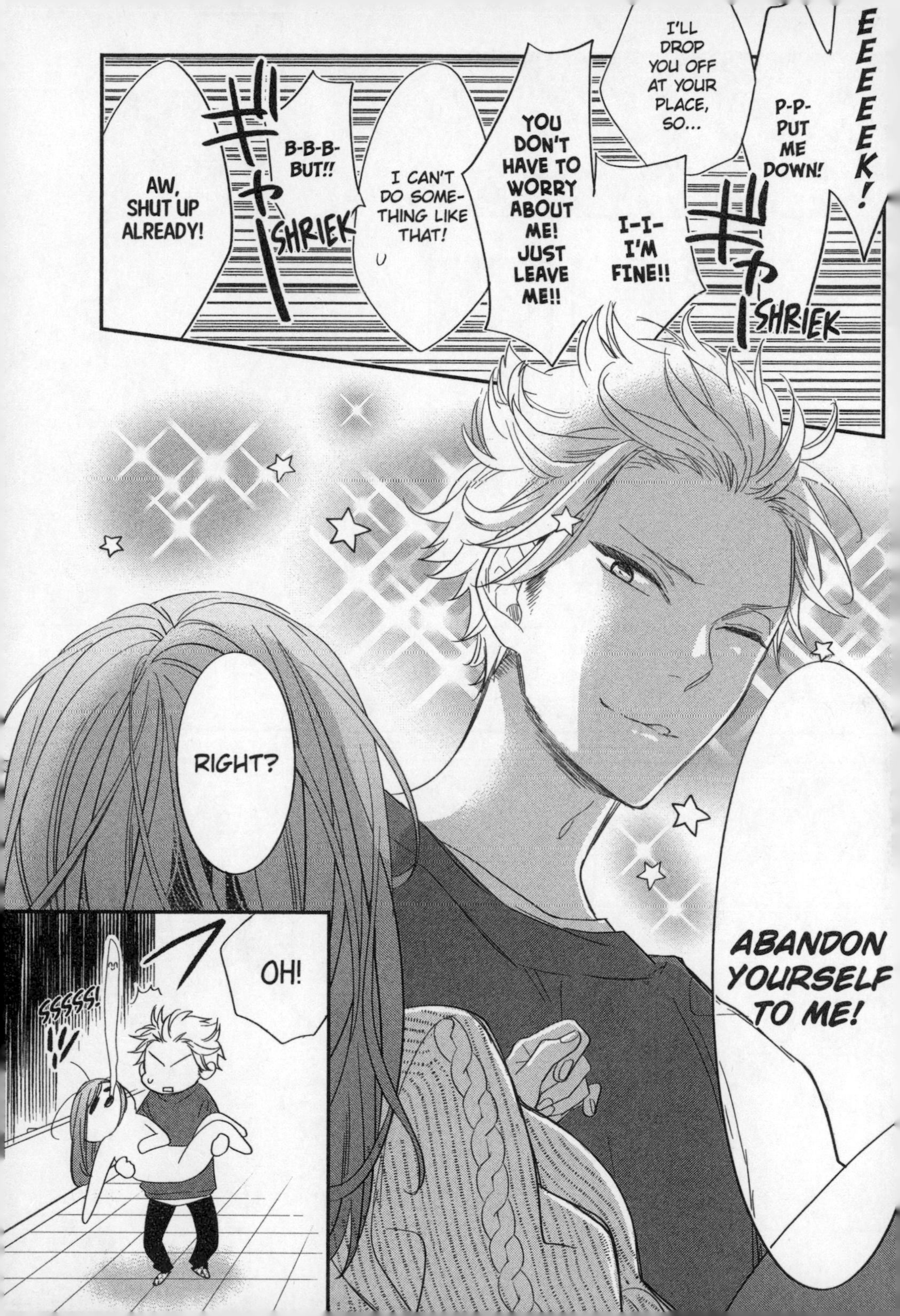
EEEEEEK!
I'LL DROP YOU OFF AT YOUR PLACE, SO...
P-P-PUT ME DOWN!
ギャー SHRIEK
I-I-I'M FINE!!
YOU DON'T HAVE TO WORRY ABOUT ME! JUST LEAVE ME!!
I CAN'T DO SOMETHING LIKE THAT!
B-B-B-BUT!!
ギャー SHRIEK
AW, SHUT UP ALREADY!
ABANDON YOURSELF TO ME!
RIGHT?
OH!
SSSSS!

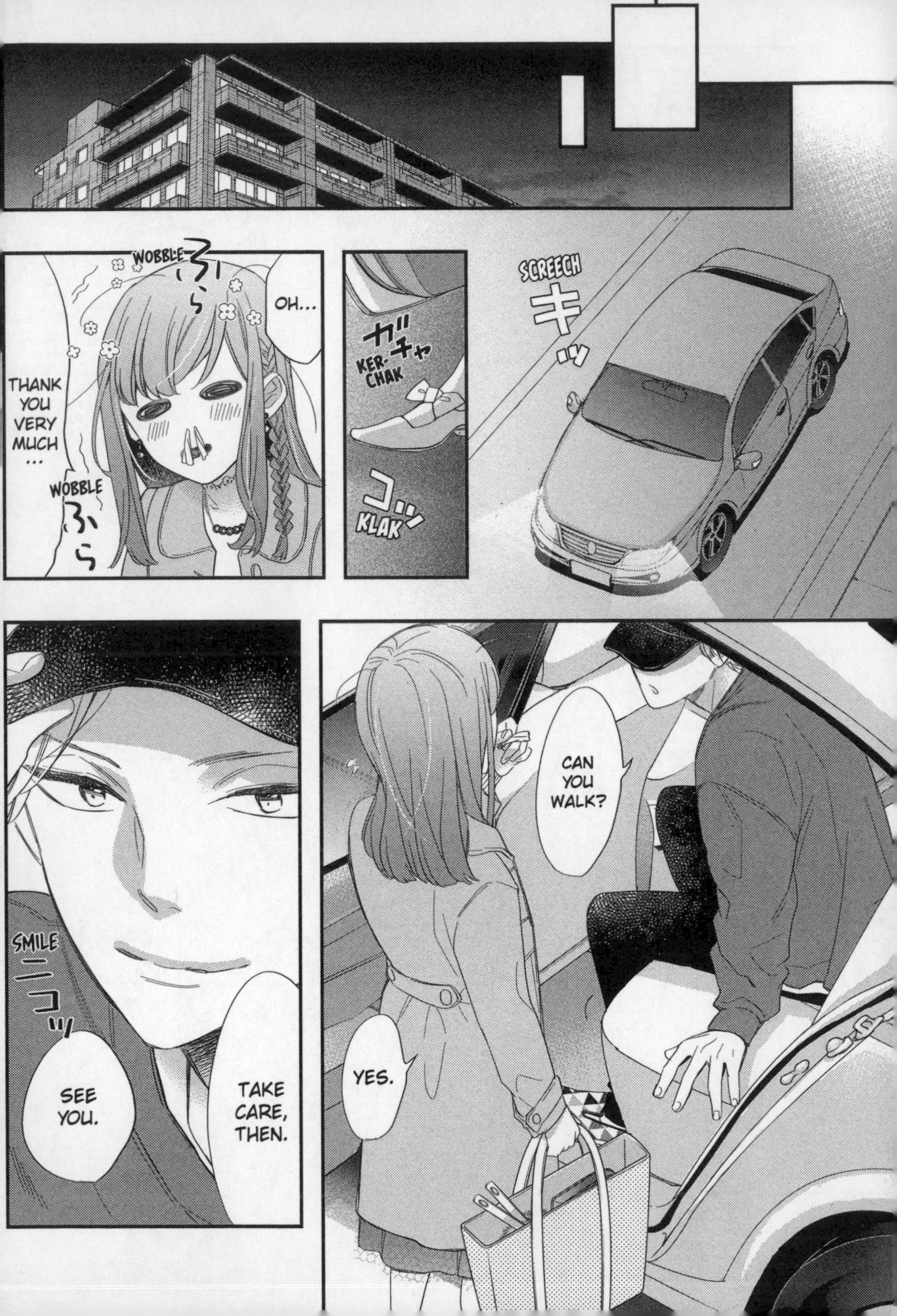
SCREECH
キッ
ガチャ
KER-CHAK
コッ
KLAK
WOBBLE
ふら
OH...
THANK YOU VERY MUCH...
WOBBLE
ふら
CAN YOU WALK?
YES.
TAKE CARE, THEN.
SMILE
ニコッ
SEE YOU.

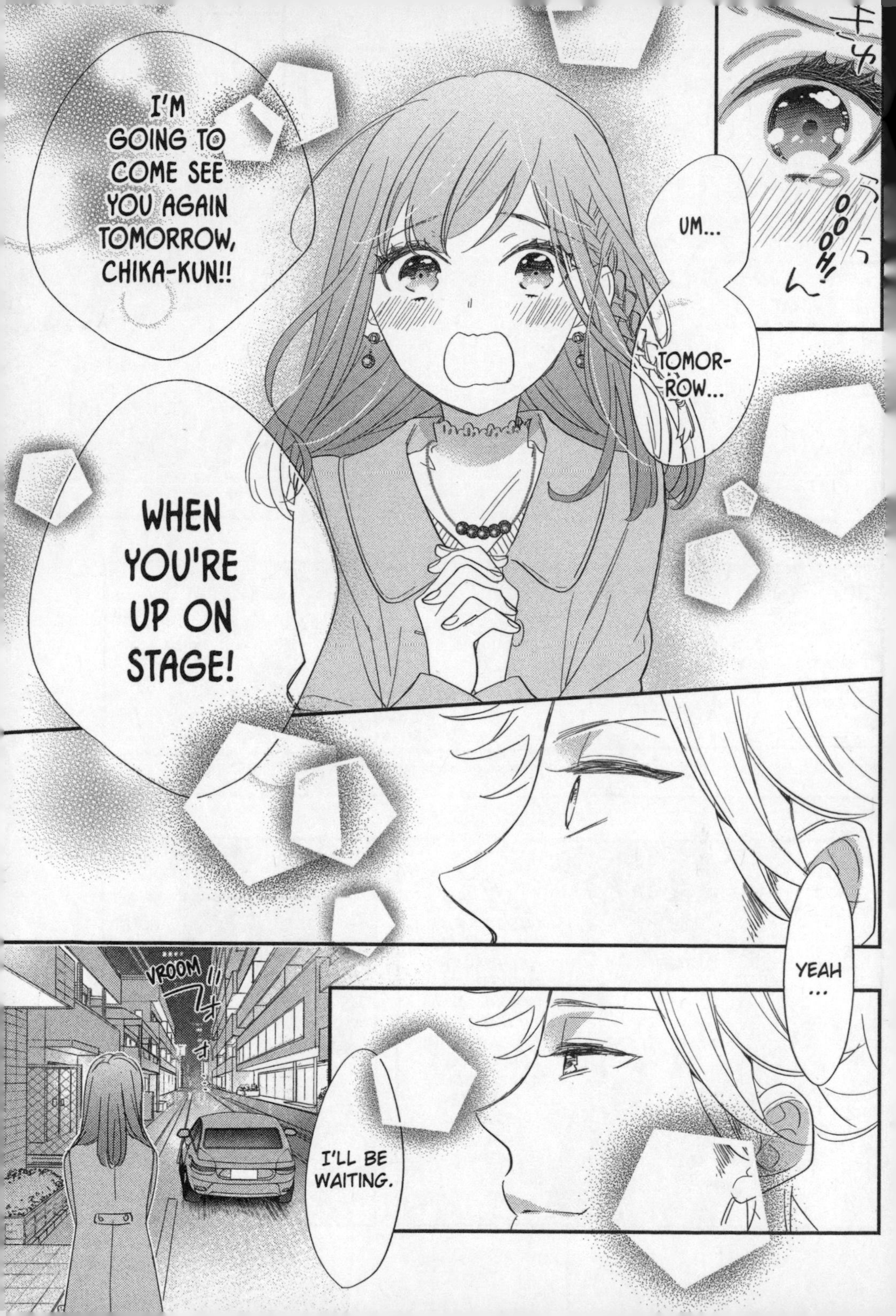
OOOH!!
UM...
TOMOR-ROW...
I'M GOING TO COME SEE YOU AGAIN TOMORROW, CHIKA-KUN!!
WHEN YOU'RE UP ON STAGE!
YEAH ...
I'LL BE WAITING.
VROOM

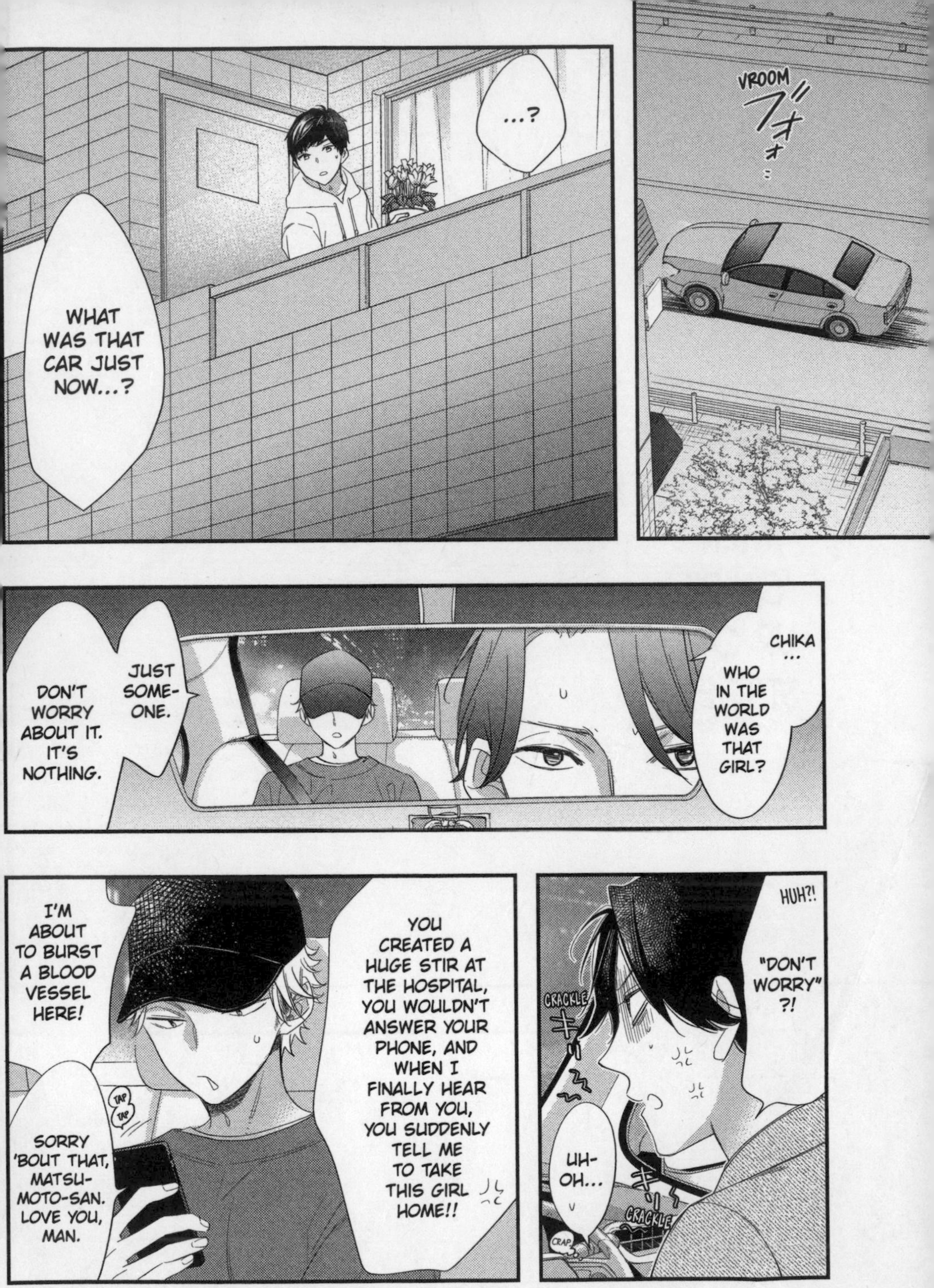
VROOM
...?
WHAT WAS THAT CAR JUST NOW...?
CHIKA... WHO IN THE WORLD WAS THAT GIRL?
JUST SOMEONE.
DON'T WORRY ABOUT IT. IT'S NOTHING.
HUH?!
"DON'T WORRY"?!
CRACKLE
UH-OH...
CRAP
CRACKLE
YOU CREATED A HUGE STIR AT THE HOSPITAL, YOU WOULDN'T ANSWER YOUR PHONE, AND WHEN I FINALLY HEAR FROM YOU, YOU SUDDENLY TELL ME TO TAKE THIS GIRL HOME!!
I'M ABOUT TO BURST A BLOOD VESSEL HERE!
TAP TAP
SORRY 'BOUT THAT, MATSUMOTO-SAN. LOVE YOU, MAN.

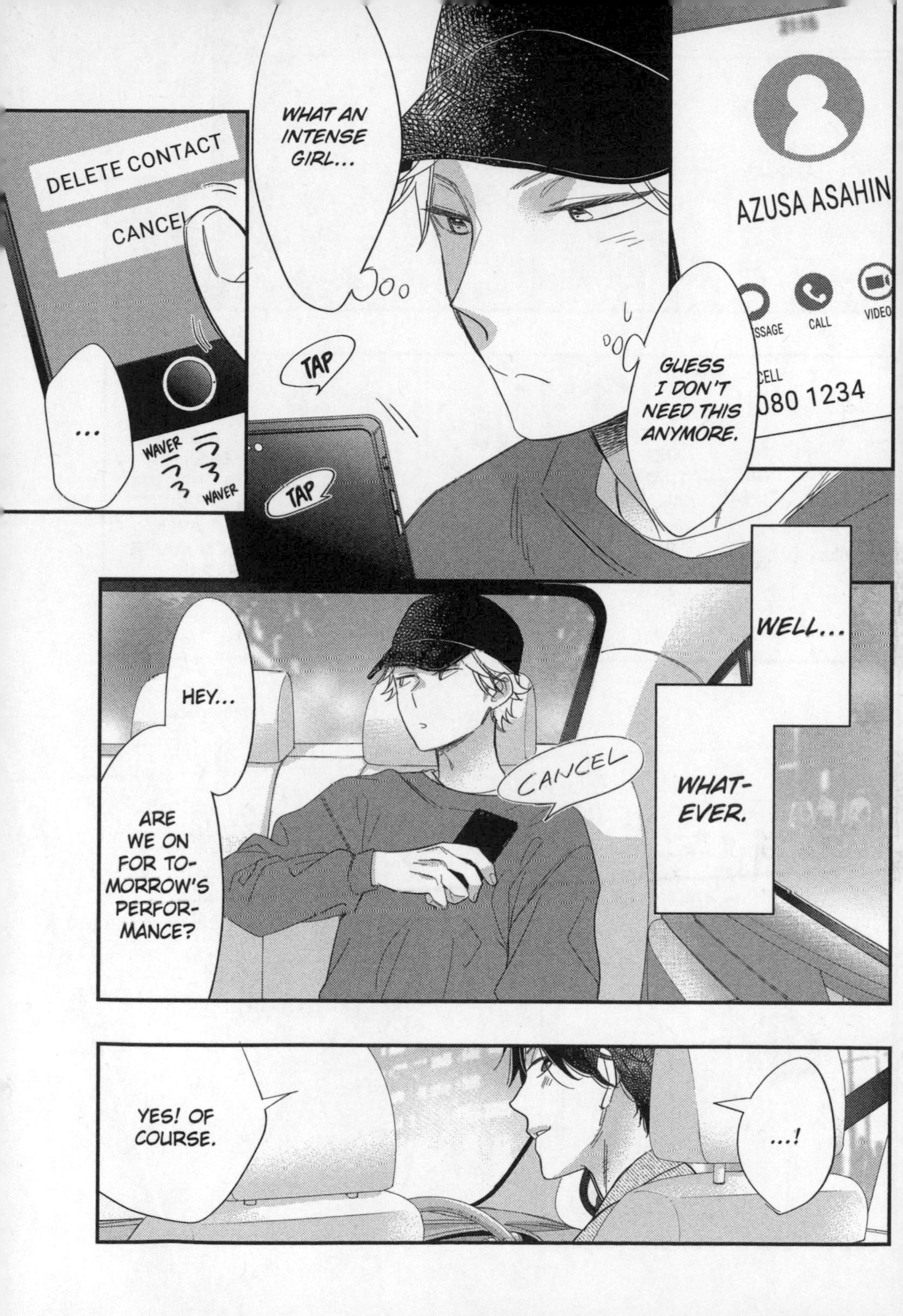
AZUSA ASAHIN
SSAGE
CALL
VIDEO
CELL
080 1234
GUESS I DON'T NEED THIS ANYMORE.
WHAT AN INTENSE GIRL...
TAP
TAP
DELETE CONTACT
CANCEL
...
WAVER
WAVER
WELL...
WHAT-EVER.
CANCEL
HEY...
ARE WE ON FOR TO-MORROW'S PERFORMANCE?
...!
YES! OF COURSE.

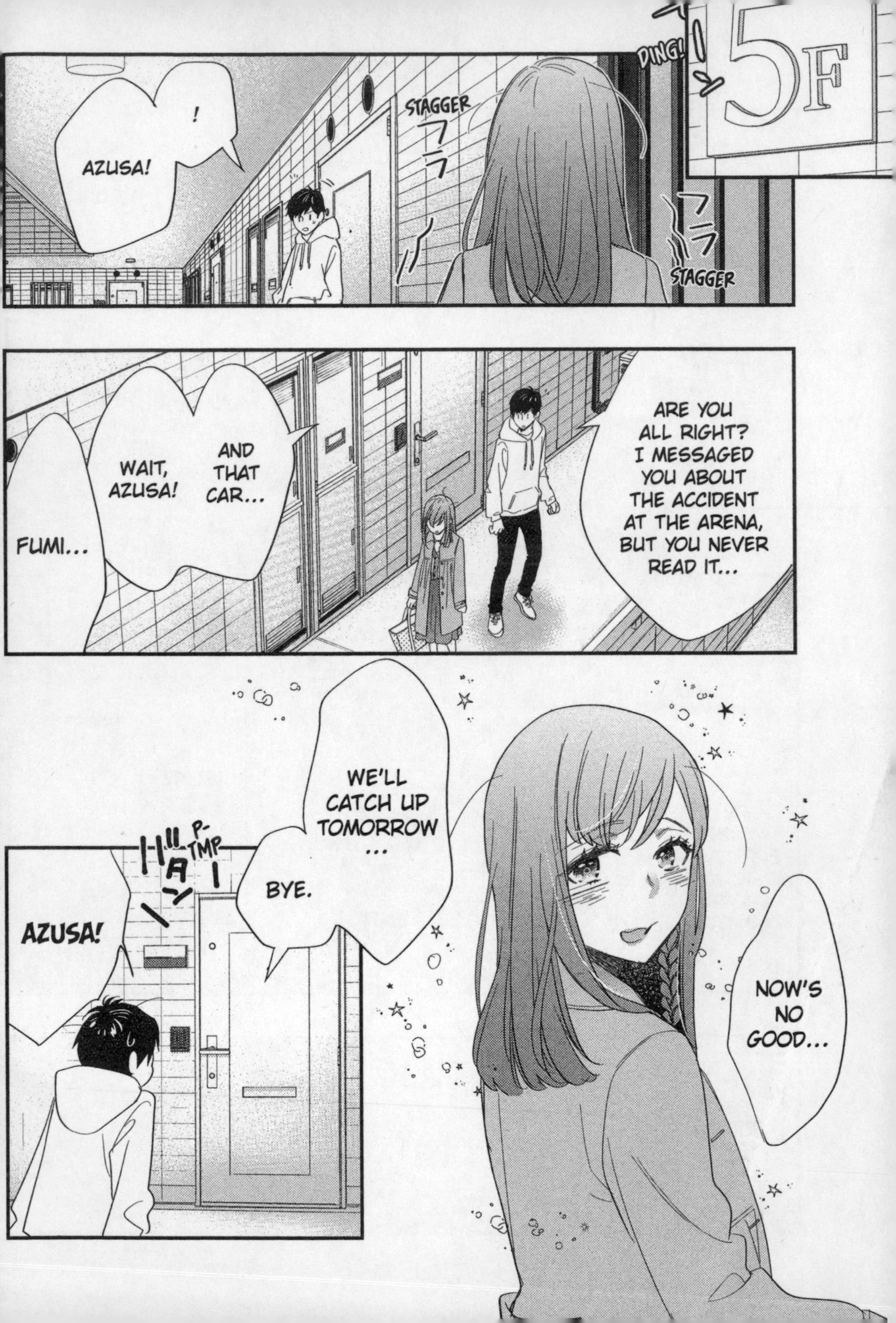
5F
DING!
STAGGER
フラ
STAGGER
フラ
!
AZUSA!
ARE YOU ALL RIGHT? I MESSAGED YOU ABOUT THE ACCIDENT AT THE ARENA, BUT YOU NEVER READ IT...
AND THAT CAR...
WAIT, AZUSA!
FUMI...
NOW'S NO GOOD...
WE'LL CATCH UP TOMORROW ...
BYE.
P-TMP
AZUSA!

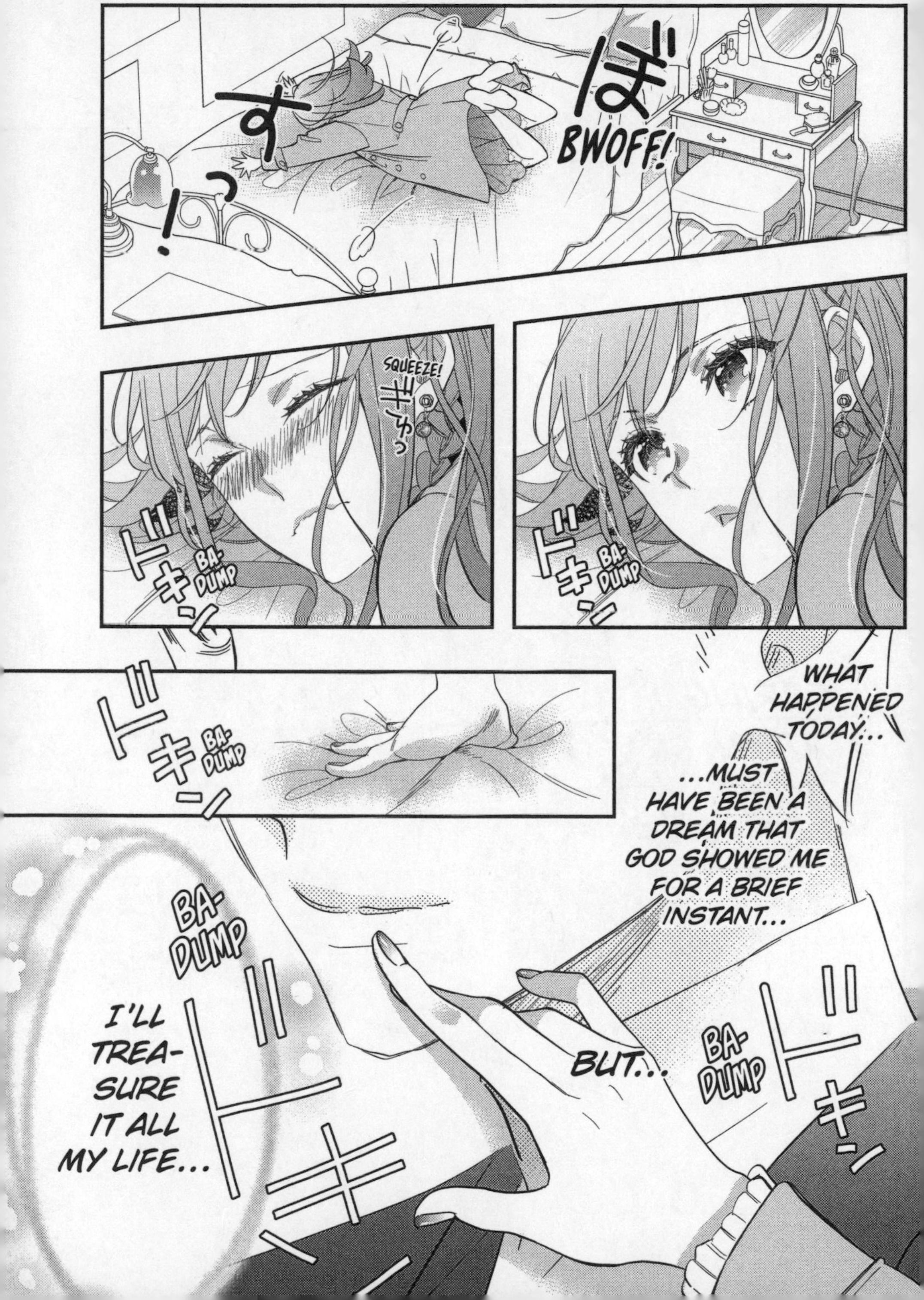
ぼ
BWOFF!
す
!?
BA-DUMP
SQUEEZE!
BA-DUMP
WHAT HAPPENED TODAY...
...MUST HAVE BEEN A DREAM THAT GOD SHOWED ME FOR A BRIEF INSTANT...
BA-DUMP
BA-DUMP
BUT...
BA-DUMP
I'LL TREA-SURE IT ALL MY LIFE...

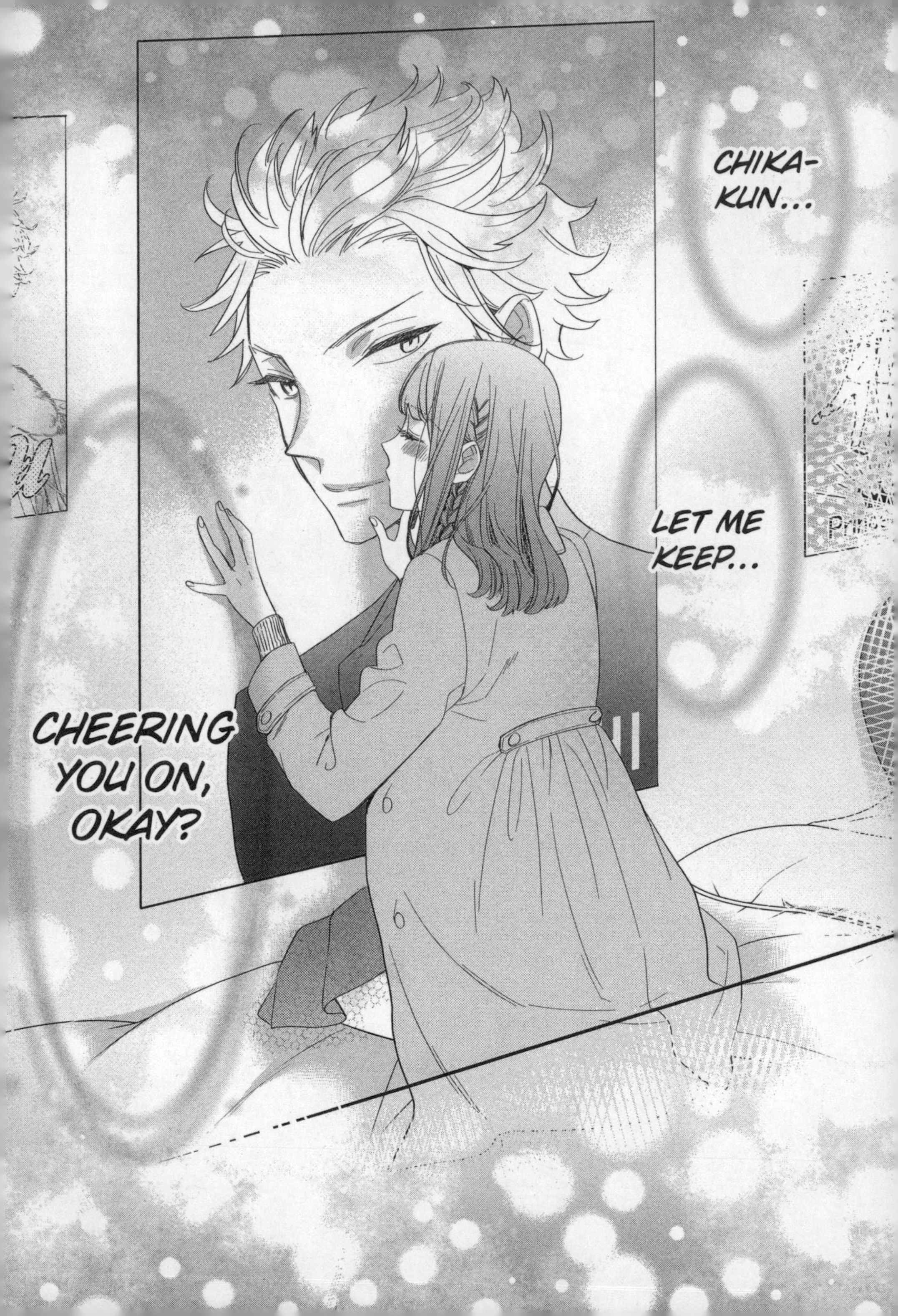
CHIKA-KUN...
LET ME KEEP...
CHEERING YOU ON, OKAY?

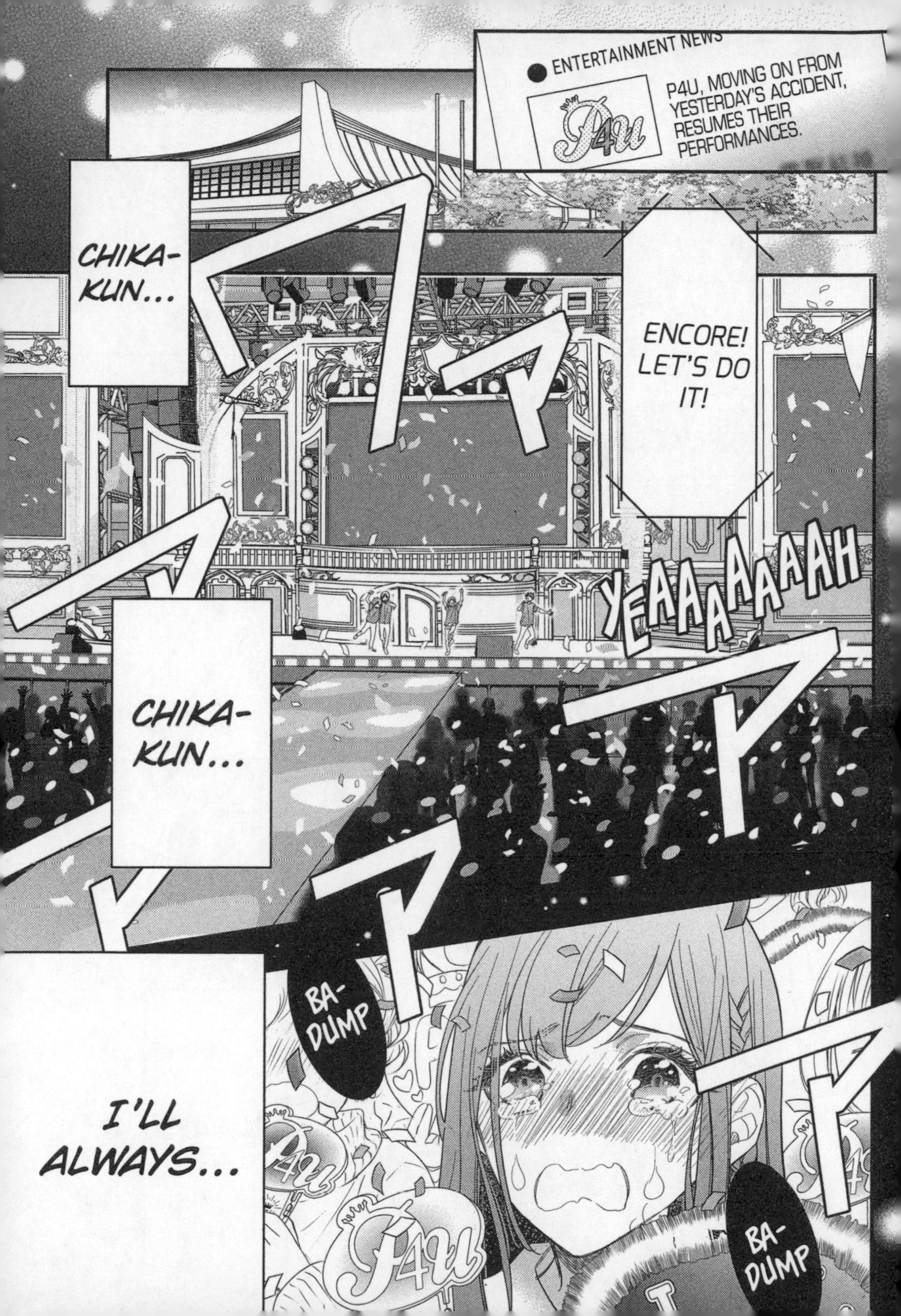
ENTERTAINMENT NEWS
P4U
P4U, MOVING ON FROM YESTERDAY'S ACCIDENT, RESUMES THEIR PERFORMANCES.
ENCORE! LET'S DO IT!
CHIKA-KUN...
YEAAAAAAAH
CHIKA-KUN...
BA-DUMP
BA-DUMP
I'LL ALWAYS...

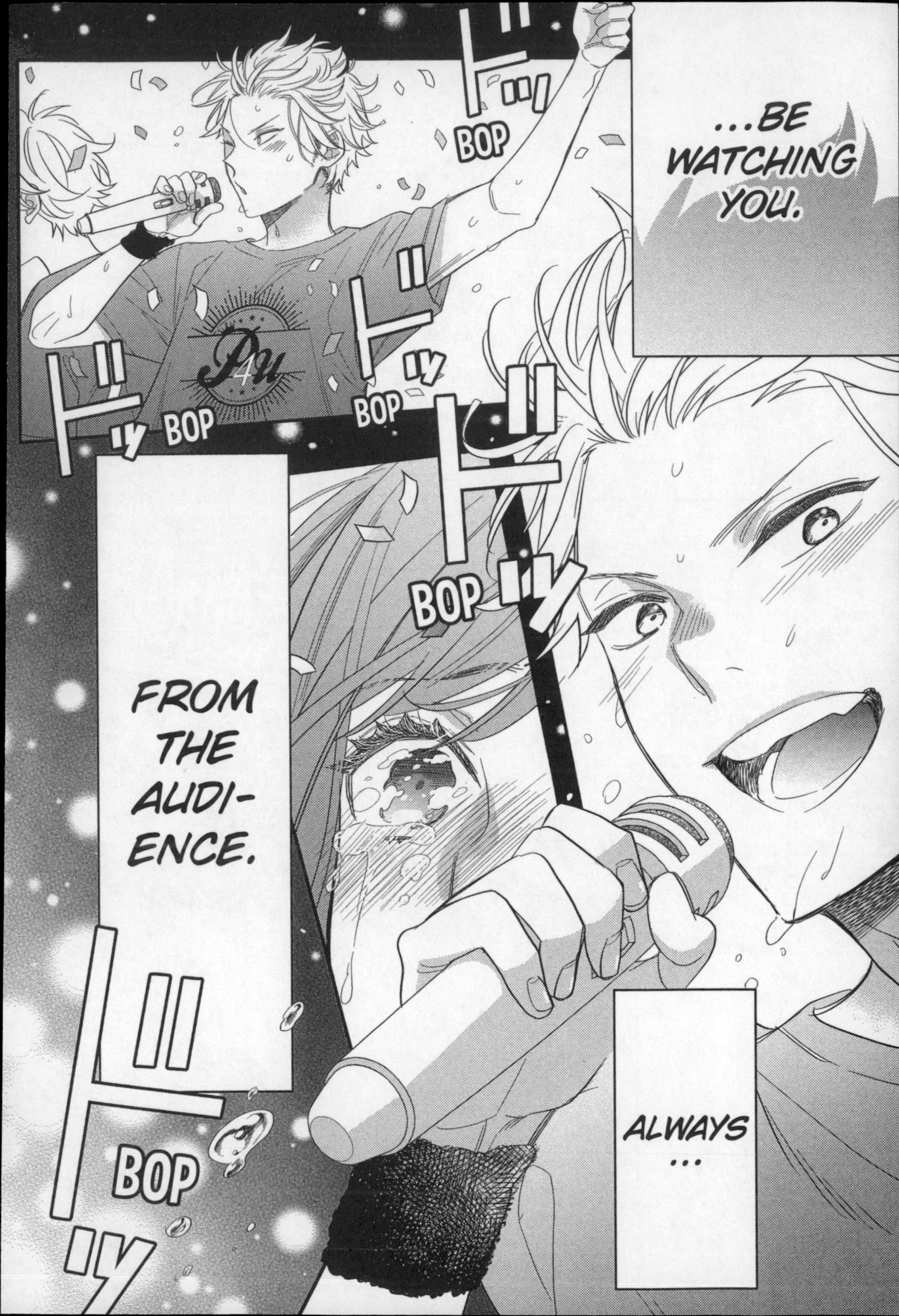

...BE WATCHING YOU.
ドッ BOP
ドッ BOP
ドッ BOP
ドッ BOP
ドッ BOP
ALWAYS ...
FROM THE AUDIENCE.
ドッ BOP

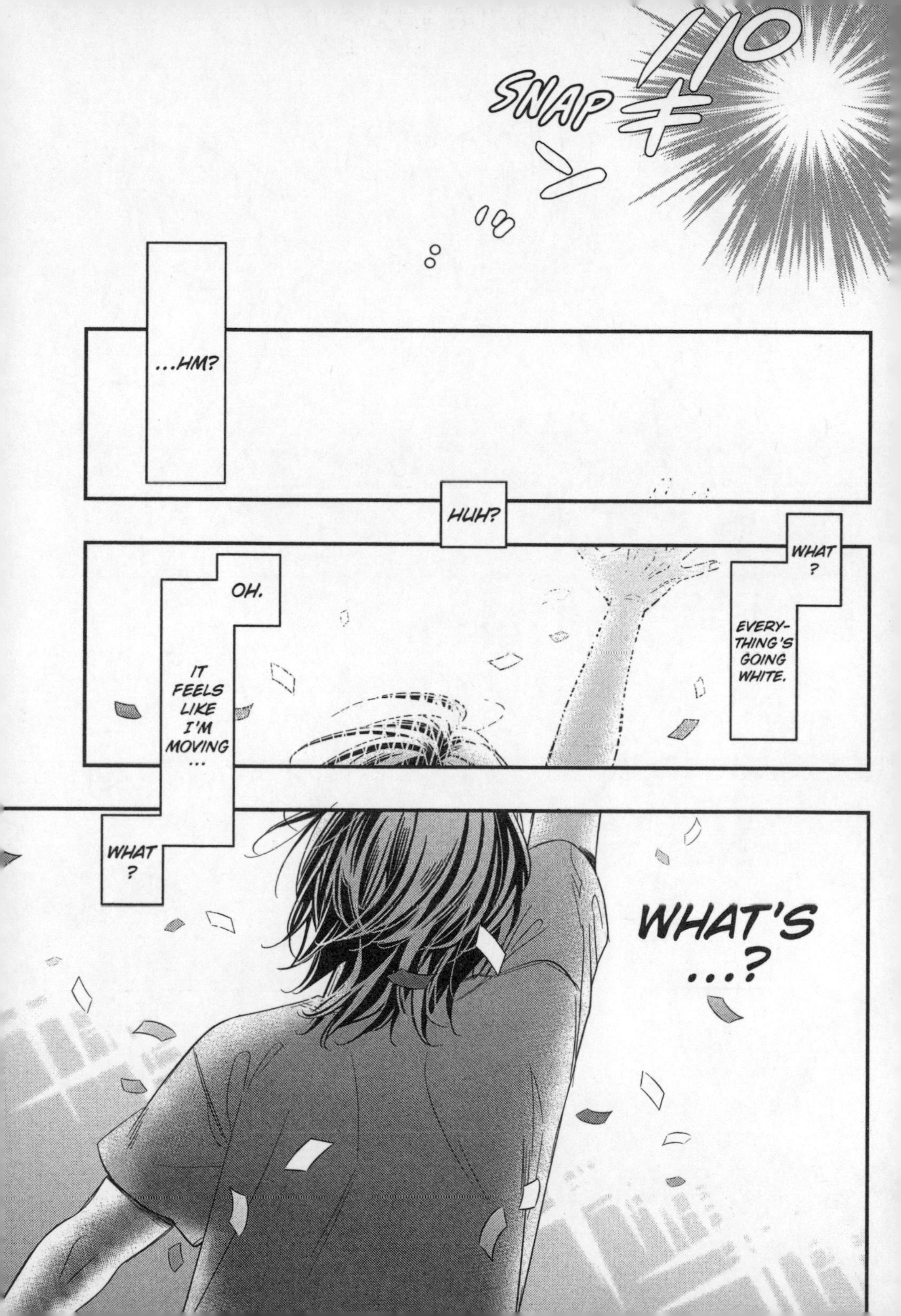
パキン
SNAP
...HM?
HUH?
WHAT?
EVERYTHING'S GOING WHITE.
OH.
IT FEELS LIKE I'M MOVING...
WHAT?
WHAT'S ...?

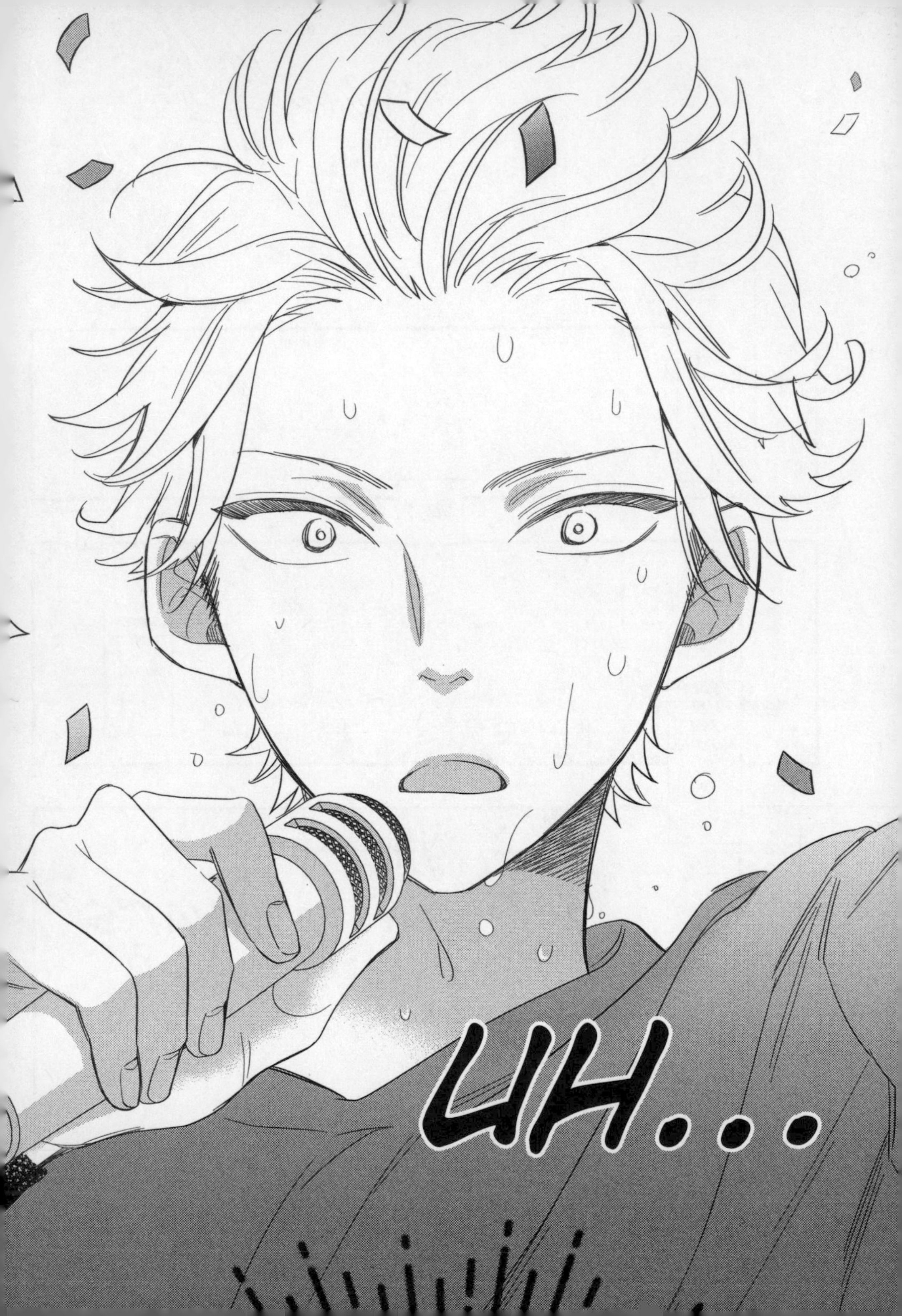
UH...

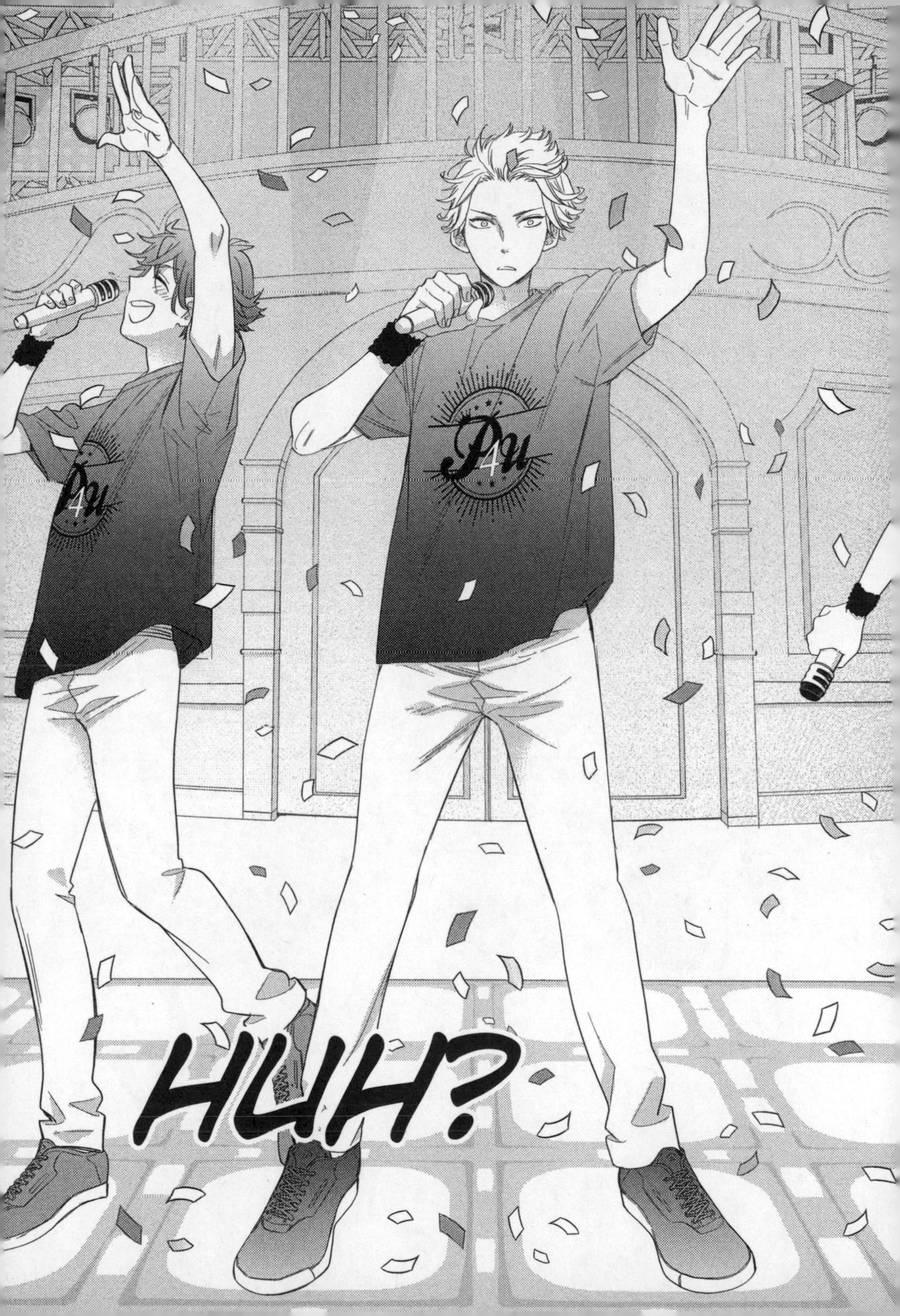
HUH?

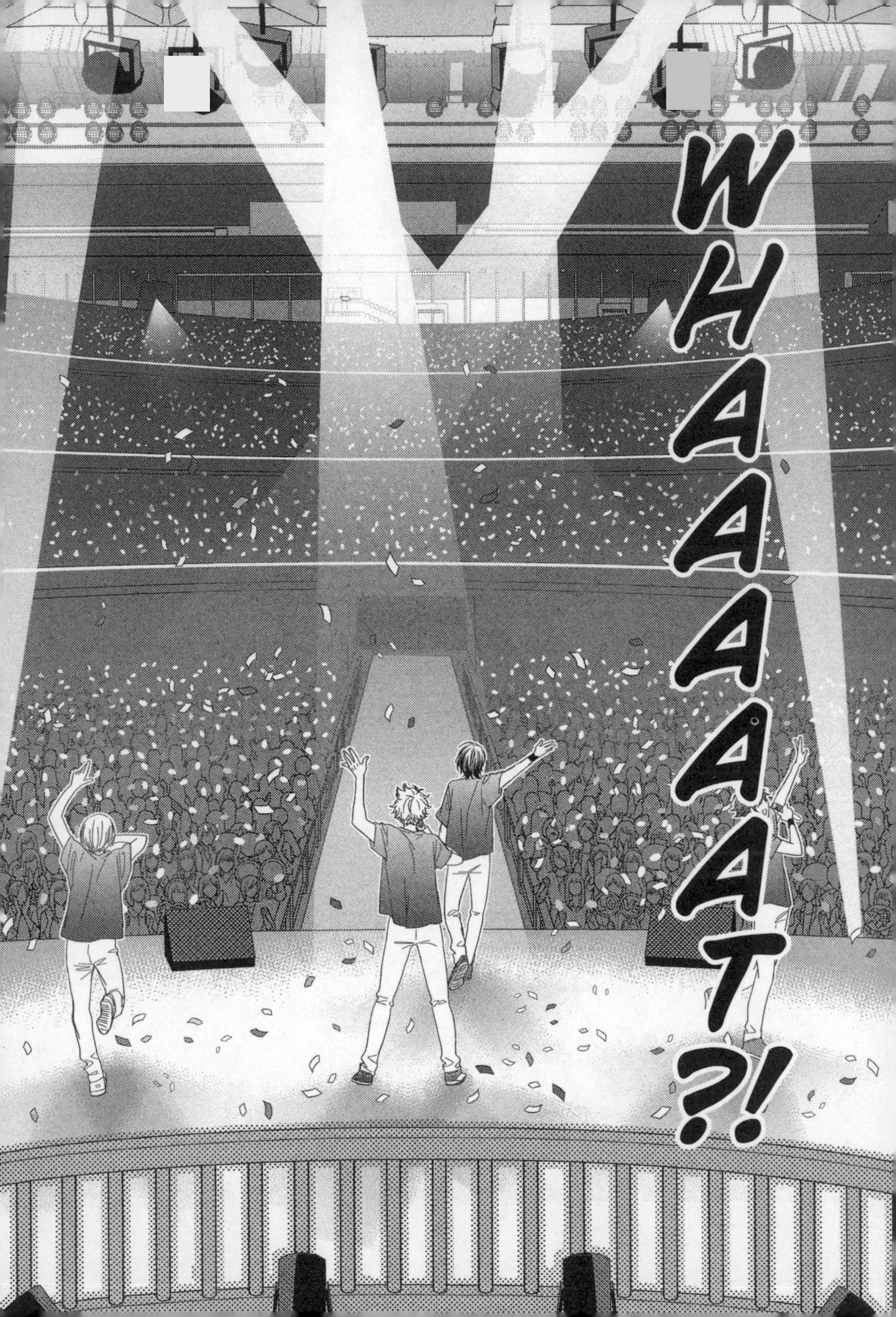
WHAAAAAT?!

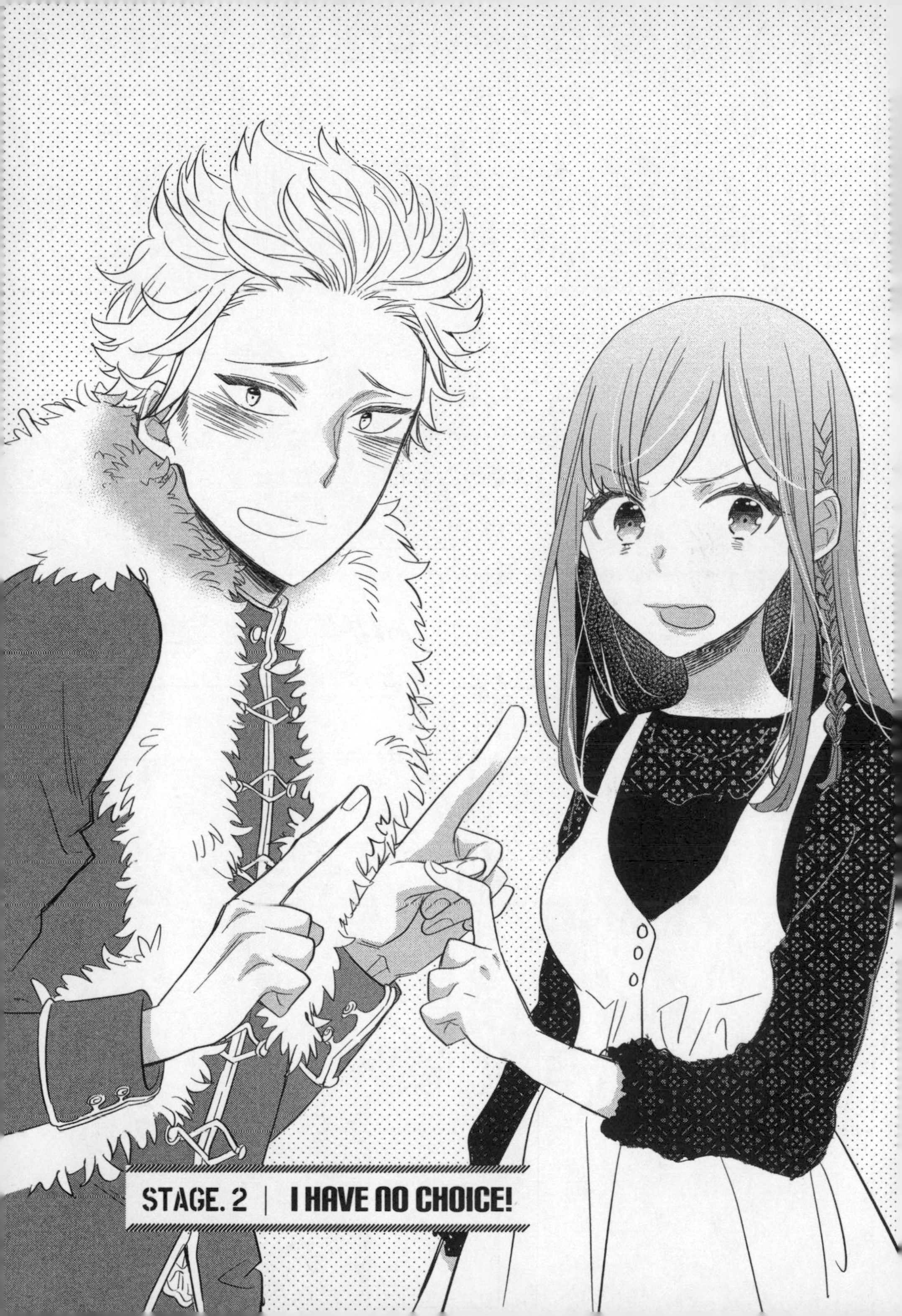
STAGE. 2
I HAVE NO CHOICE!

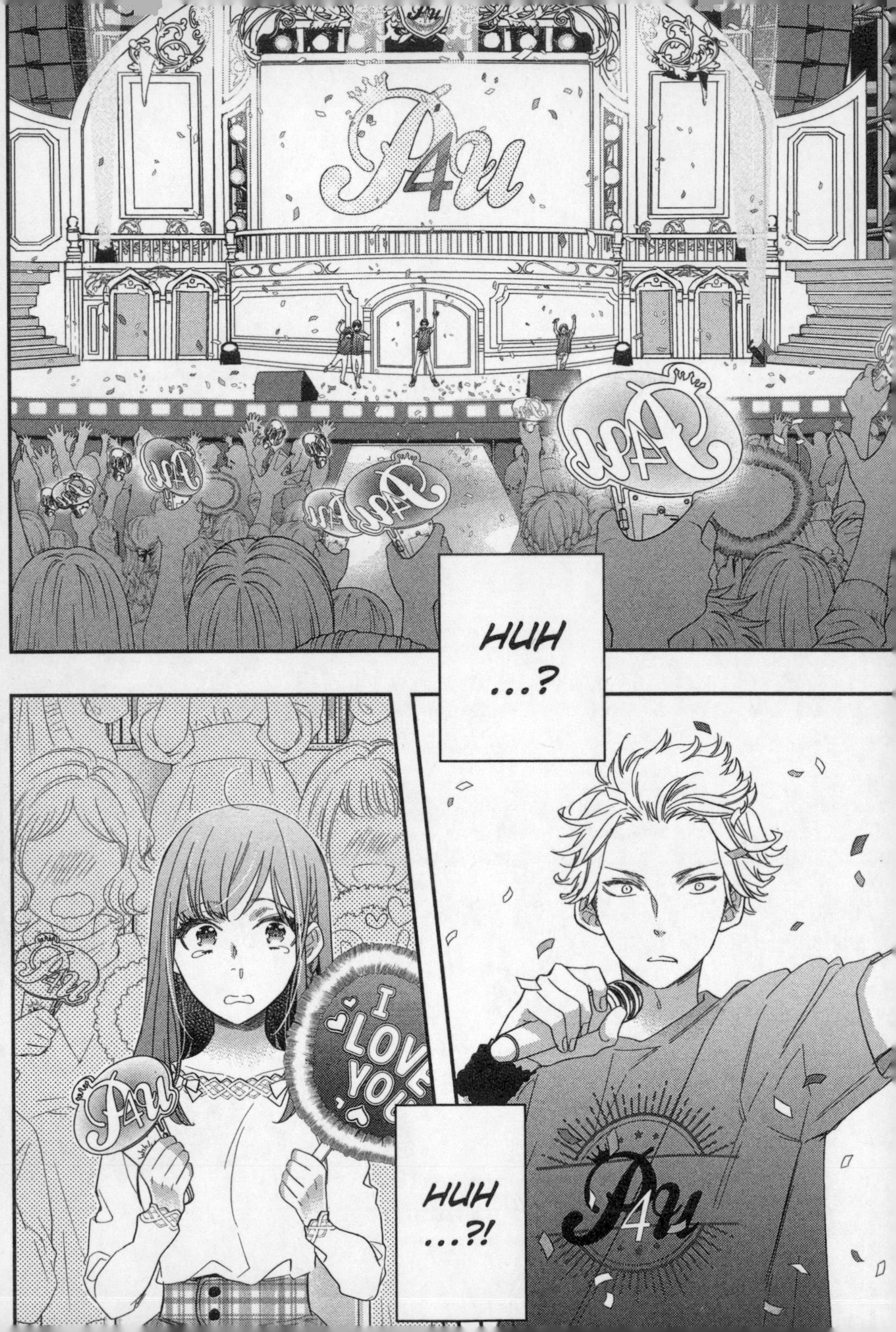
P4U
HUH ...?
HUH ...?!
P4U
P4U
I LOVE YOU

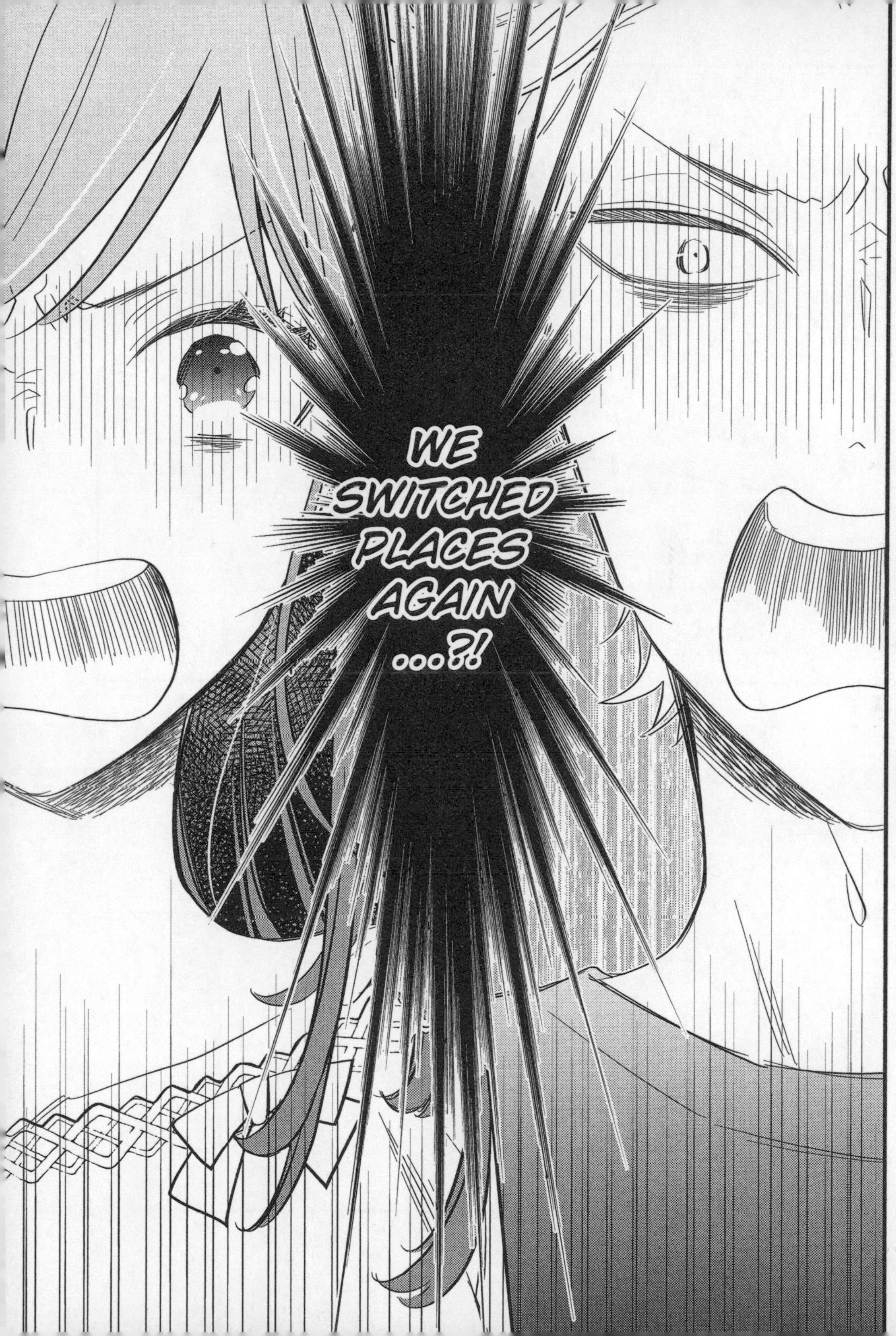
WE SWITCHED PLACES AGAIN ...?!

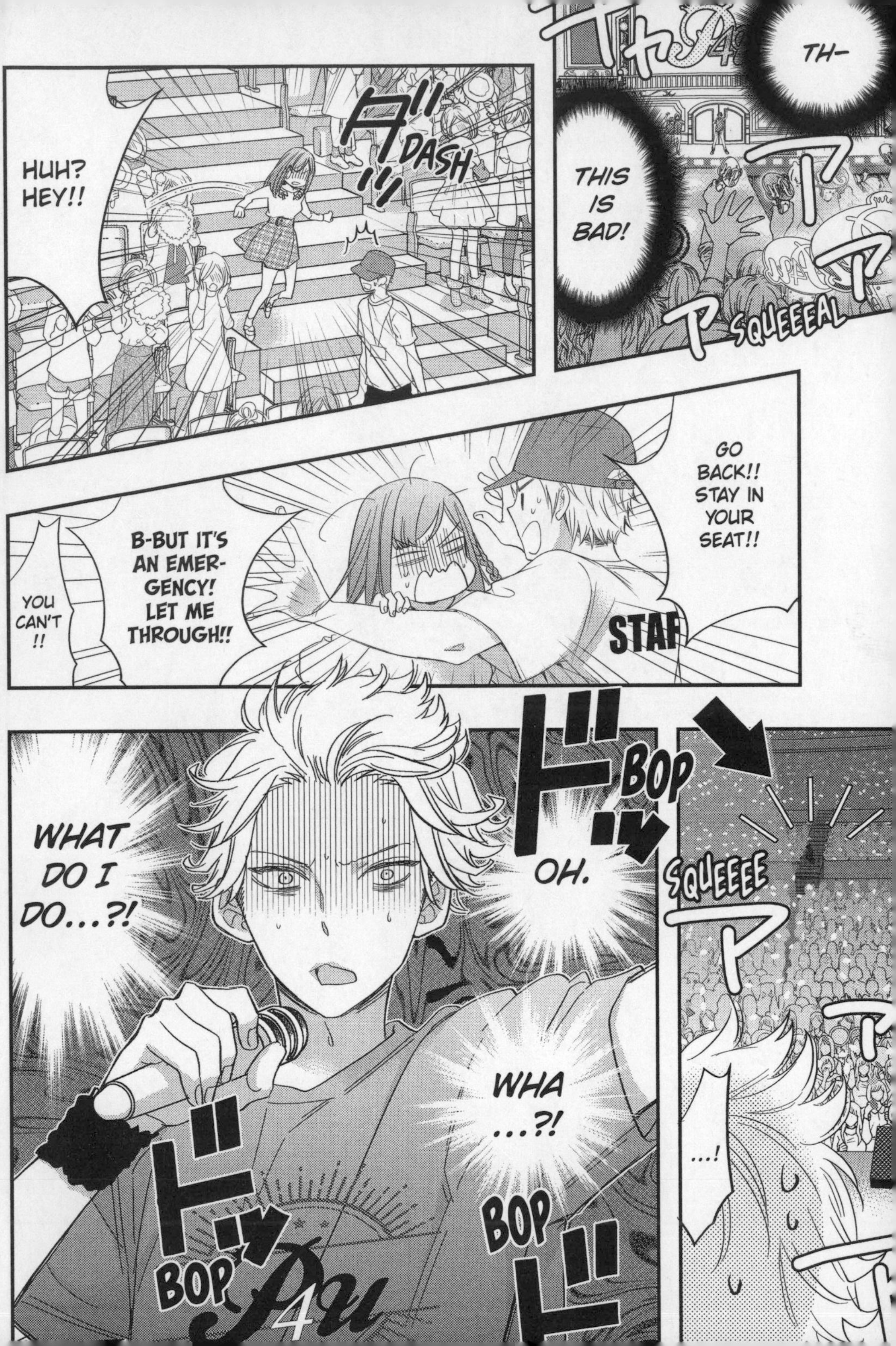
TH-
THIS IS BAD!
SQUEEEAL
DASH
HUH? HEY!!
GO BACK!! STAY IN YOUR SEAT!!
STAF
B-BUT IT'S AN EMER-GENCY! LET ME THROUGH!!
YOU CAN'T !!
SQUEEEE
...!
BOP
OH.
WHAT DO I DO...?!
WHA ...?!
BOP
BOP

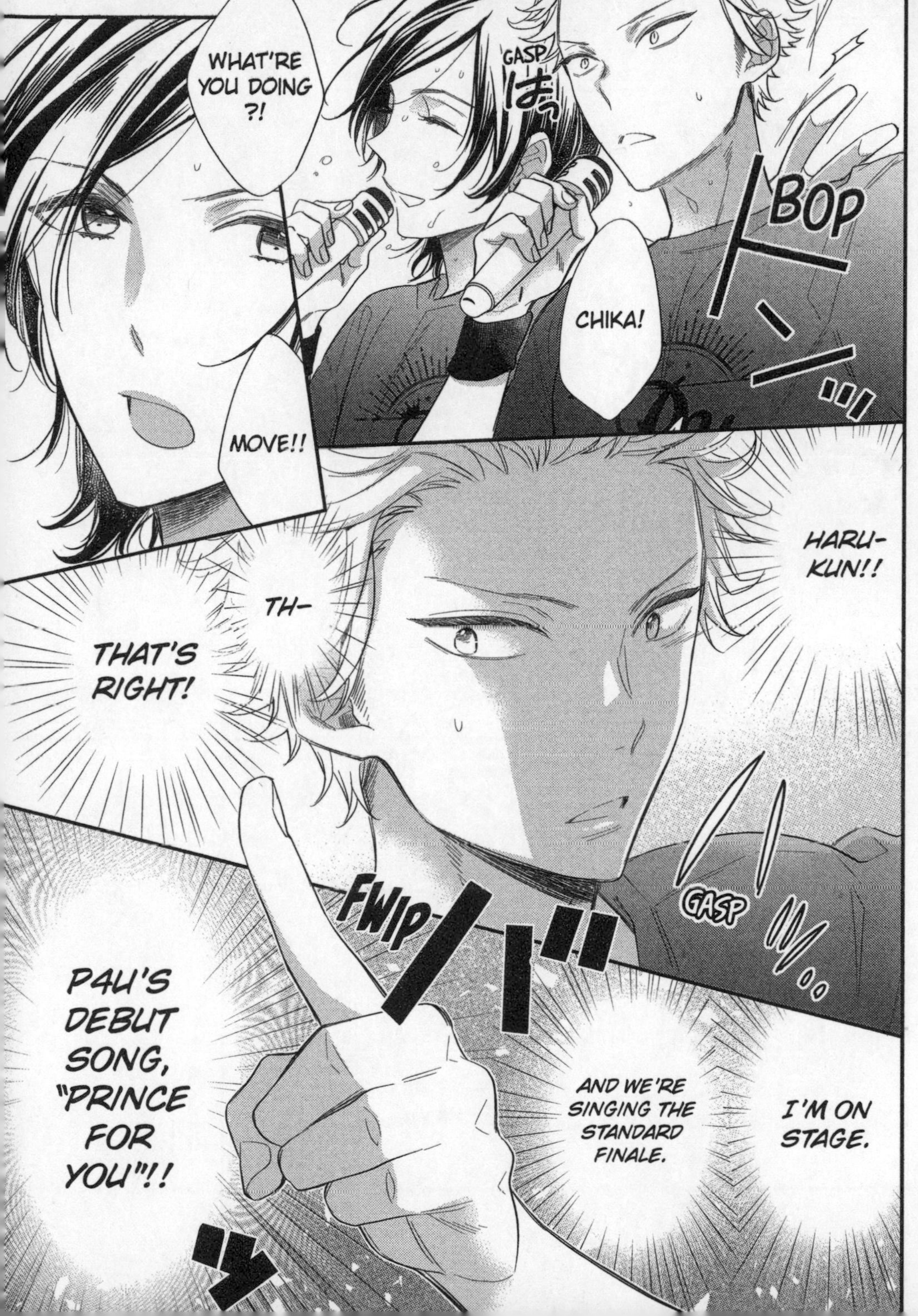
BOP
GASP
はっ
CHIKA!
WHAT'RE YOU DOING ?!
MOVE!!
HARU-KUN!!
TH-
THAT'S RIGHT!
GASP
FWIP
I'M ON STAGE.
AND WE'RE SINGING THE STANDARD FINALE.
P4U'S DEBUT SONG, "PRINCE FOR YOU"!!

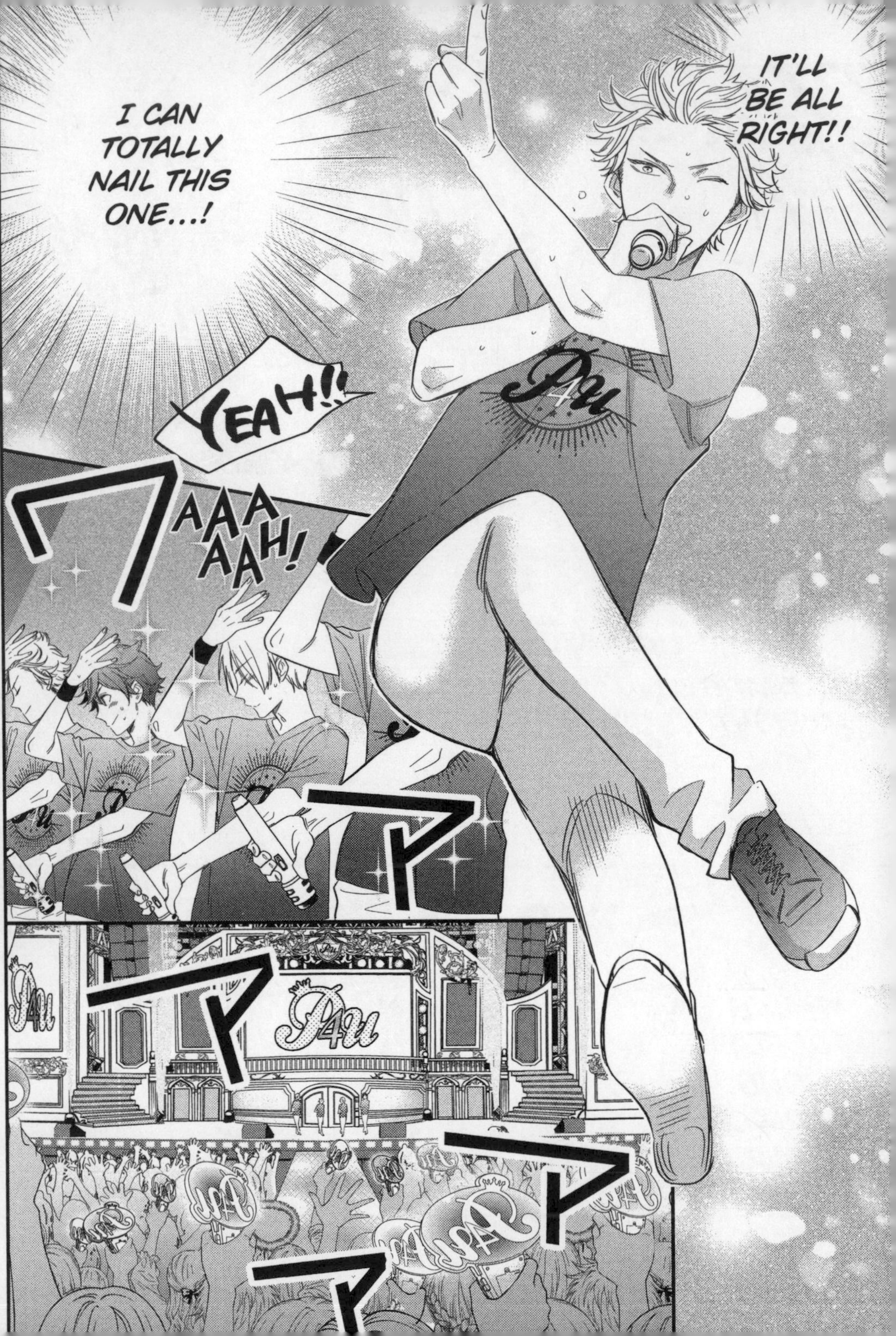
IT'LL BE ALL RIGHT!!
I CAN TOTALLY NAIL THIS ONE...!
YEAH!!
AAAAAH!

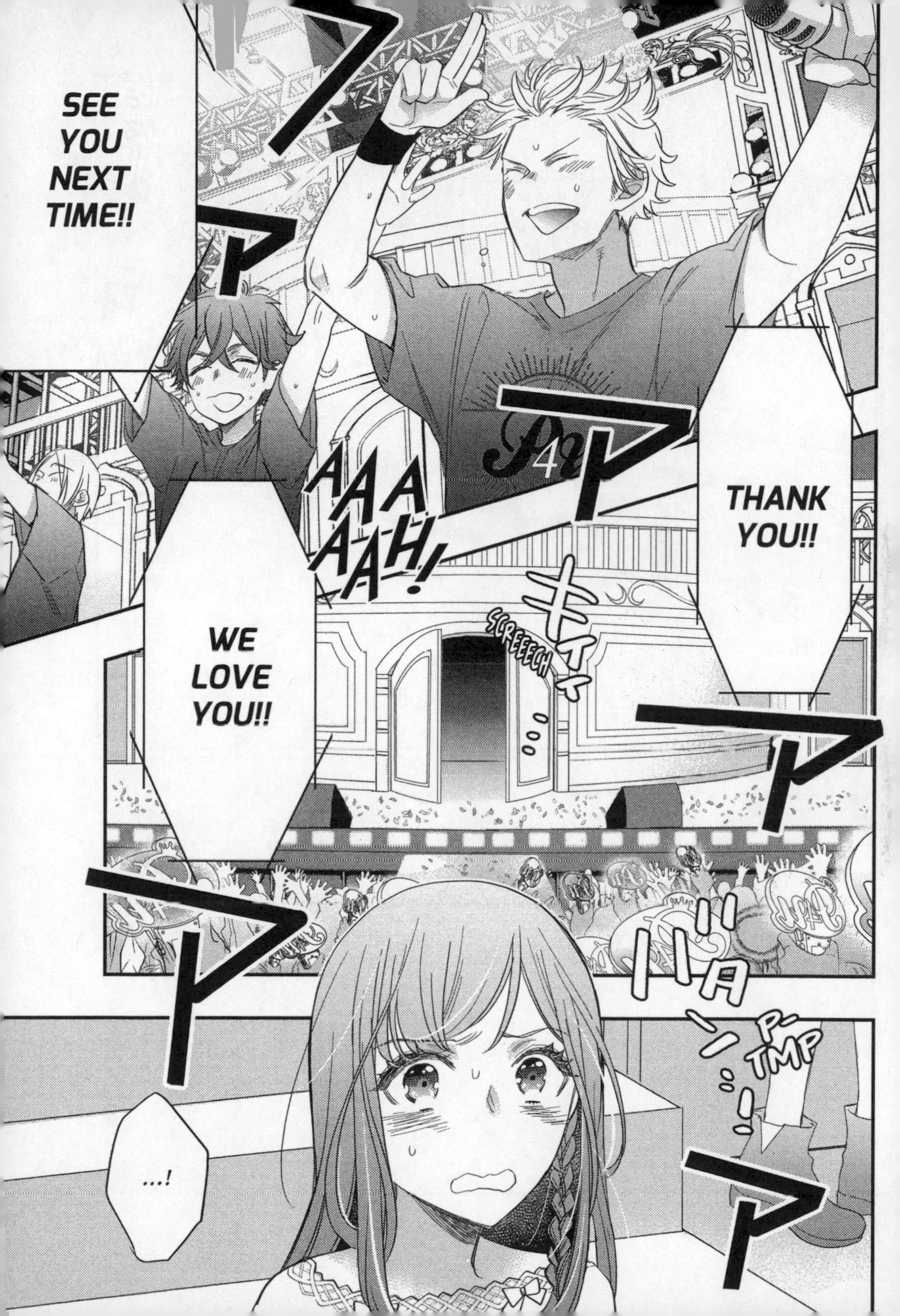
THANK YOU!!
SEE YOU NEXT TIME!!
AAAAAH!
WE LOVE YOU!!
SCREEECH
P-TMP
...!

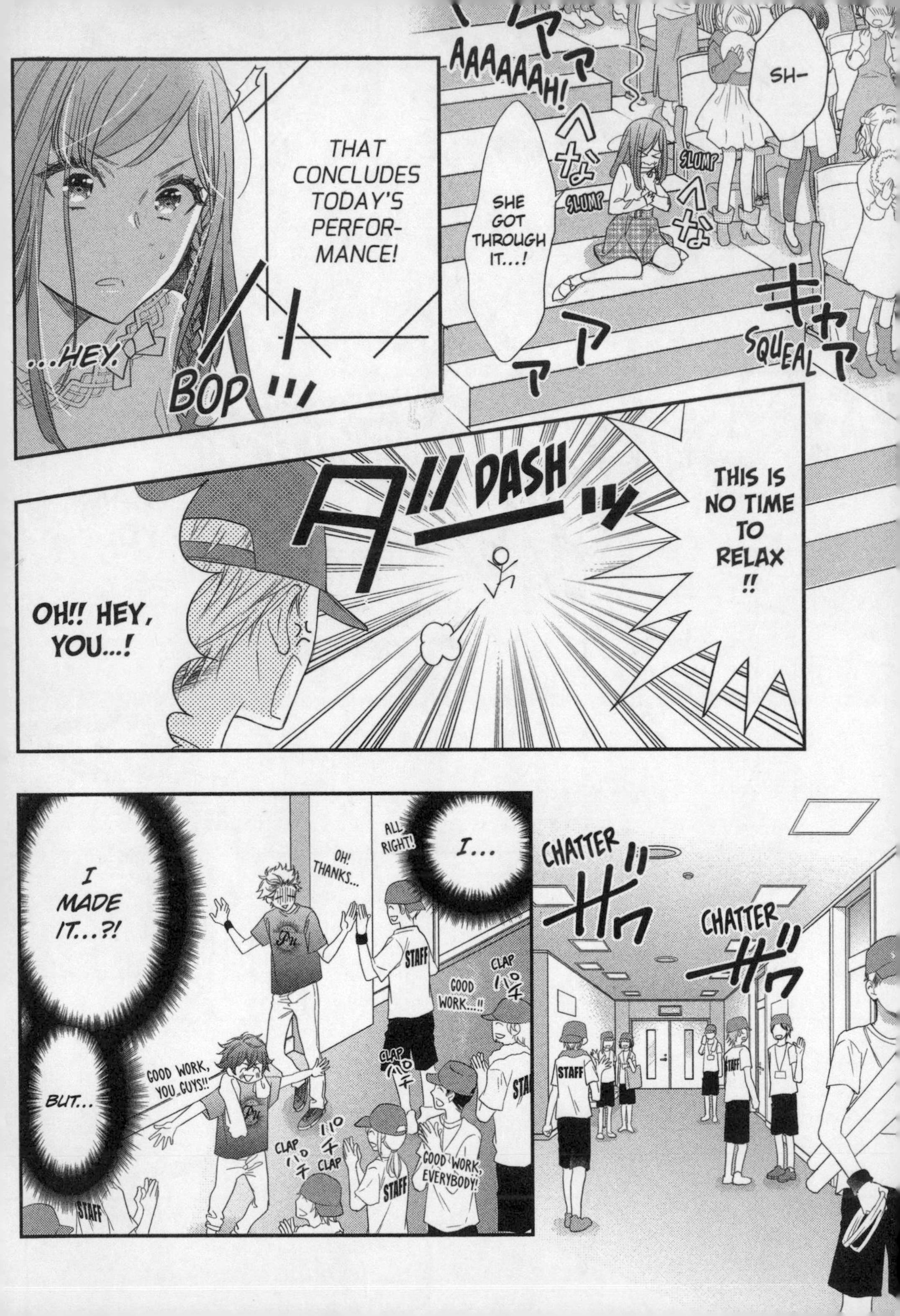

AAAAAAH!
SH-
SHE GOT THROUGH IT...!
SLUMP
SLUMP
SQUEAL
THAT CONCLUDES TODAY'S PERFORMANCE!
...HEY.
BOP
THIS IS NO TIME TO RELAX !!
DASH
OH!! HEY, YOU...!
CHATTER
CHATTER
I...
ALL RIGHT!
OH! THANKS...
I MADE IT...?!
CLAP
GOOD WORK...!!
CLAP
GOOD WORK, YOU GUYS!!
BUT...
CLAP
CLAP
GOOD WORK, EVERYBODY!
STAFF

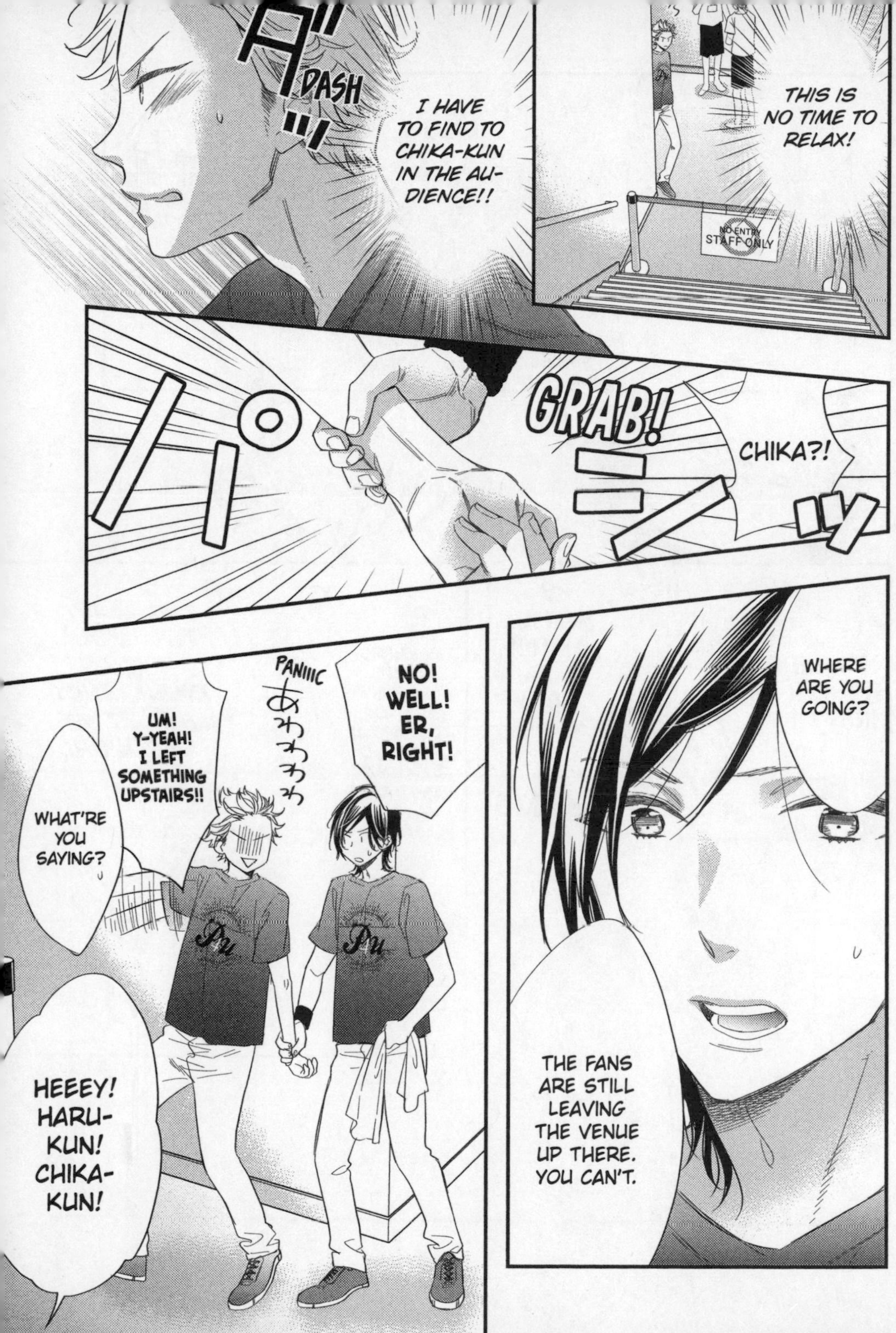
THIS IS NO TIME TO RELAX!
NO ENTRY
STAFF ONLY
DASH
I HAVE TO FIND TO CHIKA-KUN IN THE AUDIENCE!!
GRAB!
CHIKA?!
WHERE ARE YOU GOING?
THE FANS ARE STILL LEAVING THE VENUE UP THERE. YOU CAN'T.
NO! WELL! ER, RIGHT!
PANIIIC
あわわわわ
UM! Y-YEAH! I LEFT SOMETHING UPSTAIRS!!
WHAT'RE YOU SAYING?
HEEEY! HARU-KUN! CHIKA-KUN!

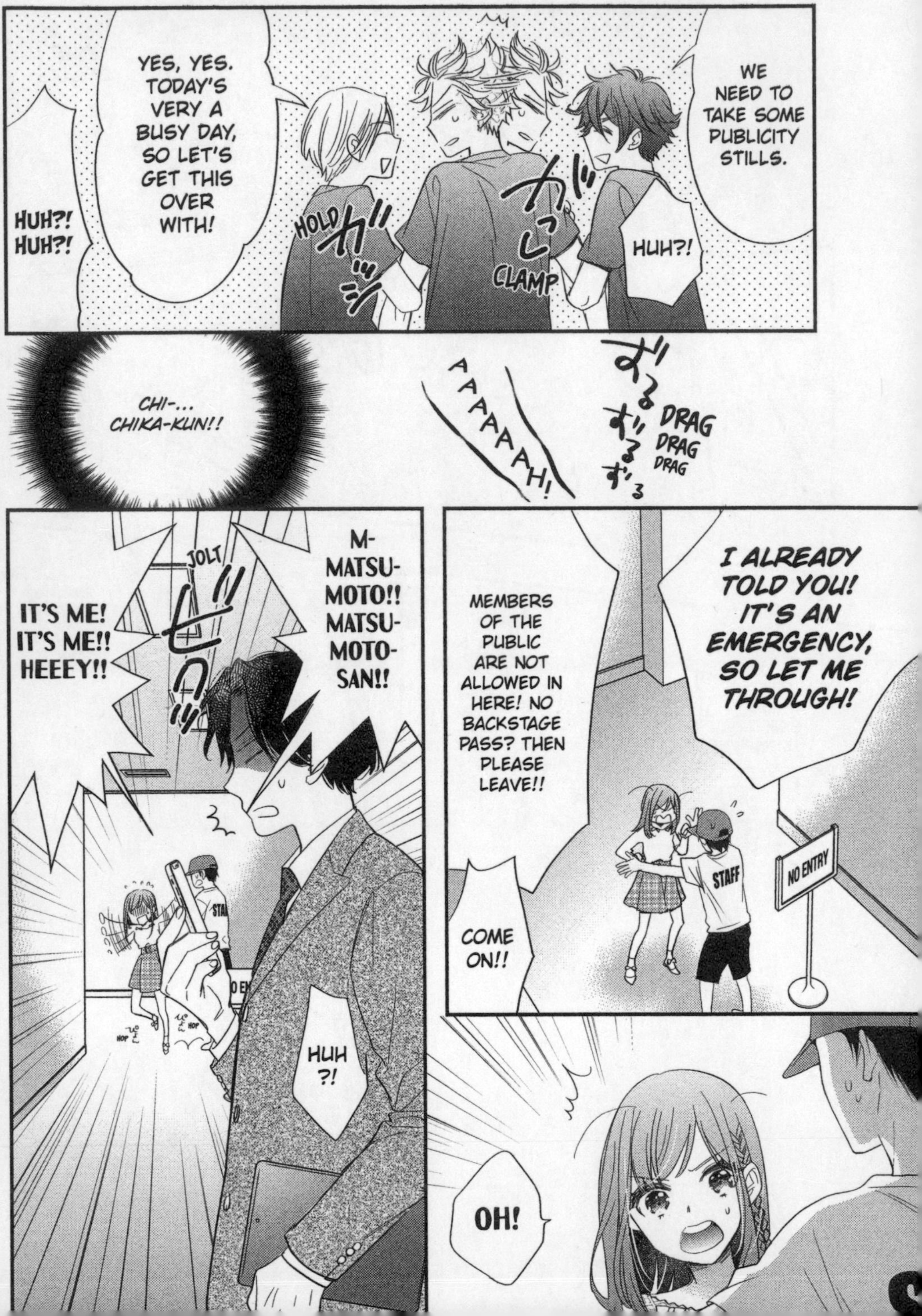
WE NEED TO TAKE SOME PUBLICITY STILLS.
HUH?!
CLAMP
HOLD
YES, YES. TODAY'S VERY A BUSY DAY, SO LET'S GET THIS OVER WITH!
HUH?! HUH?!
DRAG DRAG DRAG
AAAAAAAH!
CHI-... CHIKA-KUN!!
I ALREADY TOLD YOU! IT'S AN EMERGENCY, SO LET ME THROUGH!
MEMBERS OF THE PUBLIC ARE NOT ALLOWED IN HERE! NO BACKSTAGE PASS? THEN PLEASE LEAVE!!
STAFF
NO ENTRY
COME ON!!
OH!
M-MATSUMOTO!! MATSUMOTO-SAN!!
JOLT
IT'S ME! IT'S ME!! HEEEY!!
HOP
HOP
HUH ?!

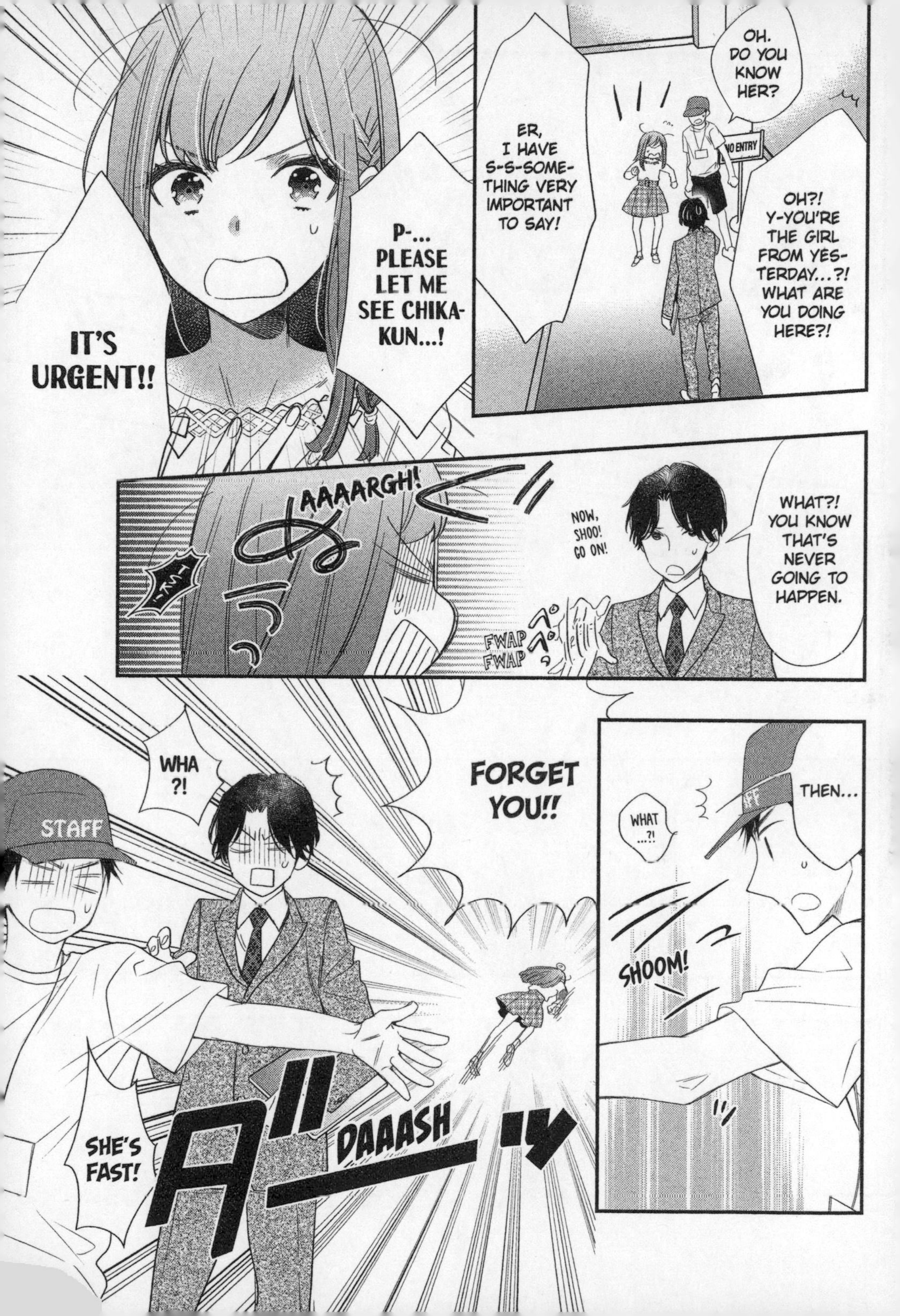
OH. DO YOU KNOW HER?
NO ENTRY
ER, I HAVE S-S-SOMETHING VERY IMPORTANT TO SAY!
OH?! Y-YOU'RE THE GIRL FROM YESTERDAY...?! WHAT ARE YOU DOING HERE?!
P-... PLEASE LET ME SEE CHIKA-KUN...!
IT'S URGENT!!
WHAT?! YOU KNOW THAT'S NEVER GOING TO HAPPEN.
NOW, SHOO! GO ON!
FWAP FWAP
AAAARGH!
THEN...
WHAT ...?!
SHOOM!
FORGET YOU!!
WHA ?!
STAFF
DAAASH
SHE'S FAST!

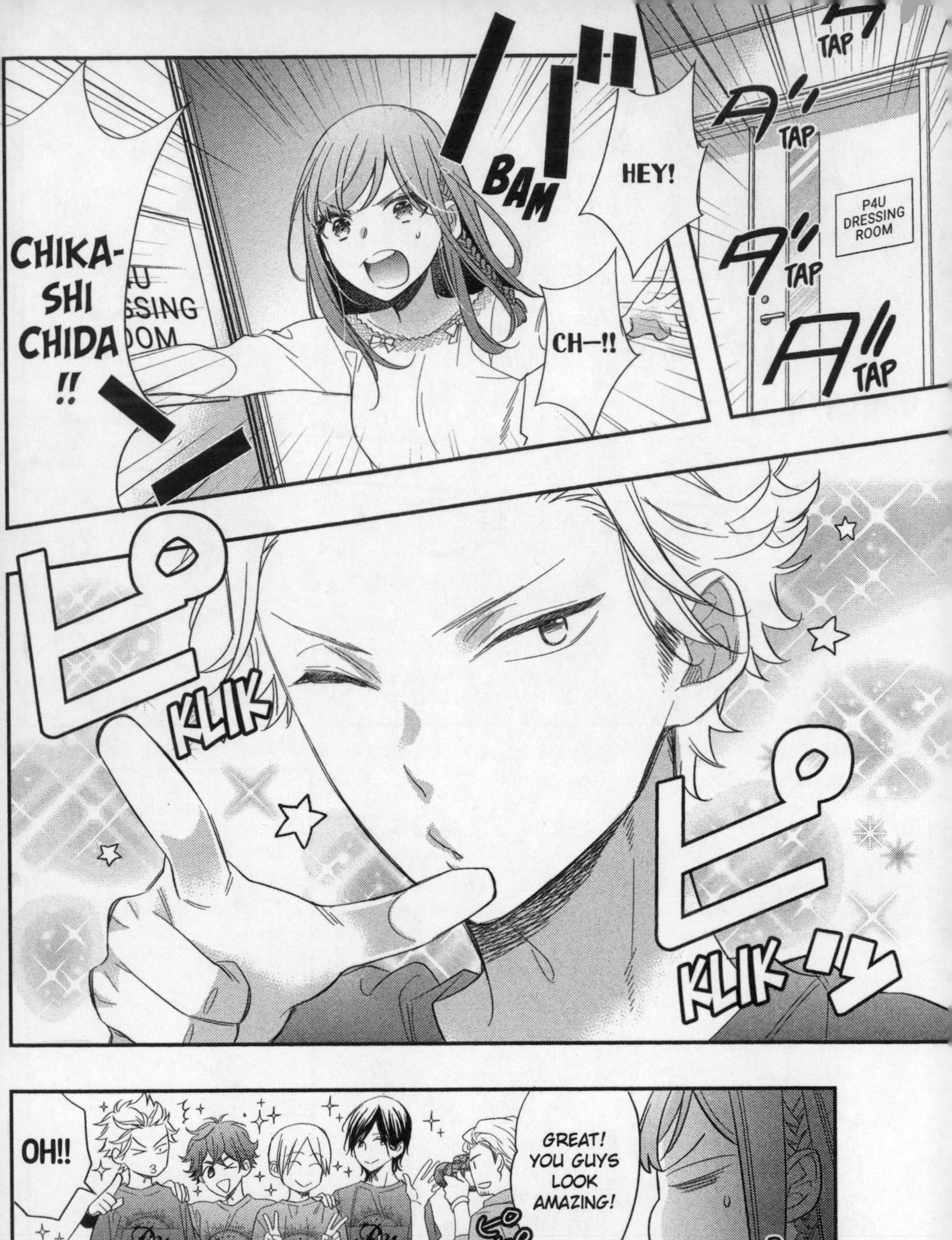
TAP
TAP
P4U DRESSING ROOM
TAP
TAP
HEY!
BAM
CH—!!
CHIKA-SHI CHIDA !!
KLIK
KLIK
...?
GREAT! YOU GUYS LOOK AMAZING!
KLIK KLIK
OH!!

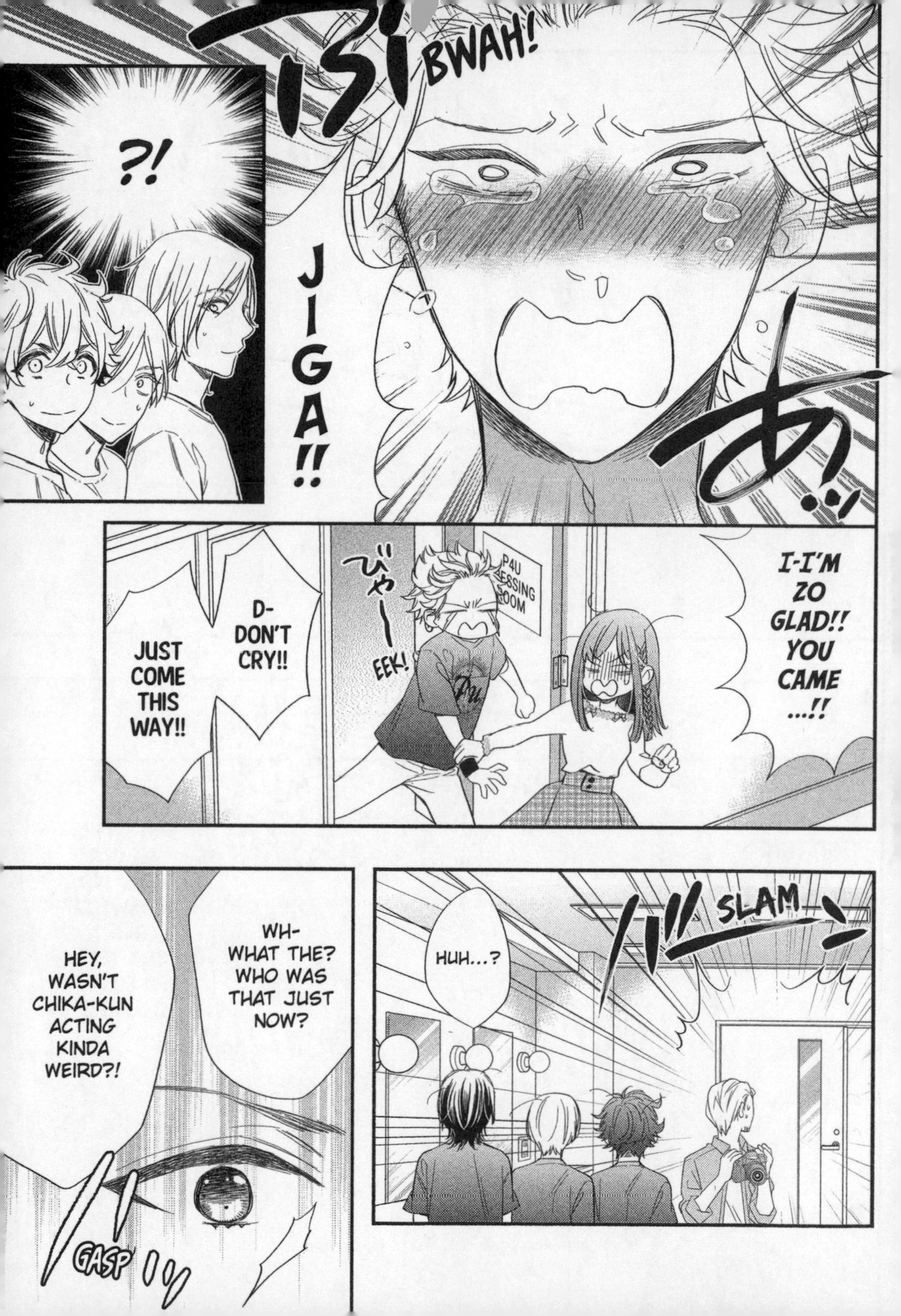
BWAH!
JIGA!!
あ…!
?!
I-I'M ZO GLAD!! YOU CAME…!!
びゃー
EEK!
D-DON'T CRY!!
JUST COME THIS WAY!!
SLAM
HUH…?
WH-WHAT THE? WHO WAS THAT JUST NOW?
HEY, WASN'T CHIKA-KUN ACTING KINDA WEIRD?!
GASP

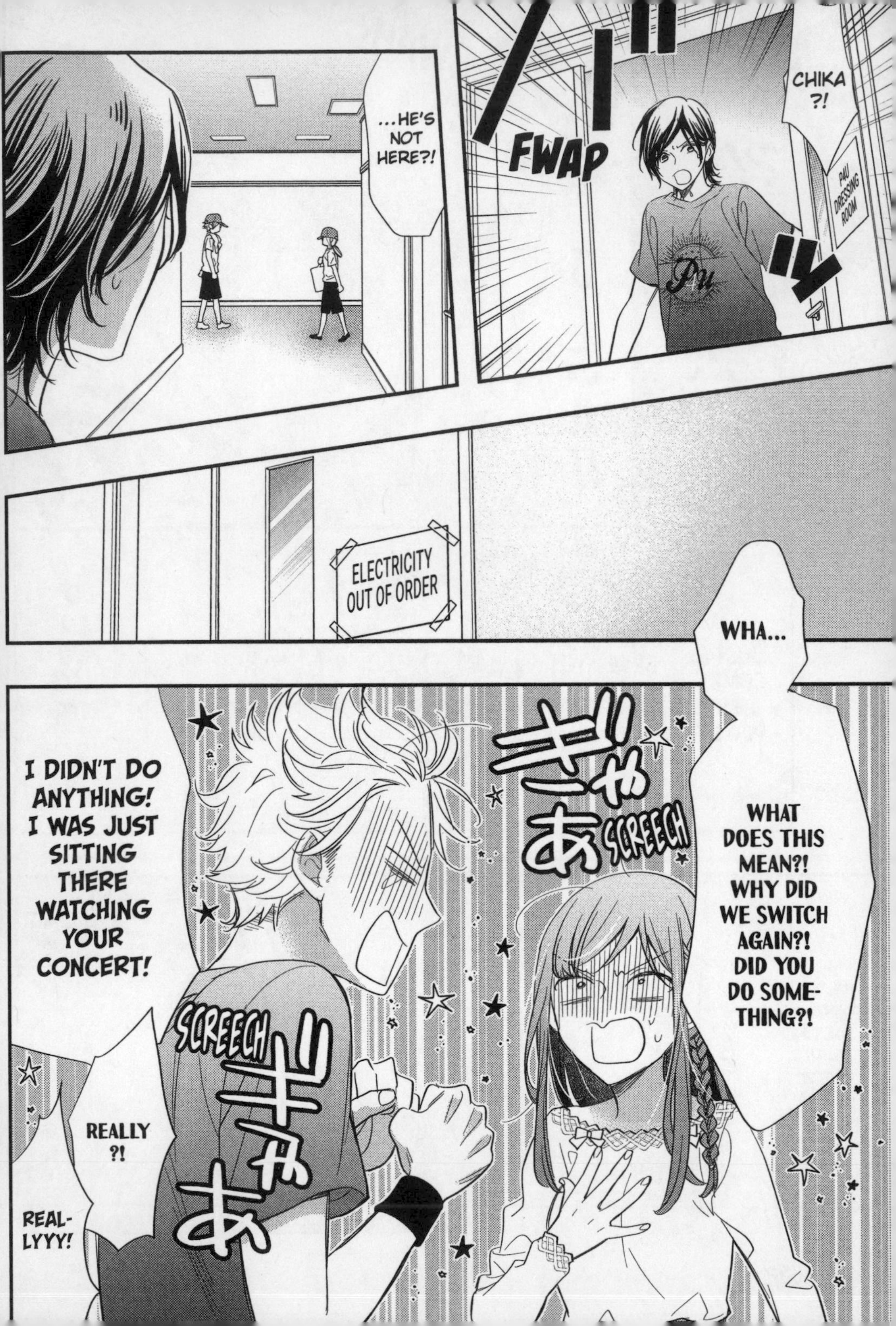

CHIKA ?!
FWAP
P4U DRESSING ROOM
...HE'S NOT HERE?!
ELECTRICITY OUT OF ORDER
WHA...
WHAT DOES THIS MEAN?! WHY DID WE SWITCH AGAIN?! DID YOU DO SOME-THING?!
SCREECH
I DIDN'T DO ANYTHING! I WAS JUST SITTING THERE WATCHING YOUR CONCERT!
SCREECH
REALLY ?!
REAL-LYYY!

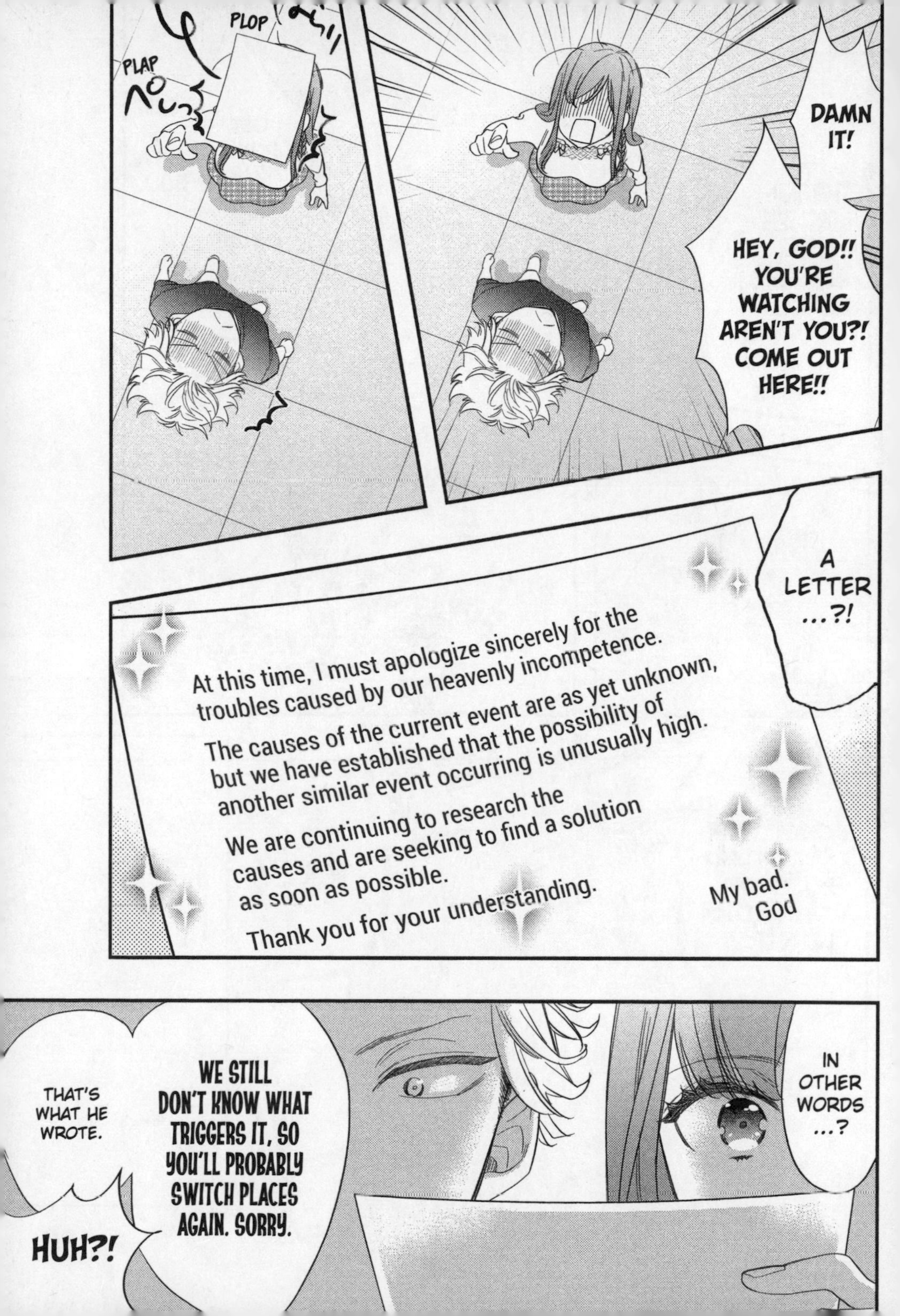
DAMN IT!
HEY, GOD!! YOU'RE WATCHING AREN'T YOU?! COME OUT HERE!!
PLOP
PLAP
A LETTER ...?!
At this time, I must apologize sincerely for the troubles caused by our heavenly incompetence.
The causes of the current event are as yet unknown, but we have established that the possibility of another similar event occurring is unusually high.
We are continuing to research the causes and are seeking to find a solution as soon as possible.
Thank you for your understanding.
My bad. God
IN OTHER WORDS ...?
WE STILL DON'T KNOW WHAT TRIGGERS IT, SO YOU'LL PROBABLY SWITCH PLACES AGAIN. SORRY.
THAT'S WHAT HE WROTE.
HUH?!

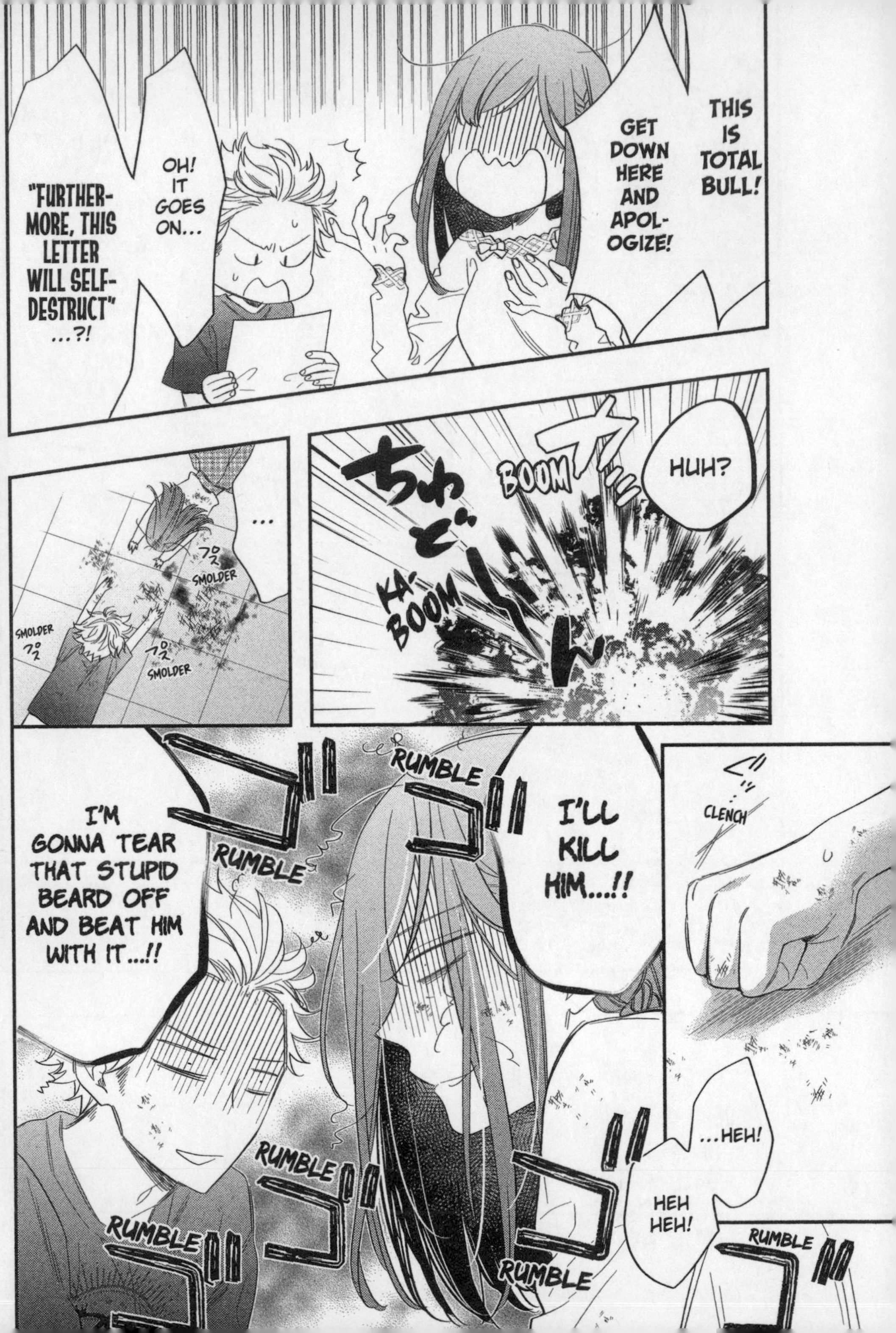
THIS IS TOTAL BULL!
GET DOWN HERE AND APOLOGIZE!
OH! IT GOES ON...
"FURTHERMORE, THIS LETTER WILL SELF-DESTRUCT"...?!
HUH?
BOOM
KA-BOOM
...
SMOLDER
SMOLDER
SMOLDER
CLENCH
...HEH!
HEH HEH!
RUMBLE
I'LL KILL HIM...!!
RUMBLE
I'M GONNA TEAR THAT STUPID BEARD OFF AND BEAT HIM WITH IT...!!
RUMBLE
RUMBLE
RUMBLE
RUMBLE

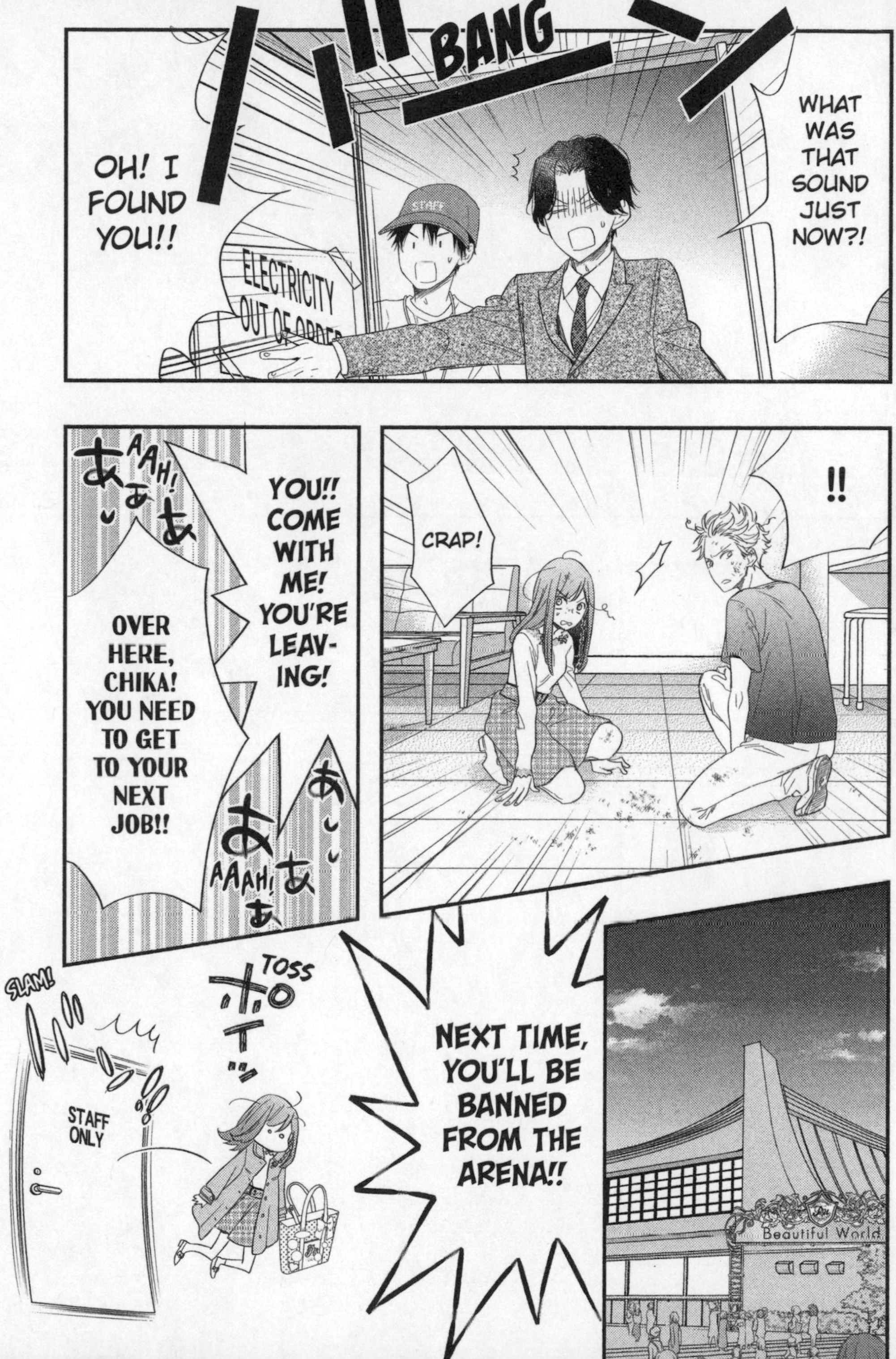
BANG
WHAT WAS THAT SOUND JUST NOW?!
OH! I FOUND YOU!!
STAFF
ELECTRICITY OUT OF ORDER
!!
CRAP!
YOU!! COME WITH ME! YOU'RE LEAV-ING!
OVER HERE, CHIKA! YOU NEED TO GET TO YOUR NEXT JOB!!
AAH!
AAAH!
Beautiful World
NEXT TIME, YOU'LL BE BANNED FROM THE ARENA!!
TOSS
SLAM!
STAFF ONLY

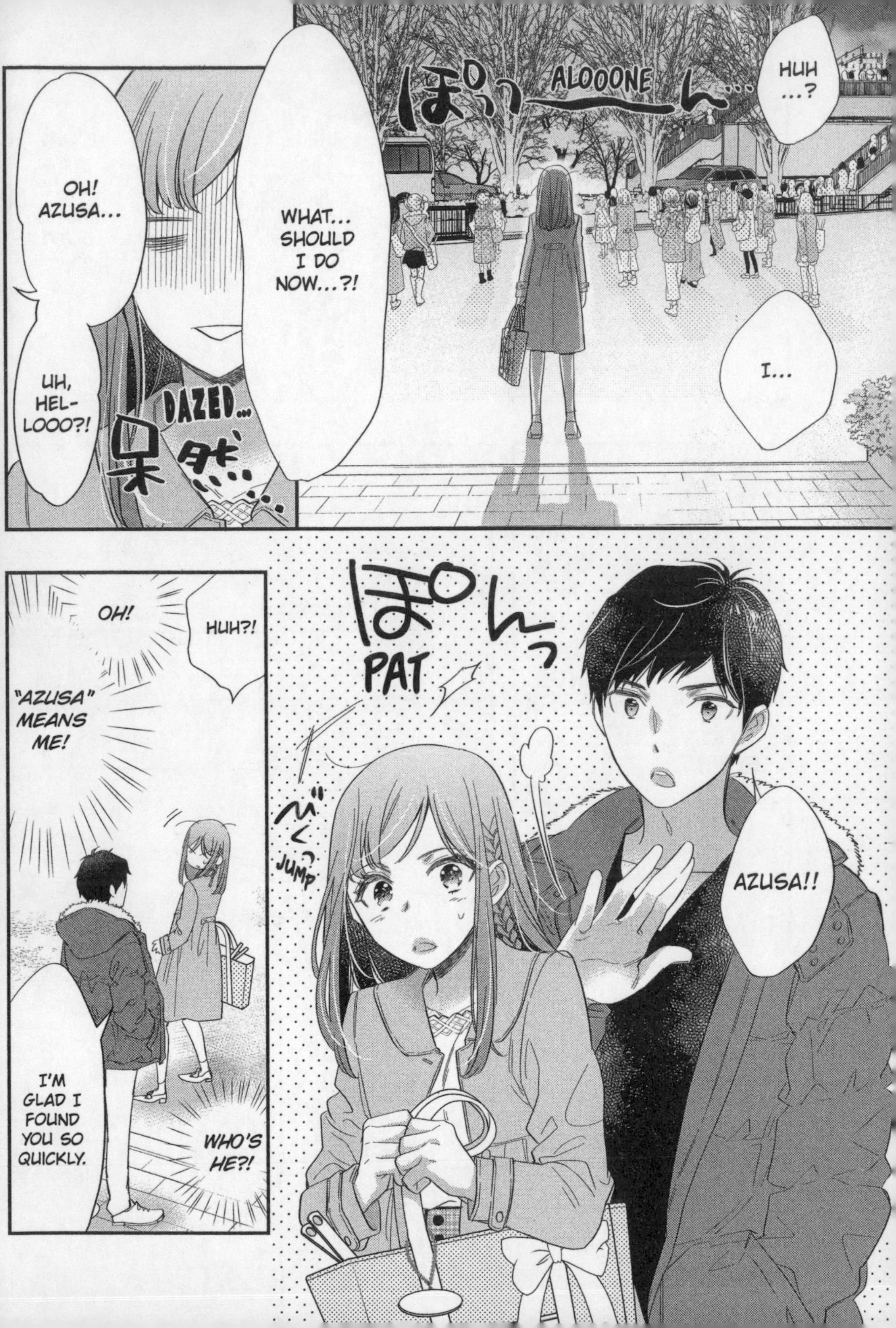
HUH ...?
ぽつ——ん
ALOOONE
I...
WHAT... SHOULD I DO NOW...?!
OH! AZUSA...
UH, HEL-LOOO?!
呆然...
DAZED...
ぽんっ
PAT
AZUSA!!
びくっ
JUMP
HUH?!
OH!
"AZUSA" MEANS ME!
I'M GLAD I FOUND YOU SO QUICKLY.
WHO'S HE?!

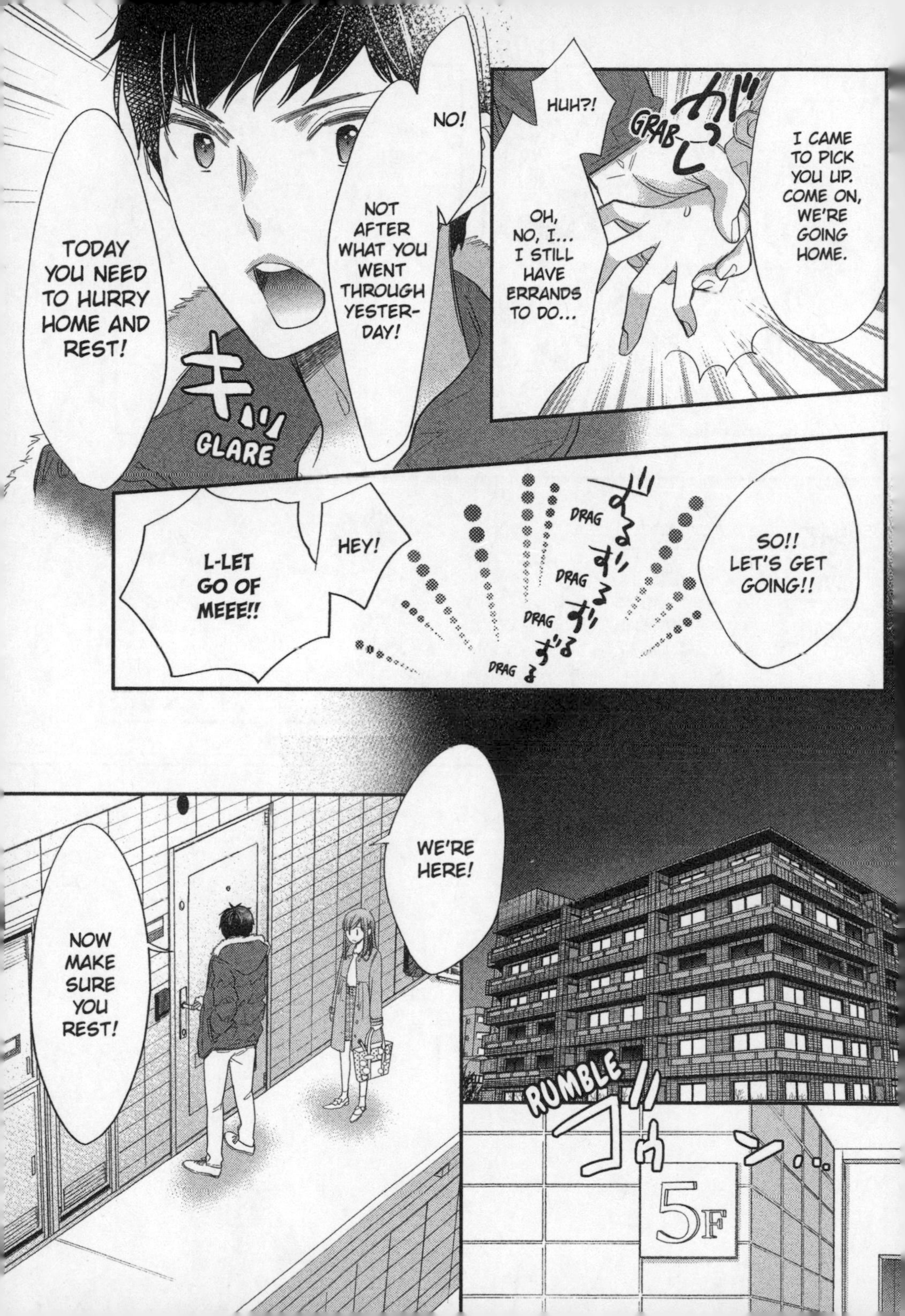
I CAME TO PICK YOU UP. COME ON, WE'RE GOING HOME.
GRAB
HUH?!
OH, NO, I... I STILL HAVE ERRANDS TO DO...
NO!
NOT AFTER WHAT YOU WENT THROUGH YESTER-DAY!
TODAY YOU NEED TO HURRY HOME AND REST!
GLARE
SO!! LET'S GET GOING!!
DRAG
DRAG
DRAG
DRAG
HEY!
L-LET GO OF MEEE!!
RUMBLE
5F
WE'RE HERE!
NOW MAKE SURE YOU REST!

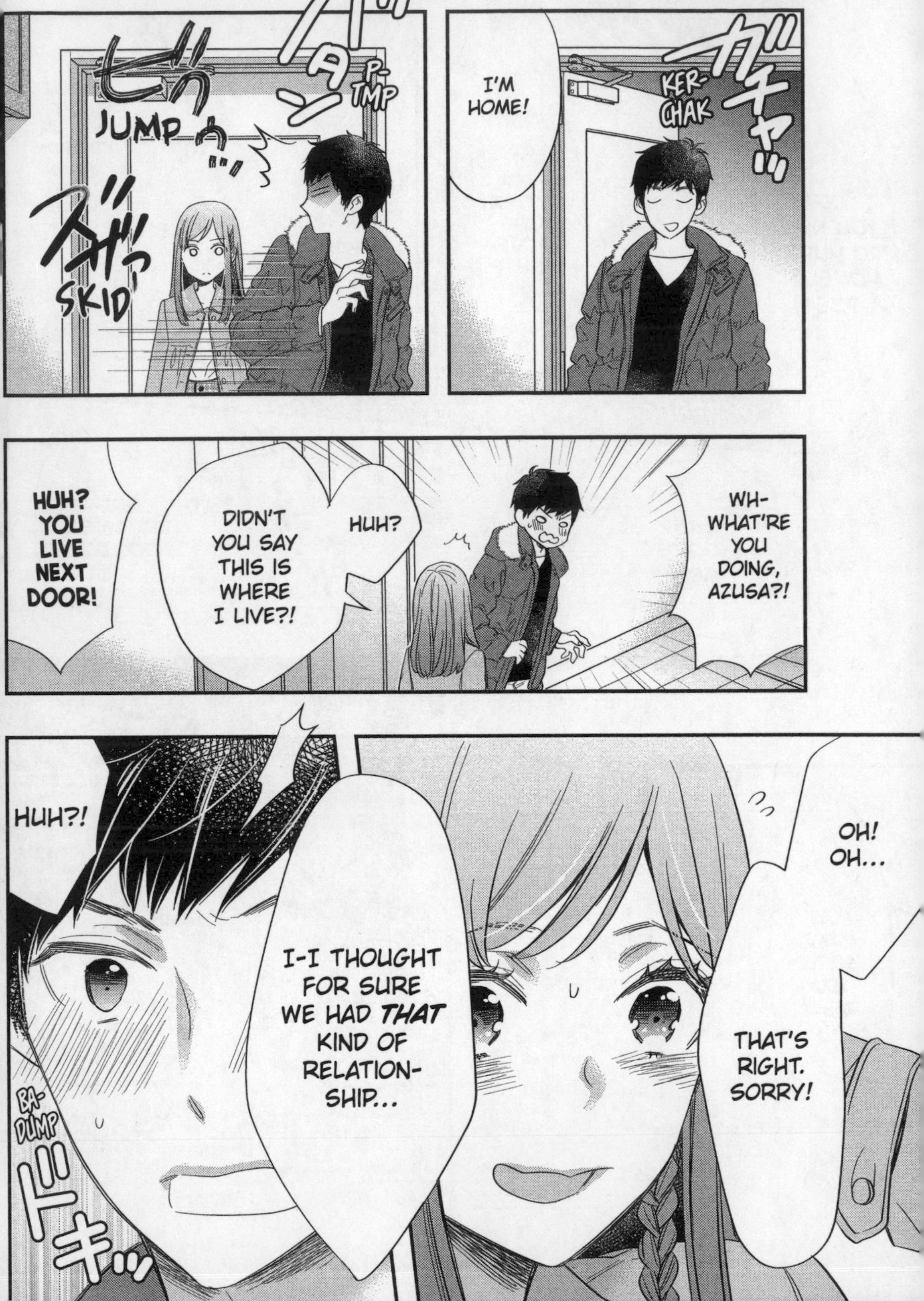

ガチャッ
KER-CHAK
I'M HOME!
バタン
P-TMP
ビクッ
JUMP
ズザッ
SKID
WH-WHAT'RE YOU DOING, AZUSA?!
HUH?
DIDN'T YOU SAY THIS IS WHERE I LIVE?!
HUH? YOU LIVE NEXT DOOR!
OH! OH...
THAT'S RIGHT. SORRY!
I-I THOUGHT FOR SURE WE HAD *THAT* KIND OF RELATION-SHIP...
HUH?!
ドキッ
BA-DUMP

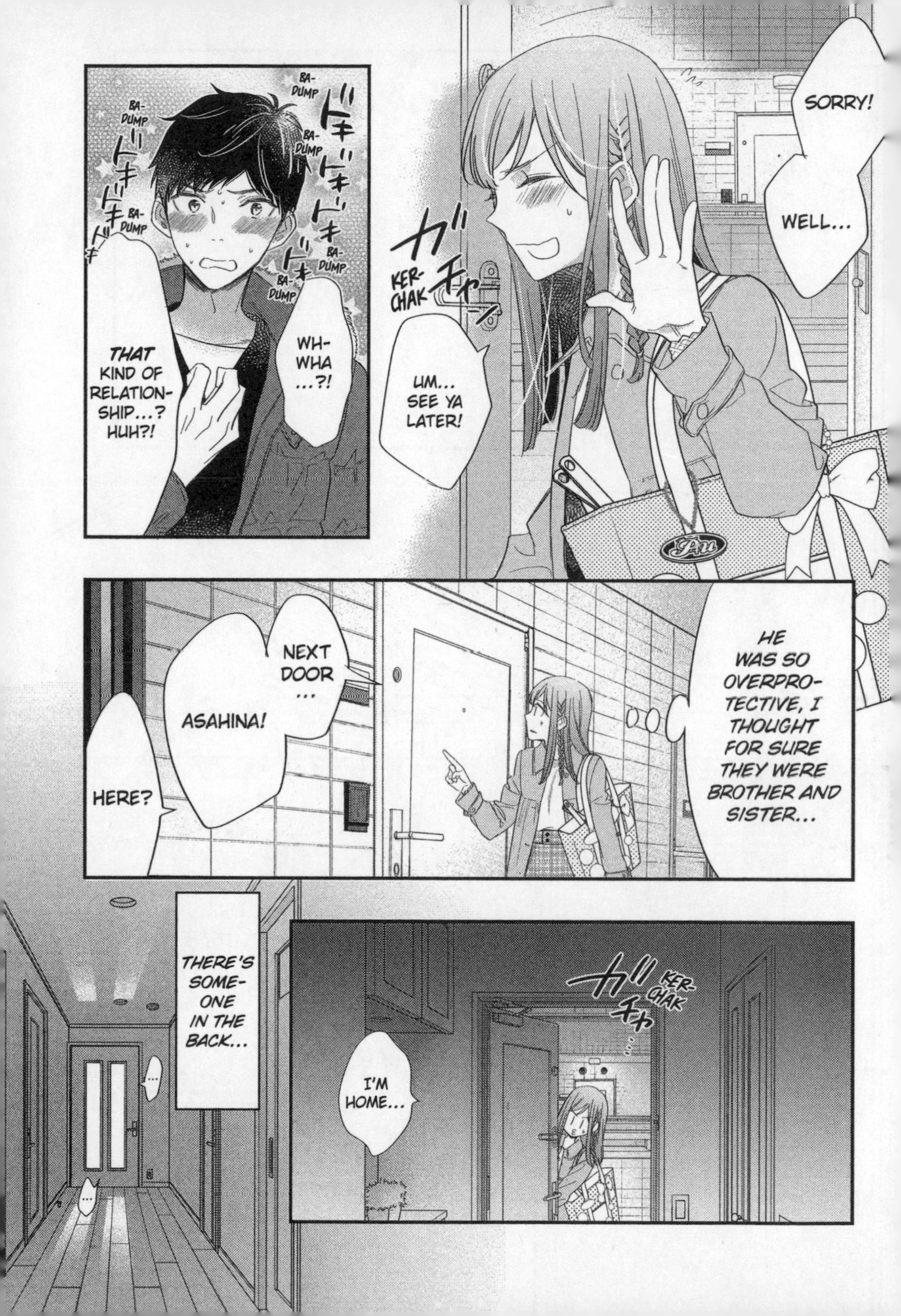
SORRY!
WELL...
KER-CHAK
UM... SEE YA LATER!
BA-DUMP
BA-DUMP
BA-DUMP
BA-DUMP
BA-DUMP
BA-DUMP
WH-WHA...?!
THAT KIND OF RELATIONSHIP...? HUH?!
HE WAS SO OVERPROTECTIVE, I THOUGHT FOR SURE THEY WERE BROTHER AND SISTER...
NEXT DOOR...
ASAHINA!
HERE?
KER-CHAK
I'M HOME...
THERE'S SOMEONE IN THE BACK...
...
...

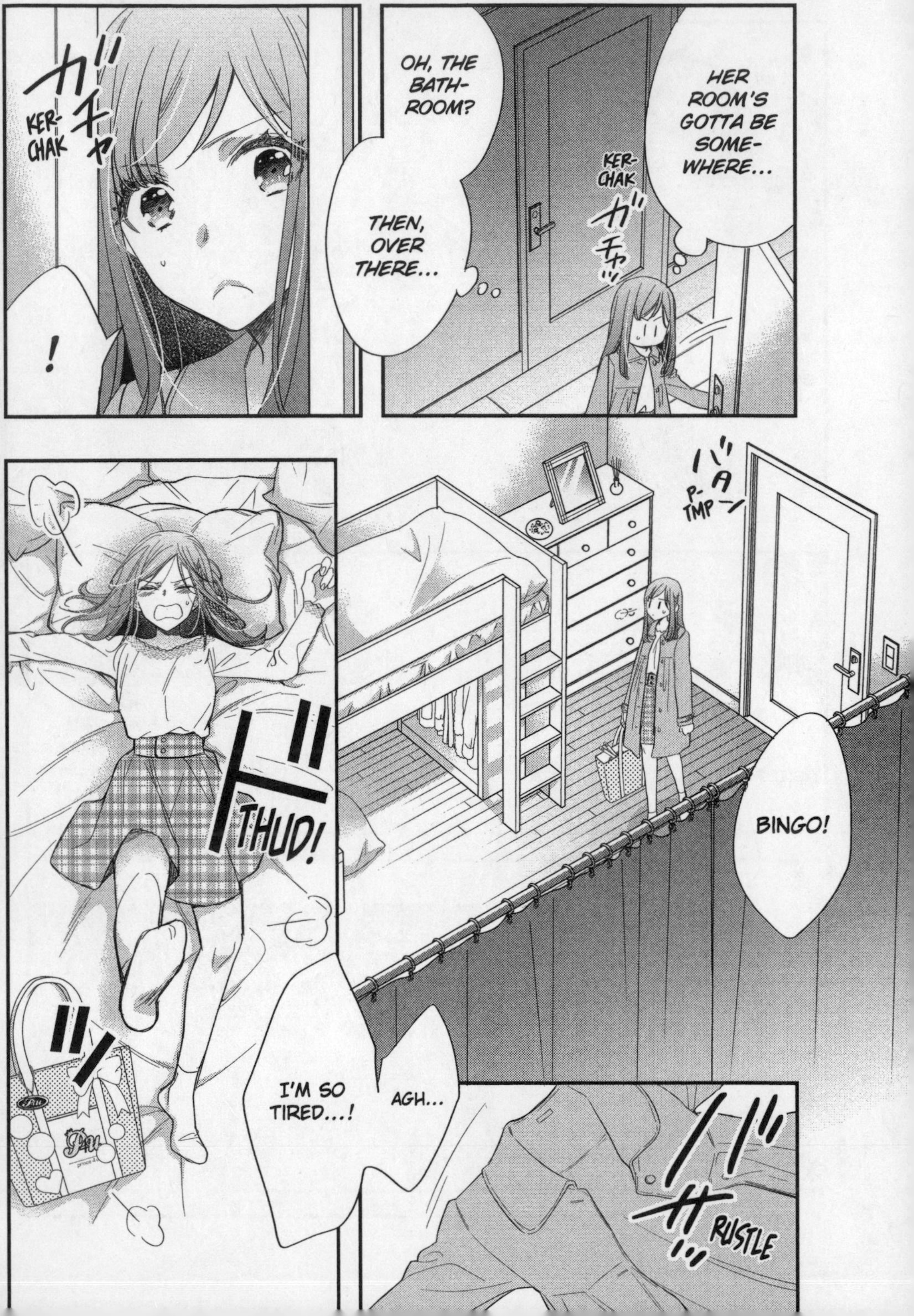

HER ROOM'S GOTTA BE SOME-WHERE...
ガチャッ
KER-CHAK
OH, THE BATH-ROOM?
THEN, OVER THERE...
ガチャ
KER-CHAK
!
バン
P-TMP
BINGO!
バサッ
RUSTLE
ドッ
THUD!
AGH...
I'M SO TIRED...!

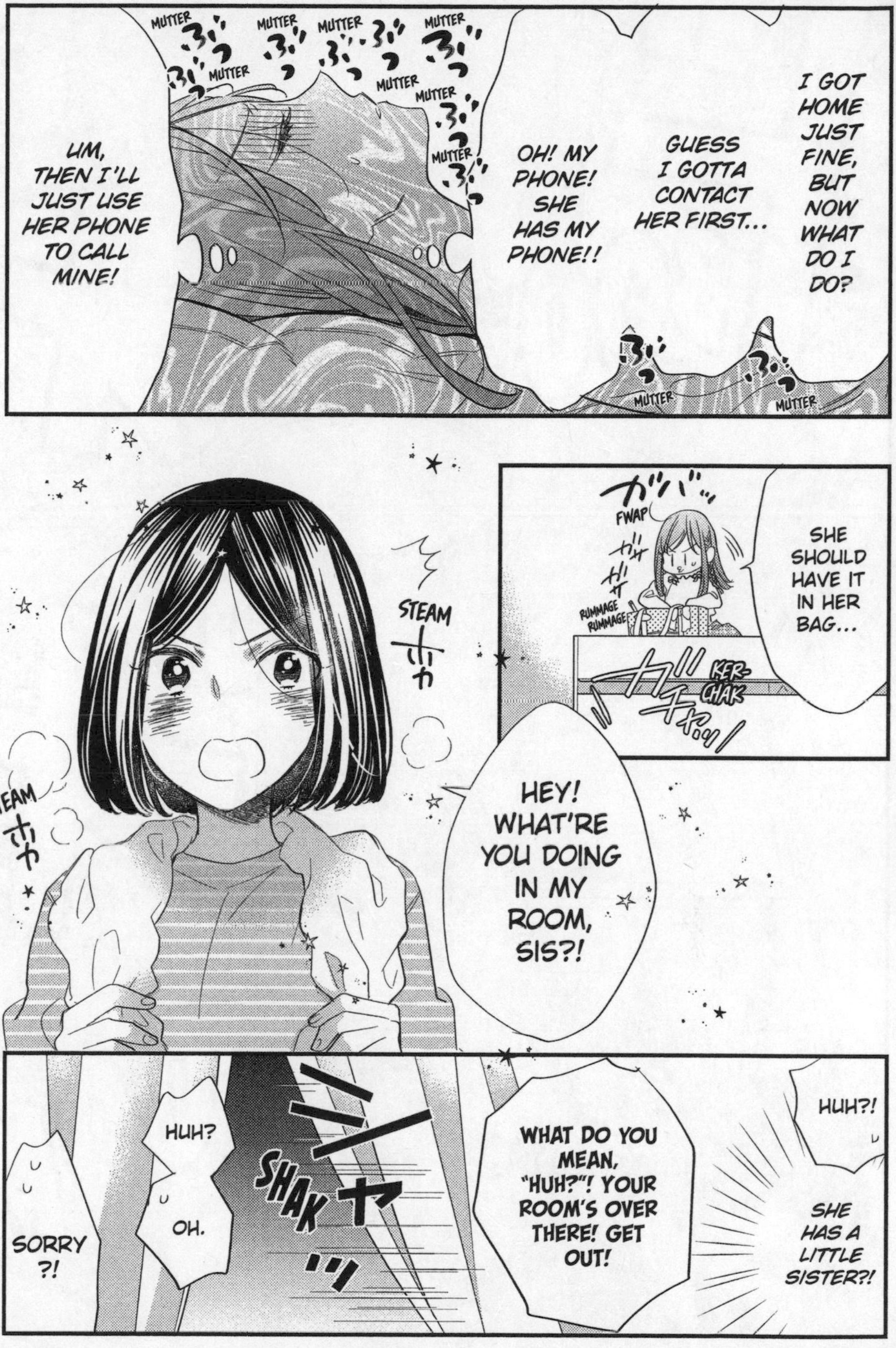
MUTTER
MUTTER
MUTTER
MUTTER
MUTTER
MUTTER
MUTTER
I GOT HOME JUST FINE, BUT NOW WHAT DO I DO?
GUESS I GOTTA CONTACT HER FIRST...
OH! MY PHONE! SHE HAS MY PHONE!!
UM, THEN I'LL JUST USE HER PHONE TO CALL MINE!
MUTTER
MUTTER
SHE SHOULD HAVE IT IN HER BAG...
FWAP
RUMMAGE RUMMAGE
KER-CHAK
STEAM
HEY! WHAT'RE YOU DOING IN MY ROOM, SIS?!
STEAM
HUH?!
SHE HAS A LITTLE SISTER?!
WHAT DO YOU MEAN, "HUH?"! YOUR ROOM'S OVER THERE! GET OUT!
SHAK
HUH?
OH.
SORRY?!

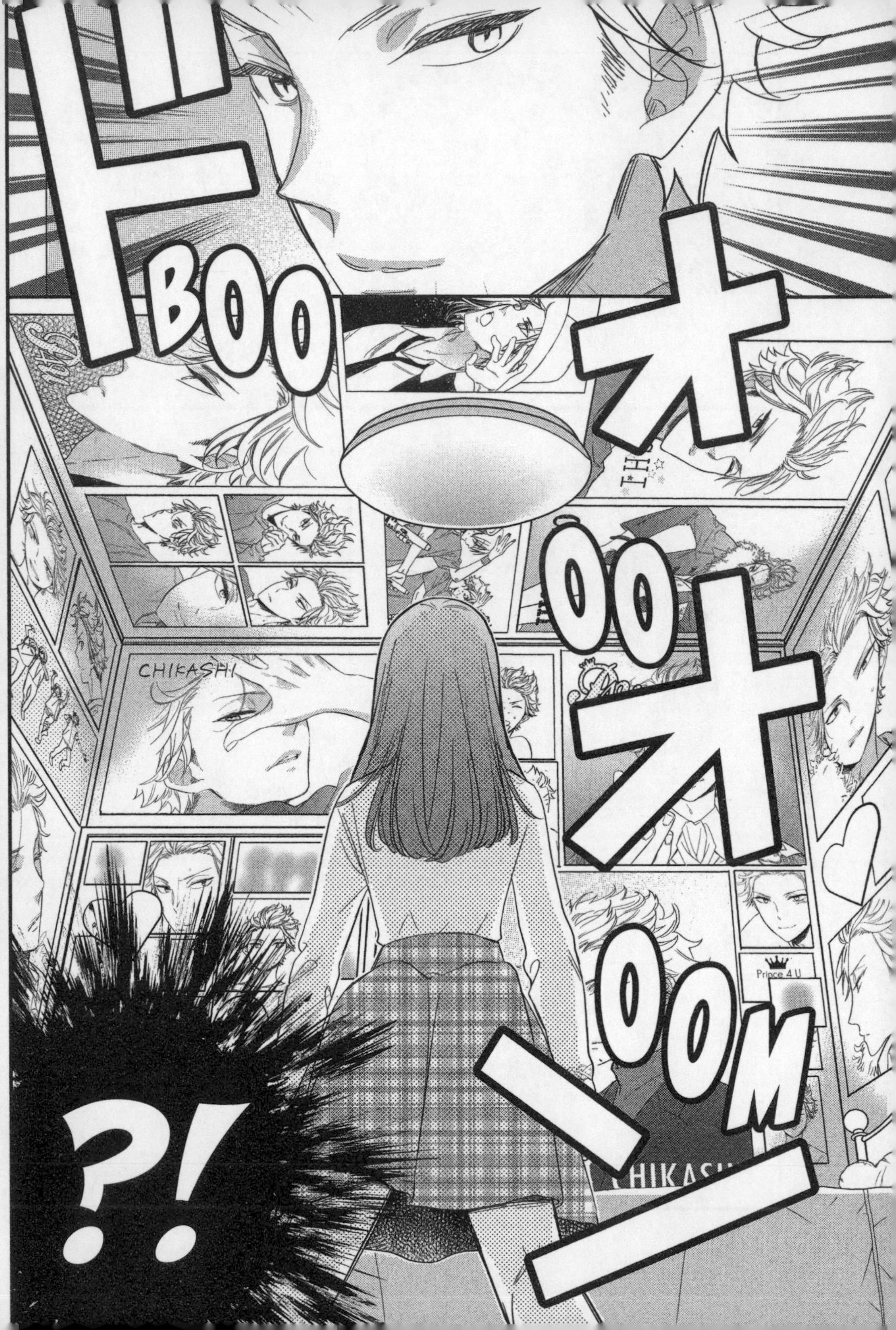
ド
BOO
オ
OO
オ
OOM
ー
CHIKASHI
Prince 4 U
CHIKASHI
?!

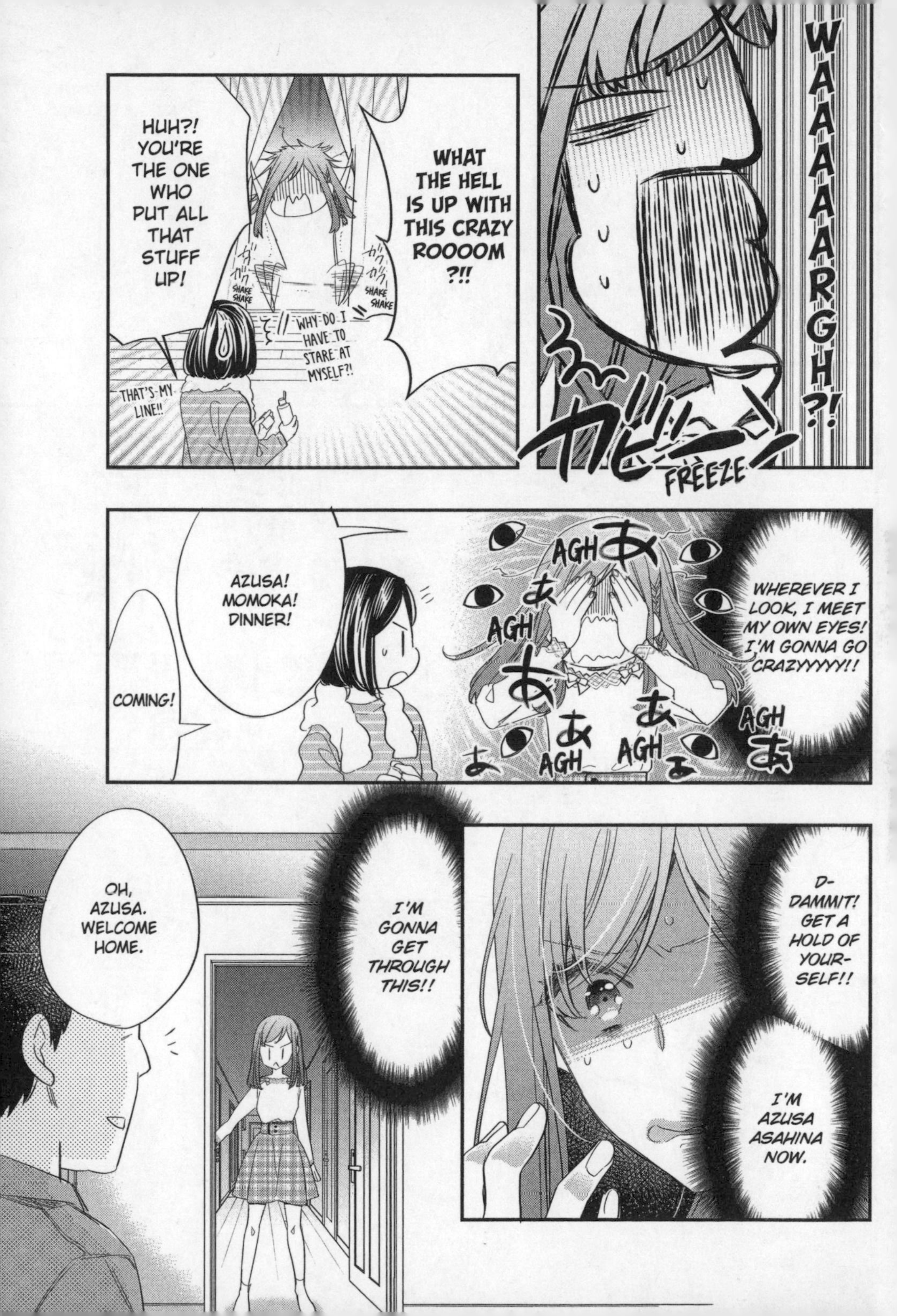
WAAAAAARGH?!
FREEZE
WHAT THE HELL IS UP WITH THIS CRAZY ROOOOM?!!
SHAKE SHAKE
WHY DO I HAVE TO STARE AT MYSELF?!
HUH?! YOU'RE THE ONE WHO PUT ALL THAT STUFF UP!
SHAKE SHAKE
THAT'S MY LINE!!
WHEREVER I LOOK, I MEET MY OWN EYES! I'M GONNA GO CRAZYYYYY!!
AGH あ
AGH あ
AGH あ
AGH あ
AGH あ
AGH あ
AZUSA! MOMOKA! DINNER!
COMING!
D-DAMMIT! GET A HOLD OF YOURSELF!!
I'M AZUSA ASAHINA NOW.
I'M GONNA GET THROUGH THIS!!
OH, AZUSA. WELCOME HOME.

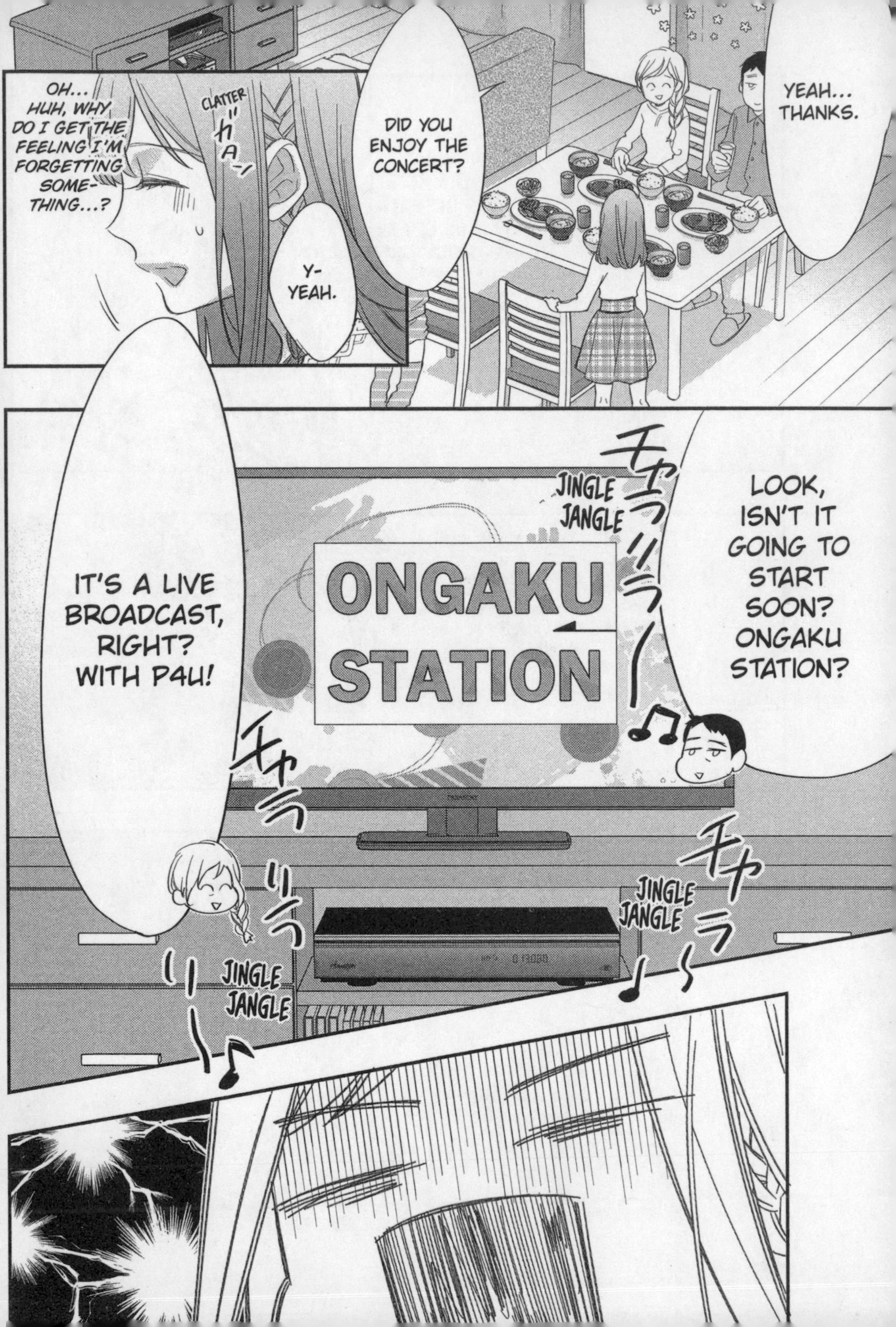
YEAH... THANKS.
DID YOU ENJOY THE CONCERT?
Y-YEAH.
CLATTER
OH... HUH, WHY DO I GET THE FEELING I'M FORGETTING SOME-THING...?
JINGLE JANGLE
LOOK, ISN'T IT GOING TO START SOON? ONGAKU STATION?
ONGAKU STATION
JINGLE JANGLE
IT'S A LIVE BROADCAST, RIGHT? WITH P4U!
JINGLE JANGLE

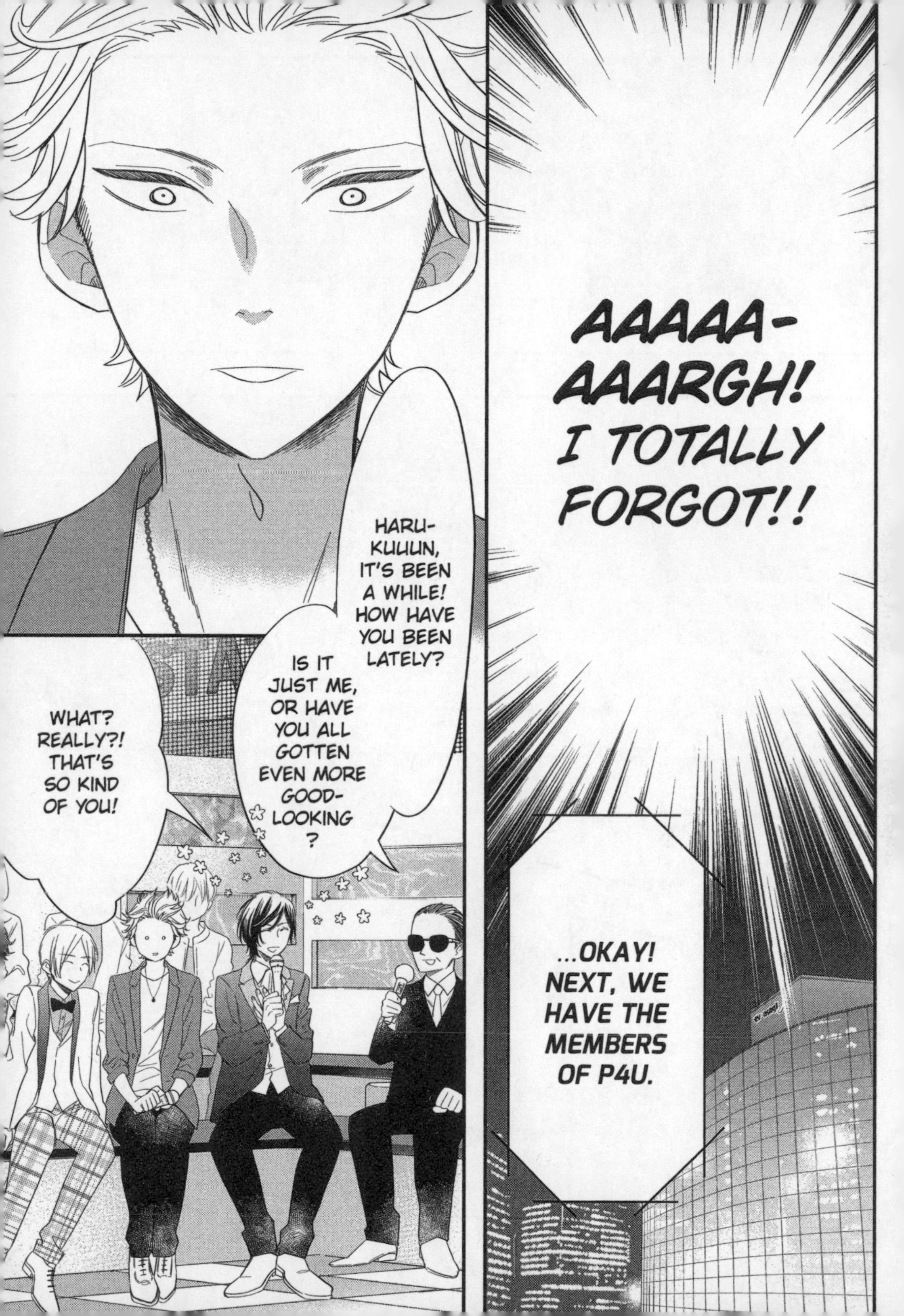
AAAAA-AAARGH! I TOTALLY FORGOT!!
...OKAY! NEXT, WE HAVE THE MEMBERS OF P4U.
HARU-KUUUN, IT'S BEEN A WHILE! HOW HAVE YOU BEEN LATELY?
IS IT JUST ME, OR HAVE YOU ALL GOTTEN EVEN MORE GOOD-LOOKING?
WHAT? REALLY?! THAT'S SO KIND OF YOU!

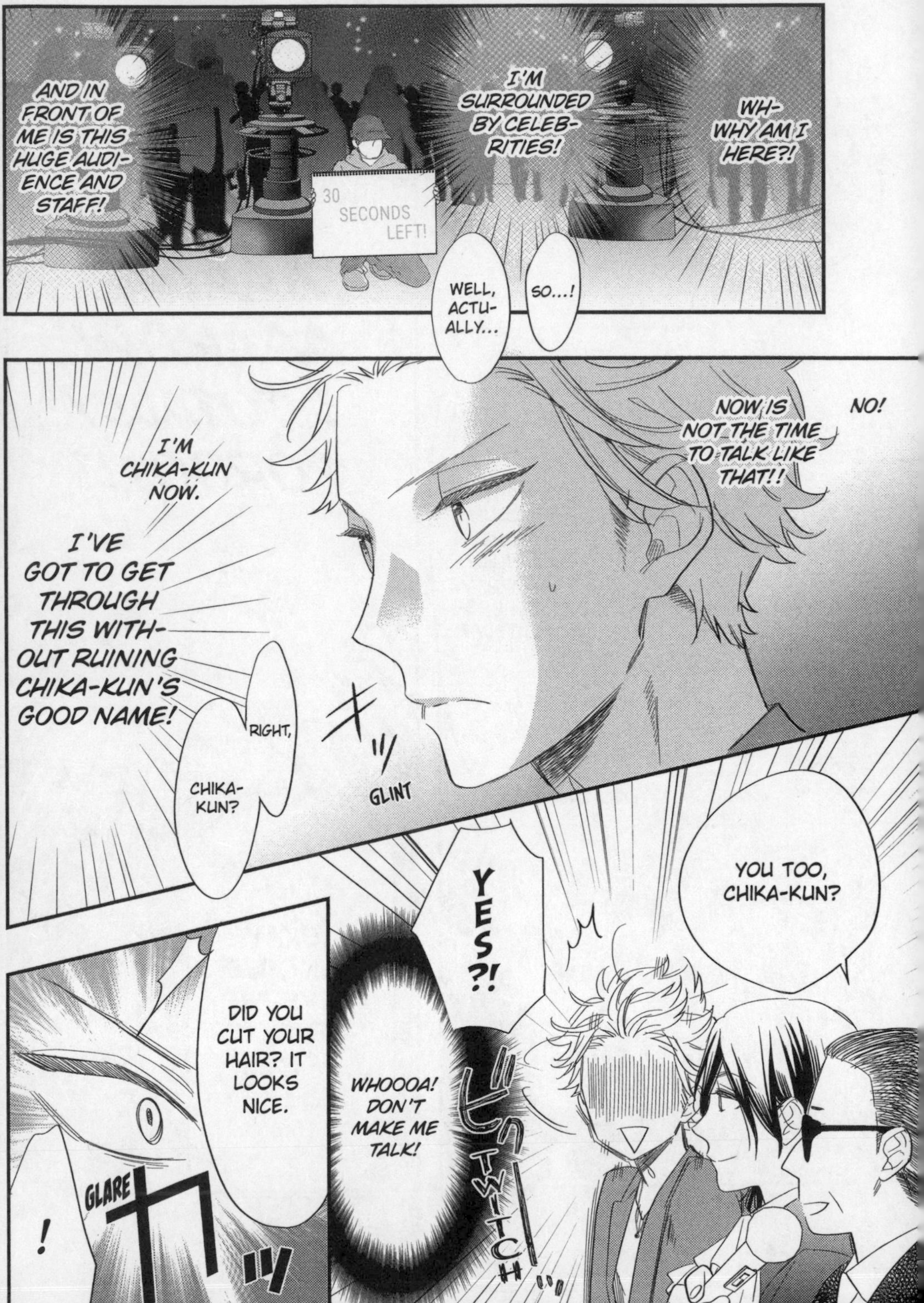
WH- WHY AM I HERE?!
I'M SURROUNDED BY CELEB-RITIES!
AND IN FRONT OF ME IS THIS HUGE AUDI-ENCE AND STAFF!
30 SECONDS LEFT!
SO...!
WELL, ACTU-ALLY...
NO!
NOW IS NOT THE TIME TO TALK LIKE THAT!!
I'M CHIKA-KUN NOW.
I'VE GOT TO GET THROUGH THIS WITH-OUT RUINING CHIKA-KUN'S GOOD NAME!
GLINT
RIGHT, CHIKA-KUN?
YOU TOO, CHIKA-KUN?
YES?!
TWITCH
WHOOOA! DON'T MAKE ME TALK!
DID YOU CUT YOUR HAIR? IT LOOKS NICE.
GLARE

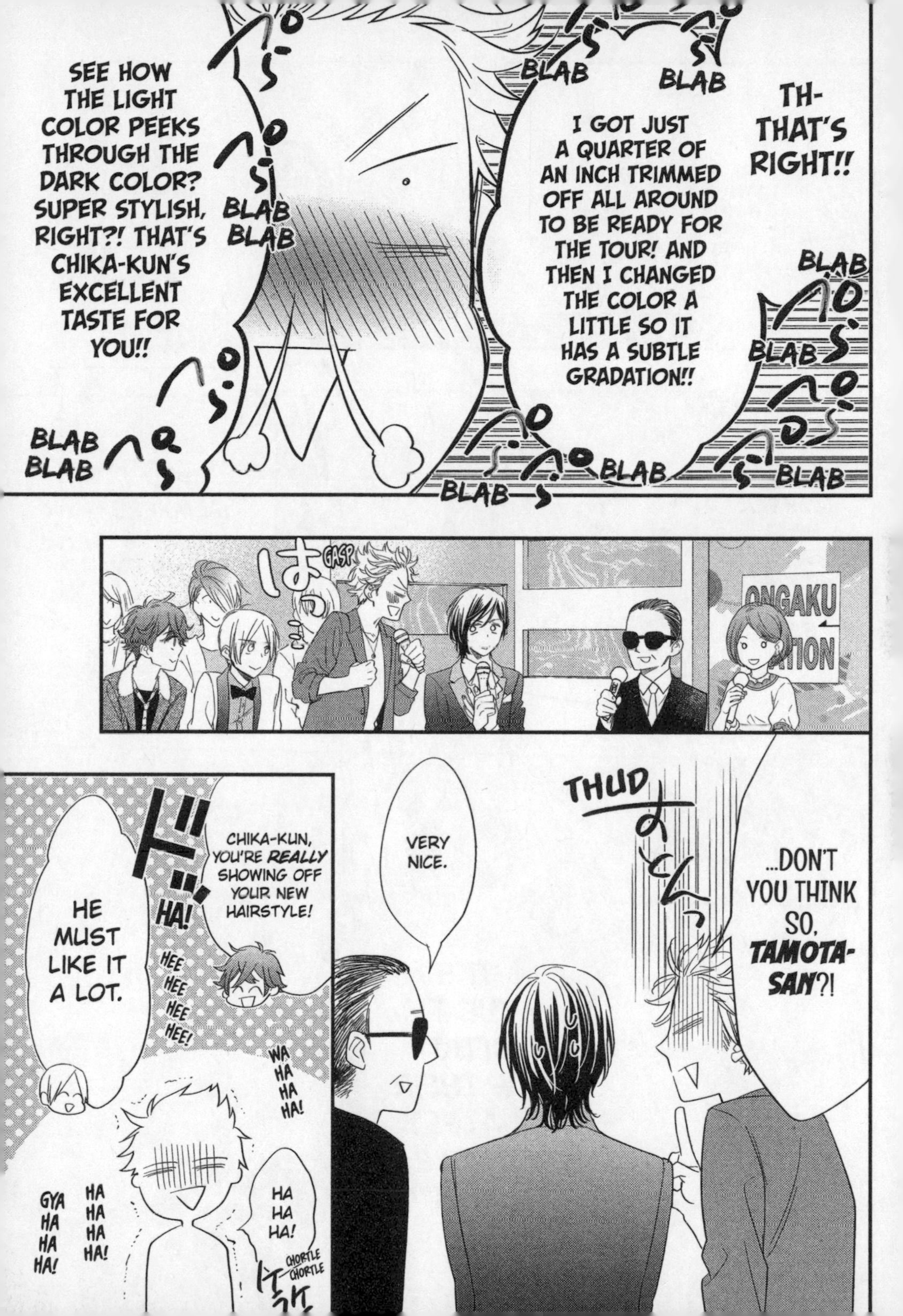
TH- THAT'S RIGHT!!
BLAB BLAB
I GOT JUST A QUARTER OF AN INCH TRIMMED OFF ALL AROUND TO BE READY FOR THE TOUR! AND THEN I CHANGED THE COLOR A LITTLE SO IT HAS A SUBTLE GRADATION!!
BLAB BLAB BLAB BLAB BLAB
BLAB BLAB
SEE HOW THE LIGHT COLOR PEEKS THROUGH THE DARK COLOR? SUPER STYLISH, RIGHT?! THAT'S CHIKA-KUN'S EXCELLENT TASTE FOR YOU!!
BLAB BLAB
GASP
はっ
ONGAKU
TION
THUD
...DON'T YOU THINK SO, TAMOTA-SAN?!
VERY NICE.
CHIKA-KUN, YOU'RE REALLY SHOWING OFF YOUR NEW HAIRSTYLE!
HA!
HE MUST LIKE IT A LOT.
HEE HEE HEE HEE!
WA HA HA HA HA!
HA HA HA!
CHORTLE CHORTLE
HA HA HA HA!
GYA HA HA HA!

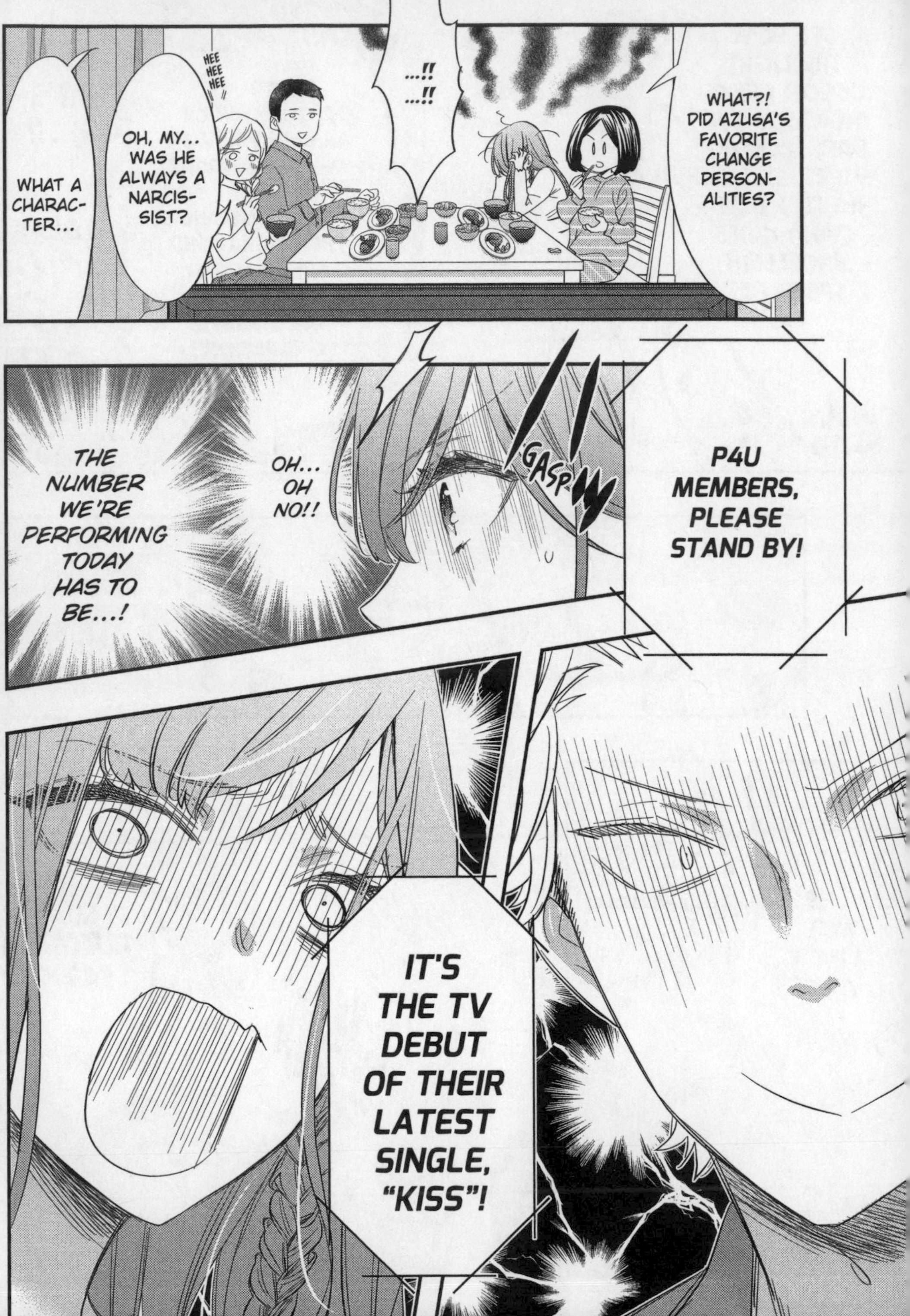
WHAT?! DID AZUSA'S FAVORITE CHANGE PERSON-ALITIES?
...!! ...!!
HEE HEE HEE
OH, MY... WAS HE ALWAYS A NARCIS-SIST?
WHAT A CHARAC-TER...
P4U MEMBERS, PLEASE STAND BY!
GASP
OH... OH NO!!
THE NUMBER WE'RE PERFORMING TODAY HAS TO BE...!
IT'S THE TV DEBUT OF THEIR LATEST SINGLE, "KISS"!

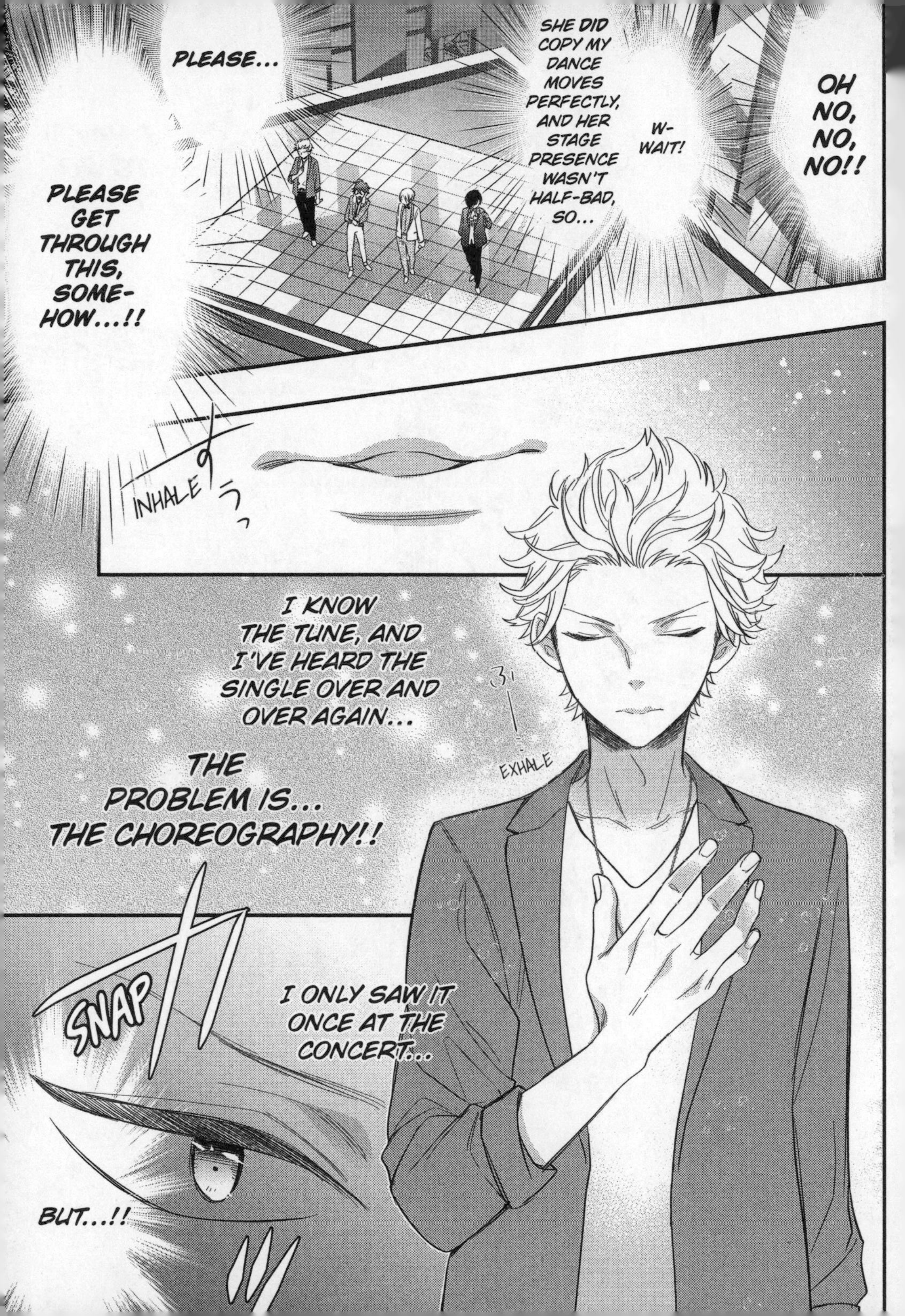
OH NO, NO, NO!!
W-WAIT!
SHE DID COPY MY DANCE MOVES PERFECTLY, AND HER STAGE PRESENCE WASN'T HALF-BAD, SO...
PLEASE...
PLEASE GET THROUGH THIS, SOME-HOW...!!
INHALE
EXHALE
I KNOW THE TUNE, AND I'VE HEARD THE SINGLE OVER AND OVER AGAIN...
THE PROBLEM IS... THE CHOREOGRAPHY!!
I ONLY SAW IT ONCE AT THE CONCERT...
SNAP
BUT...!!

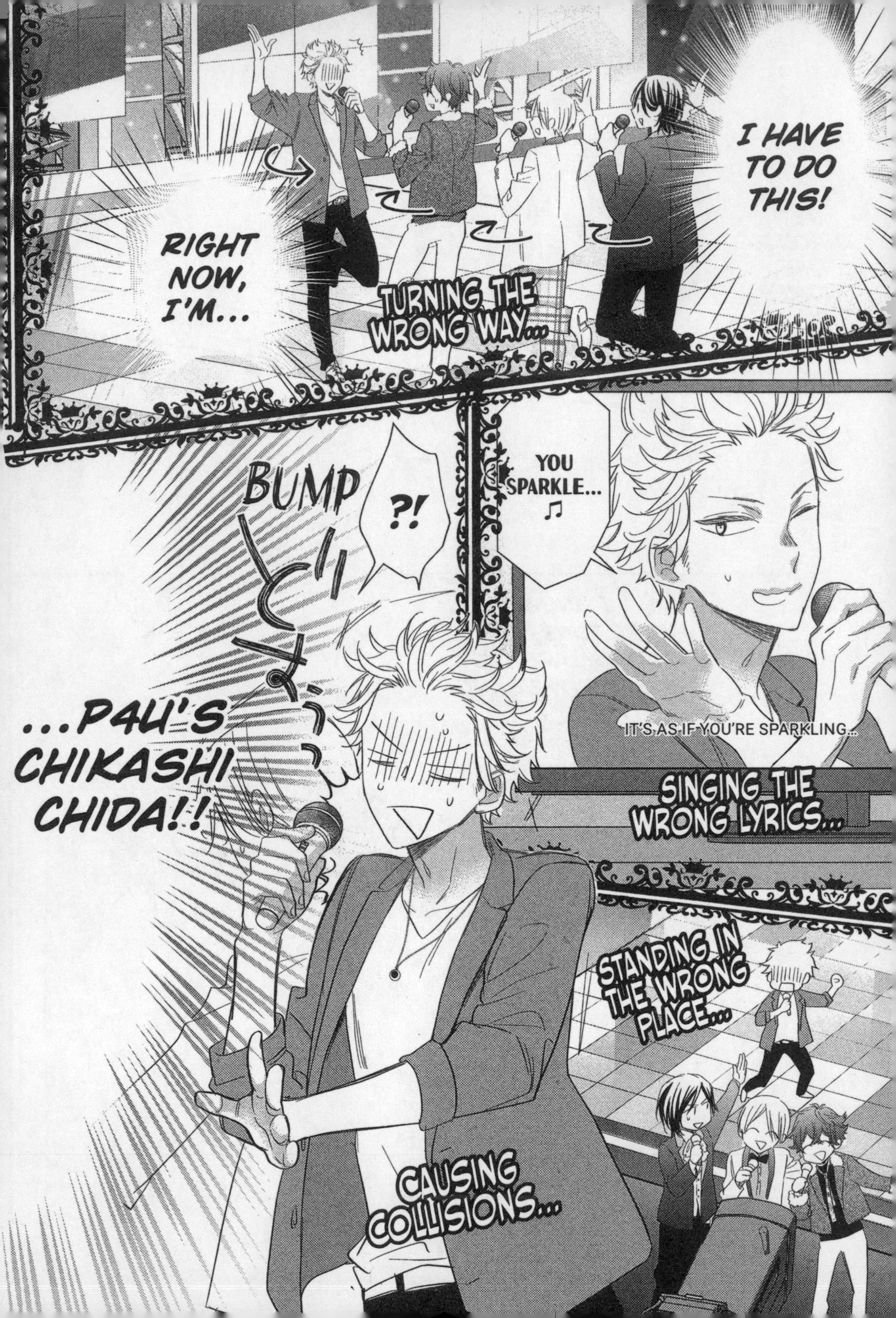
I HAVE TO DO THIS!
RIGHT NOW, I'M...
TURNING THE WRONG WAY...
YOU SPARKLE... ♫
IT'S AS IF YOU'RE SPARKLING...
SINGING THE WRONG LYRICS...
STANDING IN THE WRONG PLACE...
?!
BUMP
CAUSING COLLISIONS...
...P4U'S CHIKASHI CHIDA!!

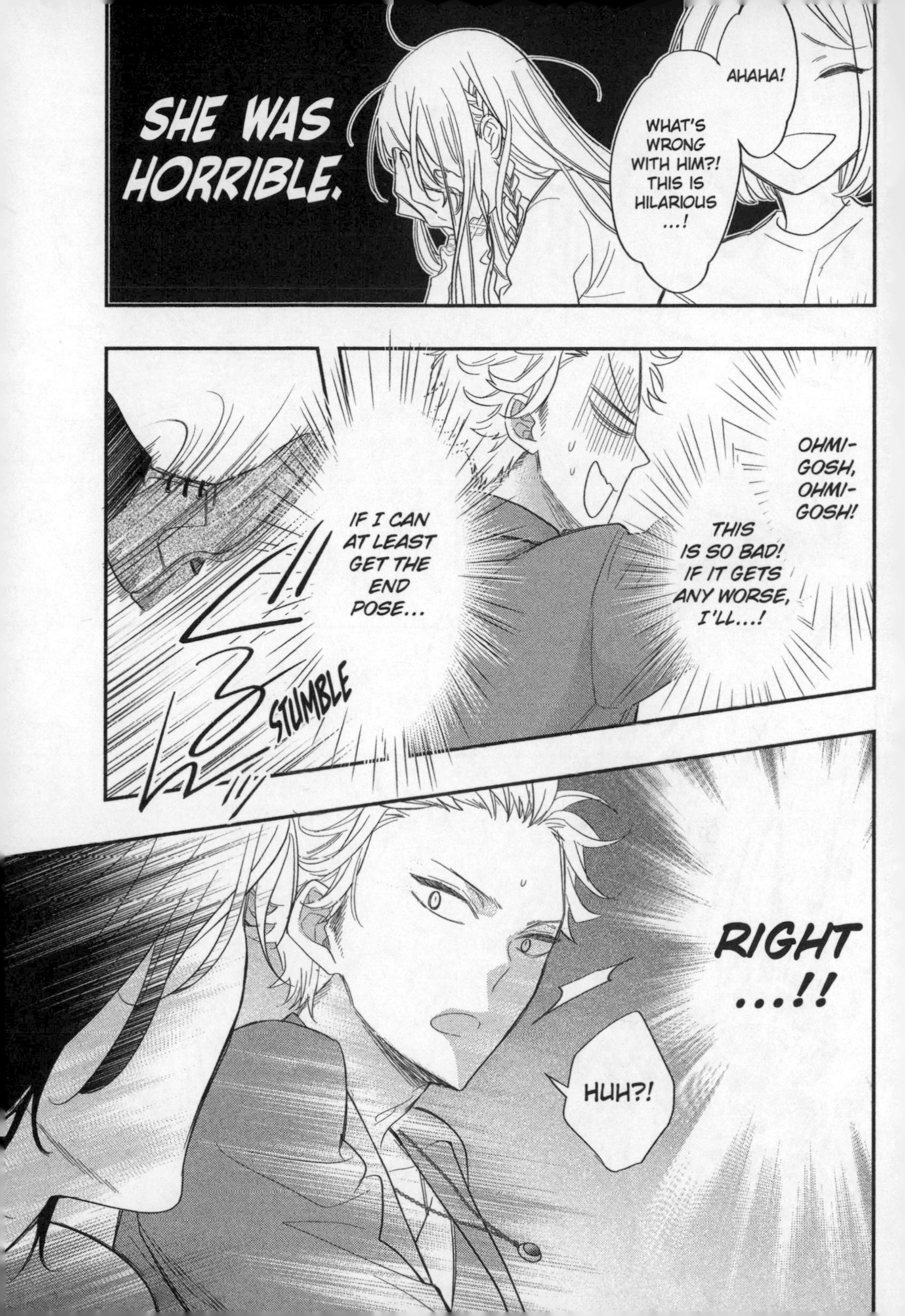
AHAHA!
WHAT'S WRONG WITH HIM?! THIS IS HILARIOUS ...!
SHE WAS HORRIBLE.
OHMI-GOSH, OHMI-GOSH!
THIS IS SO BAD! IF IT GETS ANY WORSE, I'LL...!
IF I CAN AT LEAST GET THE END POSE...
STUMBLE
RIGHT ...!!
HUH?!

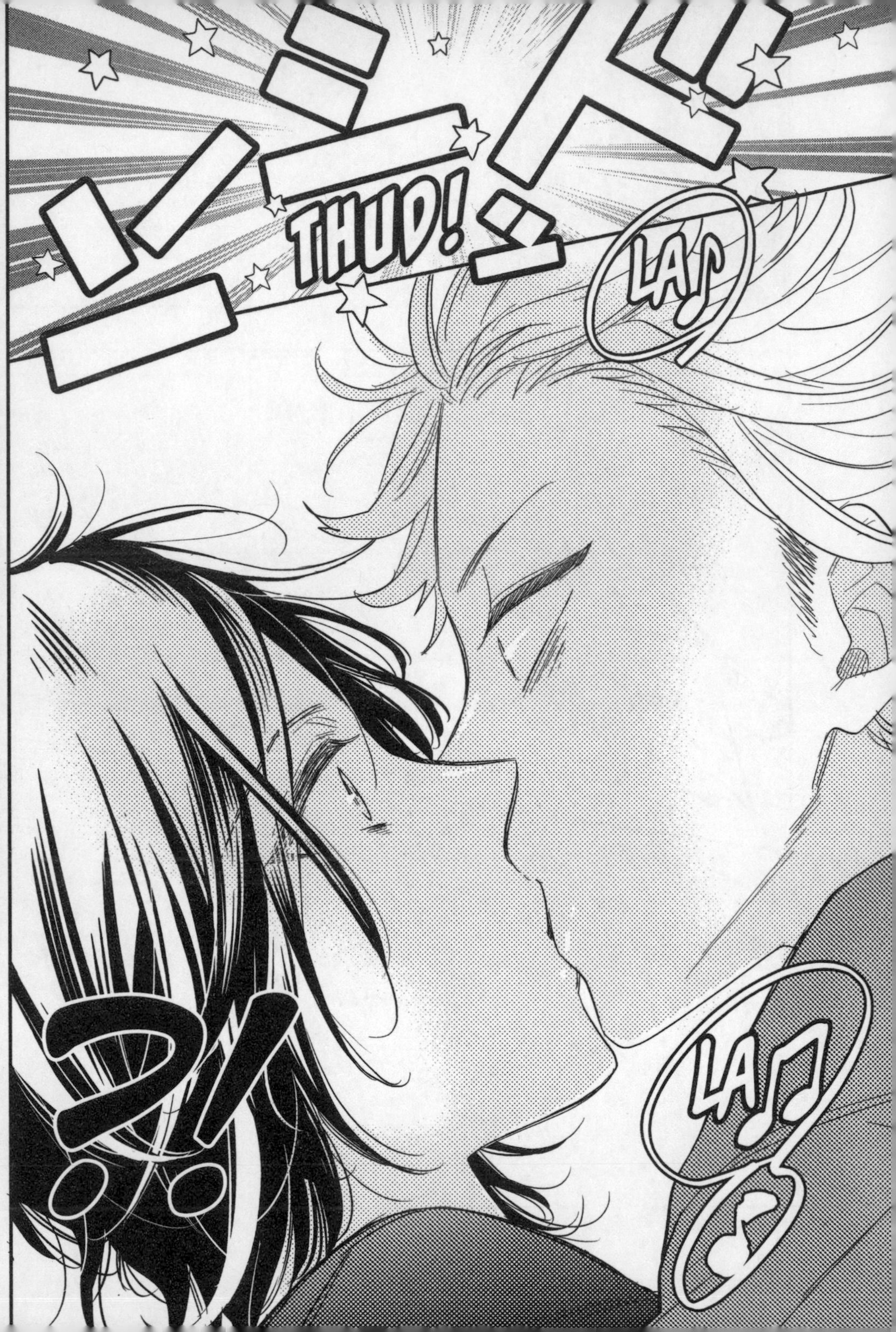
LA♪
THUD!
LA♪

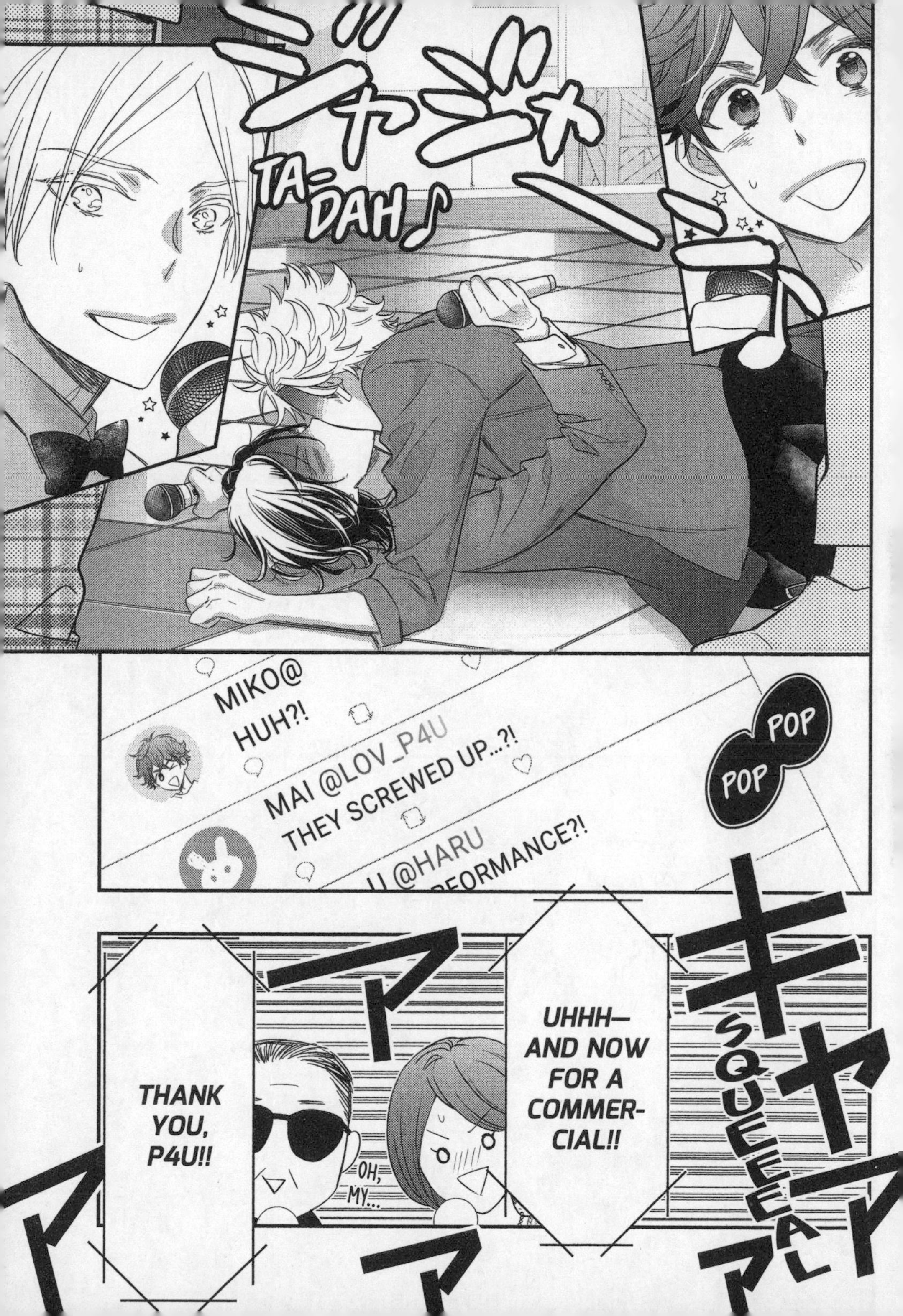
TA-DAH♪
MIKO@
HUH?!
MAI @LOV_P4U
THEY SCREWED UP...?!
@HARU
POP POP POP
SQUEEEAL
UHHH—AND NOW FOR A COMMERCIAL!!
OH, MY...
THANK YOU, P4U!!

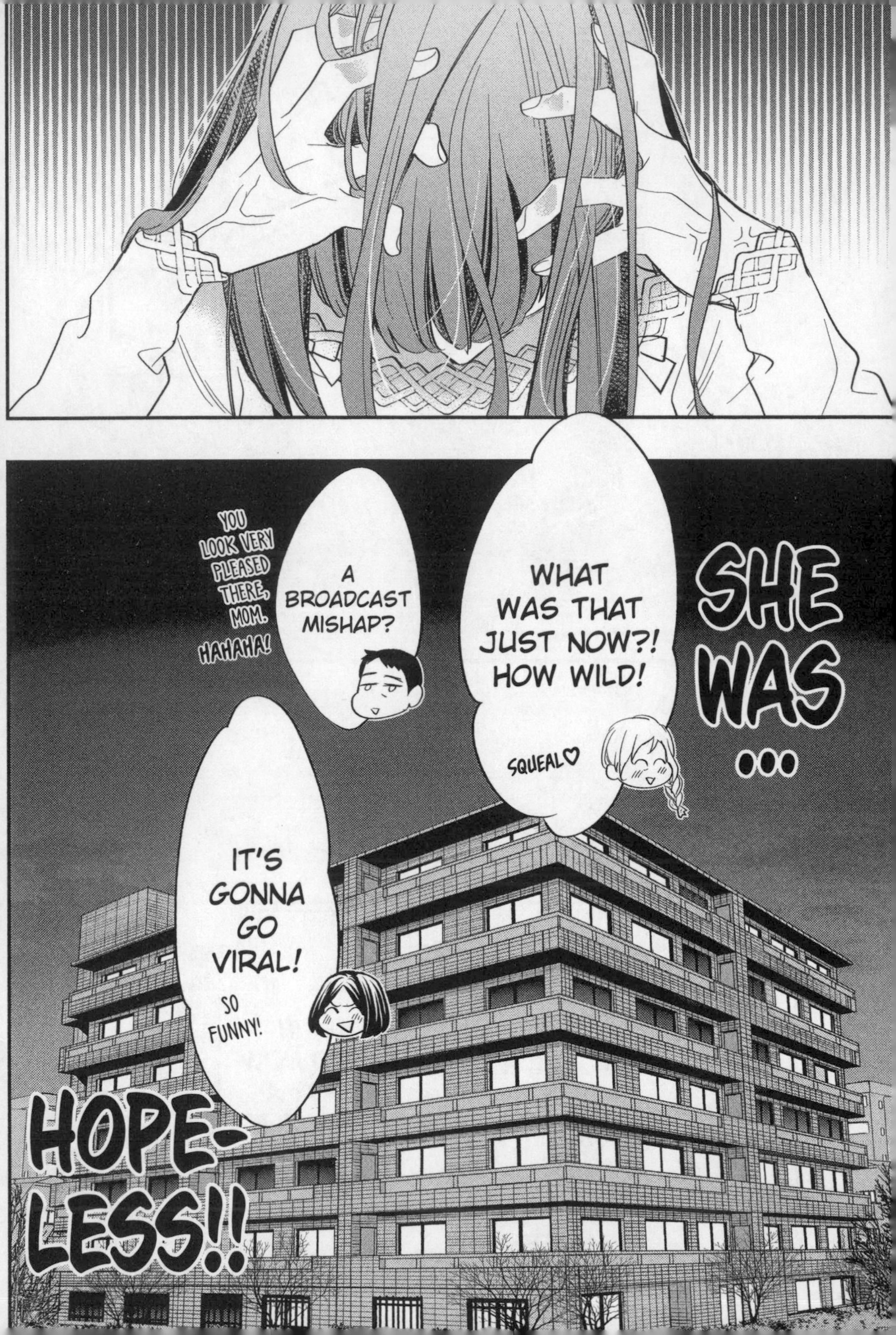
SHE WAS...
WHAT WAS THAT JUST NOW?! HOW WILD!
SQUEAL♡
A BROADCAST MISHAP?
YOU LOOK VERY PLEASED THERE, MOM.
HAHAHA!
IT'S GONNA GO VIRAL!
SO FUNNY!
HOPE-LESS!!

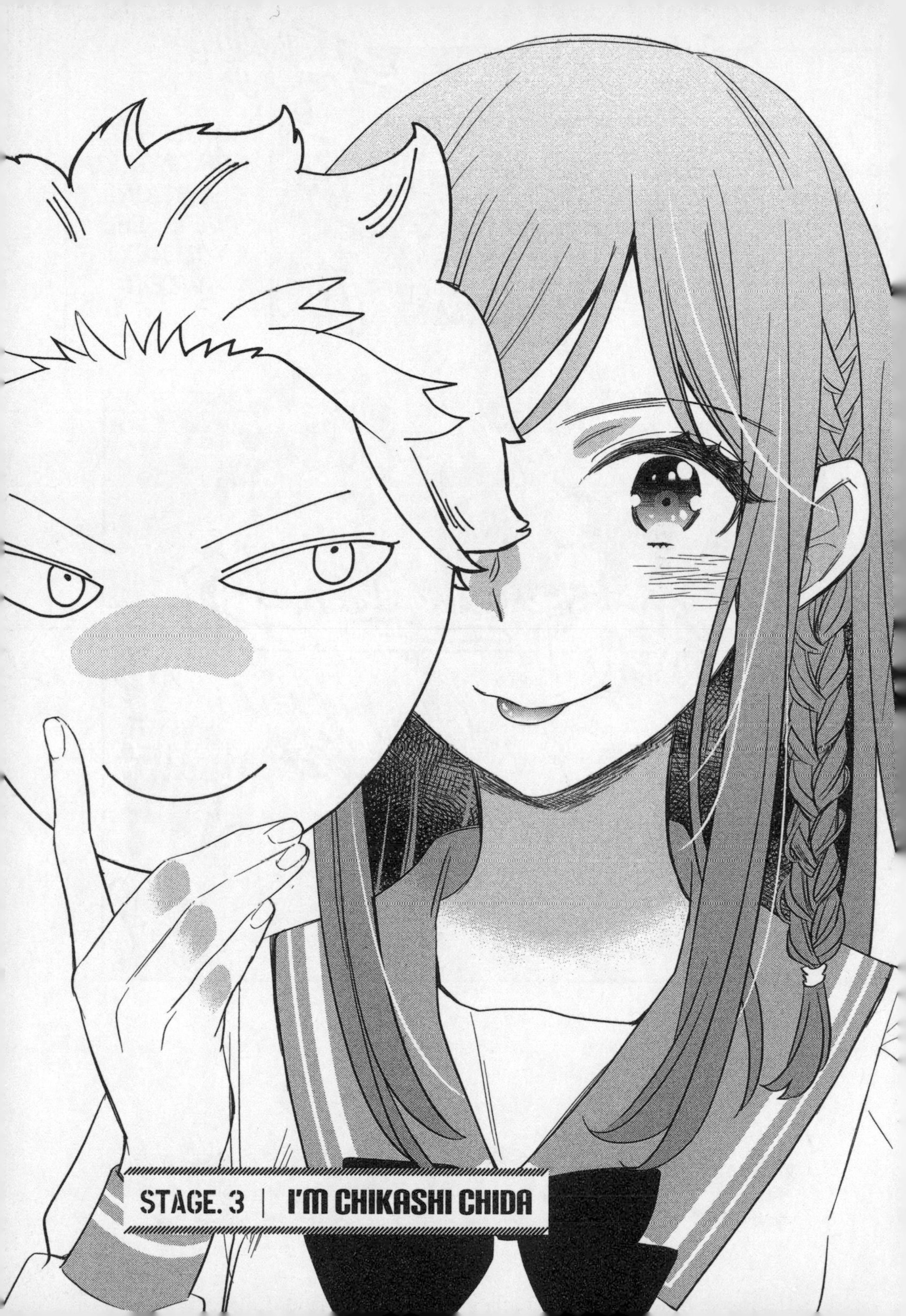
STAGE. 3 | I'M CHIKASHI CHIDA

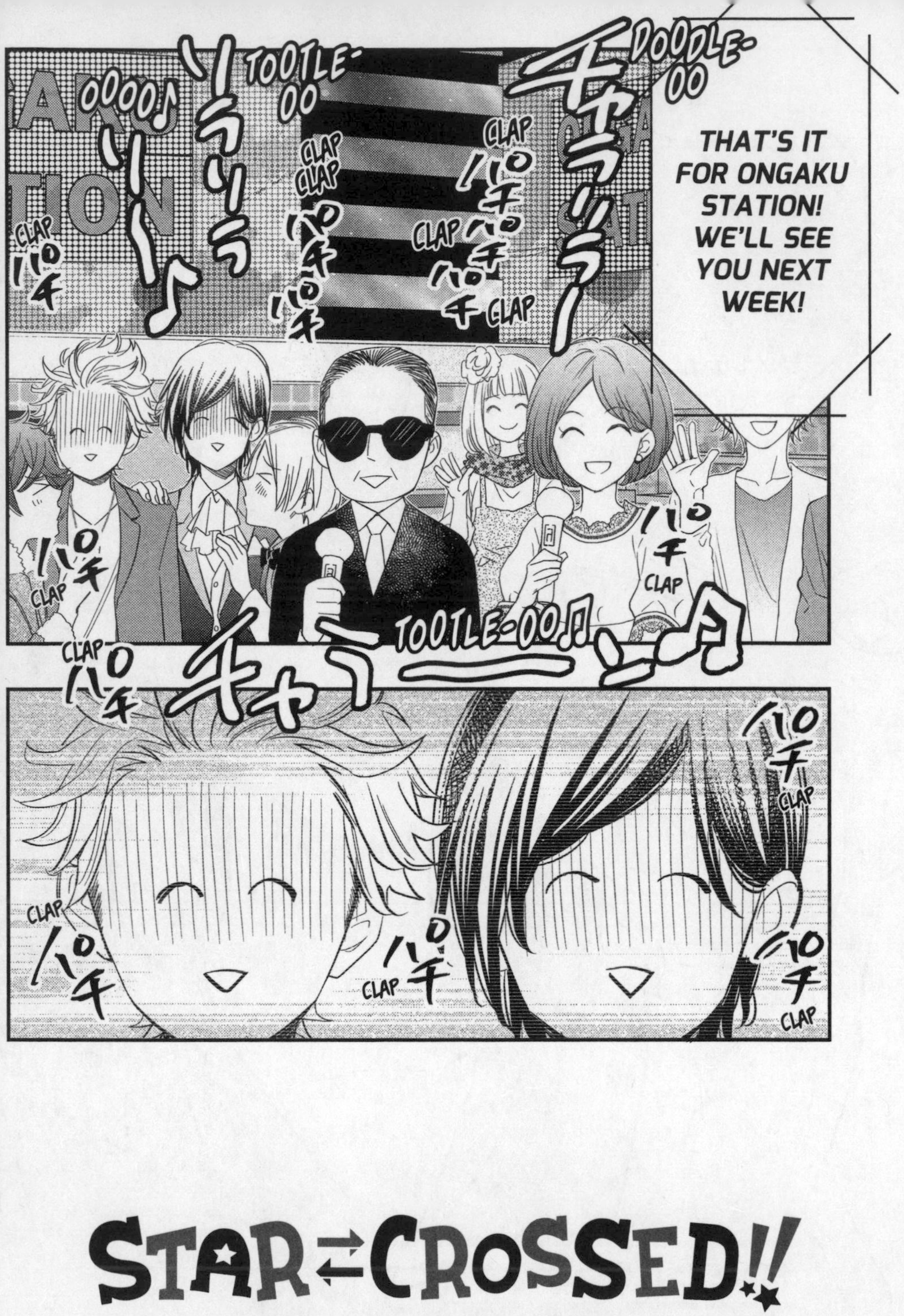
THAT'S IT FOR ONGAKU STATION! WE'LL SEE YOU NEXT WEEK!
DOODLE-OO
CLAP
CLAP
CLAP
CLAP CLAP
TOOTLE-OO
OOOO♪
CLAP
CLAP
CLAP
TOOTLE-OO♫
CLAP
CLAP
CLAP
CLAP
CLAP
CLAP

STAR⇄CROSSED!!

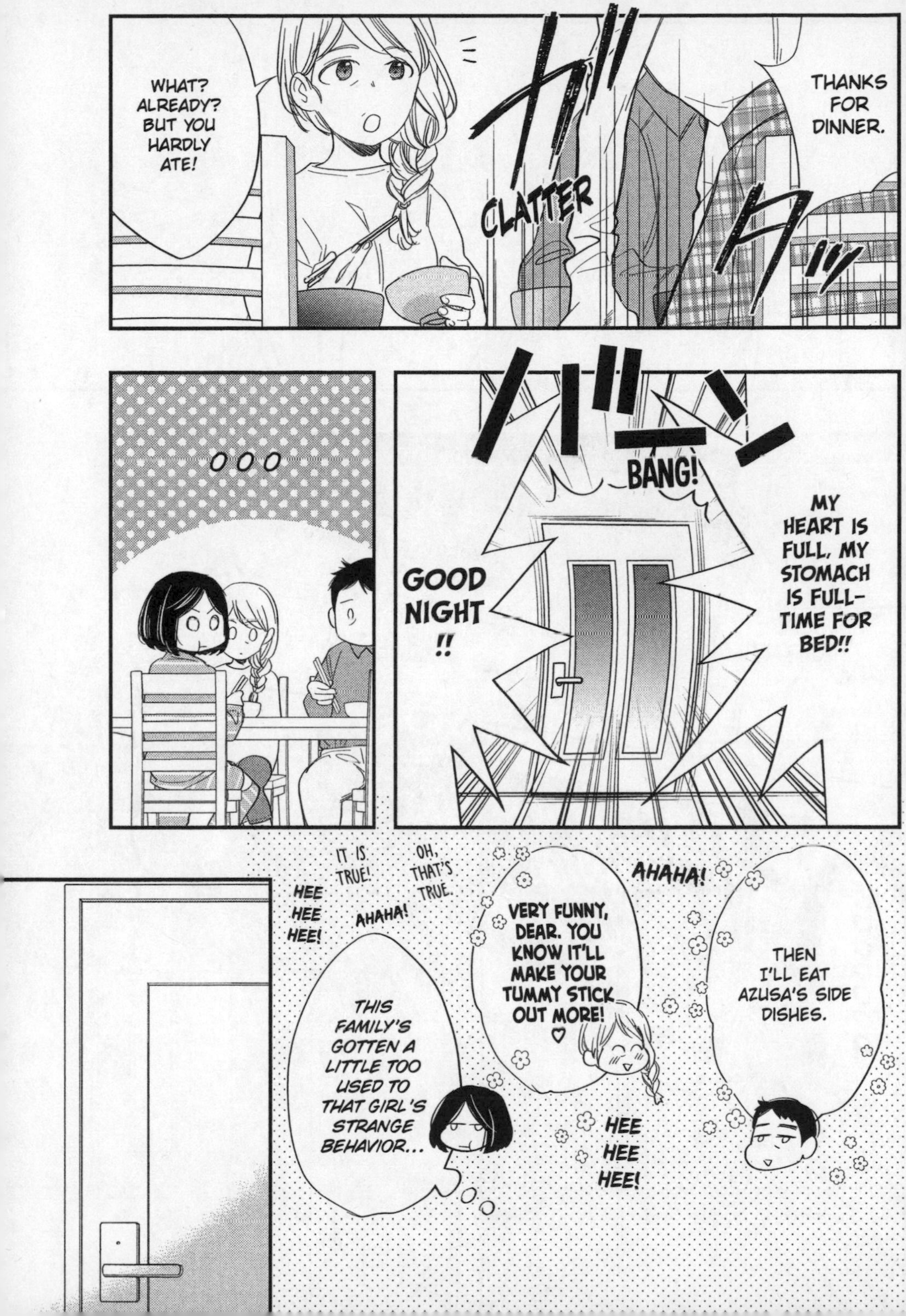
THANKS FOR DINNER.
CLATTER
WHAT? ALREADY? BUT YOU HARDLY ATE!
BANG!
MY HEART IS FULL, MY STOMACH IS FULL-TIME FOR BED!!
GOOD NIGHT !!
...
THEN I'LL EAT AZUSA'S SIDE DISHES.
AHAHA!
VERY FUNNY, DEAR. YOU KNOW IT'LL MAKE YOUR TUMMY STICK OUT MORE! ♡
HEE HEE HEE!
OH, THAT'S TRUE.
IT IS TRUE!
AHAHA!
HEE HEE HEE!
THIS FAMILY'S GOTTEN A LITTLE TOO USED TO THAT GIRL'S STRANGE BEHAVIOR...

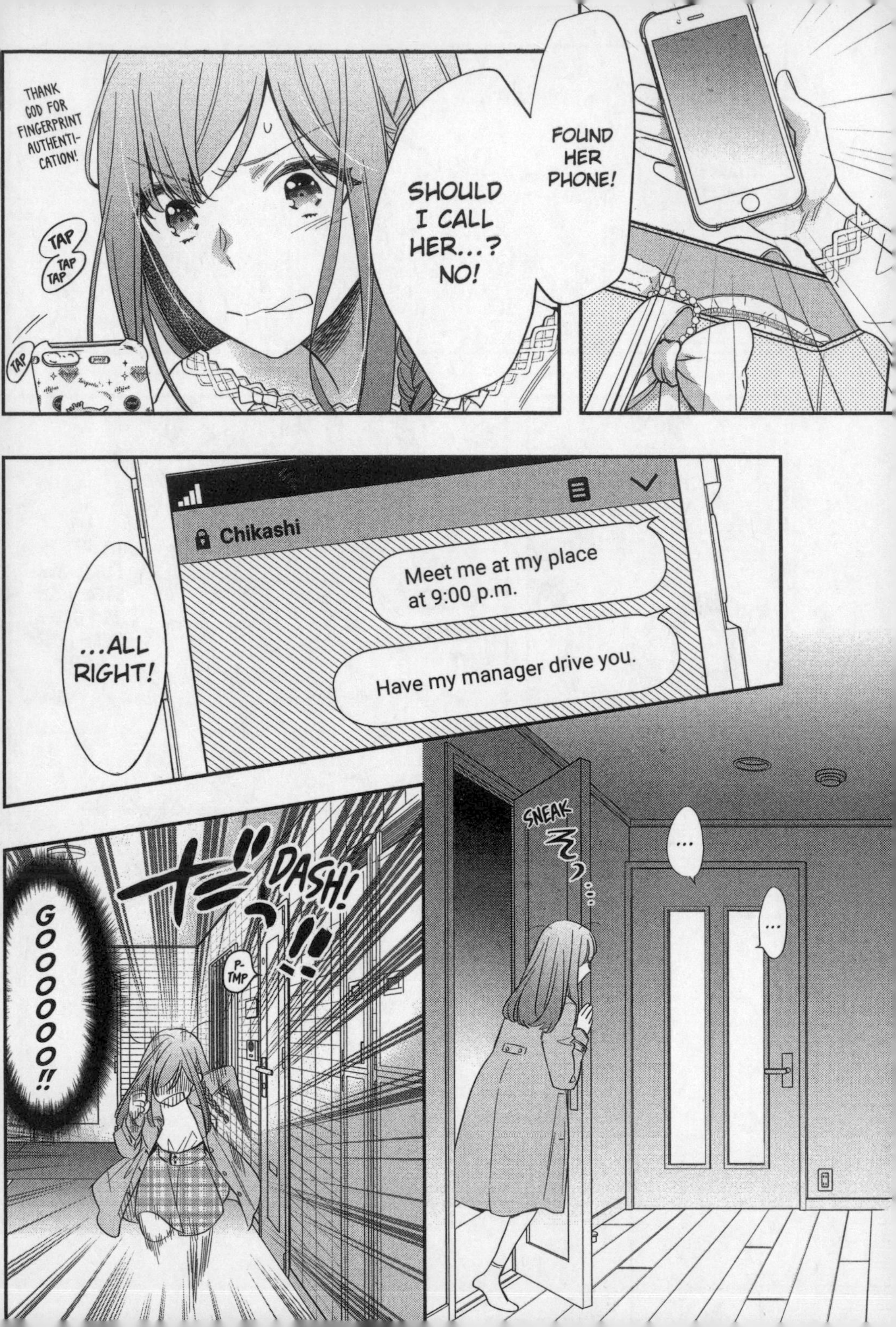
FOUND HER PHONE!
SHOULD I CALL HER...? NO!
THANK GOD FOR FINGERPRINT AUTHENTI-CATION!
TAP TAP TAP
TAP
Chikashi
Meet me at my place at 9:00 p.m.
Have my manager drive you.
...ALL RIGHT!
SNEAK
...
...
DASH!
P-TMP
GOOOOOOO!!

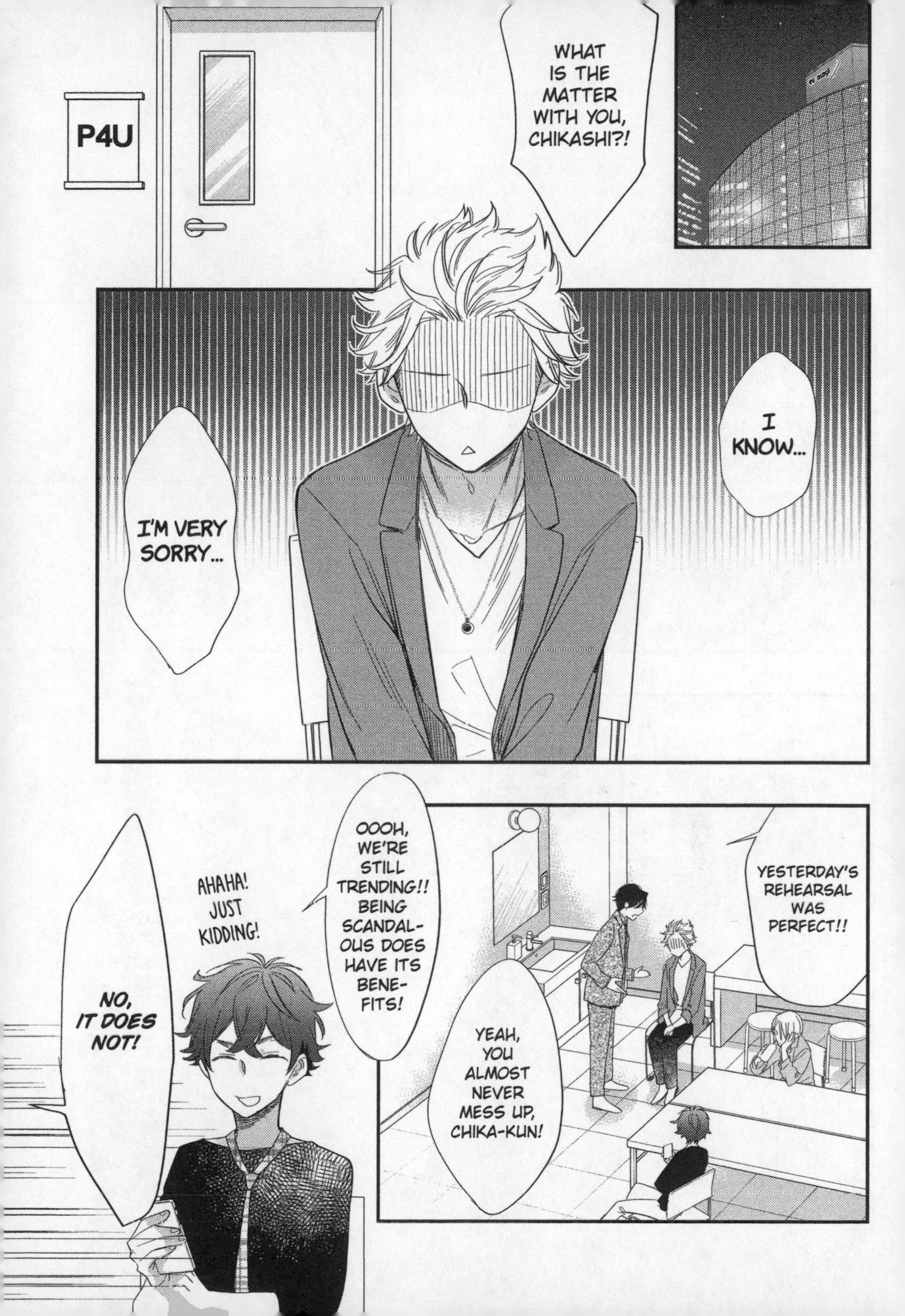
P4U
WHAT IS THE MATTER WITH YOU, CHIKASHI?!
I KNOW...
I'M VERY SORRY...
YESTERDAY'S REHEARSAL WAS PERFECT!!
YEAH, YOU ALMOST NEVER MESS UP, CHIKA-KUN!
OOOH, WE'RE STILL TRENDING!! BEING SCANDAL-OUS DOES HAVE ITS BENE-FITS!
AHAHA! JUST KIDDING!
NO, IT DOES NOT!

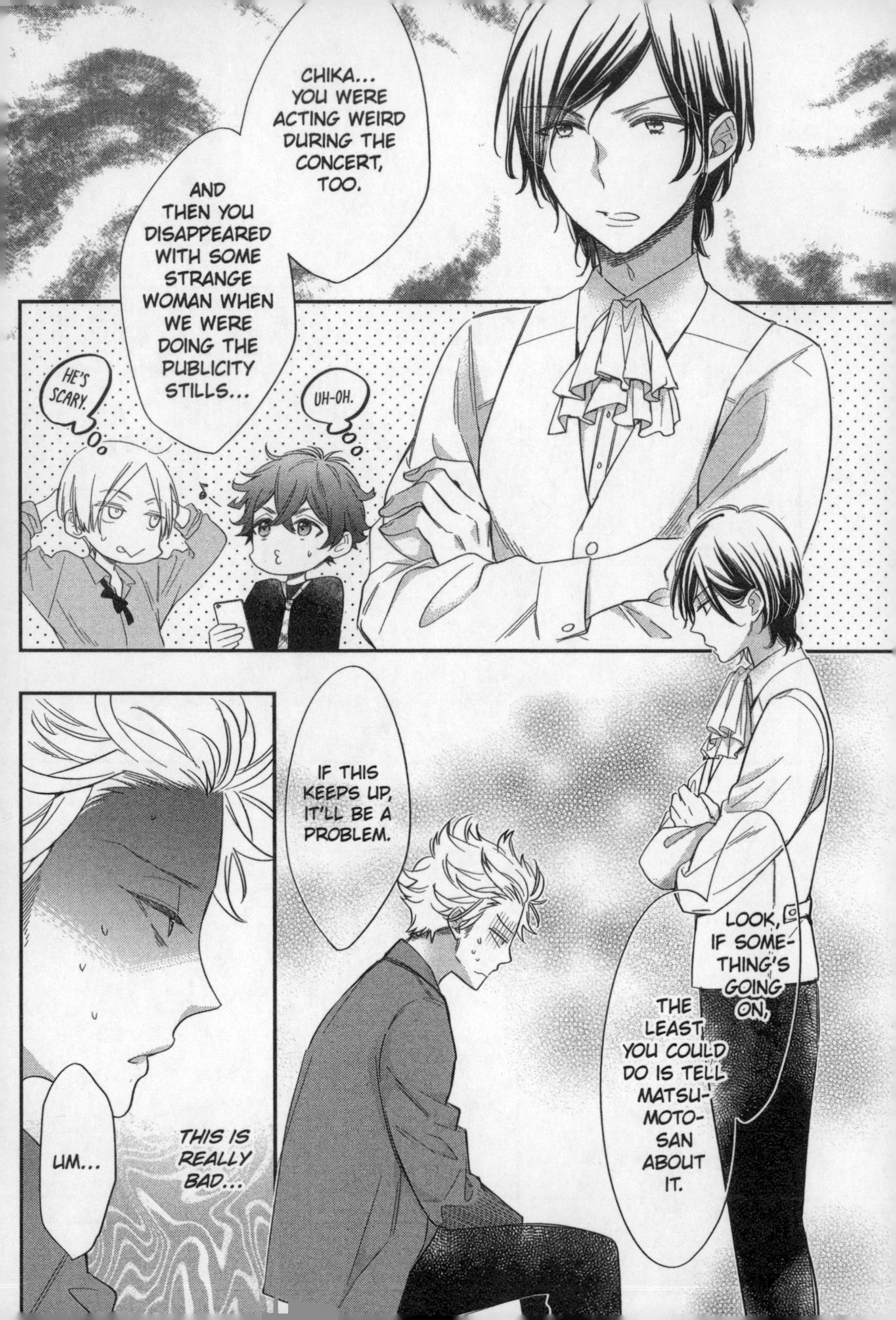
CHIKA... YOU WERE ACTING WEIRD DURING THE CONCERT, TOO.
AND THEN YOU DISAPPEARED WITH SOME STRANGE WOMAN WHEN WE WERE DOING THE PUBLICITY STILLS...
UH-OH.
HE'S SCARY.
LOOK, IF SOMETHING'S GOING ON,
THE LEAST YOU COULD DO IS TELL MATSUMOTO-SAN ABOUT IT.
IF THIS KEEPS UP, IT'LL BE A PROBLEM.
THIS IS REALLY BAD...
UM...

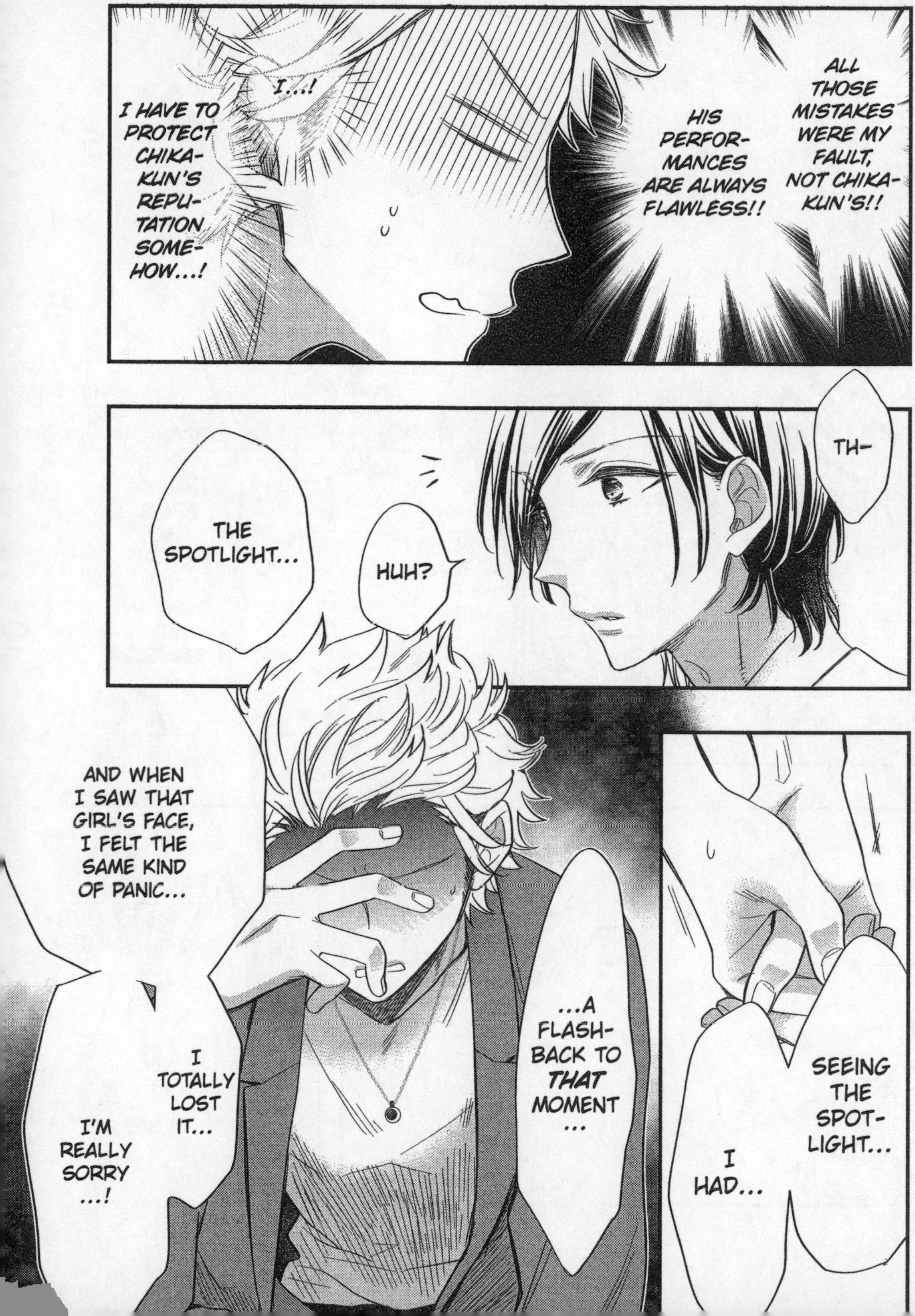
ALL THOSE MISTAKES WERE MY FAULT, NOT CHIKA-KUN'S!!
HIS PERFORMANCES ARE ALWAYS FLAWLESS!!
I...!
I HAVE TO PROTECT CHIKA-KUN'S REPUTATION SOMEHOW...!
TH-
HUH?
THE SPOTLIGHT...
SEEING THE SPOTLIGHT...
I HAD...
...A FLASHBACK TO *THAT* MOMENT...
AND WHEN I SAW THAT GIRL'S FACE, I FELT THE SAME KIND OF PANIC...
I TOTALLY LOST IT...
I'M REALLY SORRY...!

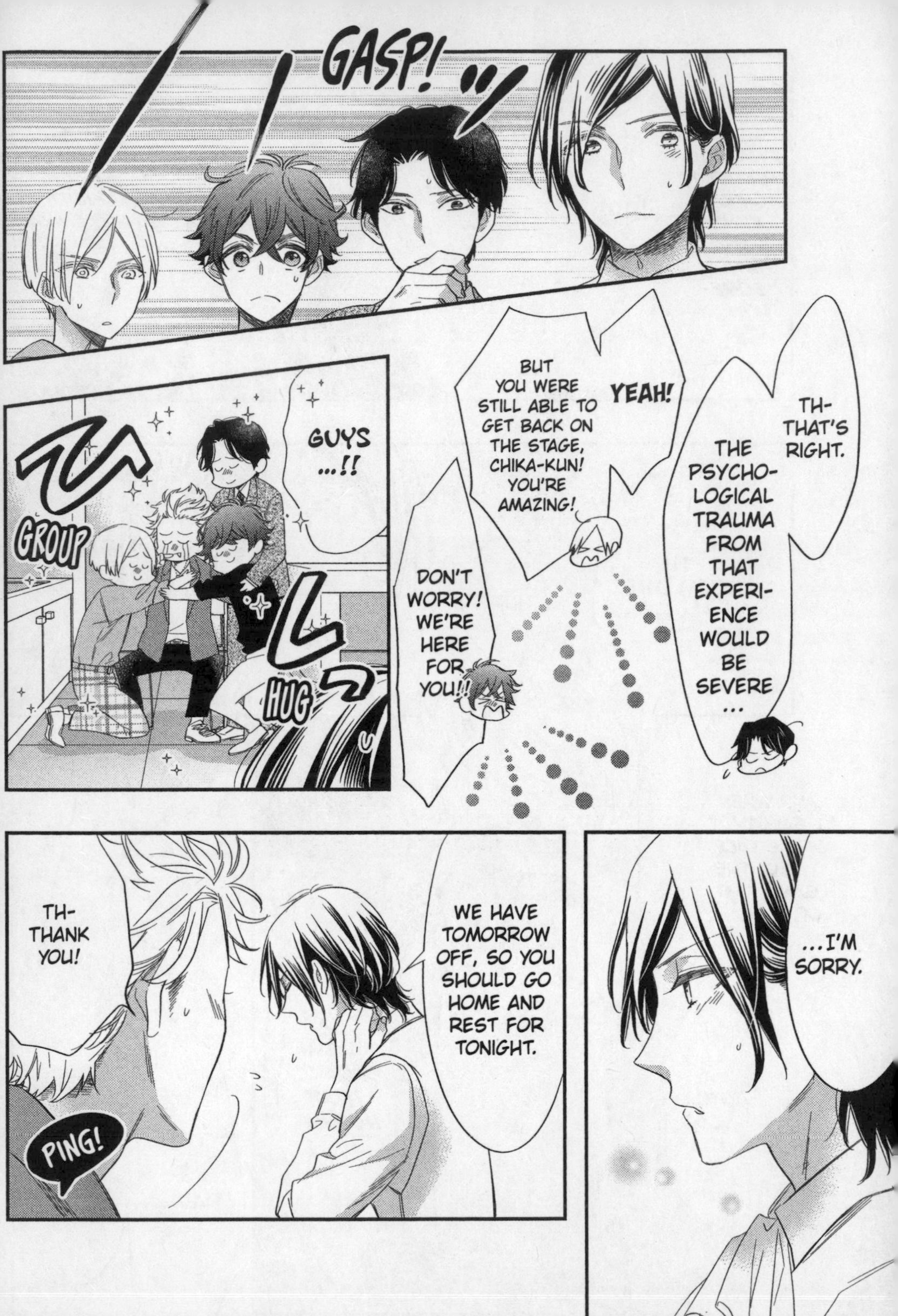
GASP!
TH- THAT'S RIGHT.
THE PSYCHOLOGICAL TRAUMA FROM THAT EXPERIENCE WOULD BE SEVERE...
YEAH!
BUT YOU WERE STILL ABLE TO GET BACK ON THE STAGE, CHIKA-KUN! YOU'RE AMAZING!
DON'T WORRY! WE'RE HERE FOR YOU!!
GUYS ...!!
GROUP
HUG
...I'M SORRY.
WE HAVE TOMORROW OFF, SO YOU SHOULD GO HOME AND REST FOR TONIGHT.
TH- THANK YOU!
PING!

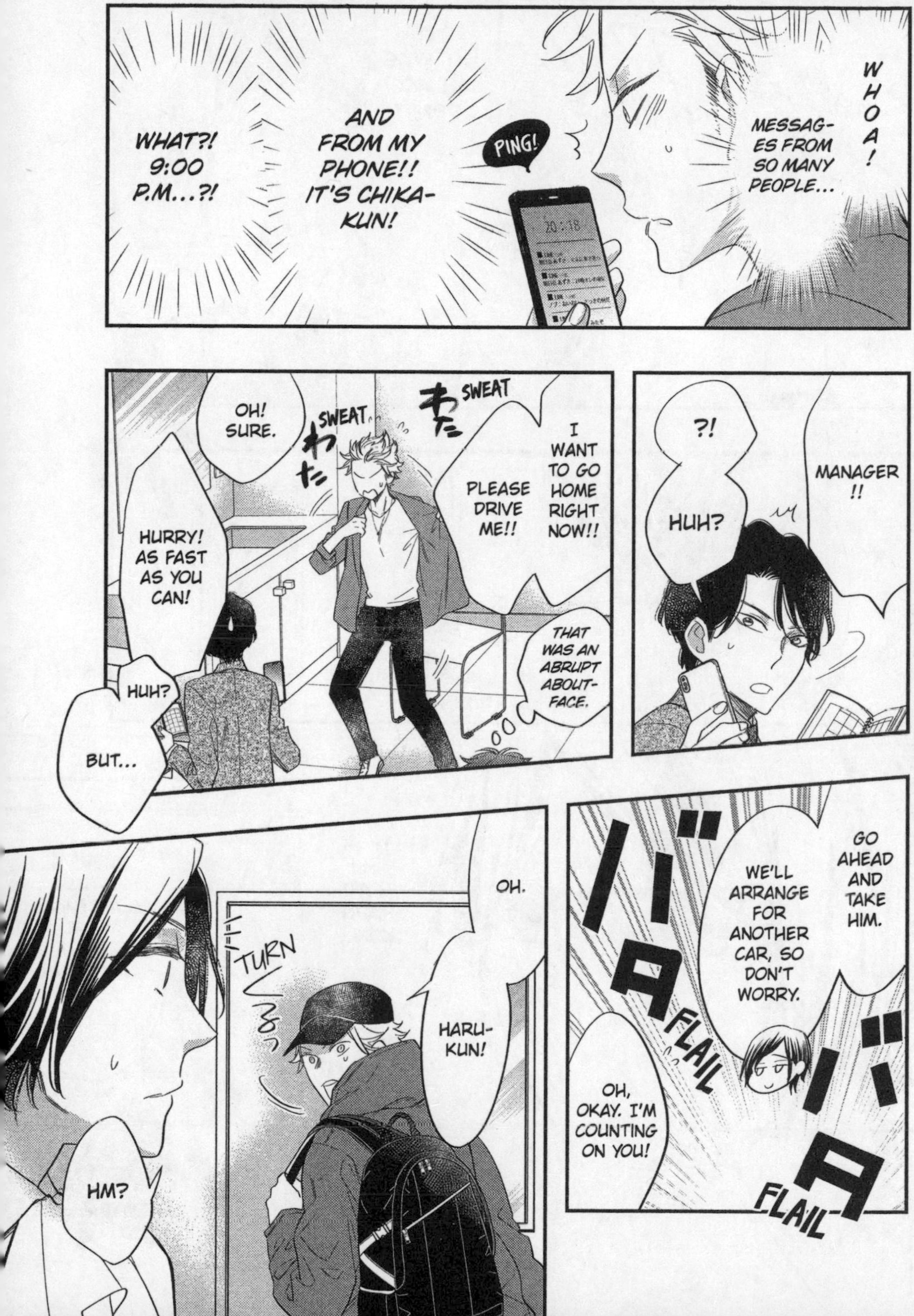

WHOA!
MESSAGES FROM SO MANY PEOPLE...
PING!
AND FROM MY PHONE!! IT'S CHIKA-KUN!
WHAT?! 9:00 P.M...?!
MANAGER!!
?!
HUH?
I WANT TO GO HOME RIGHT NOW!!
PLEASE DRIVE ME!!
SWEAT
SWEAT
OH! SURE.
THAT WAS AN ABRUPT ABOUT-FACE.
HURRY! AS FAST AS YOU CAN!
HUH?
BUT...
GO AHEAD AND TAKE HIM.
WE'LL ARRANGE FOR ANOTHER CAR, SO DON'T WORRY.
FLAIL
FLAIL
OH, OKAY. I'M COUNTING ON YOU!
OH.
HARU-KUN!
TURN
HM?

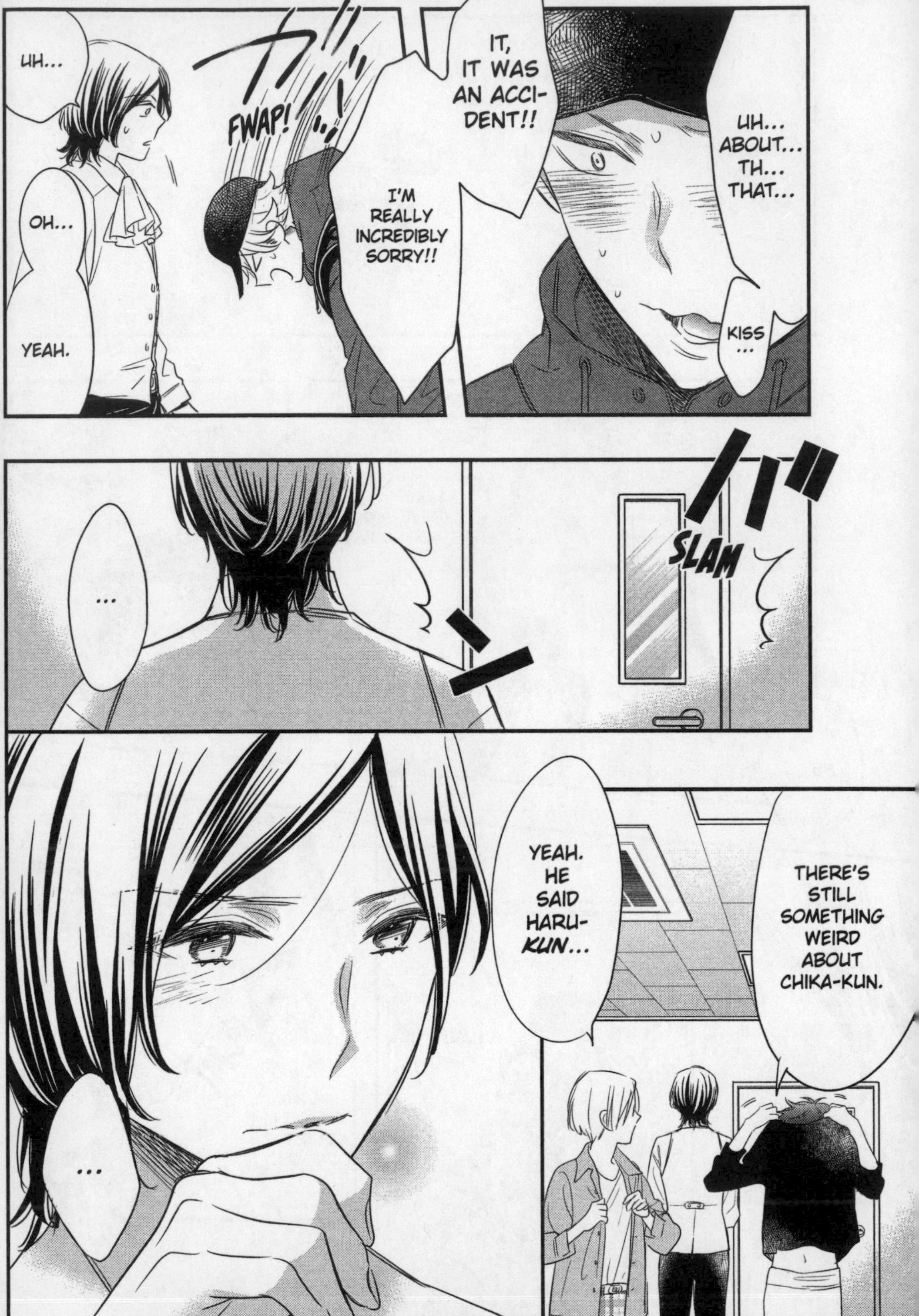

UH... ABOUT... TH... THAT...
KISS...
IT, IT WAS AN ACCI-DENT!!
I'M REALLY INCREDIBLY SORRY!!
FWAP!
UH...
OH...
YEAH.
SLAM
...
THERE'S STILL SOMETHING WEIRD ABOUT CHIKA-KUN.
YEAH. HE SAID HARU-KUN...
...

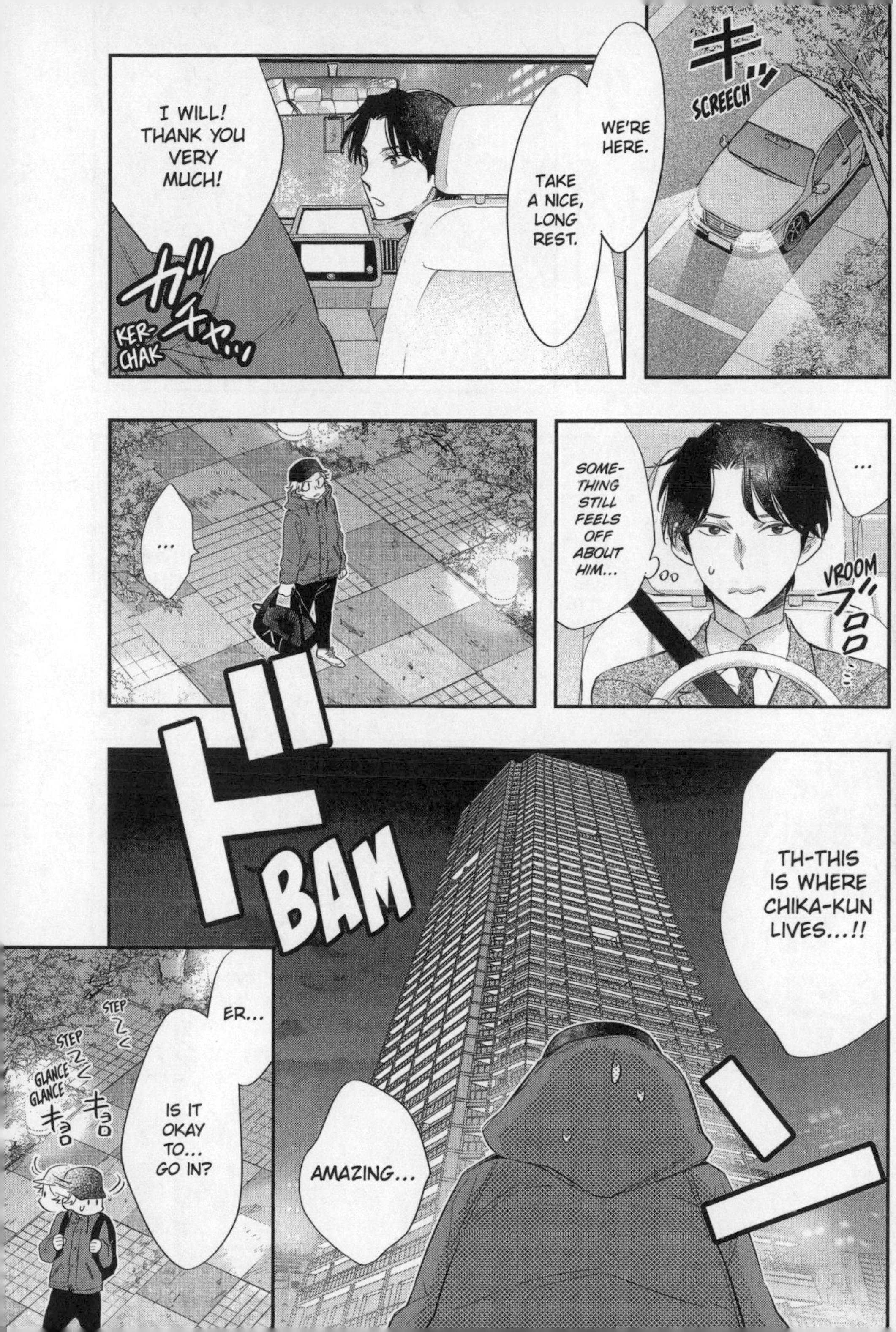
キッ
SCREECH
WE'RE HERE.
TAKE A NICE, LONG REST.
I WILL! THANK YOU VERY MUCH!
ガチャ…
KER-CHAK
…
SOMETHING STILL FEELS OFF ABOUT HIM…
VROOM
ブロロ…
…
ド
BAM
TH-THIS IS WHERE CHIKA-KUN LIVES…!!
AMAZING…
ER…
IS IT OKAY TO… GO IN?
STEP STEP
GLANCE GLANCE
キョロキョロ

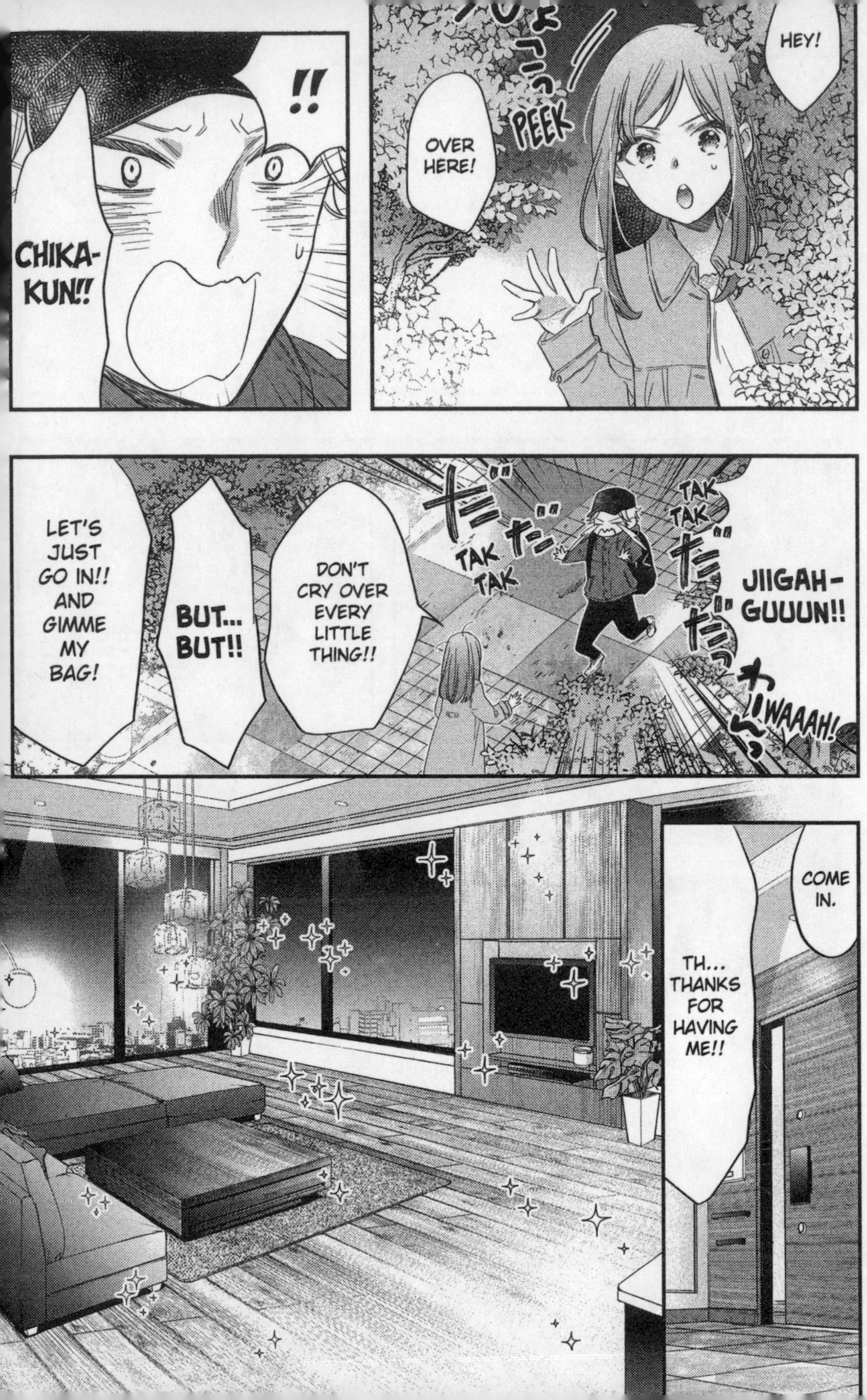
HEY!
OVER HERE!
PEEK
!!
CHIKA-KUN!!
TAK TAK
JIIGAH-GUUUN!!
WAAAH!
TAK TAK
DON'T CRY OVER EVERY LITTLE THING!!
BUT... BUT!!
LET'S JUST GO IN!! AND GIMME MY BAG!
COME IN.
TH... THANKS FOR HAVING ME!!

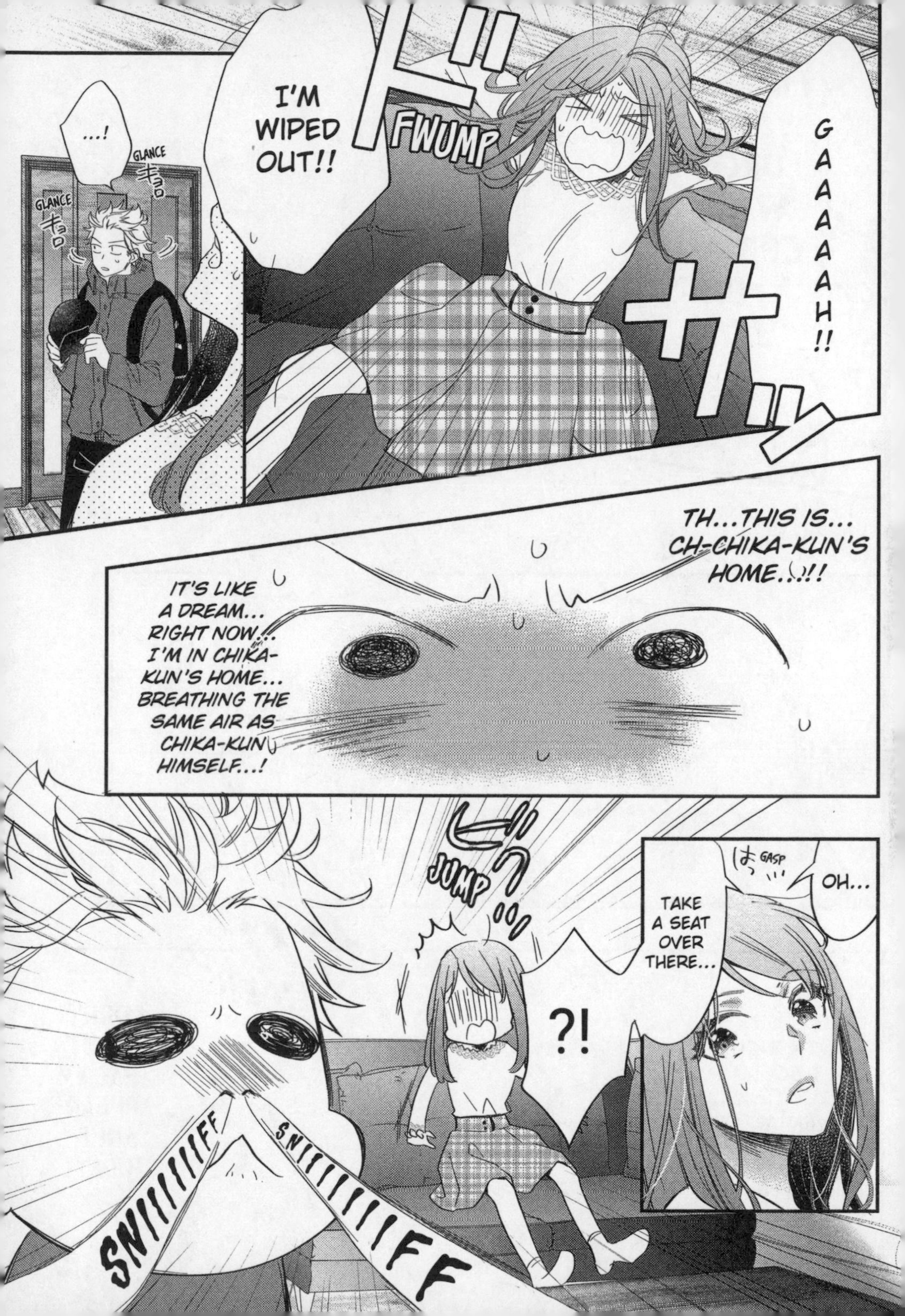
GAAAAAH!!
FWUMP
I'M WIPED OUT!!
...!
GLANCE
GLANCE
TH...THIS IS... CH-CHIKA-KUN'S HOME...!!
IT'S LIKE A DREAM... RIGHT NOW... I'M IN CHIKA-KUN'S HOME... BREATHING THE SAME AIR AS CHIKA-KUN HIMSELF...!
GASP
OH...
TAKE A SEAT OVER THERE...
JUMP
?!
SNIIIIIIFF
SNIIIIIIIIFF

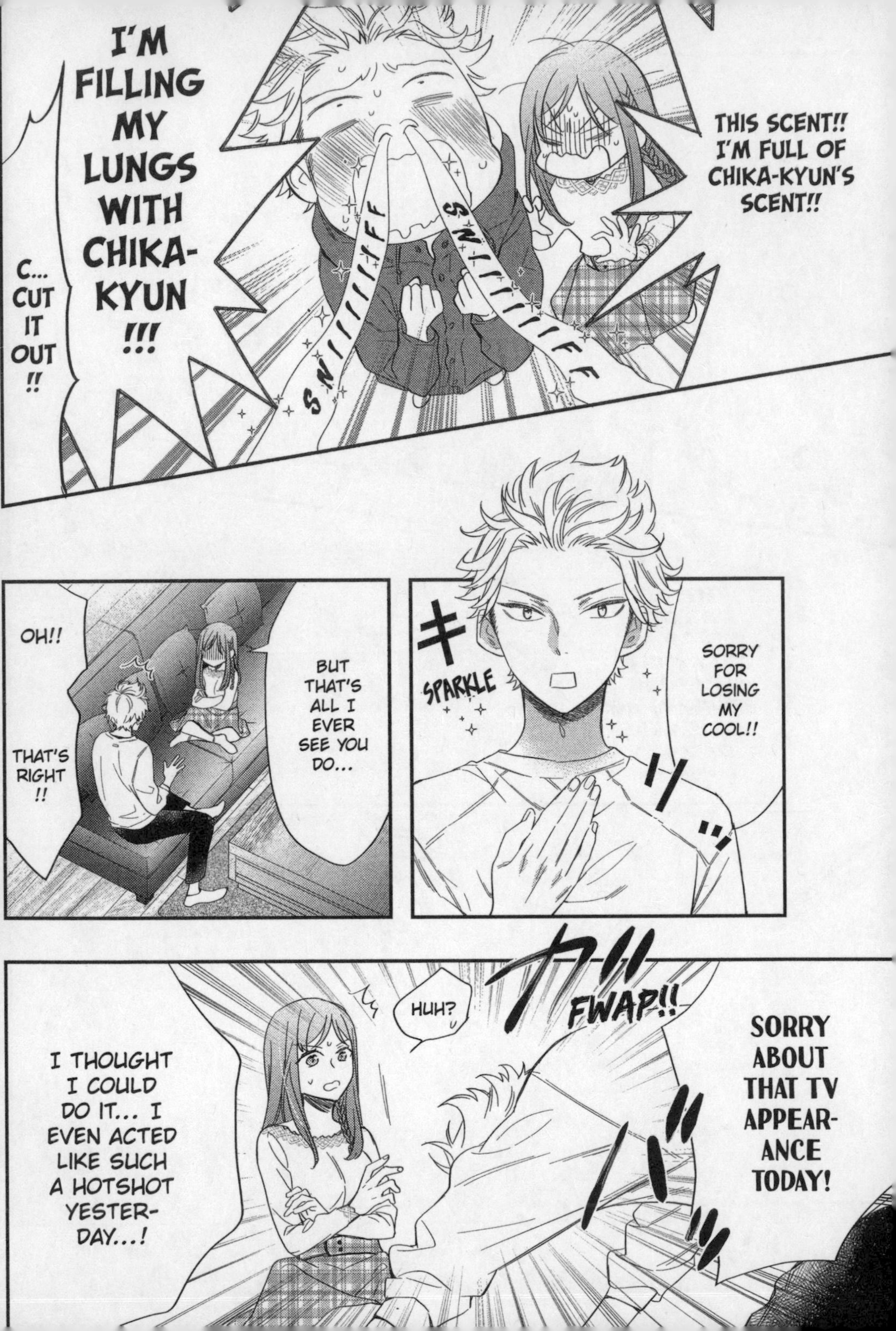
THIS SCENT!! I'M FULL OF CHIKA-KYUN'S SCENT!!
SNIIIIIFF
SNIIIIIFF
I'M FILLING MY LUNGS WITH CHIKA-KYUN!!!
C... CUT IT OUT!!
SORRY FOR LOSING MY COOL!!
SPARKLE
BUT THAT'S ALL I EVER SEE YOU DO...
OH!!
THAT'S RIGHT!!
FWAP!!
SORRY ABOUT THAT TV APPEAR-ANCE TODAY!
HUH?
I THOUGHT I COULD DO IT... I EVEN ACTED LIKE SUCH A HOTSHOT YESTER-DAY...!

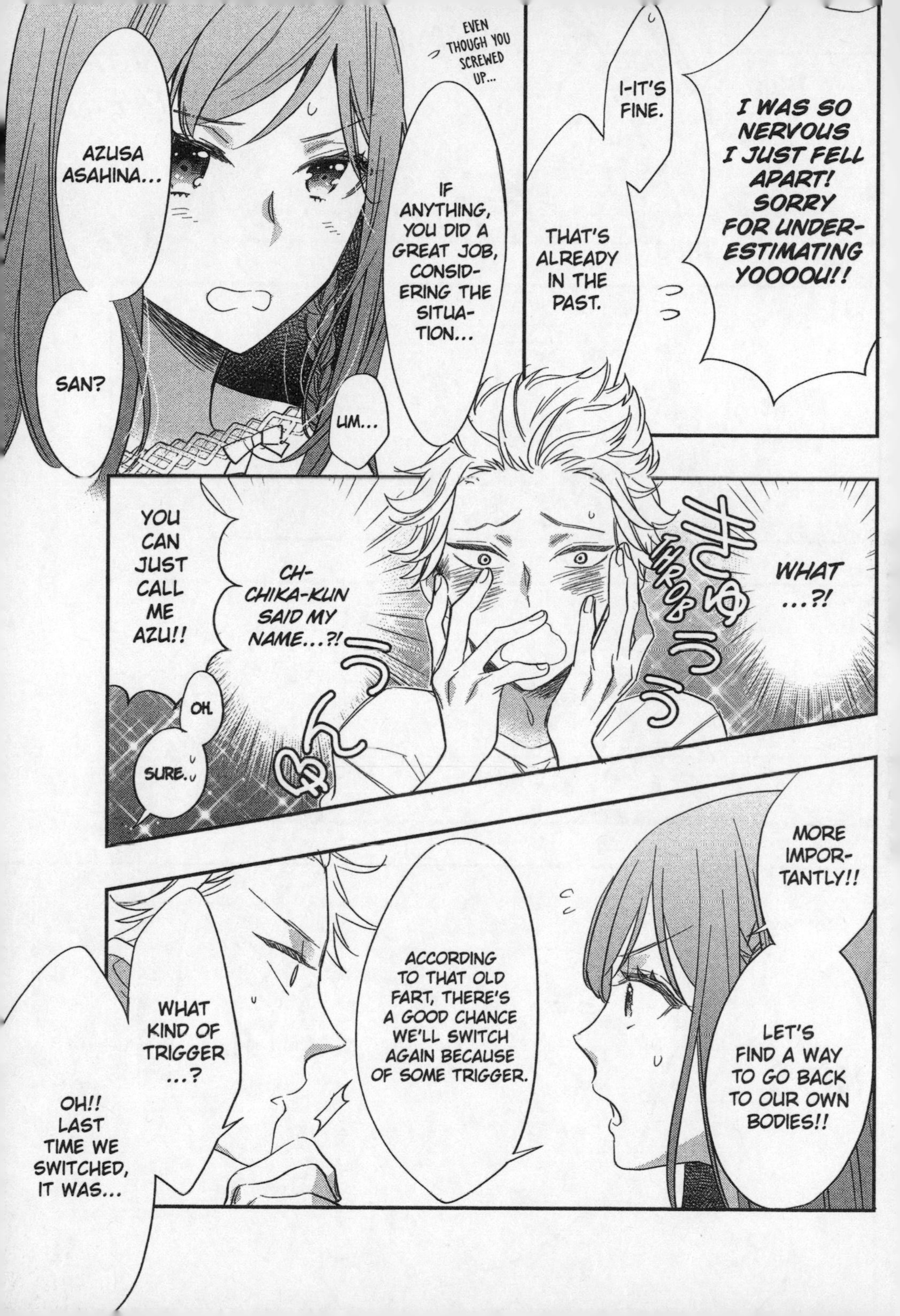
I WAS SO NERVOUS I JUST FELL APART! SORRY FOR UNDER-ESTIMATING YOOOOU!!
I-IT'S FINE.
THAT'S ALREADY IN THE PAST.
EVEN THOUGH YOU SCREWED UP...
IF ANYTHING, YOU DID A GREAT JOB, CONSID-ERING THE SITUA-TION...
UM...
AZUSA ASAHINA...
SAN?
WHAT ...?!
きゅうう
THROB
CH-CHIKA-KUN SAID MY NAME...?!
YOU CAN JUST CALL ME AZU!!
OH.
SURE.
MORE IMPOR-TANTLY!!
LET'S FIND A WAY TO GO BACK TO OUR OWN BODIES!!
ACCORDING TO THAT OLD FART, THERE'S A GOOD CHANCE WE'LL SWITCH AGAIN BECAUSE OF SOME TRIGGER.
WHAT KIND OF TRIGGER ...?
OH!! LAST TIME WE SWITCHED, IT WAS...

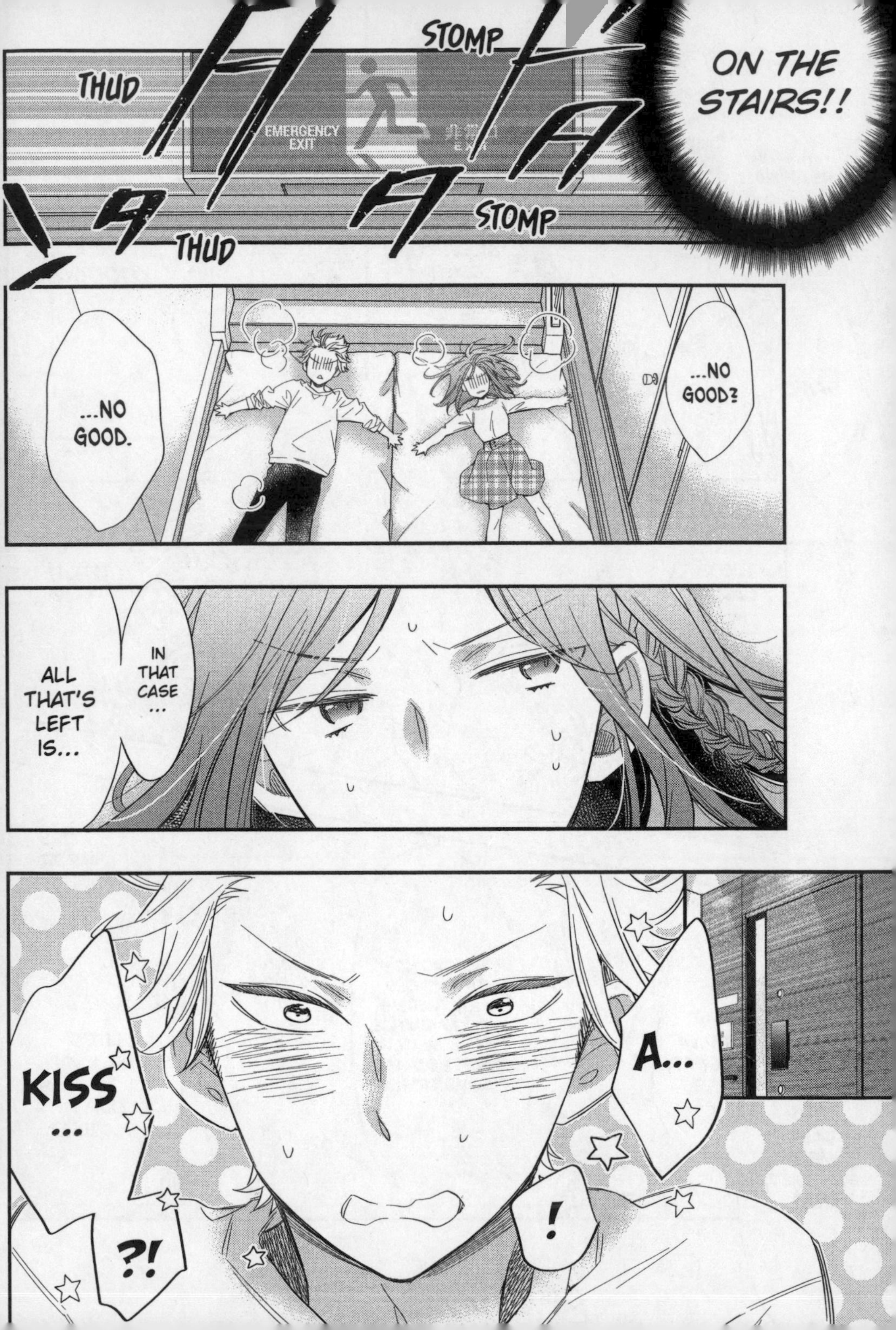
ON THE STAIRS!!
STOMP
STOMP
EMERGENCY EXIT
THUD
THUD
...NO GOOD?
...NO GOOD.
IN THAT CASE...
ALL THAT'S LEFT IS...
A...
!
KISS...
?!

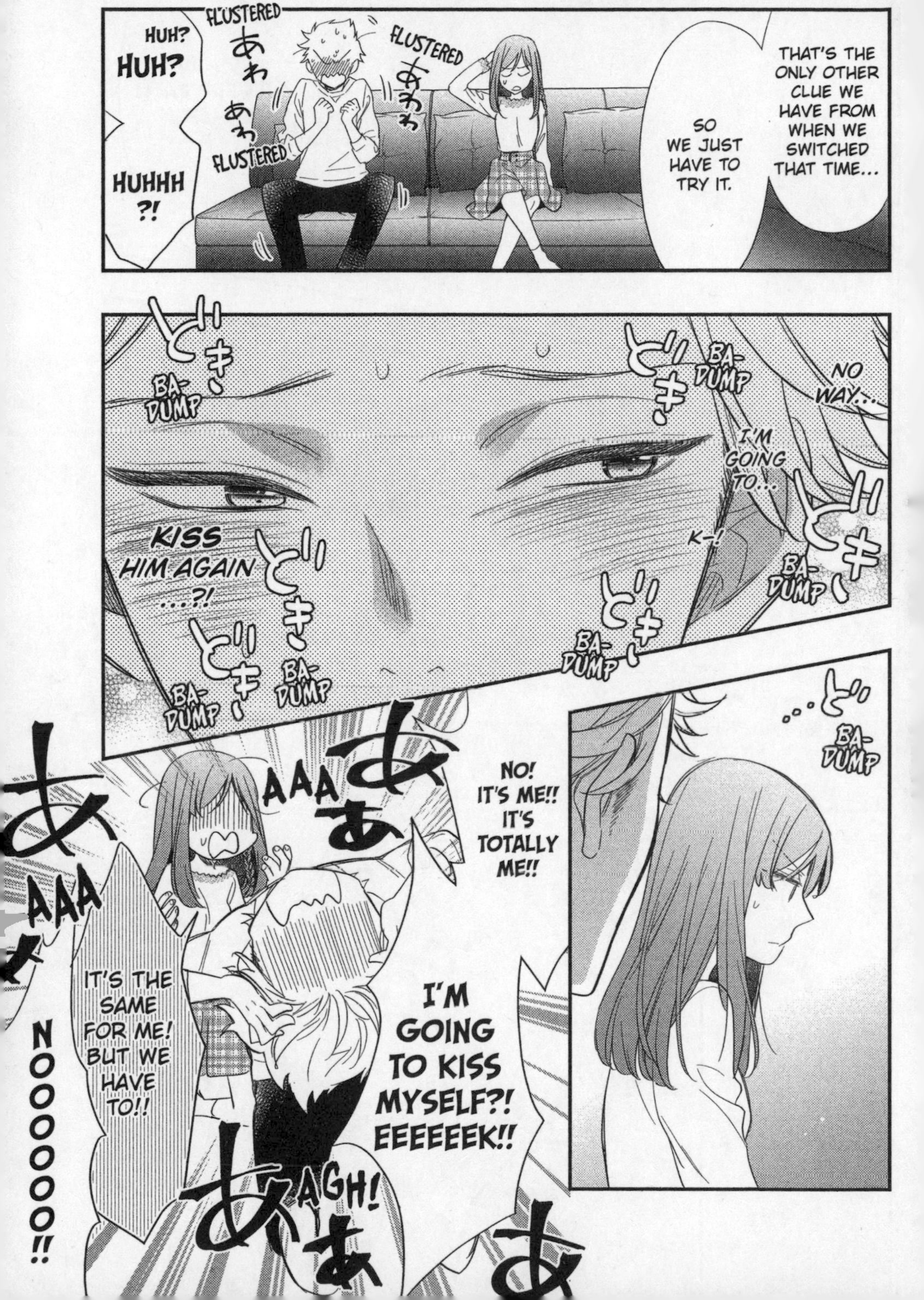
THAT'S THE ONLY OTHER CLUE WE HAVE FROM WHEN WE SWITCHED THAT TIME...
SO WE JUST HAVE TO TRY IT.
FLUSTERED あわわ
FLUSTERED あわ
あわ FLUSTERED
HUH? HUH?
HUHHH ?!
どき BA-DUMP
NO WAY...
I'M GOING TO...
K-!
どき BA-DUMP
どき BA-DUMP
どき BA-DUMP
KISS HIM AGAIN ...?!
どき BA-DUMP
どき BA-DUMP
...ど BA-DUMP
NO! IT'S ME!! IT'S TOTALLY ME!!
あ AAA あ
I'M GOING TO KISS MYSELF?! EEEEEEK!!
あ AGH! あ あ
IT'S THE SAME FOR ME! BUT WE HAVE TO!!
あ AAA
NOOOOOOO!!

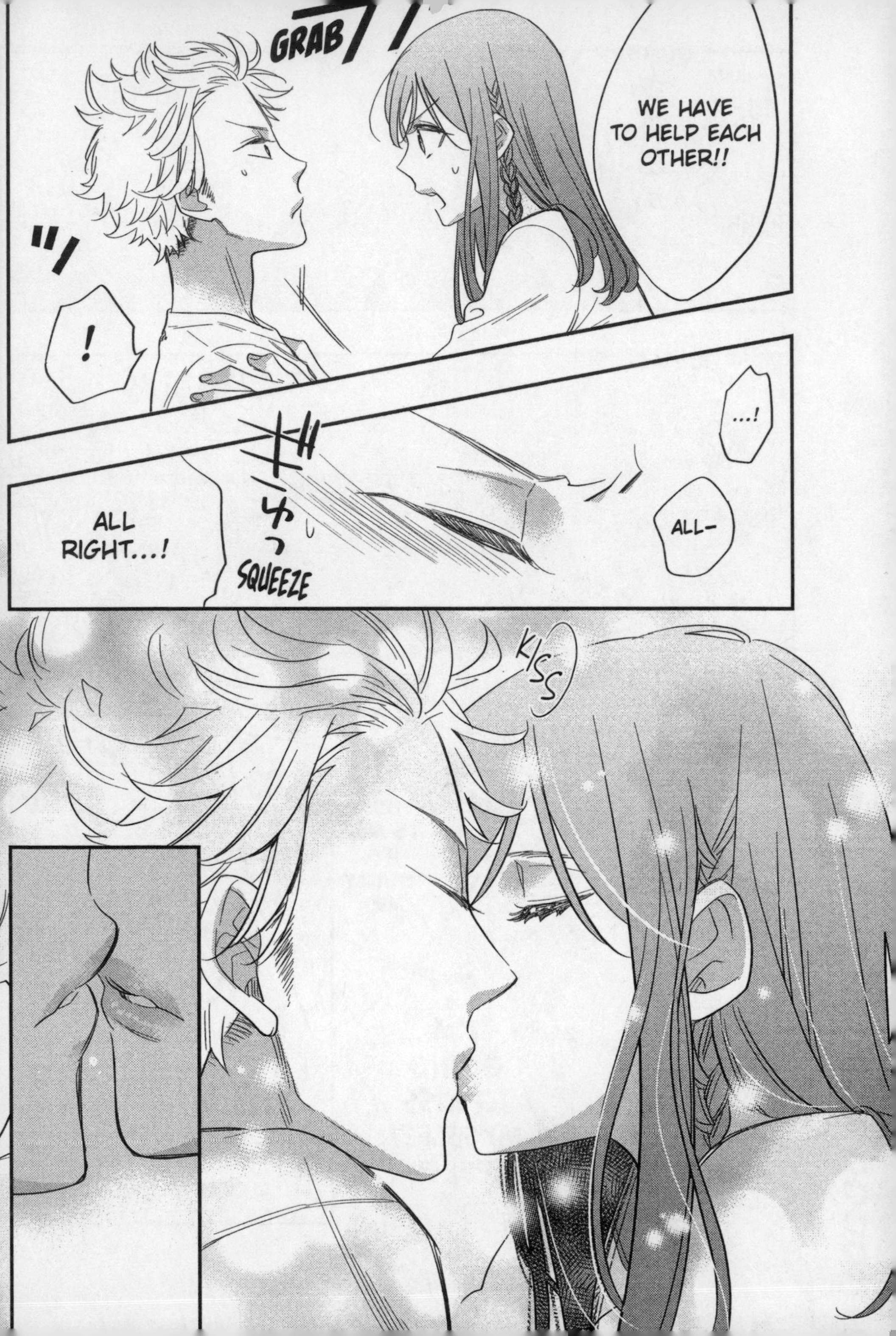
WE HAVE TO HELP EACH OTHER!!
GRAB
!
...!
ALL-
SQUEEZE
ALL RIGHT...!
KISS

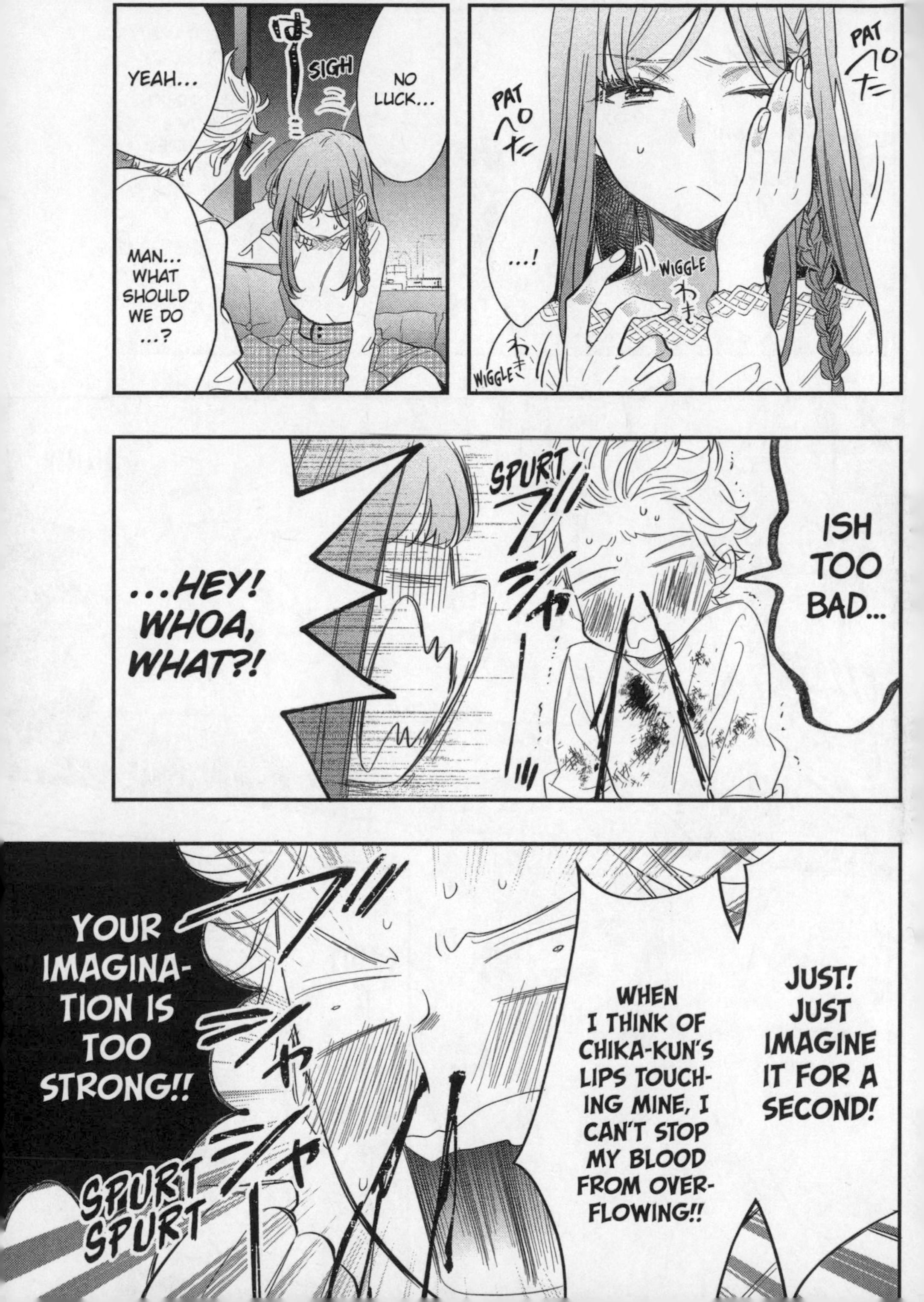
PAT
PAT
...!
WIGGLE
WIGGLE
NO LUCK...
SIGH
YEAH...
MAN... WHAT SHOULD WE DO ...?
ISH TOO BAD...
SPURT
...HEY! WHOA, WHAT?!
JUST! JUST IMAGINE IT FOR A SECOND!
WHEN I THINK OF CHIKA-KUN'S LIPS TOUCHING MINE, I CAN'T STOP MY BLOOD FROM OVERFLOWING!!
YOUR IMAGINATION IS TOO STRONG!!
SPURT SPURT

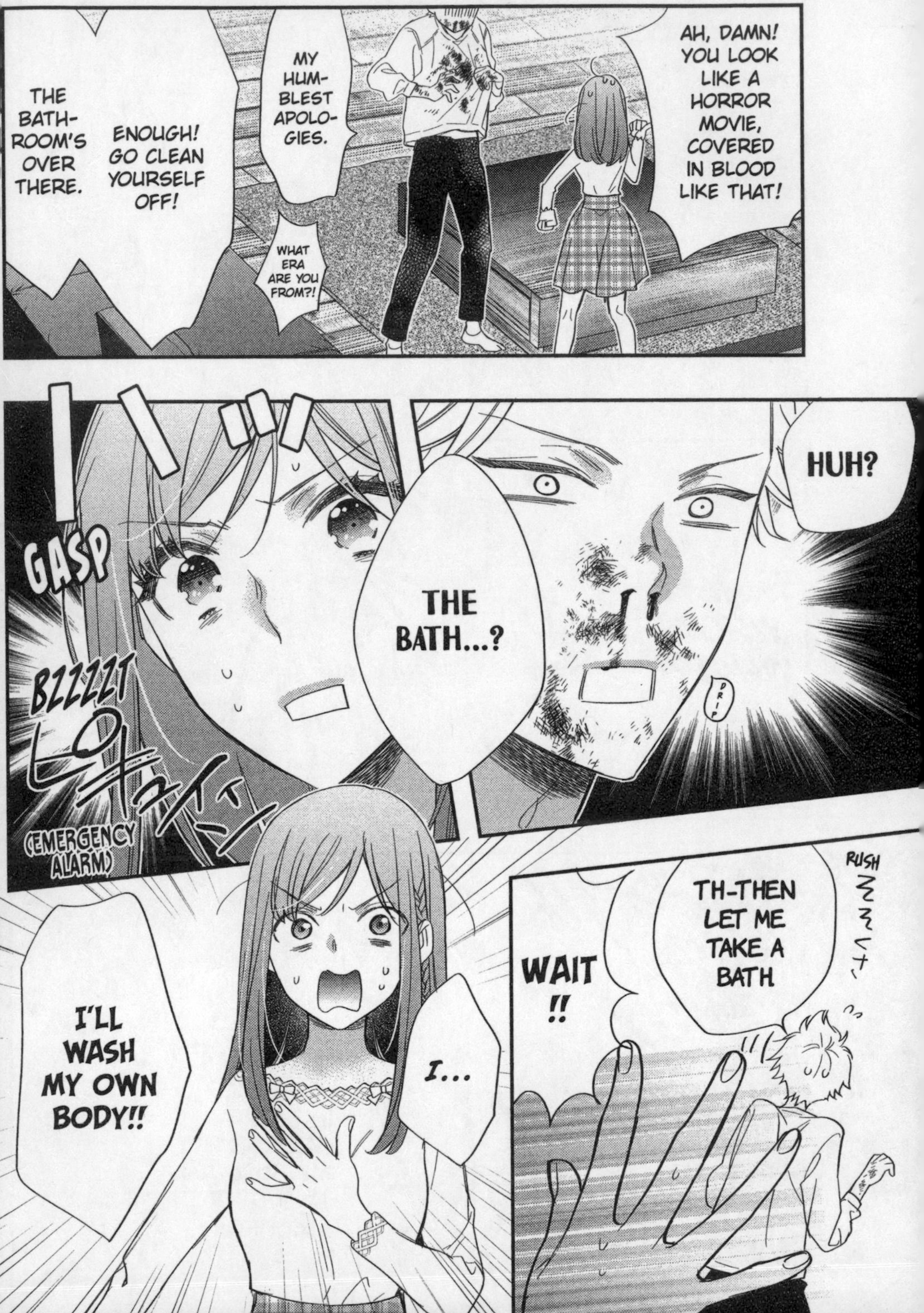
AH, DAMN! YOU LOOK LIKE A HORROR MOVIE, COVERED IN BLOOD LIKE THAT!
MY HUM-BLEST APOLO-GIES.
WHAT ERA ARE YOU FROM?!
ENOUGH! GO CLEAN YOURSELF OFF!
THE BATH-ROOM'S OVER THERE.
HUH?
THE BATH...?
DRIP
GASP
BZZZZT
(EMERGENCY ALARM)
RUSH
TH-THEN LET ME TAKE A BATH
WAIT!!
I...
I'LL WASH MY OWN BODY!!

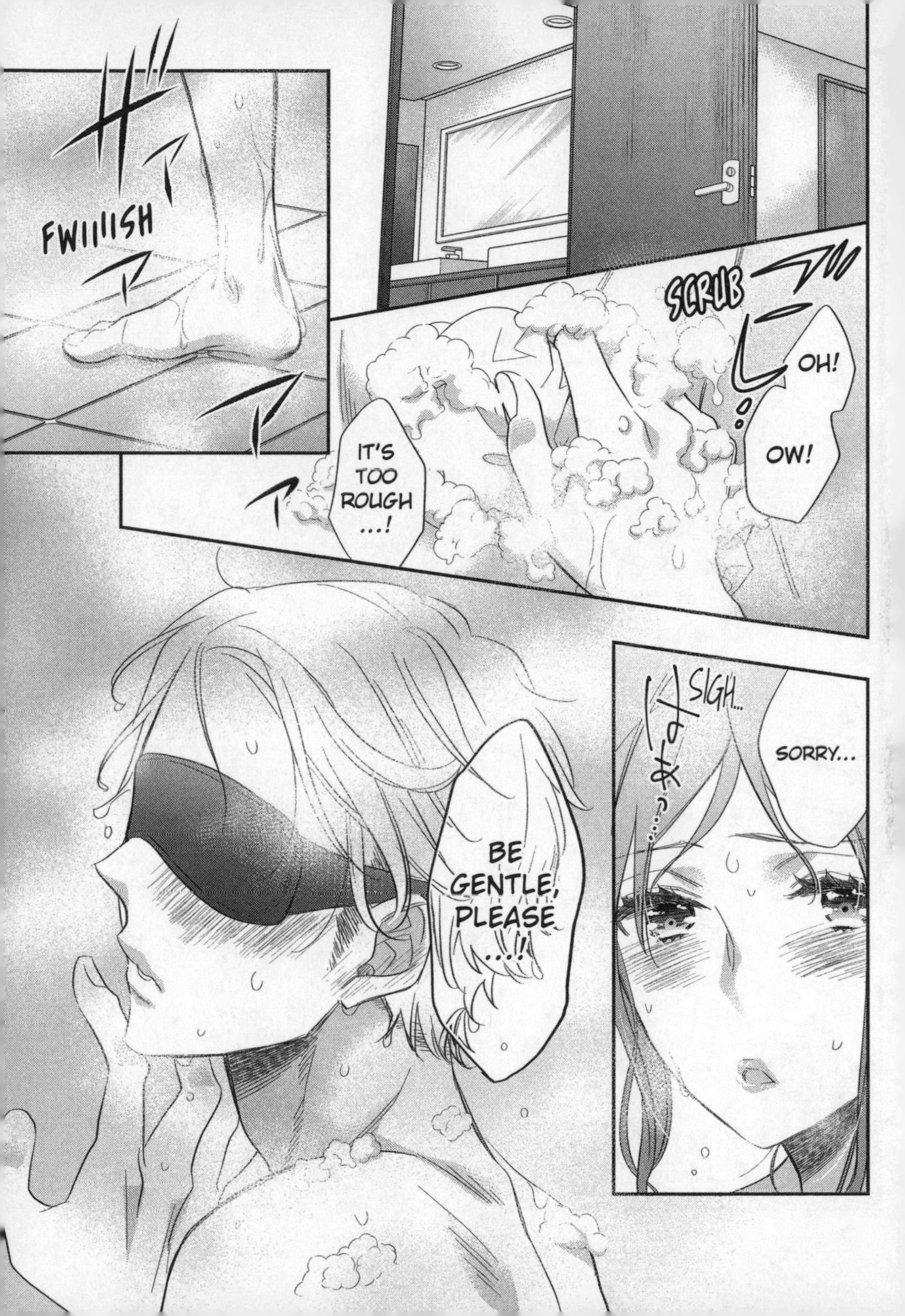
FWIIIISH
SCRUB
OH!
OW!
IT'S TOO ROUGH ...!
SIGH...
SORRY...
BE GENTLE, PLEASE ...!!

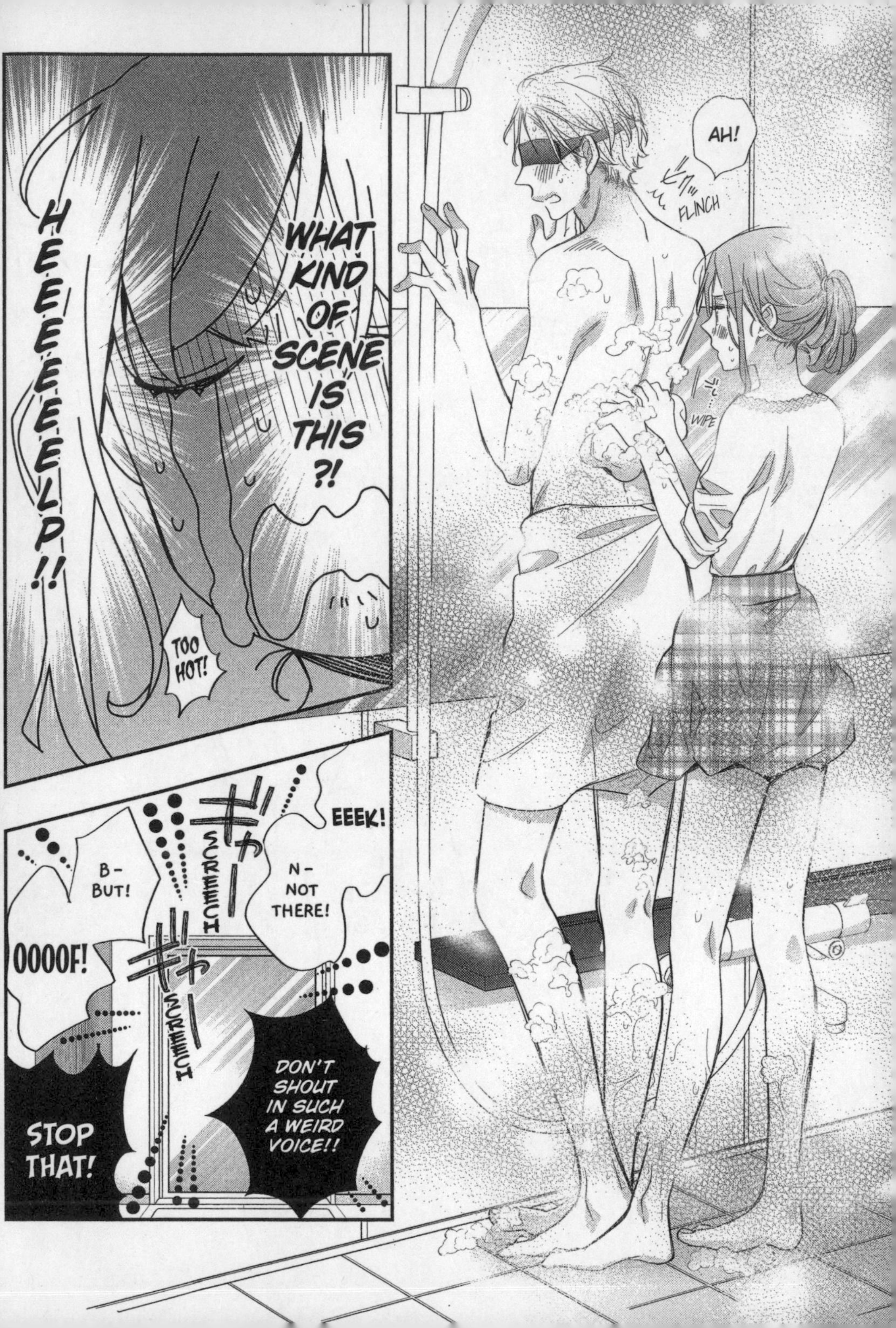
AH!
FLINCH
WIPE
WHAT KIND OF SCENE IS THIS?!
HEEEEEEELP!!
TOO HOT!
EEEK!
N-NOT THERE!
SCREEECH
B-BUT!
SCREEECH
OOOOF!
DON'T SHOUT IN SUCH A WEIRD VOICE!!
STOP THAT!

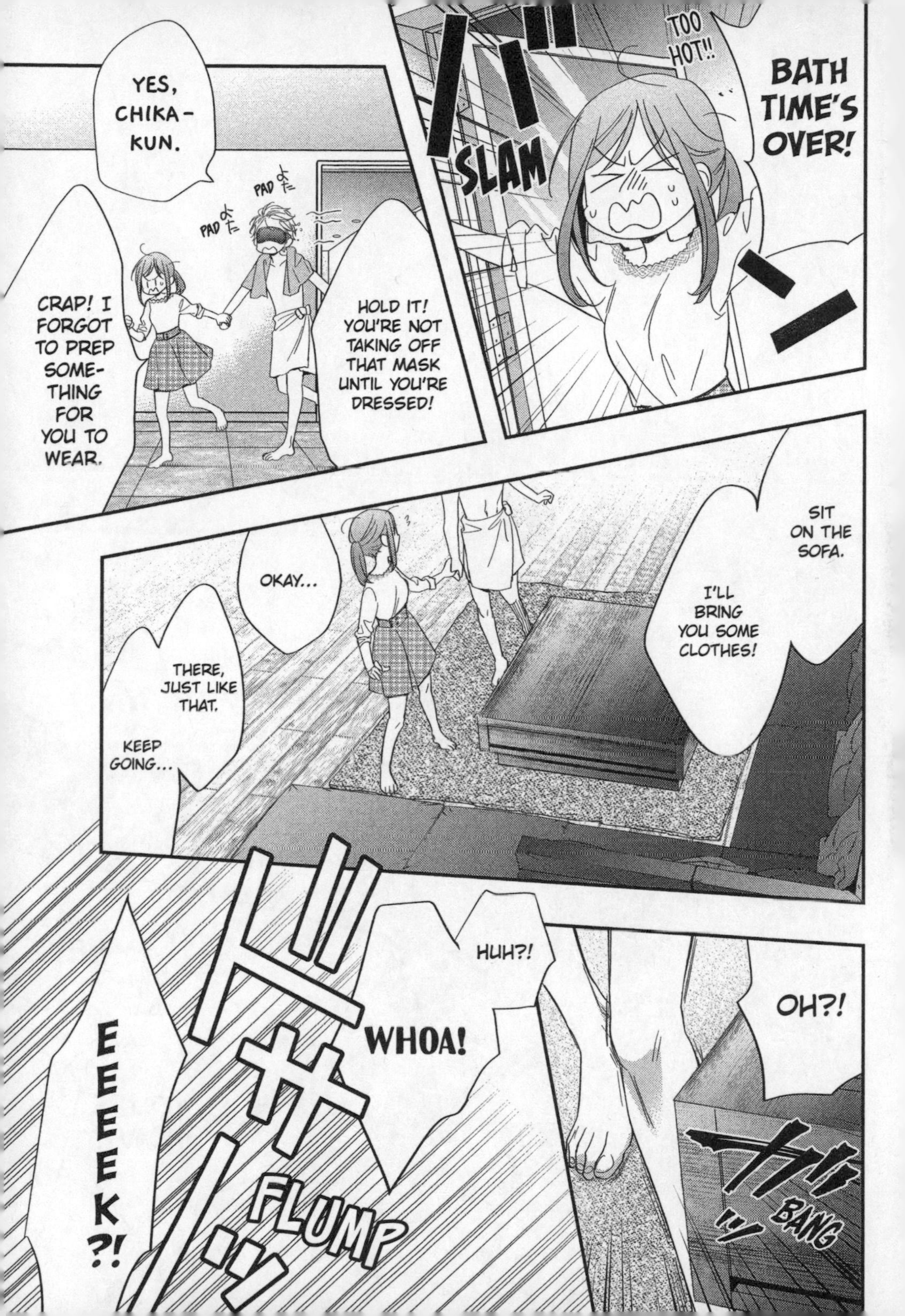
BATH TIME'S OVER!
TOO HOT!!
SLAM
HOLD IT! YOU'RE NOT TAKING OFF THAT MASK UNTIL YOU'RE DRESSED!
YES, CHIKA-KUN.
PAD
PAD
CRAP! I FORGOT TO PREP SOME-THING FOR YOU TO WEAR.
SIT ON THE SOFA.
I'LL BRING YOU SOME CLOTHES!
OKAY...
THERE, JUST LIKE THAT.
KEEP GOING...
OH?!
BANG
HUH?!
WHOA!
FLUMP
EEEEK?!

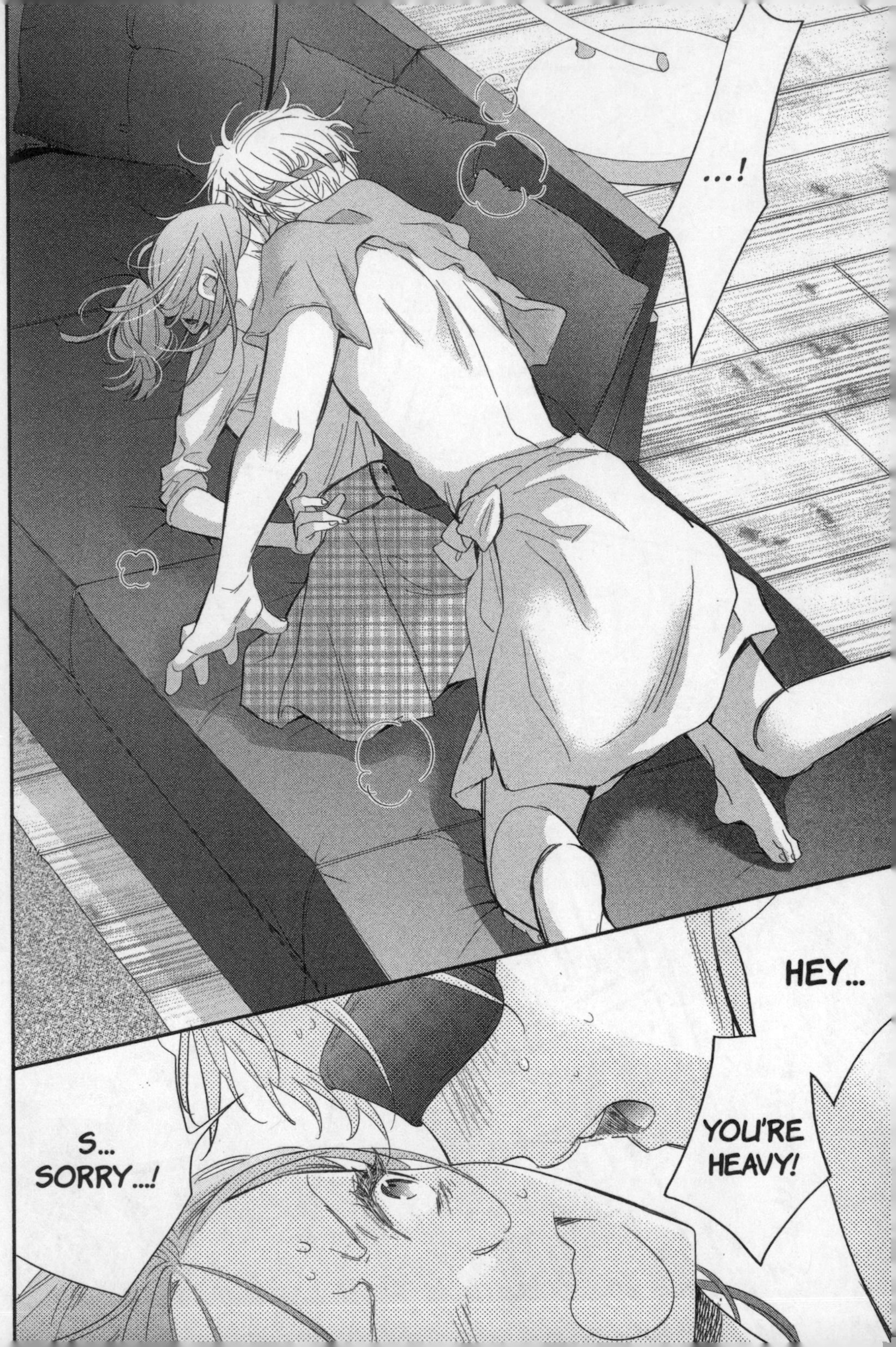
...!
HEY...
YOU'RE HEAVY!
S... SORRY...!

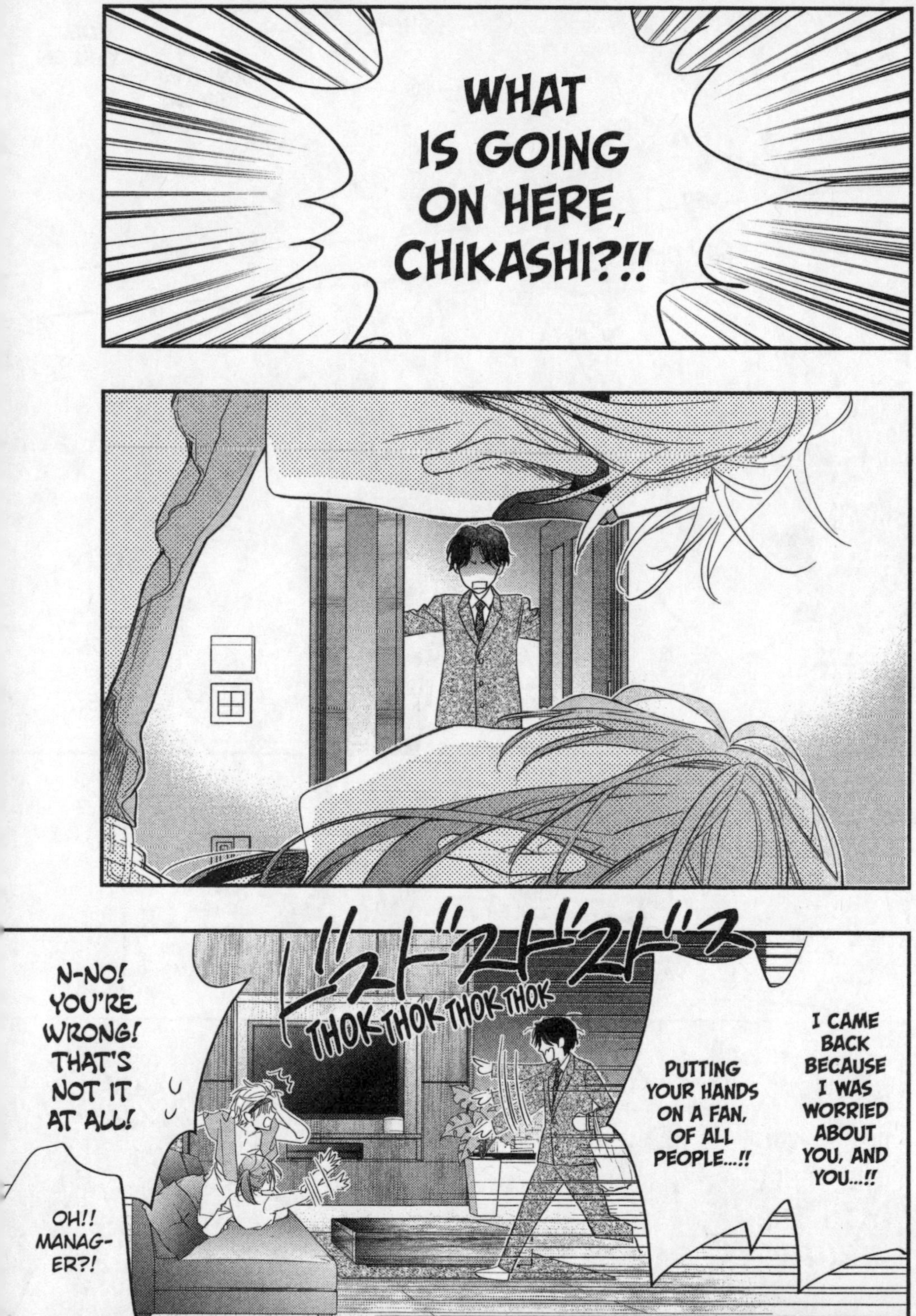
WHAT IS GOING ON HERE, CHIKASHI?!!
ドスドスドスドス
THOK THOK THOK THOK
I CAME BACK BECAUSE I WAS WORRIED ABOUT YOU, AND YOU...!!
PUTTING YOUR HANDS ON A FAN, OF ALL PEOPLE...!!
N-NO! YOU'RE WRONG! THAT'S NOT IT AT ALL!
OH!! MANAGER?!

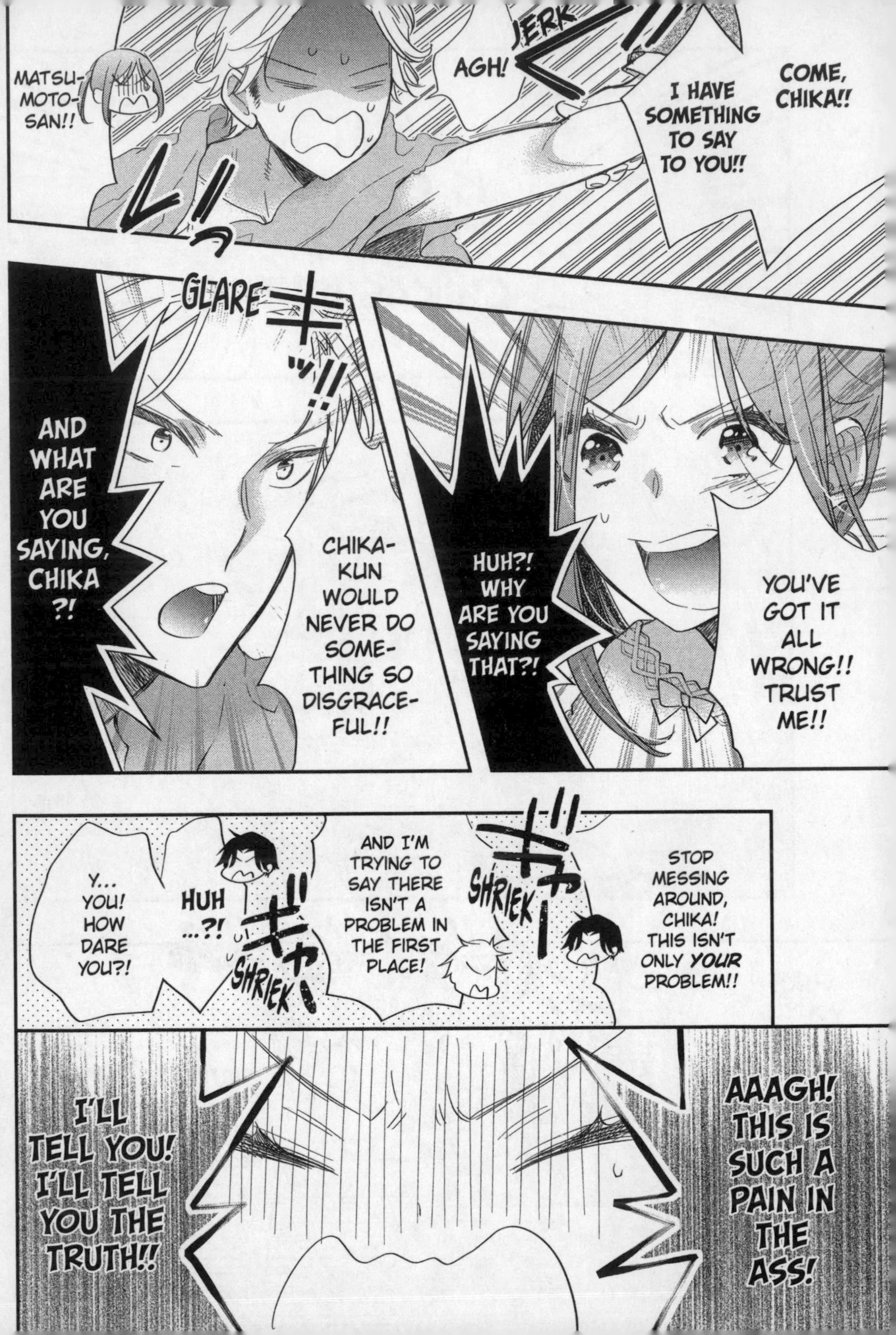

COME, CHIKA!!
I HAVE SOMETHING TO SAY TO YOU!!
JERK
AGH!
MATSU-MOTO-SAN!!
YOU'VE GOT IT ALL WRONG!! TRUST ME!!
HUH?! WHY ARE YOU SAYING THAT?!
GLARE
CHIKA-KUN WOULD NEVER DO SOME-THING SO DISGRACE-FUL!!
AND WHAT ARE YOU SAYING, CHIKA?!
STOP MESSING AROUND, CHIKA! THIS ISN'T ONLY *YOUR* PROBLEM!!
SHRIEK
AND I'M TRYING TO SAY THERE ISN'T A PROBLEM IN THE FIRST PLACE!
SHRIEK
HUH ...?!
Y... YOU! HOW DARE YOU?!
AAAGH! THIS IS SUCH A PAIN IN THE ASS!
I'LL TELL YOU! I'LL TELL YOU THE TRUTH!!

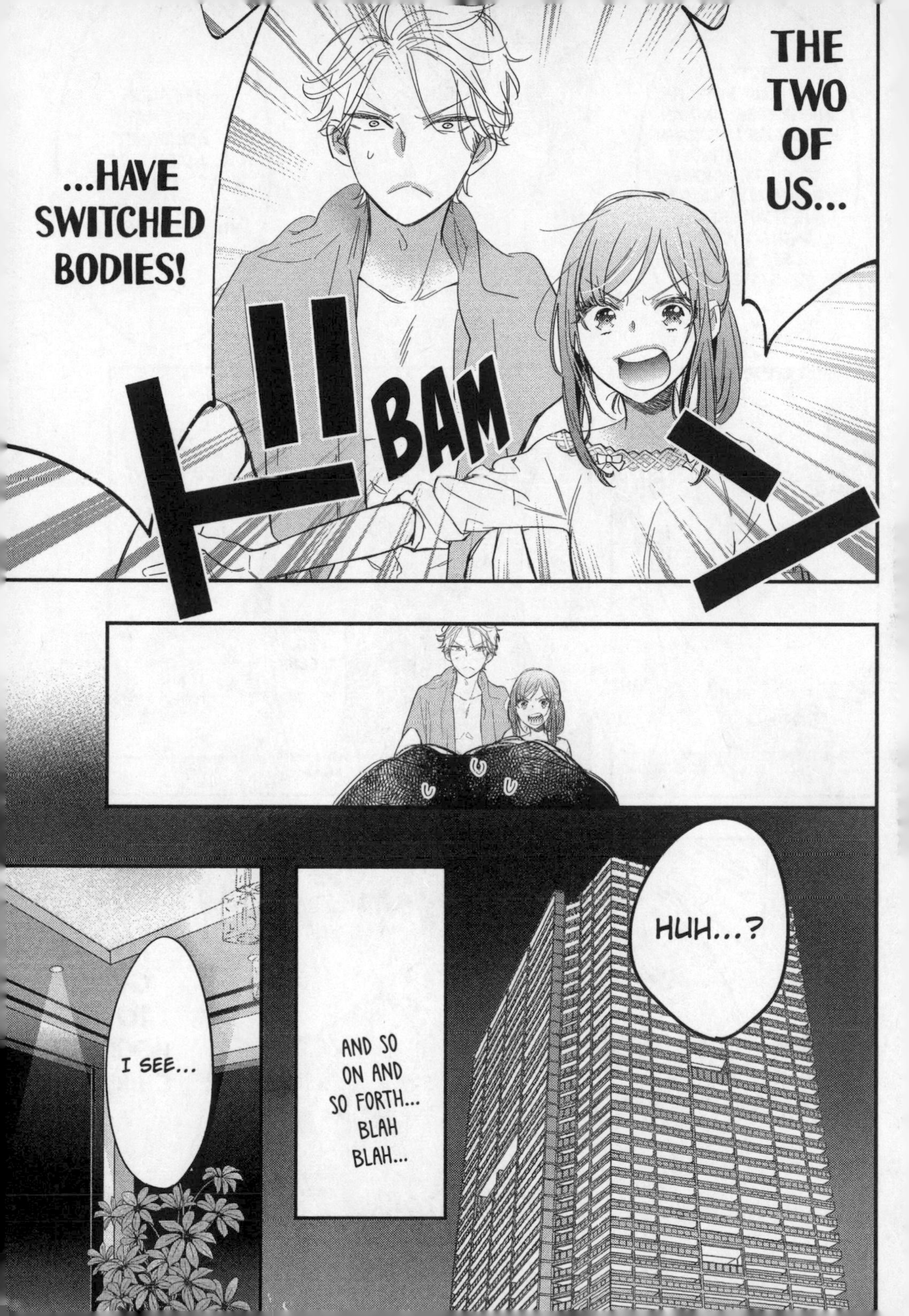
THE TWO OF US...
...HAVE SWITCHED BODIES!
BAM
HUH...?
AND SO ON AND SO FORTH... BLAH BLAH...
I SEE...

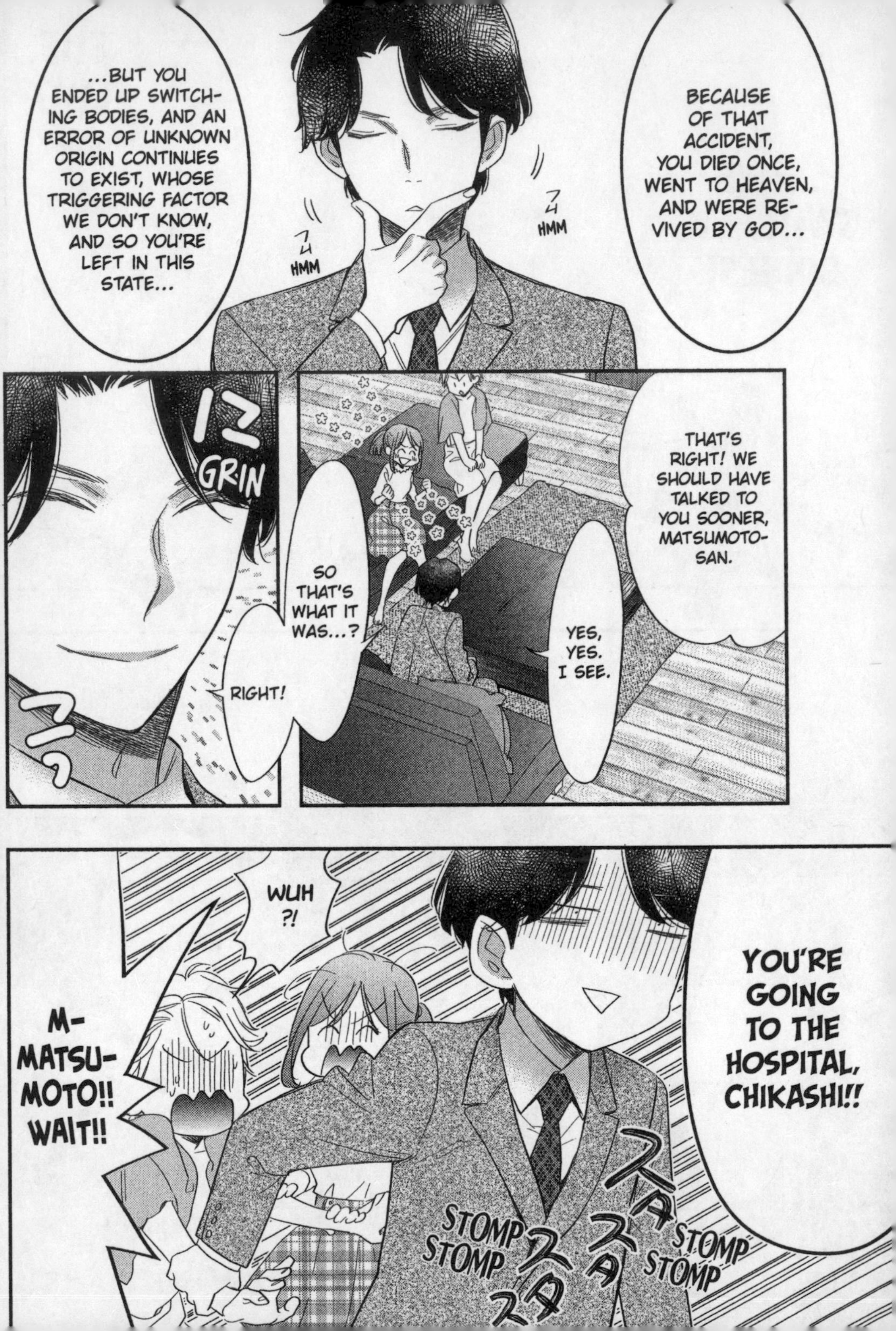
BECAUSE OF THAT ACCIDENT, YOU DIED ONCE, WENT TO HEAVEN, AND WERE RE-VIVED BY GOD...
HMM
HMM
...BUT YOU ENDED UP SWITCH-ING BODIES, AND AN ERROR OF UNKNOWN ORIGIN CONTINUES TO EXIST, WHOSE TRIGGERING FACTOR WE DON'T KNOW, AND SO YOU'RE LEFT IN THIS STATE...
THAT'S RIGHT! WE SHOULD HAVE TALKED TO YOU SOONER, MATSUMOTO-SAN.
YES, YES. I SEE.
SO THAT'S WHAT IT WAS...?
RIGHT!
GRIN
YOU'RE GOING TO THE HOSPITAL, CHIKASHI!!
WUH ?!
M-MATSUMOTO!! WAIT!!
STOMP STOMP
STOMP STOMP

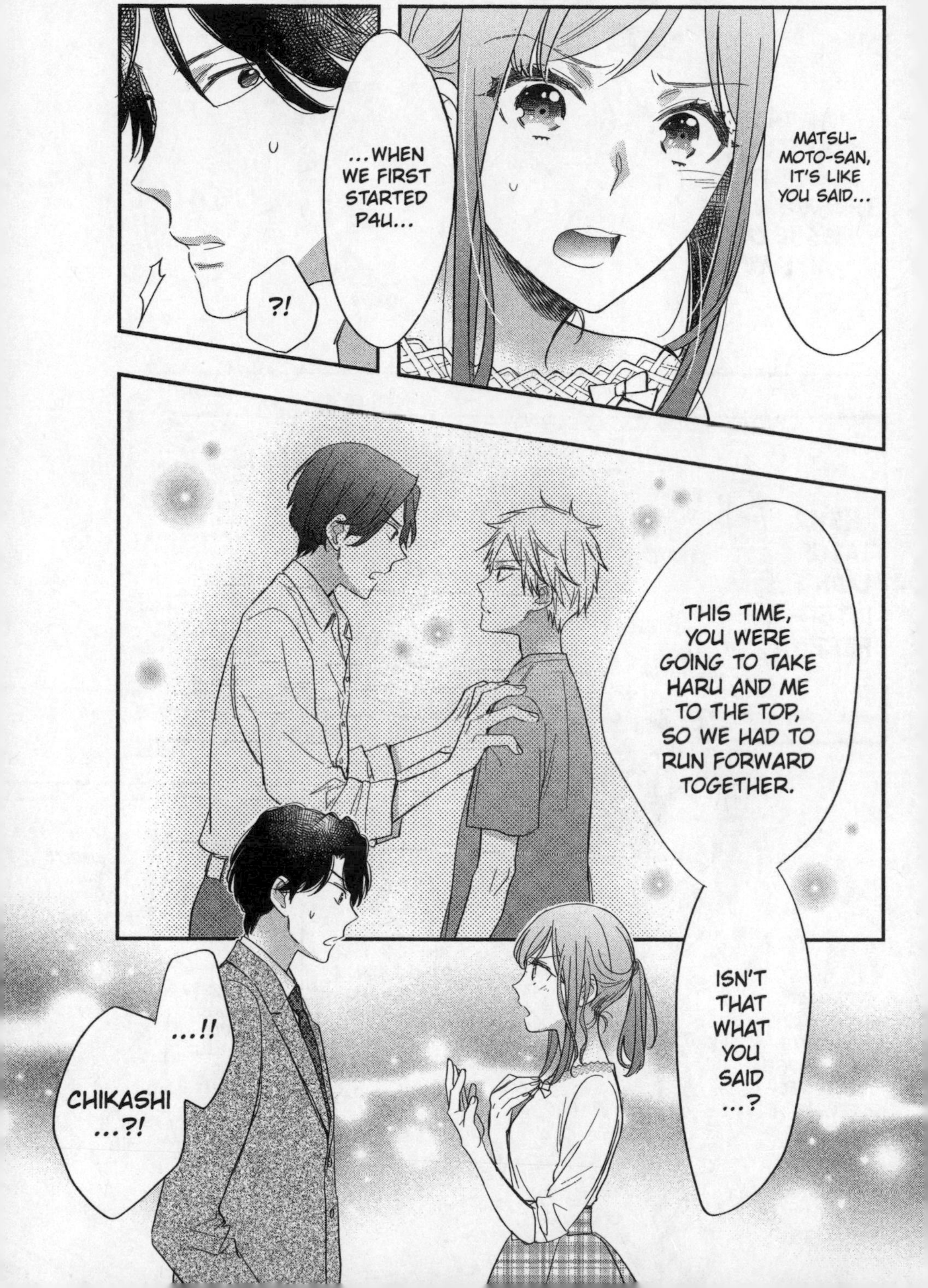
MATSU-MOTO-SAN, IT'S LIKE YOU SAID...
...WHEN WE FIRST STARTED P4U...
?!
THIS TIME, YOU WERE GOING TO TAKE HARU AND ME TO THE TOP, SO WE HAD TO RUN FORWARD TOGETHER.
ISN'T THAT WHAT YOU SAID ...?
...!!
CHIKASHI ...?!

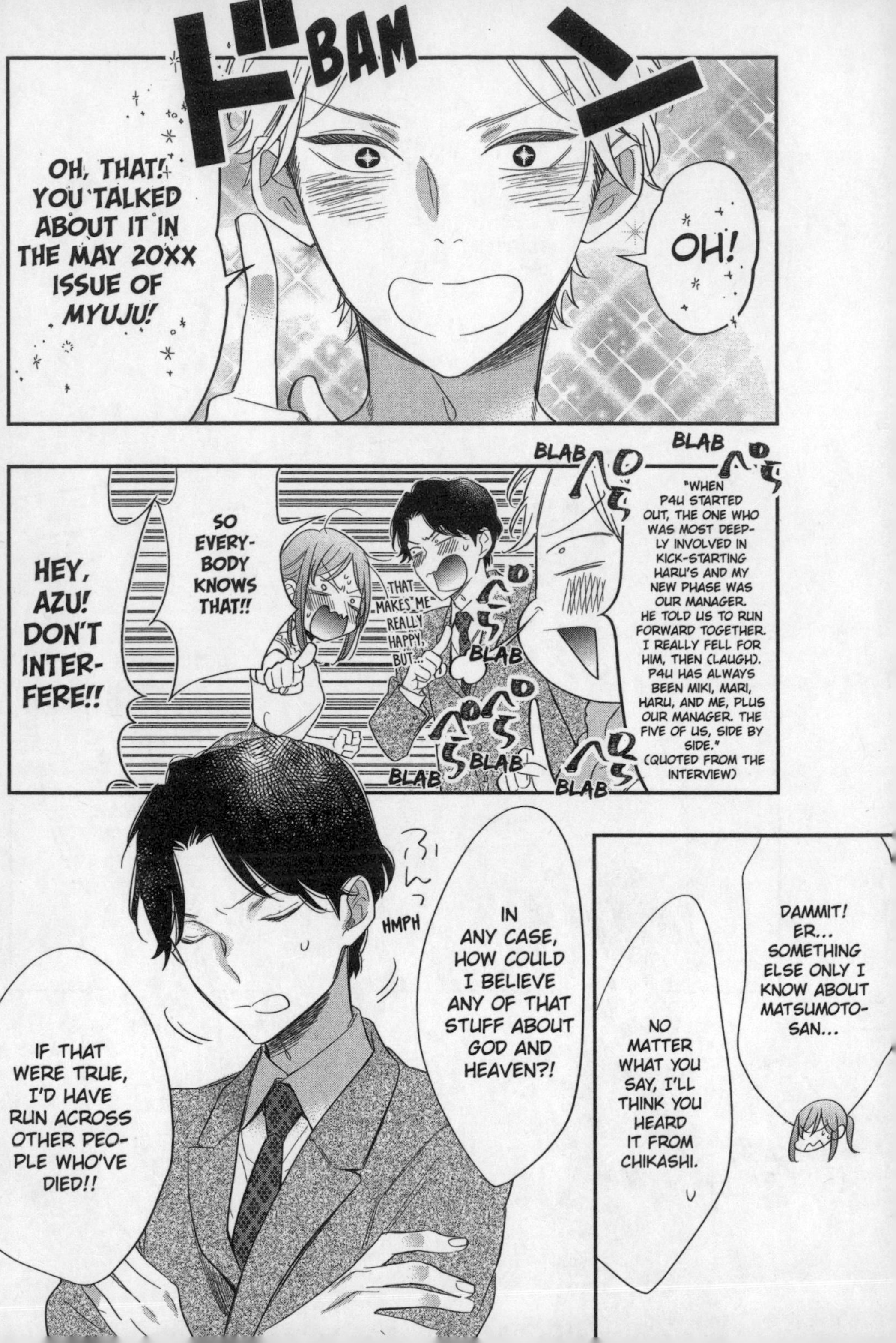
BAM
OH!
OH, THAT! YOU TALKED ABOUT IT IN THE MAY 20XX ISSUE OF MYUJU!
BLAB
BLAB
"WHEN P4U STARTED OUT, THE ONE WHO WAS MOST DEEPLY INVOLVED IN KICK-STARTING HARU'S AND MY NEW PHASE WAS OUR MANAGER. HE TOLD US TO RUN FORWARD TOGETHER. I REALLY FELL FOR HIM, THEN (LAUGH). P4U HAS ALWAYS BEEN MIKI, MARI, HARU, AND ME, PLUS OUR MANAGER. THE FIVE OF US, SIDE BY SIDE."
(QUOTED FROM THE INTERVIEW)
BLAB
BLAB
BLAB
BLAB
THAT MAKES ME REALLY HAPPY, BUT...
SO EVERYBODY KNOWS THAT!!
HEY, AZU! DON'T INTERFERE!!
DAMMIT! ER... SOMETHING ELSE ONLY I KNOW ABOUT MATSUMOTO-SAN...
NO MATTER WHAT YOU SAY, I'LL THINK YOU HEARD IT FROM CHIKASHI.
HMPH
IN ANY CASE, HOW COULD I BELIEVE ANY OF THAT STUFF ABOUT GOD AND HEAVEN?!
IF THAT WERE TRUE, I'D HAVE RUN ACROSS OTHER PEOPLE WHO'VE DIED!!

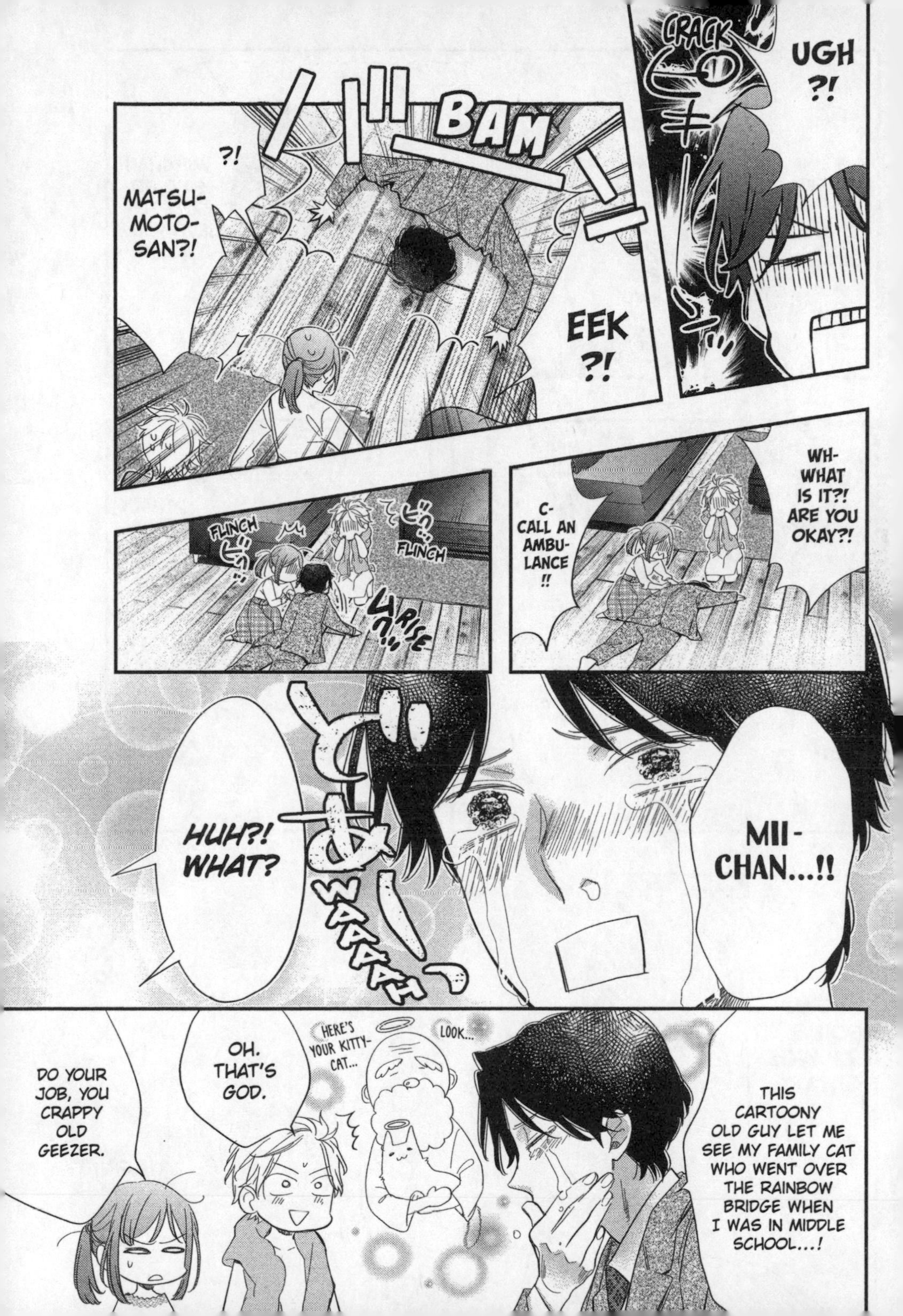
CRACK
UGH ?!
BAM
?!
MATSU-MOTO-SAN?!
EEK ?!
WH-WHAT IS IT?! ARE YOU OKAY?!
C-CALL AN AMBULANCE !!
FLINCH
FLINCH
RISE
MII-CHAN...!!
WAAAAH
HUH?! WHAT?
THIS CARTOONY OLD GUY LET ME SEE MY FAMILY CAT WHO WENT OVER THE RAINBOW BRIDGE WHEN I WAS IN MIDDLE SCHOOL...!
LOOK...
HERE'S YOUR KITTY-CAT...
OH. THAT'S GOD.
DO YOUR JOB, YOU CRAPPY OLD GEEZER.

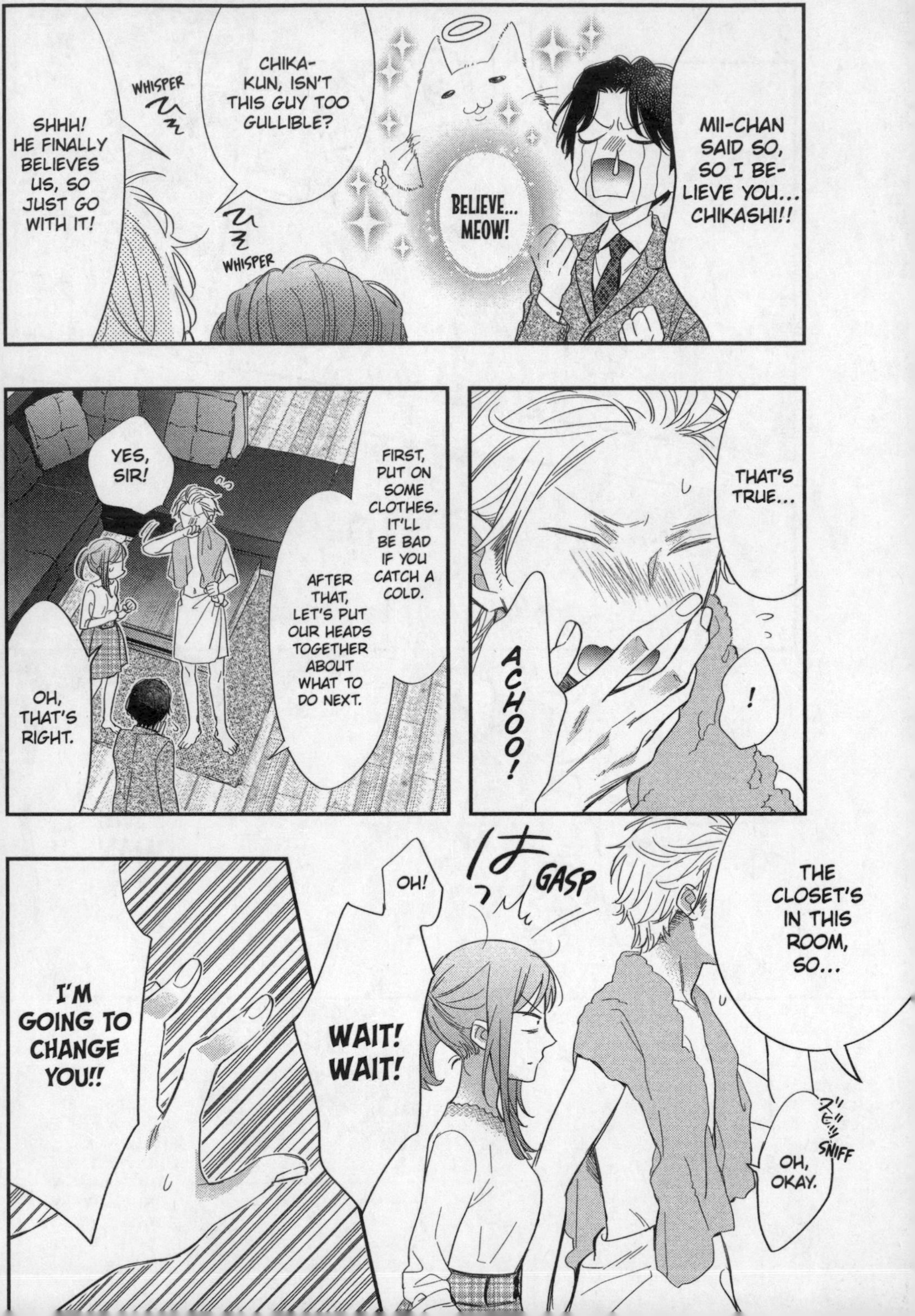
MII-CHAN SAID SO, SO I BE-LIEVE YOU... CHIKASHI!!
BELIEVE... MEOW!
CHIKA-KUN, ISN'T THIS GUY TOO GULLIBLE?
WHISPER
SHHH! HE FINALLY BELIEVES US, SO JUST GO WITH IT!
WHISPER
THAT'S TRUE...
ACHOO!
!
FIRST, PUT ON SOME CLOTHES. IT'LL BE BAD IF YOU CATCH A COLD.
AFTER THAT, LET'S PUT OUR HEADS TOGETHER ABOUT WHAT TO DO NEXT.
YES, SIR!
OH, THAT'S RIGHT.
THE CLOSET'S IN THIS ROOM, SO...
SNIFF
OH, OKAY.
GASP
OH!
WAIT! WAIT!
I'M GOING TO CHANGE YOU!!

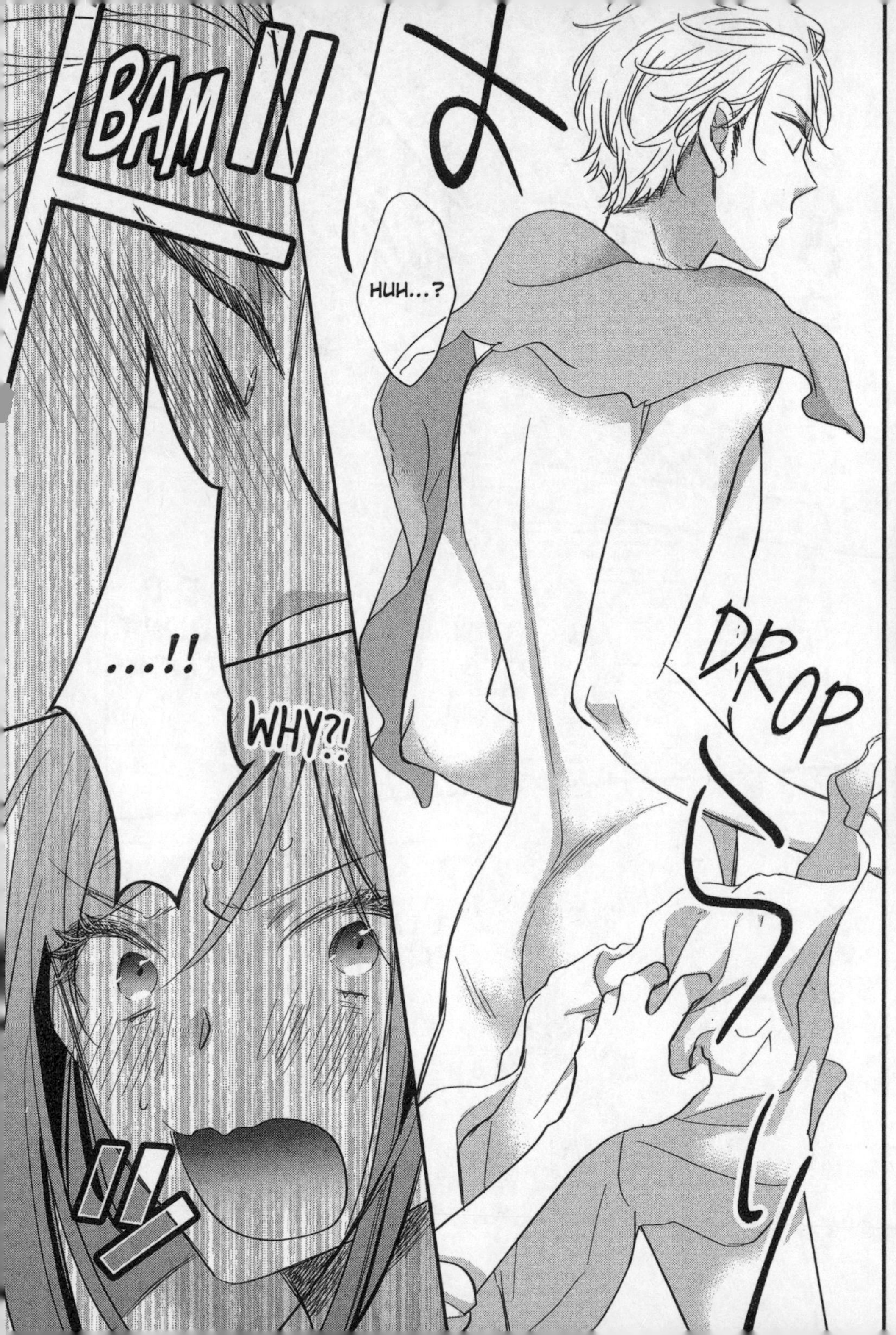
HUH...?
DROP
BAM!!
...!!
WHY?!

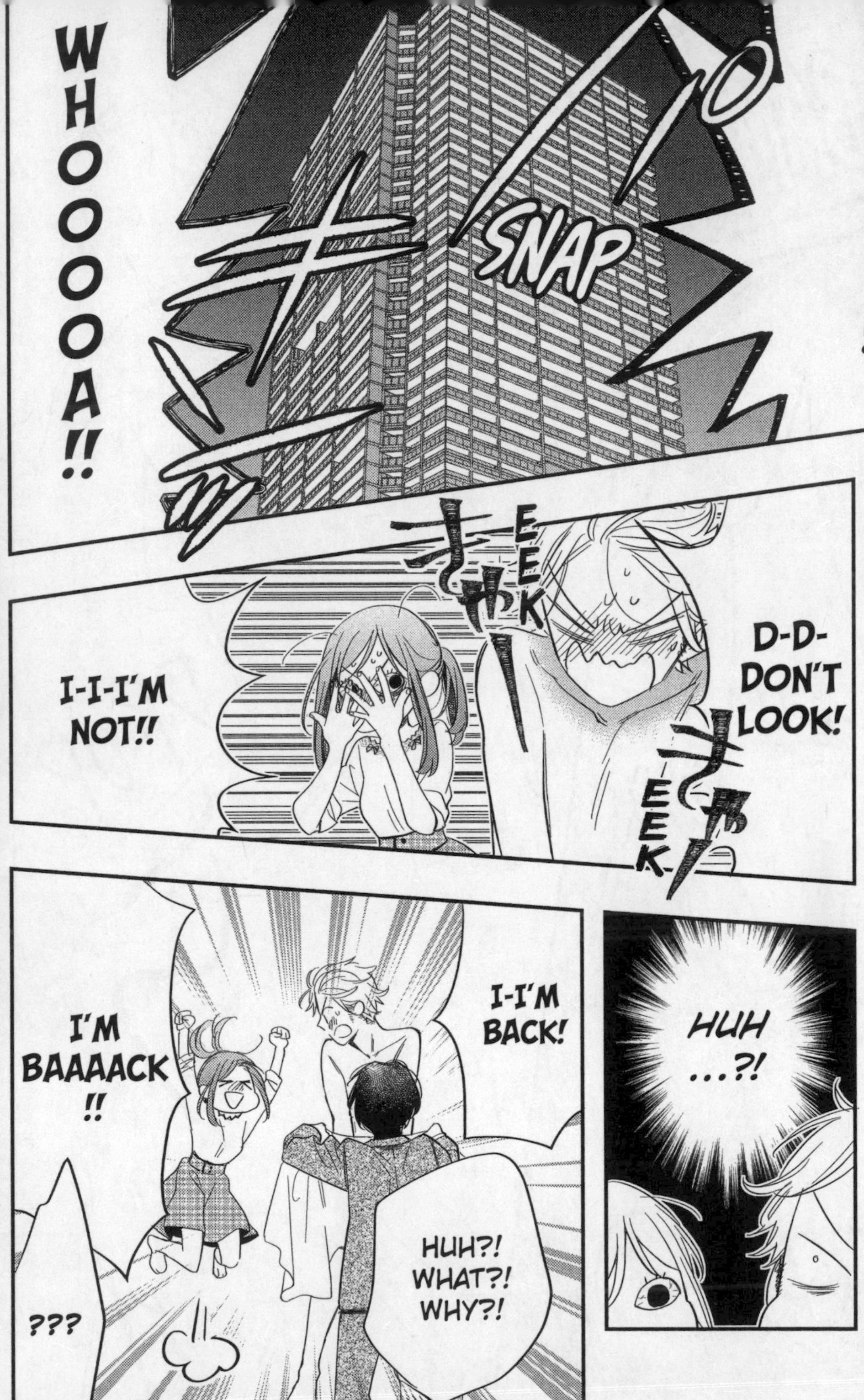
EEEEEK!!!
SNAP
WHOOOOOA!!
EEEK
D-D-DON'T LOOK!
EEEK
I-I-I'M NOT!!
HUH ...?!
I-I'M BACK!
I'M BAAAACK!!
HUH?! WHAT?! WHY?!
???

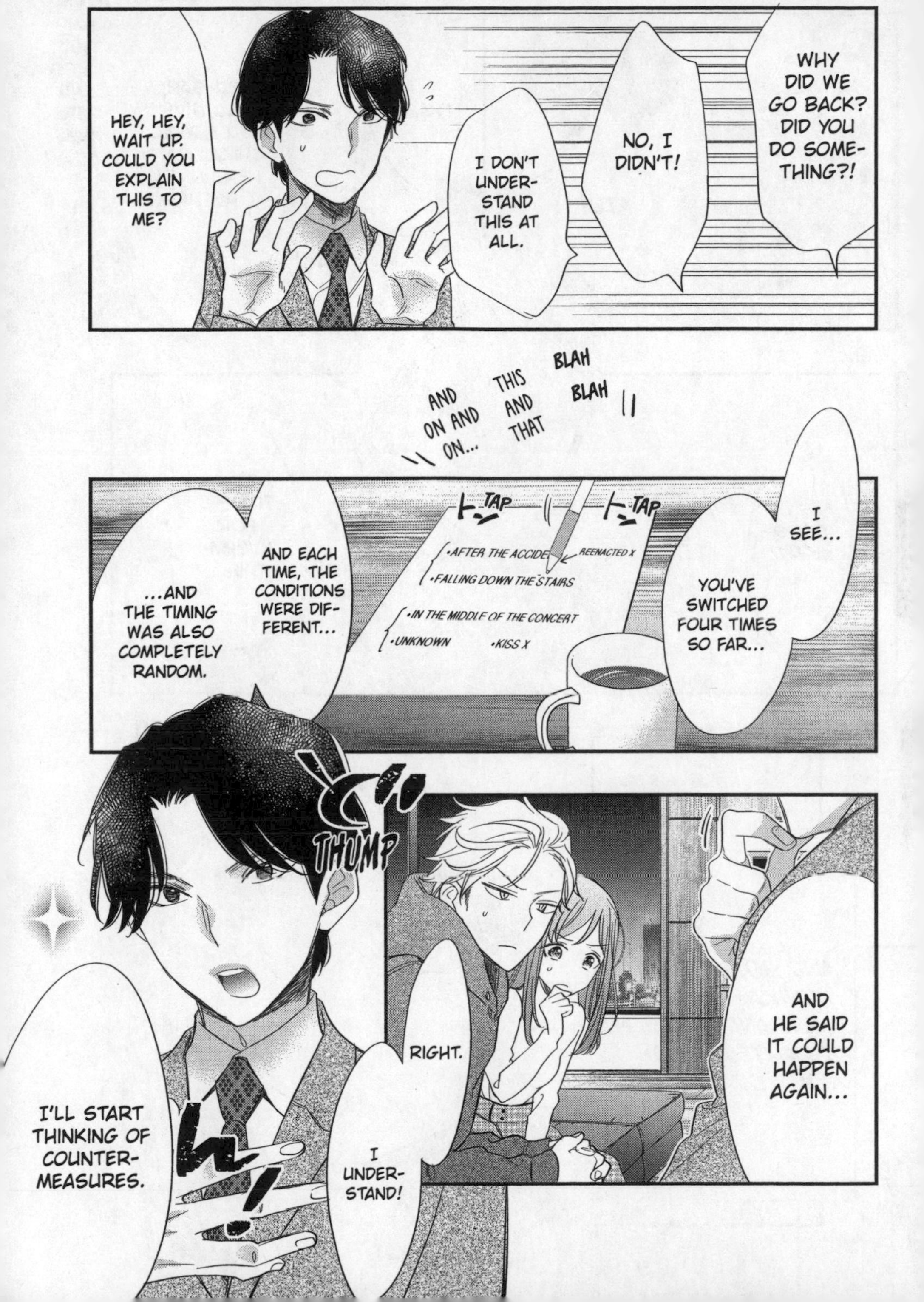
WHY DID WE GO BACK? DID YOU DO SOMETHING?!
NO, I DIDN'T!
I DON'T UNDERSTAND THIS AT ALL.
HEY, HEY, WAIT UP. COULD YOU EXPLAIN THIS TO ME?
BLAH BLAH
THIS AND THAT
AND ON AND ON...
I SEE...
YOU'VE SWITCHED FOUR TIMES SO FAR...
TAP
TAP
•AFTER THE ACCIDE
REENACTED X
•FALLING DOWN THE STAIRS
•IN THE MIDDLE OF THE CONCERT
•UNKNOWN
•KISS X
AND EACH TIME, THE CONDITIONS WERE DIFFERENT...
...AND THE TIMING WAS ALSO COMPLETELY RANDOM.
AND HE SAID IT COULD HAPPEN AGAIN...
RIGHT.
I UNDERSTAND!
THUMP
I'LL START THINKING OF COUNTERMEASURES.

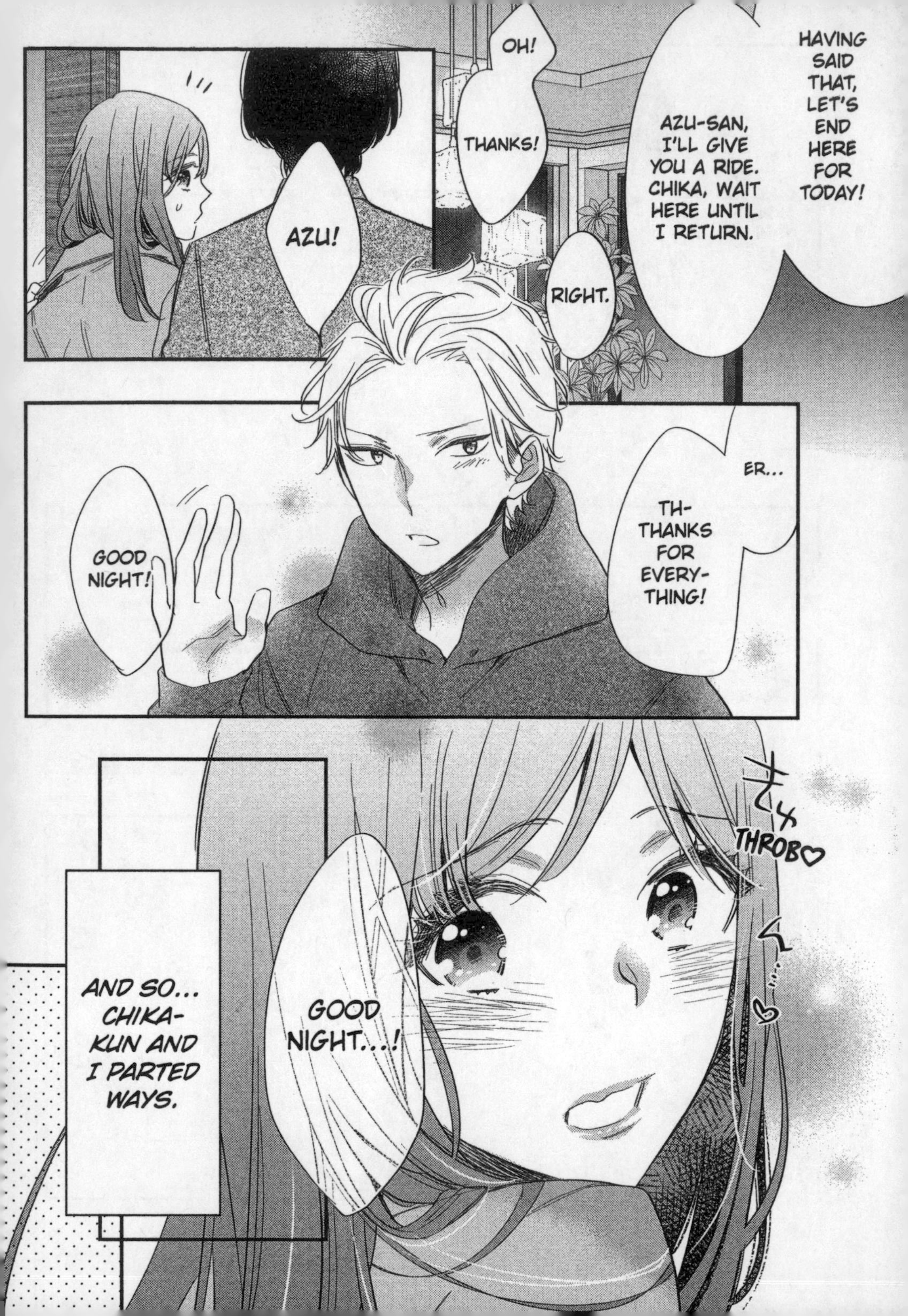
HAVING SAID THAT, LET'S END HERE FOR TODAY!
AZU-SAN, I'LL GIVE YOU A RIDE. CHIKA, WAIT HERE UNTIL I RETURN.
OH!
THANKS!
RIGHT.
AZU!
ER...
TH-THANKS FOR EVERYTHING!
GOOD NIGHT!
THROB
GOOD NIGHT...!
AND SO... CHIKA-KUN AND I PARTED WAYS.

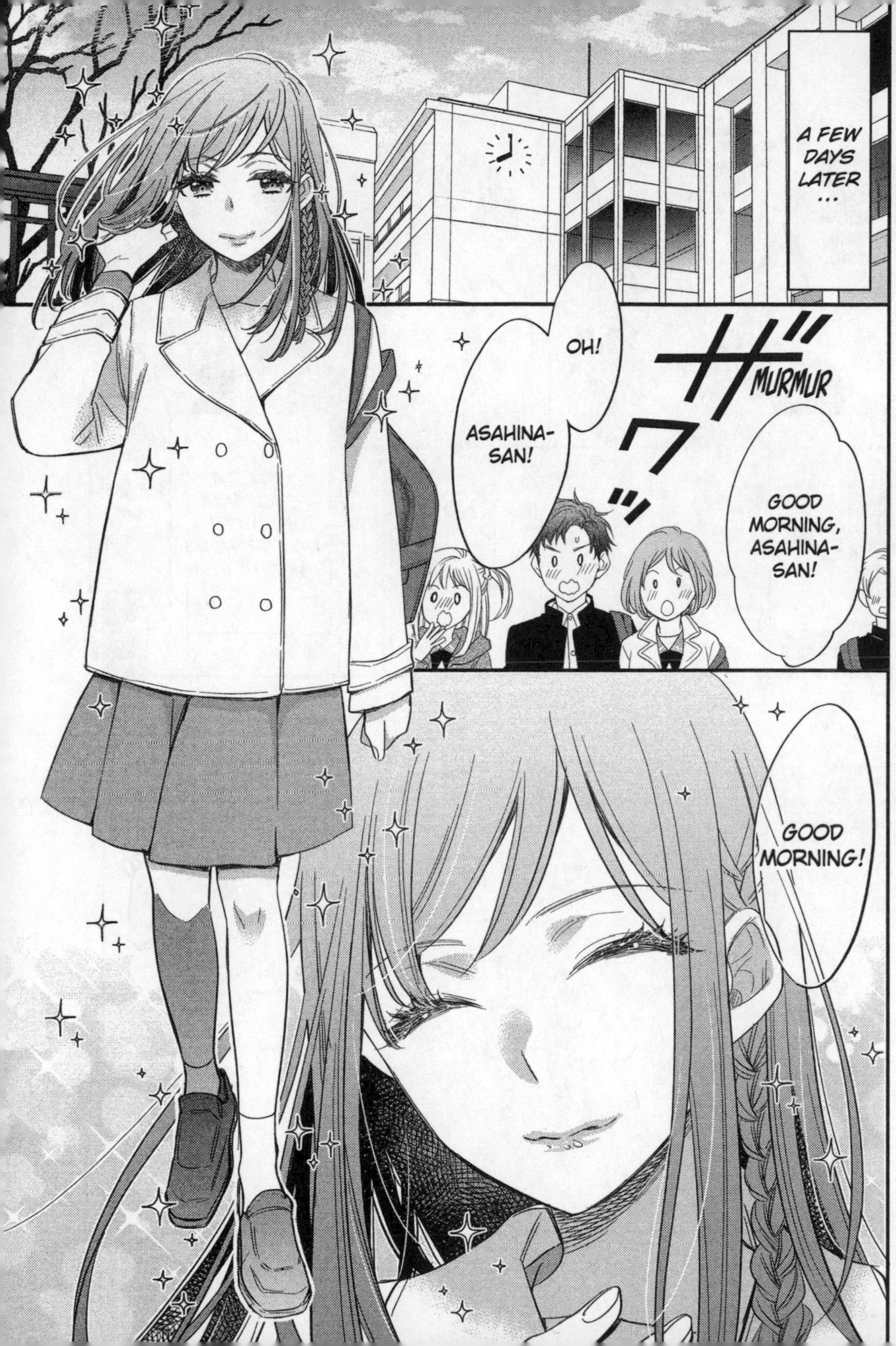
A FEW DAYS LATER...
GOOD MORNING, ASAHINA-SAN!
ザワッ
MURMUR
OH! ASAHINA-SAN!
GOOD MORNING!

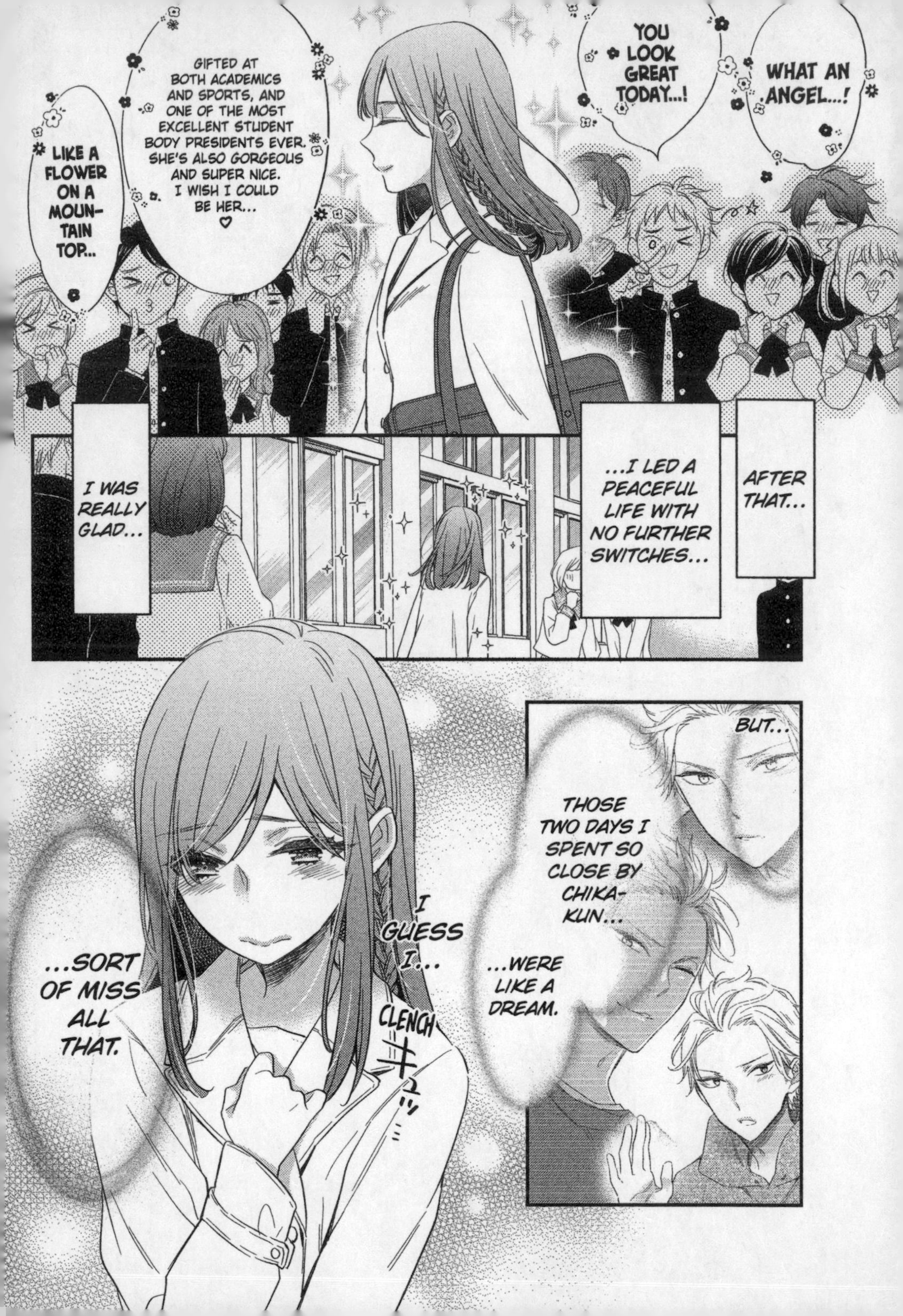
WHAT AN ANGEL...!
YOU LOOK GREAT TODAY...!
GIFTED AT BOTH ACADEMICS AND SPORTS, AND ONE OF THE MOST EXCELLENT STUDENT BODY PRESIDENTS EVER. SHE'S ALSO GORGEOUS AND SUPER NICE. I WISH I COULD BE HER... ♡
LIKE A FLOWER ON A MOUNTAIN TOP...
AFTER THAT...
...I LED A PEACEFUL LIFE WITH NO FURTHER SWITCHES...
I WAS REALLY GLAD...
BUT...
THOSE TWO DAYS I SPENT SO CLOSE BY CHIKA-KUN...
...WERE LIKE A DREAM.
I GUESS I...
CLENCH
...SORT OF MISS ALL THAT.

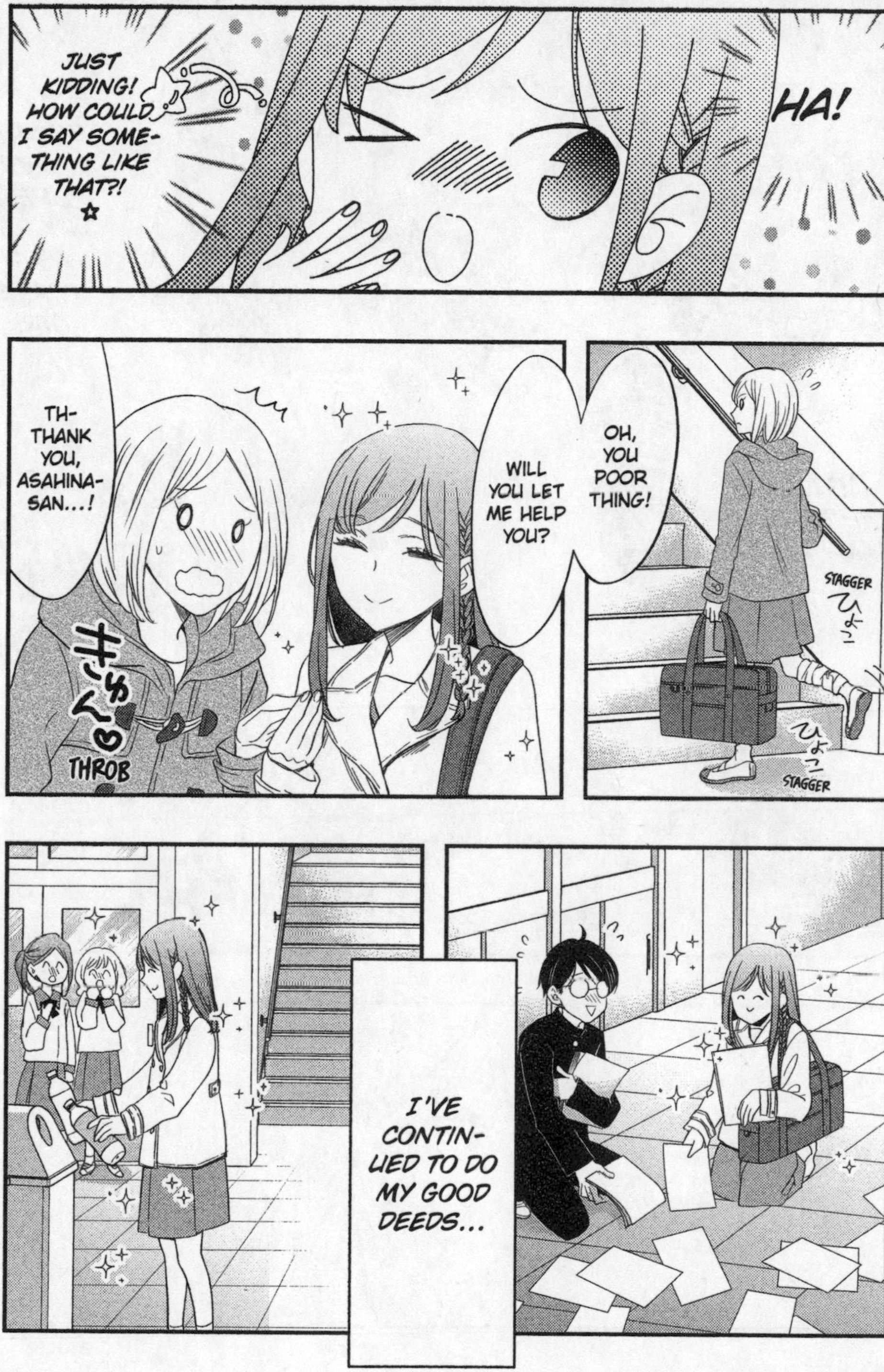
JUST KIDDING! HOW COULD I SAY SOMETHING LIKE THAT?! ☆
HA!
ひょこ
STAGGER
ひょこ
STAGGER
OH, YOU POOR THING!
WILL YOU LET ME HELP YOU?
TH-THANK YOU, ASAHINA-SAN...!
きゅん♡
THROB
I'VE CONTINUED TO DO MY GOOD DEEDS...

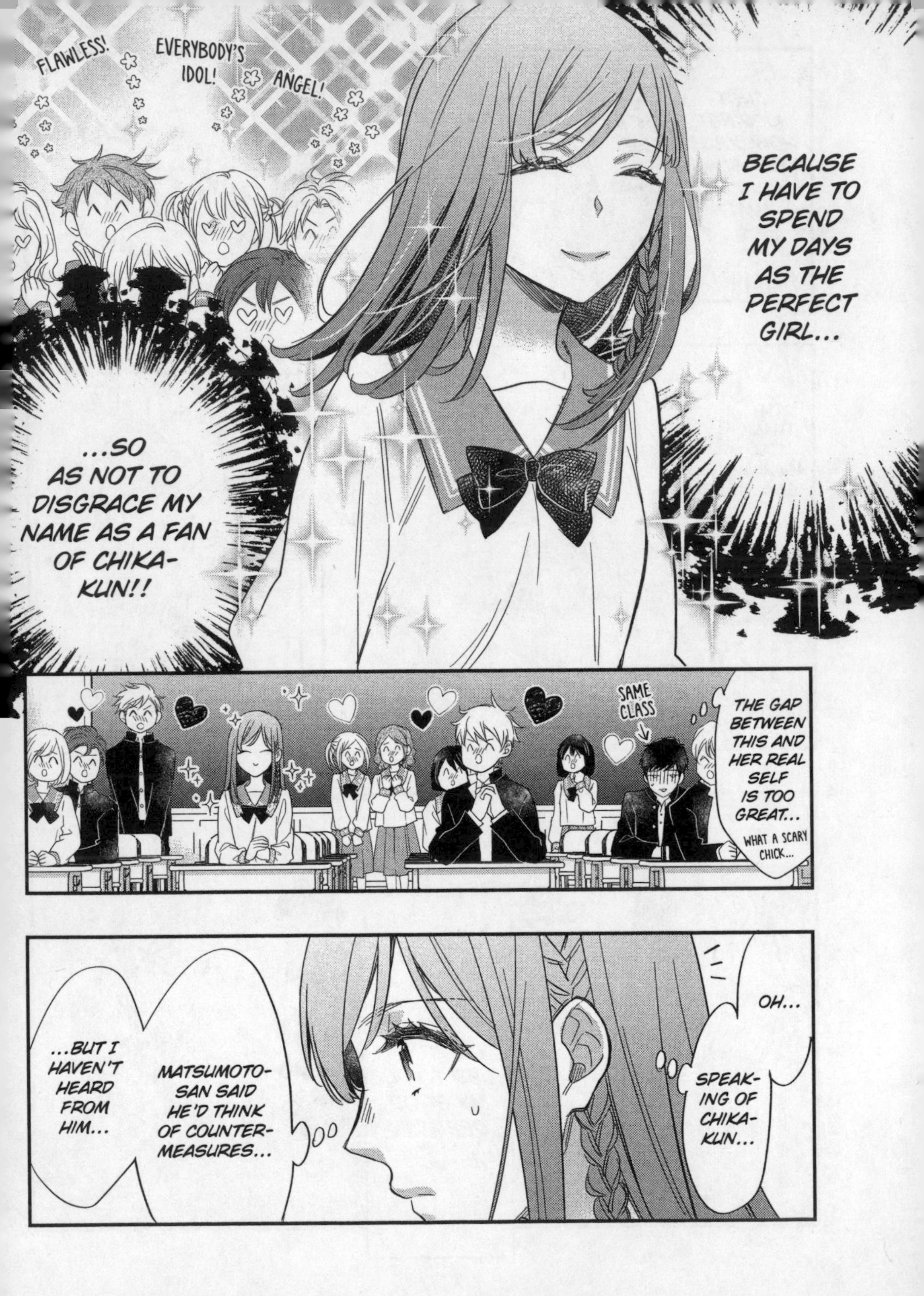
BECAUSE I HAVE TO SPEND MY DAYS AS THE PERFECT GIRL...
ANGEL!
EVERYBODY'S IDOL!
FLAWLESS!
...SO AS NOT TO DISGRACE MY NAME AS A FAN OF CHIKA-KUN!!
THE GAP BETWEEN THIS AND HER REAL SELF IS TOO GREAT...
WHAT A SCARY CHICK...
SAME CLASS
OH...
SPEAK-ING OF CHIKA-KUN...
MATSUMOTO-SAN SAID HE'D THINK OF COUNTER-MEASURES...
...BUT I HAVEN'T HEARD FROM HIM...

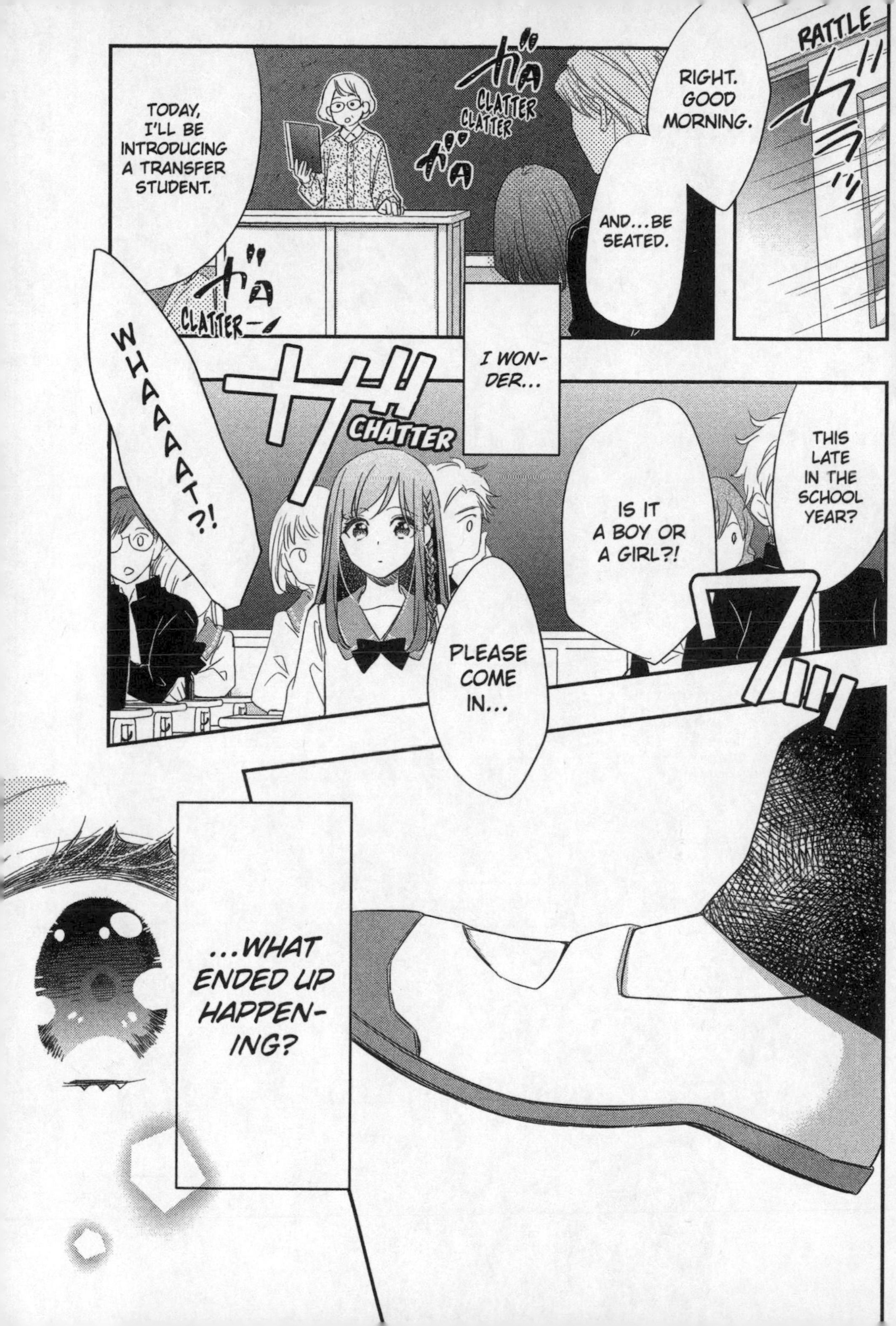
RATTLE
RIGHT. GOOD MORNING.
AND...BE SEATED.
CLATTER
CLATTER
TODAY, I'LL BE INTRODUCING A TRANSFER STUDENT.
CLATTER—
WHAAAAAT?!
THIS LATE IN THE SCHOOL YEAR?
IS IT A BOY OR A GIRL?!
I WONDER...
CHATTER
PLEASE COME IN...
...WHAT ENDED UP HAPPENING?

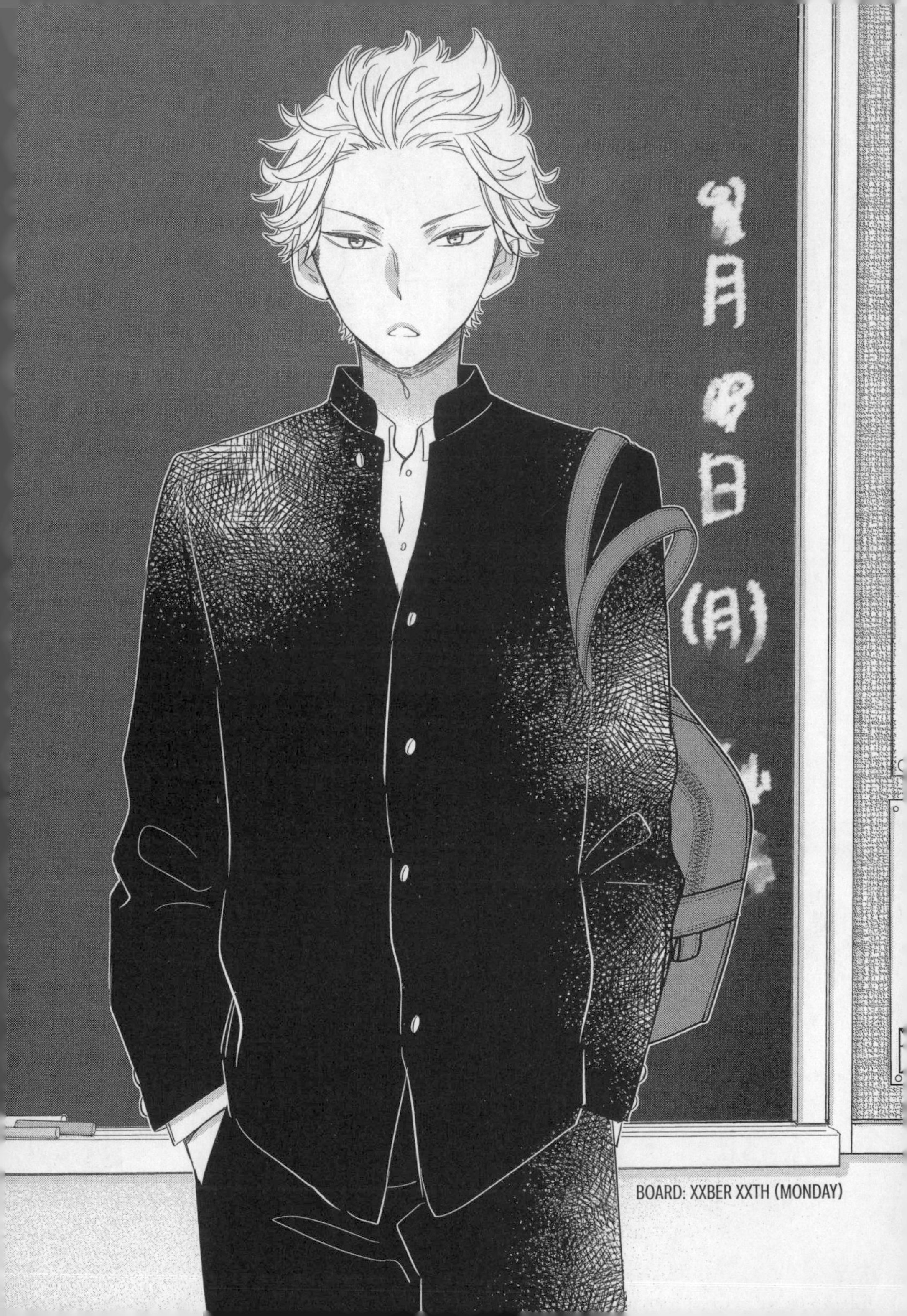
BOARD: XXBER XXTH (MONDAY)

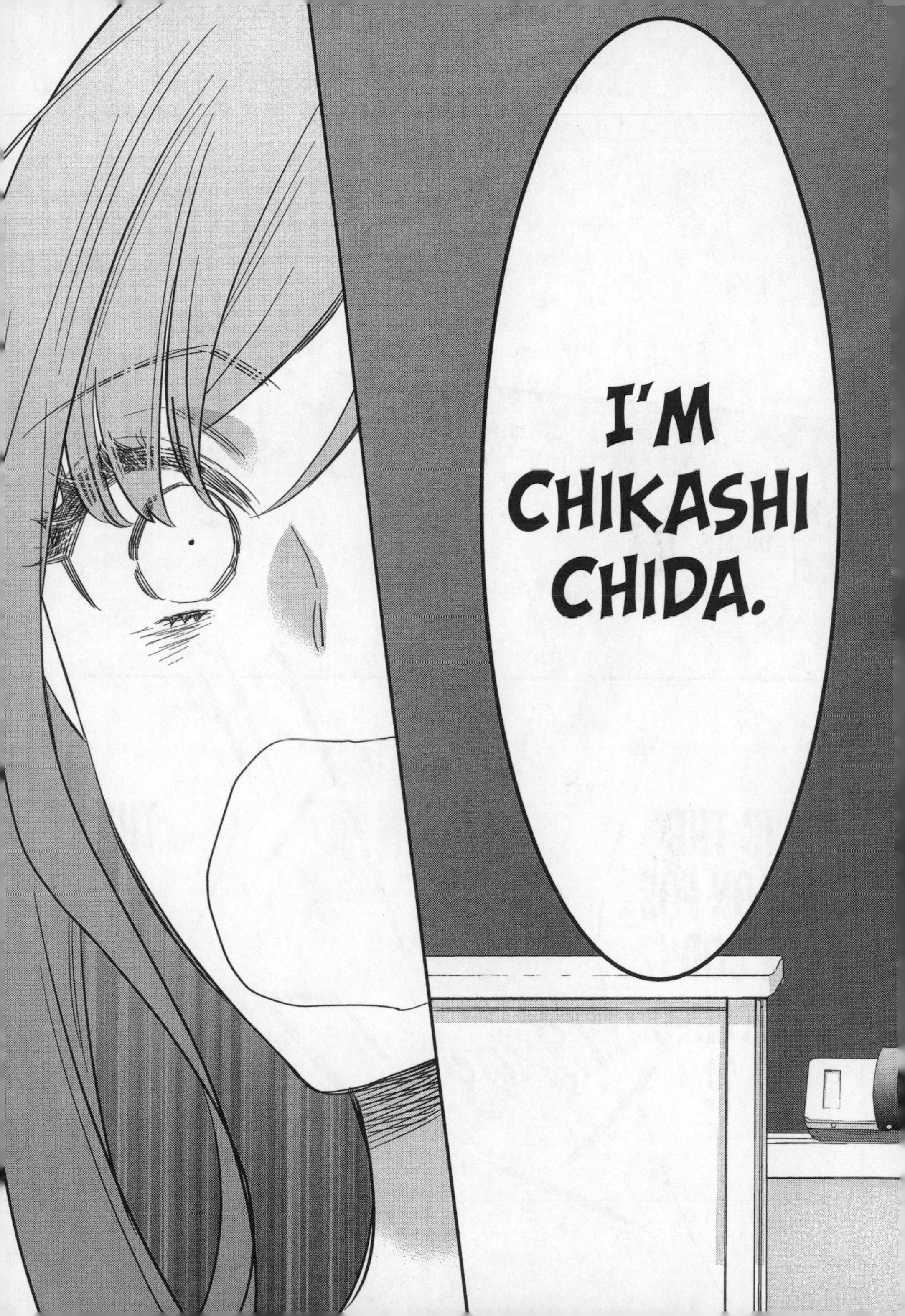
I'M CHIKASHI CHIDA.

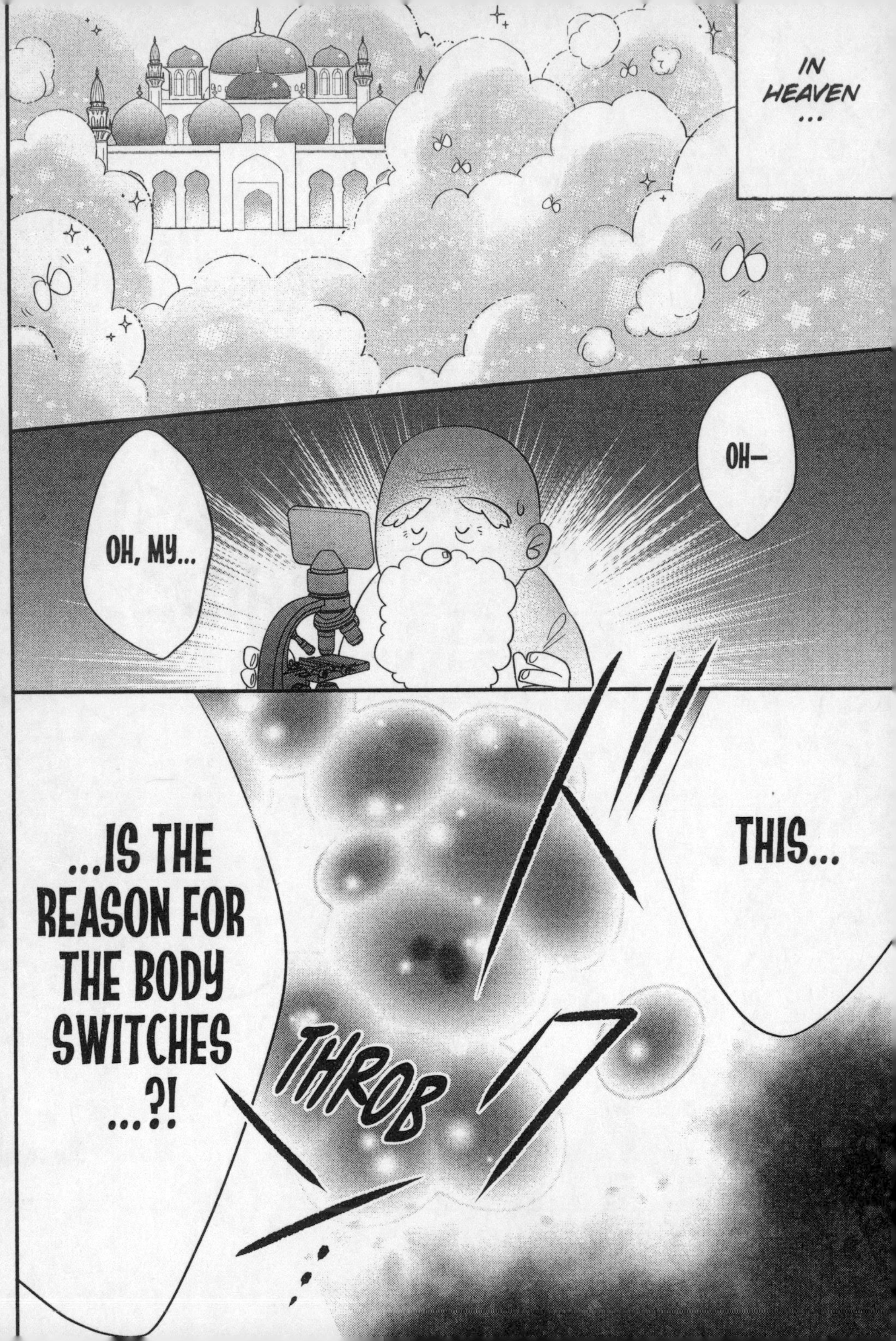
IN HEAVEN ...
OH—
OH, MY...
THIS...
THROB
...IS THE REASON FOR THE BODY SWITCHES ...?!

STAR⇄CROSSED!!

 will continue in Volume 2

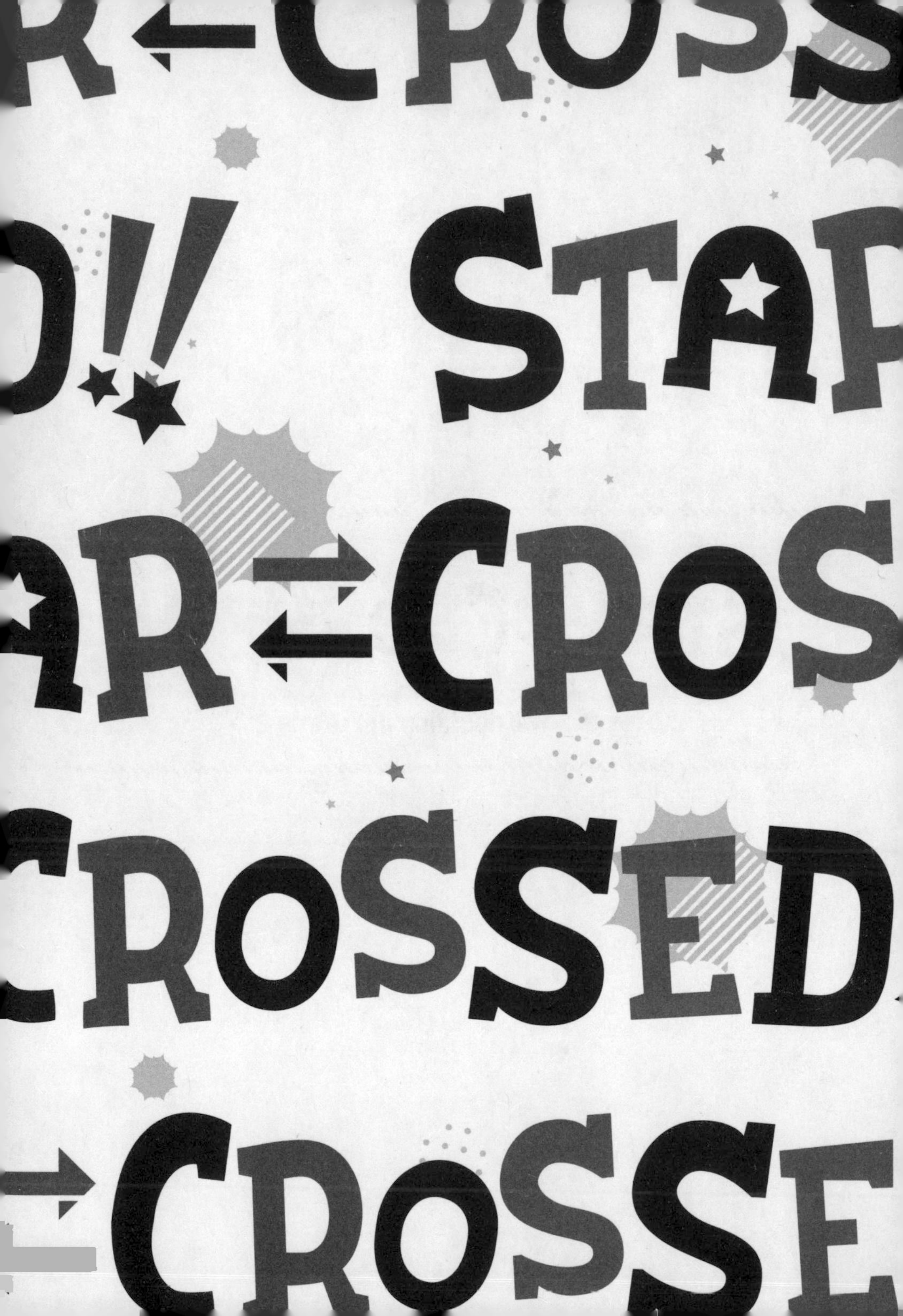
R⇄CROSS
D!! STAR
AR⇄CROS
CROSSED
⇄CROSSE

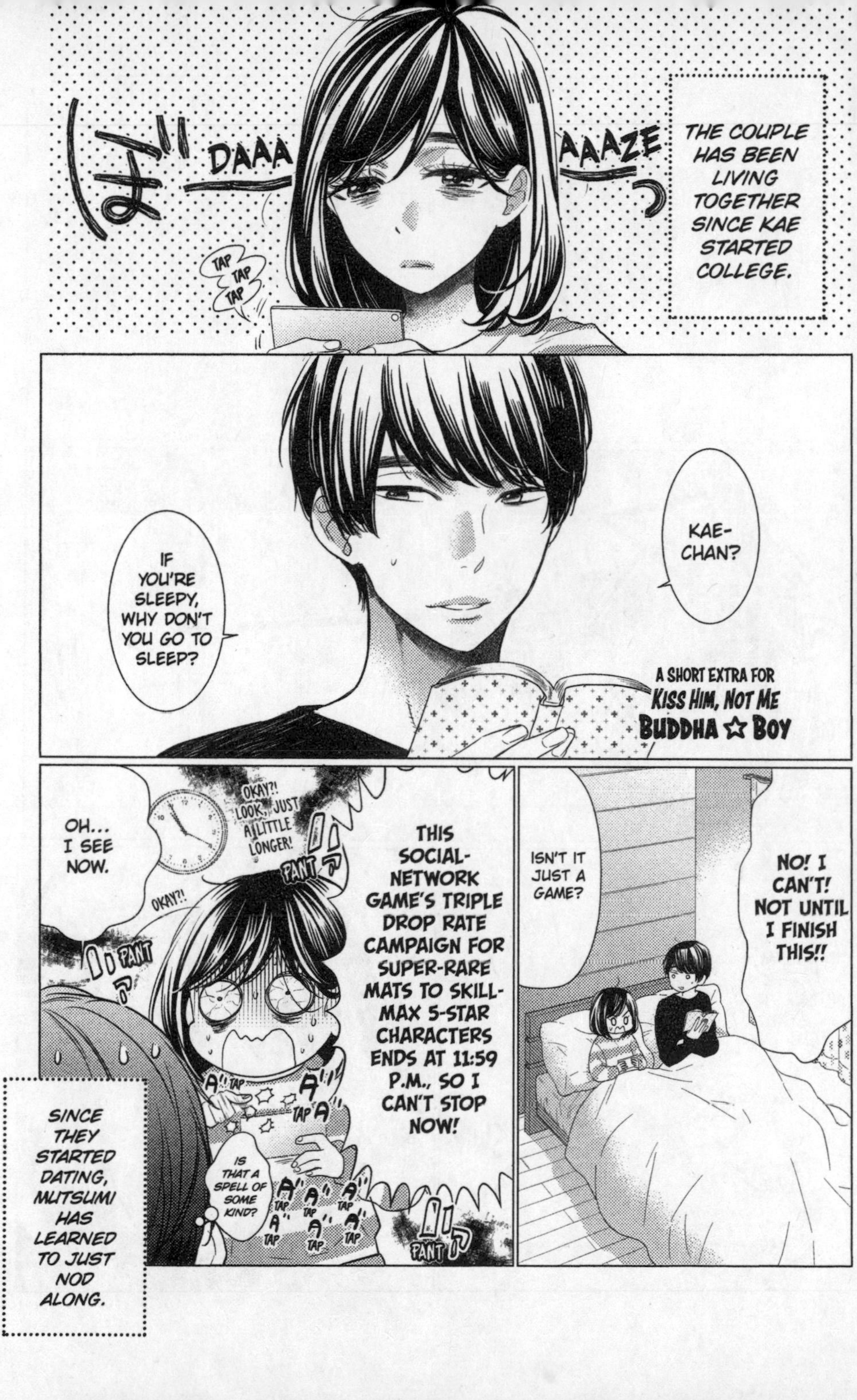

THE COUPLE HAS BEEN LIVING TOGETHER SINCE KAE STARTED COLLEGE.
DAAA AAAZE
TAP TAP TAP
KAE-CHAN?
IF YOU'RE SLEEPY, WHY DON'T YOU GO TO SLEEP?
A SHORT EXTRA FOR
Kiss Him, Not Me
BUDDHA ☆ BOY
NO! I CAN'T! NOT UNTIL I FINISH THIS!!
ISN'T IT JUST A GAME?
THIS SOCIAL-NETWORK GAME'S TRIPLE DROP RATE CAMPAIGN FOR SUPER-RARE MATS TO SKILL-MAX 5-STAR CHARACTERS ENDS AT 11:59 P.M., SO I CAN'T STOP NOW!
OKAY?! LOOK, JUST A LITTLE LONGER!
PANT
OH... I SEE NOW.
OKAY?!
PANT
TAP TAP
IS THAT A SPELL OF SOME KIND?
TAP TAP TAP TAP TAP TAP
PANT
SINCE THEY STARTED DATING, MUTSUMI HAS LEARNED TO JUST NOD ALONG.

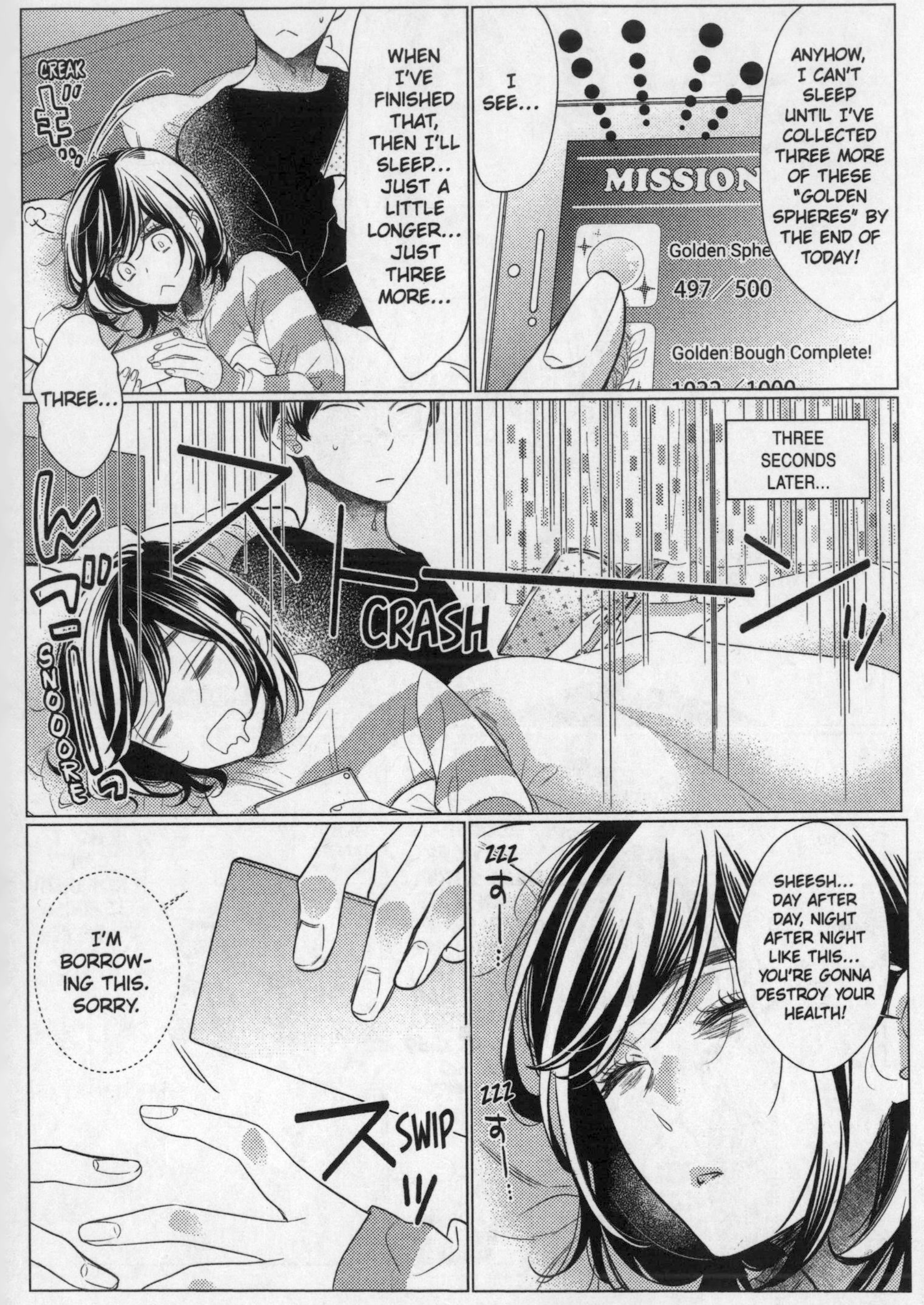
ANYHOW, I CAN'T SLEEP UNTIL I'VE COLLECTED THREE MORE OF THESE "GOLDEN SPHERES" BY THE END OF TODAY!
MISSION
Golden Sphe
497／500
Golden Bough Complete!
I SEE...
WHEN I'VE FINISHED THAT, THEN I'LL SLEEP... JUST A LITTLE LONGER... JUST THREE MORE...
CREAK
THREE...
THREE SECONDS LATER...
CRASH
SNOOORE
SHEESH... DAY AFTER DAY, NIGHT AFTER NIGHT LIKE THIS... YOU'RE GONNA DESTROY YOUR HEALTH!
ZZZ
ZZZ
I'M BORROWING THIS. SORRY.
SWIP

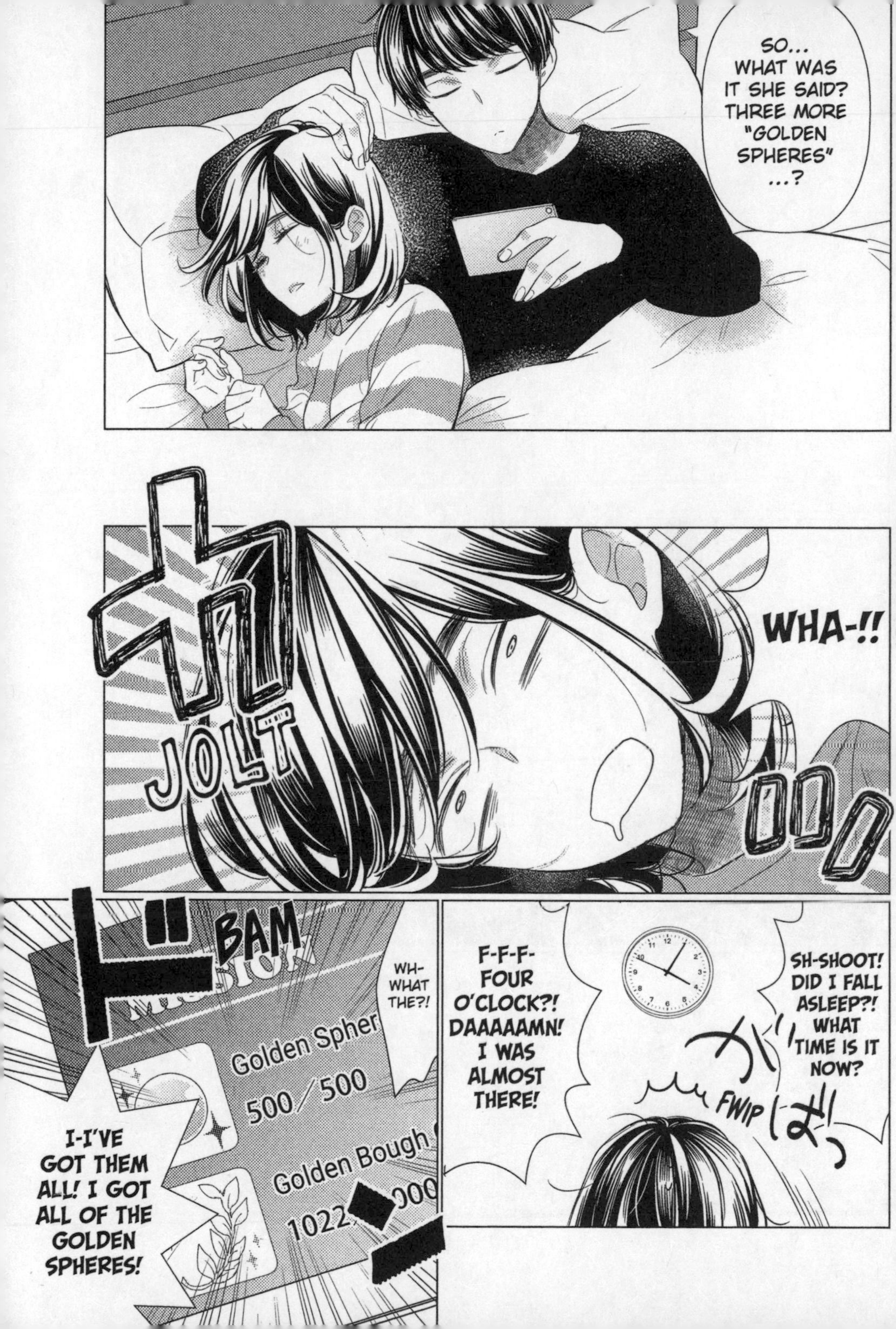
SO... WHAT WAS IT SHE SAID? THREE MORE "GOLDEN SPHERES" ...?
WHA-!!
JOLT
SH-SHOOT! DID I FALL ASLEEP?! WHAT TIME IS IT NOW?
FWIP
F-F-F-FOUR O'CLOCK?! DAAAAAMN! I WAS ALMOST THERE!
BAM
WH-WHAT THE?!
Golden Spher
500／500
Golden Bough
1022
000
I-I'VE GOT THEM ALL! I GOT ALL OF THE GOLDEN SPHERES!

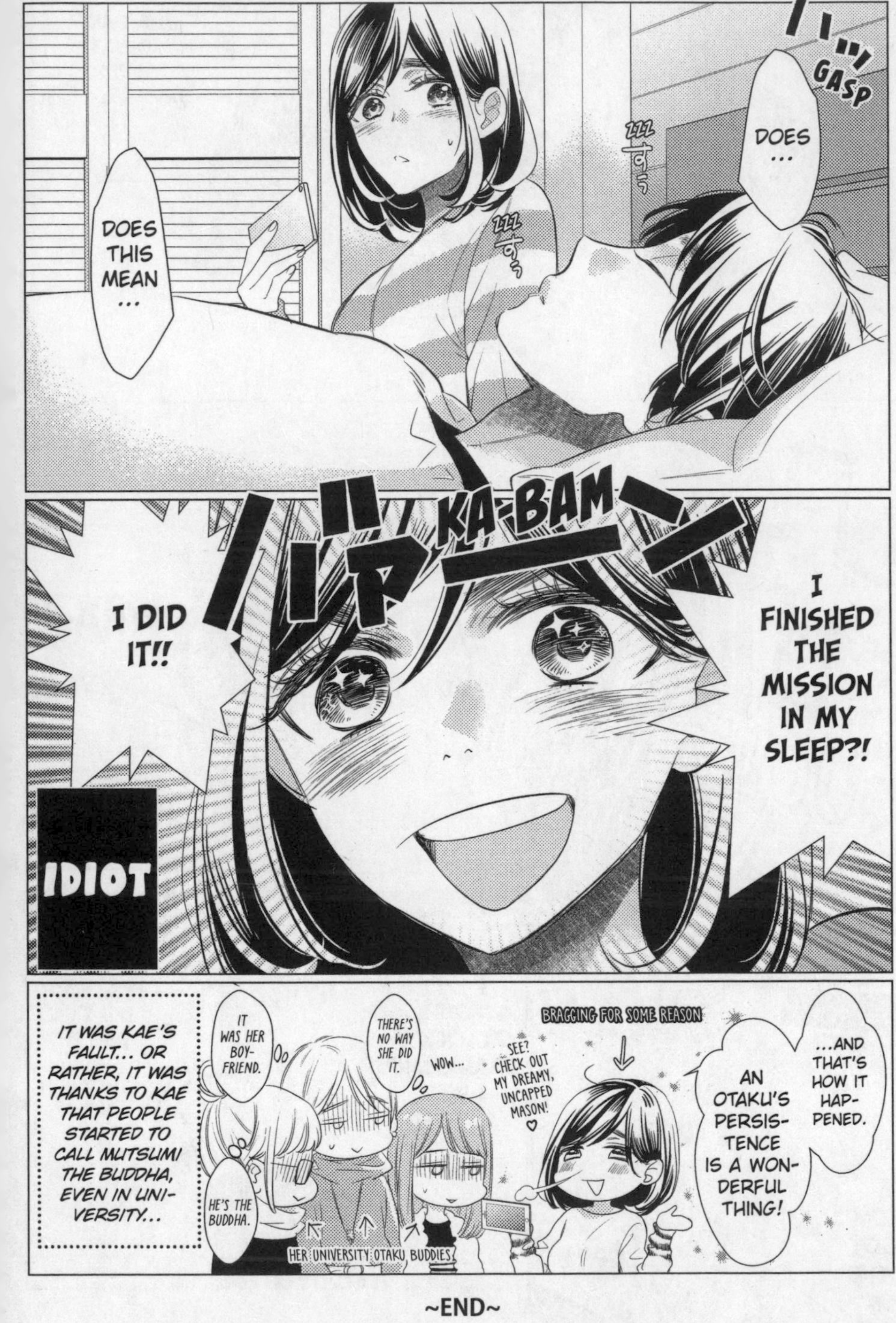
GASP
DOES...
ZZZ
ZZZ
DOES THIS MEAN...
KA-BAM
I FINISHED THE MISSION IN MY SLEEP?!
I DID IT!!
IDIOT
...AND THAT'S HOW IT HAPPENED.
AN OTAKU'S PERSISTENCE IS A WONDERFUL THING!
BRAGGING FOR SOME REASON
SEE? CHECK OUT MY DREAMY, UNCAPPED MASON! ♡
WOW...
THERE'S NO WAY SHE DID IT.
IT WAS HER BOYFRIEND.
HE'S THE BUDDHA.
HER UNIVERSITY OTAKU BUDDIES
IT WAS KAE'S FAULT... OR RATHER, IT WAS THANKS TO KAE THAT PEOPLE STARTED TO CALL MUTSUMI THE BUDDHA, EVEN IN UNIVERSITY...

~END~

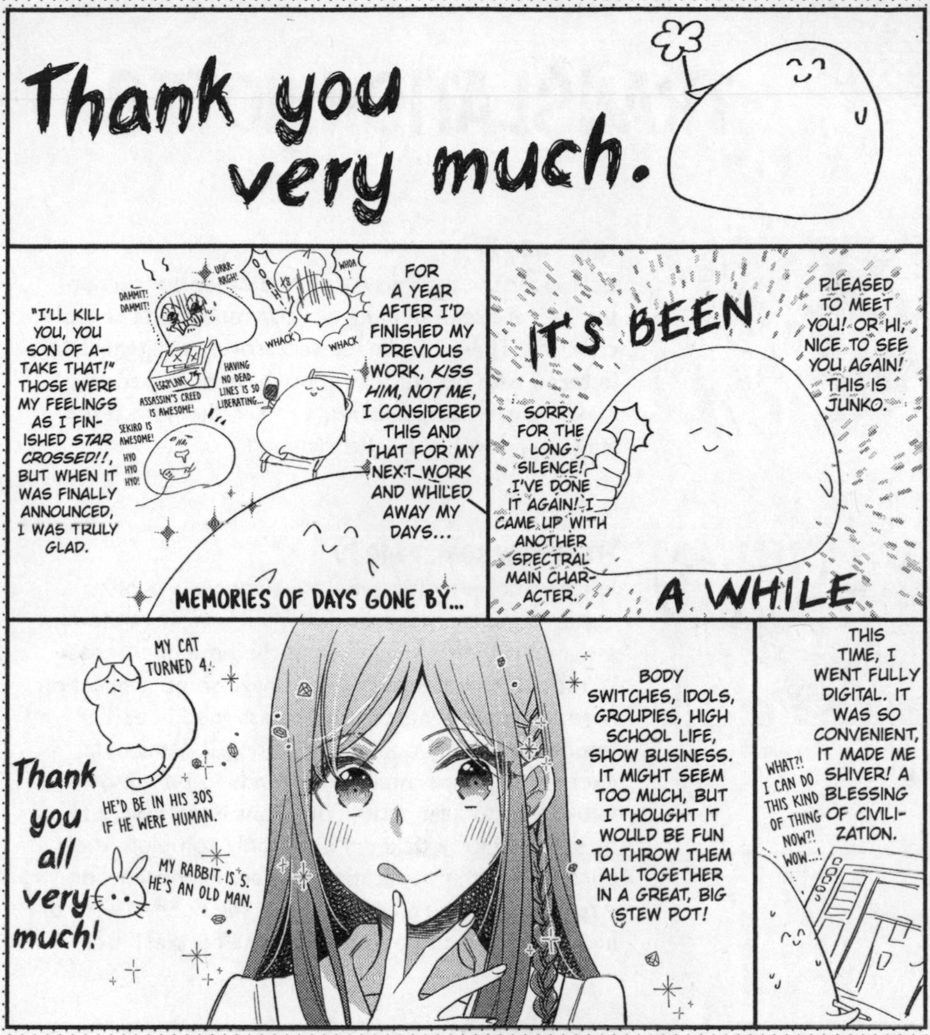
Thank you very much.
IT'S BEEN A WHILE
PLEASED TO MEET YOU! OR HI, NICE TO SEE YOU AGAIN! THIS IS JUNKO.
SORRY FOR THE LONG SILENCE! I'VE DONE IT AGAIN! I CAME UP WITH ANOTHER SPECTRAL MAIN CHARACTER.
FOR A YEAR AFTER I'D FINISHED MY PREVIOUS WORK, *KISS HIM, NOT ME*, I CONSIDERED THIS AND THAT FOR MY NEXT WORK AND WHILED AWAY MY DAYS...
WHOA!
URRR-RGH!
OOAH
DAMMIT! DAMMIT!
WHACK
WHACK
HAVING NO DEADLINES IS SO LIBERATING...
ASSASSIN'S CREED IS AWESOME!
SEKIRO IS AWESOME!
HYO HYO HYO!
"I'LL KILL YOU, YOU SON OF A-TAKE THAT!" THOSE WERE MY FEELINGS AS I FINISHED *STAR CROSSED!!*, BUT WHEN IT WAS FINALLY ANNOUNCED, I WAS TRULY GLAD.
MEMORIES OF DAYS GONE BY...
THIS TIME, I WENT FULLY DIGITAL. IT WAS SO CONVENIENT, IT MADE ME SHIVER! A BLESSING OF CIVILIZATION.
WHAT?! I CAN DO THIS KIND OF THING NOW?! WOW...!
BODY SWITCHES, IDOLS, GROUPIES, HIGH SCHOOL LIFE, SHOW BUSINESS. IT MIGHT SEEM TOO MUCH, BUT I THOUGHT IT WOULD BE FUN TO THROW THEM ALL TOGETHER IN A GREAT, BIG STEW POT!
MY CAT TURNED 4.
HE'D BE IN HIS 30S IF HE WERE HUMAN.
MY RABBIT IS 5. HE'S AN OLD MAN.
Thank you all very much!

Special Thanks!

☆SPECIAL ADVISER☆
EIKI EIKI-SENSEI
☆ASSISTANTS☆
UZUKI-SAN, AKI-SAN, MIKAN-SAN, SHIROE-SAN, ROKKU-SAN (FIRST CHAPTER)
☆SUPERVISING EDITOR☆
SATO-SAN
☆DESIGNER☆
HASE-PRO
AND EVERYONE ELSE WHO WAS INVOLVED☆
☆☆ & YOU!

TRANSLATION NOTES

I
LOVE
YOU

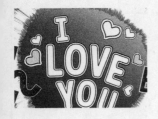

Fan, page 8

Uchiwa, or the flat fans Azusa and other concert attendees are seen holding, are common sights at idol concerts. These handmade accessories are generally lettered with big cutouts of bright neon paper, which makes it easy for performers to see them from the stage, even with the lights dimmed.

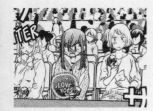

Front-row seat, page 19

In Japan, ticketing for events like concerts is often done via a lottery system, where seating is randomly assigned rather than chosen at the time of purchase. "First-come, first-served" does have some application here, as better seats tend to be assigned in earlier (more exclusive) rounds of ticketing. If demand far exceeds the seats available, as tends to be the case for extremely popular artists, then fans must first apply to be selected for a ticket and can only complete their purchase if their application number is chosen. For Azusa to get such a coveted seat, she needed a lot of luck to be able to conquer all those hurdles!

JINGLE
JANGLE
ONGAKU
STATION

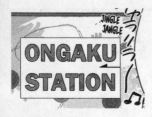

Ongaku Station, page 102

Ongaku is Japanese for "music," making this program title a play on the Japanese TV program officially titled "Music Station," which uses the English word. The format of the show (artist interview followed by performance) and the likenesses of the hosts are quite similar.

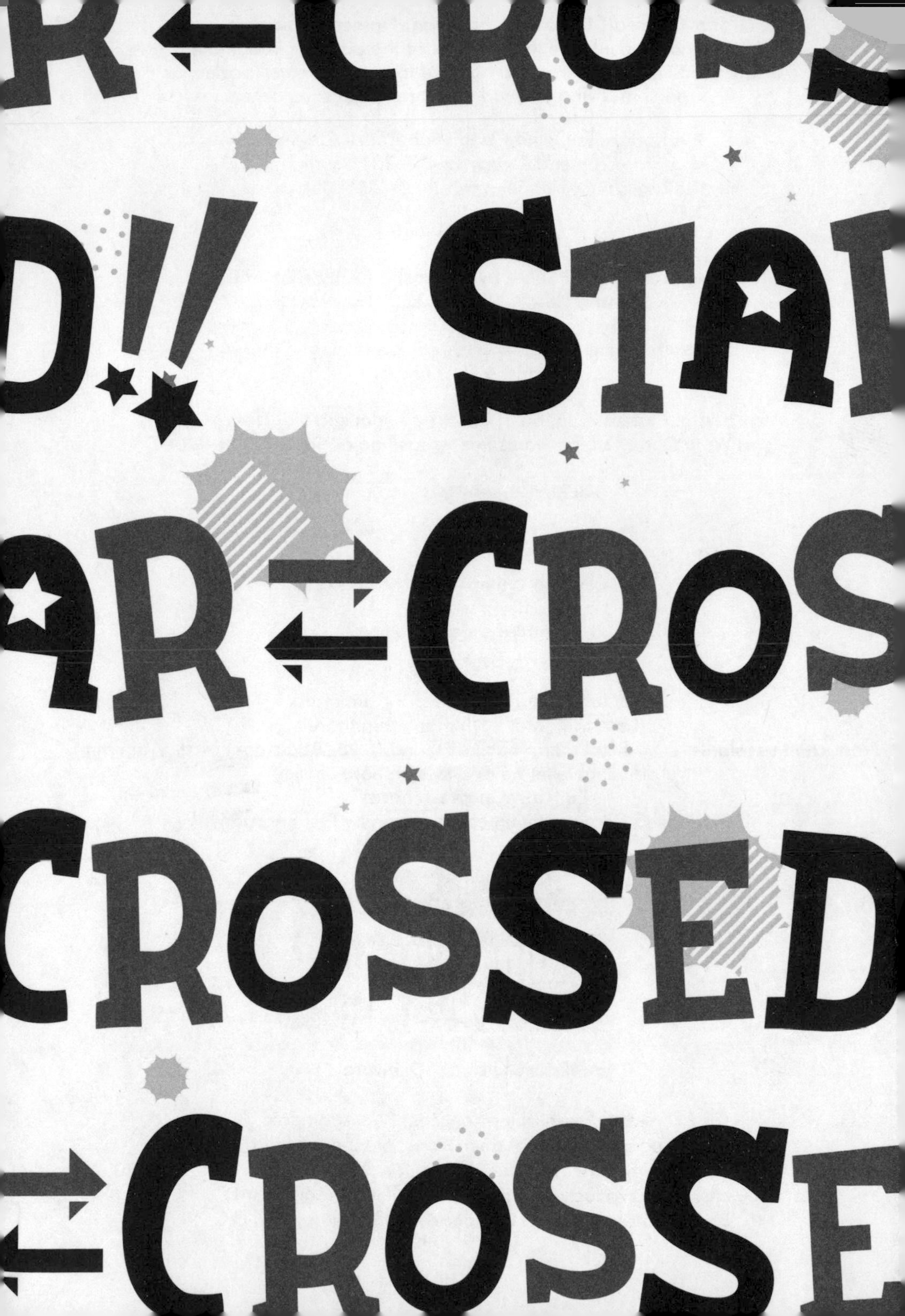
R⇄CROS
D!! STA
AR⇄CROS
CROSSED
⇄CROSSE

A Kodansha Comics Trade Paperback Original
Star-Crossed!! 1 copyright © 2019 Junko
English translation copyright © 2021 Junko

All rights reserved.

Published in the United States by Kodansha Comics, an imprint of Kodansha USA Publishing, LLC, New York.

Publication rights for this English edition arranged through Kodansha Ltd., Tokyo.

First published in Japan in 2019 by Kodansha Ltd., Tokyo as *Wota Doru, Oshiga watashide watashiga oshide*, volume 1.

ISBN 978-1-64651-187-7

Original cover design by HASEPRO

Printed in the United States of America.

www.kodanshacomics.com

9 8 7 6 5 4 3 2 1
Translation: Barbara Vincent / amimaru
Lettering: Mohit Dhiman / amimaru
Production assistants: Dani Brockman, Monika Hegedusova, Adam Jankowski / amimaru
Additional lettering and layout: Sara Linsley
Editing: Vanessa Tenazas
Kodansha Comics edition cover design by Phil Balsman

Publisher: Kiichiro Sugawara

Director of publishing services: Ben Applegate
Associate director of operations: Stephen Pakula
Publishing services managing editor: Noelle Webster
Assistant production manager: Emi Lotto, Angela Zurlo
Logo and character art ©Kodansha USA Publishing, LLC